PROTECTING
AMERICA'S HEALTH

ALSO BY PHILIP J. HILTS

Smokescreen

Memory's Ghost

Scientific Temperaments

PROTECTING AMERICA'S HEALTH

•

The FDA, Business, and One Hundred
Years of Regulation

PHILIP J. HILTS

The University of North Carolina Press
Chapel Hill and London

Photos and drawings provided by the
Food and Drug Administration.

The paper in this book meets the guidelines for permanence
and durability of the Committee on Production Guidelines
for Book Longevity of the Council on Library Resources.

The Library of Congress has cataloged the
original edition of this book as follows:

Hilts, Philip J.
Protecting America's health : the FDA, business,
and one hundred years of regulation / Philip J. Hilts
p.   cm.
Includes bibliographical references and index.
1. United States. Food and Drug Administration.
2. Food law and legislation—United States.
3. Drugs—Law and legislation—United States.
4. Pharmaceutical industry—Quality control.
5. Food adulteration and inspection—United States.
I. Title.
RA11.H54 2003
353.9'97'0973—dc 21
2002029859

ISBN 0-8078-5582-0 (pbk.: alk. paper)

08 07 06 05 04   5 4 3 2 1

To Carisa

Contents

Contents

•

Introduction

THE BEGINNING OF REGULATION

IN 1882, Theodore Roosevelt was a young, inexperienced legislator in New York State. By his own account, he had until that time believed and acted in accordance with the conventional conservative theories about the world, accepting laissez-faire doctrine as his own. He favored low wages for workers, low taxes for those better off, and few social services. That year, a bill was introduced that would have reduced from fifteen to twelve the number of hours streetcar conductors in New York City were required to work each day. He opposed it, saying it was a socialist measure that interfered with the workings of the free market. To Roosevelt, as Nathan Miller writes, "The degradation of the workingman was the result of natural law—or character—rather than economic or social injustice." Any improvements in the condition of citizens were not to come from government action but from each individual's own efforts.

Soon Roosevelt was facing another workers' issue. At the time, cigar companies in New York City required some of their employees to manufacture cigars in their tenement homes. Those workers described how they had to store their tools and bulky bundles of leaves (and whatever insects came with them) in their already overcrowded apartments. The companies did not want to build factories and warehouses to accommodate these cigar makers, who were paid by the piece, so those who didn't agree to work at home didn't work.

The union activist Samuel Gompers succeeded in getting a bill introduced in the New York legislature that would have banned tenement-house cigar manufacture, on the grounds that it put a terrible burden on the cigar workers. The bill was referred to a committee, to which Roosevelt was assigned, probably because it was thought his anti-labor attitudes would help kill the proposed legislation. He said he did not believe for a moment that the workers' living conditions were as described by the union members. But he was a man who was intellectually as well as physically game, and when challenged by Gompers to see the conditions for himself, he accepted. He liked the idea of testing arguments against evidence.

His tour of tenements was his first adult confrontation with the deleterious effects of raw capitalism, and what he saw astonished and revolted him. He visited the tenements twice on committee business, and then returned twice on his own. It wasn't just the cigar issue. The realization that hardworking people who were neither lazy nor corrupt could nevertheless find themselves in such awful living conditions began to bring a change in Roosevelt's thinking. Until then, he said, he had believed that the bill to ban tenement manufacture of cigars was "contrary to the political principles of the *laissez-faire* kind," that the businessmen he talked to were right in saying the bill was a terrible thing designed to prevent a man from doing as he wished with property that was his own. But, as he wrote later:

> My first visits to the tenement-house districts in question made me feel that, whatever the theories might be, as a matter of practical common sense, I could not conscientiously vote for the continuance of the conditions which I saw. These conditions rendered it impossible for the families of the tenement-house workers to live so that the children might grow up fitted for the exacting duties of American citizenship. . . . In the overwhelming majority of cases . . . the work of manufacturing the tobacco by men, women and children went on day and night in the eating, living and sleeping rooms—sometimes in one room. I have always remembered one room in which two families were living.

Roosevelt was astonished to learn that besides the two families and the tobacco business in the one room, a boarder had been taken in to help make ends meet. "There were several children, three men and two women in this room. The tobacco was stowed about everywhere, alongside the foul bedding and in a corner where there were scraps of food. The men, women and children in this room worked by day and far into the evening, and they slept and ate there." He soon concluded that the bill had some merit. "Instead of opposing the bill I ardently championed it." The bill passed, but the courts struck down the measure as an unconstitutional attack on the "hallowed" spaces of the home.

·   ·   ·

Roosevelt came to understand something about government and society in that unexpected encounter. He had never had the slightest patience with weakness, but he learned that self-sufficiency and competitive spirit, important as ideals, are negated when the rules are unfair. For Roosevelt, it became clear there were two kinds of weakness to be avoided in a vigorous society—that of the indolent and that of the bully.

This became a principle for Roosevelt in many affairs of government: free commerce was essential, but it would come to nothing, worse than nothing, if the rules of enterprise favored one group and bullied another. Roosevelt liked to speak of the nation in a grand way, as if it had a single character, which he wanted to shape. He came to feel that not only enterprise but also fairness was required if toughness of spirit was not to slacken into laziness or arrogance.

Roosevelt, an enthusiast of business and an admirer of progress, feared that the streak of unfairness he sometimes saw displayed in nineteenth-century capitalism, in its harshness and self-concern, would be the unmaking of the whole American enterprise. He had already seen war and the start of revolutions elsewhere; riots had taken place in America and had been brutally suppressed without addressing the matters of fairness involved. He argued, cajoled, and threatened on behalf of fairness. Still, some of his friends in business simply ignored him.

But in the first years of the twentieth century, Roosevelt got the chance to act on his philosophy of combined enterprise and fairness. The opportunity came in the most basic of trades—the sale of food and medicine. Circumstances had conspired to degrade the quality of food in the markets, so too often the food was contaminated, adulterated, or simply rotting but cleverly doctored. And much of the medicine that was sold was worthless; the few vital ingredients that could be effective were often diluted with other substances, faked, or mixed with dangerous ingredients. There were no national rules about hygiene, purity, or honesty in labeling foods and drugs. The result was a protest movement, with outraged citizens petitioning a Congress that was firmly in the pocket of giant national companies and disinclined to provide rules to ensure clean food and pure drugs.

The struggle over the issue led to the creation of the Pure Food and Drug Act, and later the Food and Drug Administration (FDA), the first citizen-protection agency of the federal government. A cadre of chemists and inspectors were thereby commissioned to ensure that, whatever economic theory dictated, businesses would provide unadulterated, uncontaminated food and potent and safe medicines.

The FDA was born in a period of reform, but it was opposed bitterly because it was clear that the organization represented a precedent. The progressives, in trying to combat the seemingly intractable special interests, had successfully enlisted the weight of the federal government against businesses, or rather, against businesses willing to use abusive practices. The new agency was the people's investigator, with the specific mission of intervening on behalf of citizens and against businesses when necessary. In creating a regime of food and drug regulation Roosevelt and Congress were establishing the principle that it was now the job of government not just to champion commerce but also to intervene when it got out of hand.

For years, the government had talked about benefiting the common citizen, but with this gesture, combined with reforms that kept new regulatory agencies independent of political patronage, the rhetoric was put into practice (not that wealth and influence were to disappear). These agencies and those that followed were established as nonpolitical bodies with standing in law and with the power to act. In practice, most of the time they were beyond political influence, and they began to give neutrality and stability to government policymaking, much as the existence of an independent judiciary had done for criminal and civil law.

Other regulatory bodies built on the FDA model, more or less, include the Environmental Protection Agency, the Consumer Product Safety Commission, the Federal Trade Commission, and the Securities and Exchange Commission. The regulatory agencies and their role have evolved over the past century. Central to that evolution has been the idea that empirical evidence, based on testing, should be the foundation of decision-making. That, and the right to interfere in commerce, may be as important in scale as the creation of the civil service that freed decision-makers from political influence, or as the provision of free public education.

This book describes the most significant events in the history of the Food and Drug Administration. But a few facts about the agency will help frame the tale. It has always been small. It began in the nineteenth century with a few scientists at the Bureau of Chemistry in the Department of Agriculture performing lab tests and issuing reports on the quality of American foods and drugs. Just after the turn of the century, as I've said, Congress changed the mission of this little bureau. After it became the FDA it was transferred from the Agriculture Department to the federal department of health—called Health, Education and Welfare, and later, Health and Human Services.

It is the growth of commerce and its new challenges that has led Congress to the FDA for scientific and technical expertise. Since the original 1902 and 1906 acts that set out the bureau's new mission, Congress has passed more than forty additional laws giving the agency more duties—from testing the toxicity of coloring and chemicals added to food, to policing product tampering and medical devices. Its work has grown in direct proportion to the number of products it has been asked to oversee: as they have proliferated in number, kind, and complexity, so has the work of the agency.

Some of its work has made headlines, and each era in American life has had one or two famous FDA cases. Over a few months in late 1919 and early 1920, twenty-five men, women, and children died in an outbreak of botulism; the FDA traced the outbreak to California olive-packing plants and eliminated its cause. In 1937 more than a hundred people, most of them children, were killed by a new antibiotic sold by a Tennessee company that had not tested the compound; FDA investigators tracked down and destroyed all but a few bottles of the deadly syrup. When a polio vaccine was first offered to America in 1954, an error at the manufacturing plant in California produced vaccine that caused 260 cases of polio, including eleven deaths. FDA investigators halted the sale of the vaccine, and discovered that the manufacturers had changed to a cheaper filter, one that incidentally allowed an occasional live particle of poliovirus to leak into the vaccine.

It was the FDA that set up the monitoring of radiation escaping from the Three Mile Island nuclear plant in 1979. When a killer in Chicago murdered seven people in 1982 by putting cyanide in Tylenol capsules, the FDA devised a method to locate contaminated capsules without opening the bottles, facilitating the inspection of millions of Tylenol bottles in a few days and the identification of additional poisoned capsules. When terrorists threatened to kill athletes taking part in the Olympic Games in Atlanta in 1996, FDA inspectors worked around the clock testing food and water for sabotage.

But while occasional cases are famous, most of the work of the FDA passes without much public attention; it is simply expected that food and medicine will be safe. As one writer found, the FDA's work may be vital but remains prosaic in appearance. At the FDA district office in Baltimore inspectors routinely sniff black tiger shrimp from Thailand and select samples of crabmeat to test for botulism. In Philadelphia, cases of grapes are opened to scan them for mold and rot. At other times, it is companies that call on the agency for help, as in cases of tampering that send their sales into sharp decline until products can be carefully screened and the tamperer stopped. Sometimes what it takes is an investigation just to stop a rumor, as when the FDA exposed a hoax about syringes turning up in Pepsi cans.

Watching daily FDA activity is like fast-forwarding a film—hazards caught and averted as they come streaming in. One recent glimpse at the FDA records turned up a routine sampling of problems the agency caught and corrected: In Mississippi, botulism was found in peppered catfish fillets on several sequential inspections of one plant. In Kansas, blood contaminated with hepatitis C was being sent out from a blood bank because of faulty inspections. In a Los Angeles clinic, mammography machines were failing tests and records were missing. In a Colorado pharmaceutical plant, the quality-control system broke down and bad batches of medicine were made and nearly sent out. In California, a company sold eyedrops claiming to cure macular degeneration without an active ingredient to accomplish that. In New York, cattle carcasses showed up at market contaminated with excessively high levels of several antibiotics.

The purview of the agency is now broad. It is required to keep tabs on the products of about 95,000 businesses, amounting to about $1 trillion worth of goods a year, about a quarter of the American economy. By the turn of the twenty-first century, the FDA was annually cataloging more than 200,000 reports of harmful effects from prescription drugs and medical devices each year. It was also fielding 70,000 consumer questions, 40,000 Freedom of Information Act requests, and 180 citizens' petitions per year. Annually, several hundred hazardous drugs and medical devices as well as food products are turned away from the American market.

The FDA was the first agency in the world to attempt broad scientific review of foods and drugs, and its standards have remained the highest. It is the most known, watched, and imitated of regulatory bodies. Because of its influence outside the United States, it has also been described as the most important regulatory agency in the world.

Beyond cleaning up the trade in food and drugs, the FDA has established the scientific base for industry—defining what is safe and what works or does not. In contrast to its reputation in industry and among conservatives as an adversary of business, the agency is a force in the maintenance of successful industries, invaluable in establishing their credibility, and often the vital stimulus that moves business to a new level.

The FDA is still organized mainly by the products it works with. Medical drug review and monitoring fall under the Center for Drug Evaluation and Research; food safety, foodborne illness, nutrition, and labeling, under the Center for Food Safety and Applied Nutrition; safety of medical devices from pacemakers to contact lenses, mammography machines to microwaves, under the Center for Devices and Radiological Health; safety of the blood supply, tissues for transplant, and vaccines under the Center for Biologics Evaluation and Research; drugs for animals, and problems related to animals such as antibiotic resistance and mad cow disease, under the Center for Veterinary Medicine.

The agency's 9,000 employees are concentrated in five regional offices and the headquarters near Washington, D.C. Including smaller outposts, the FDA has about 170 sites in the United States. In comparison with other government agencies, the FDA is tiny. It constitutes less than one half of one percent of the federal government's 2 million workers and has a budget of about $1.3 billion, less than ½₅₀th that of the Defense Department. Even the Agriculture Department, which focuses on a far narrower range of products and activities, is ten times larger in personnel and fifty times larger in budget. The Army Corps of Engineers has a budget three times that of the FDA; NASA's budget is about a dozen times larger. Over the years, tasks have been routinely assigned to the agency by Congress without the funds to carry them out, so a central problem of the agency over the past century has been to spread the very limited budget over an increasing array of jobs. Its chief failures to this day result from the lack of people and resources to carry out the tasks mandated. The cost of the FDA's services in America is about $4 per taxpayer annually.

Above and beyond this daily labor, and arising from it, there are larger social issues about food and drugs, about business and regulation, about the governance of human behavior. To address those takes more than looking at the daily work of such an agency. It requires the longer view of accumulated history.

Recently, a rump movement in America, led by hard conservatives, has been reviling the consumer protection agencies and refusing to accept science as the basis of policy. In particular, Ronald Reagan targeted the FDA in a campaign to return to unfettered, unregulated capitalism like that of the nineteenth century. Any regulations, regardless of their history and usefulness, became suspect.

(In 1975, for example, in a televised press conference, he said the FDA was needlessly killing Americans, and cited as evidence the drug Rifampin. "I think something more than 40,000 tuberculars alone have died in this country who conceivably could have been saved by a drug that has been used widely in the last few years throughout Europe." In fact, the drug had been on the market in America for five years. The manufacturer had applied for approval in 1970 and the FDA had awarded it within five months. In any case, the idea that 40,000 people had died of tuberculosis because of the lack of this drug was absurd. The number of those who had died of tuberculosis, with or without Rifampin, was fewer than 28,000 during the decade between 1968 and 1978. And most of those who died of the disease were diagnosed too late, not because of a drug they were or were not given.)

In the mid-1990s, remarkably, proposals were put forward in Congress to dismantle the agency altogether, and Congress did take some steps backward to the nineteenth century. For example, it stripped food and drug law of all meaningful regulation of herbal remedies and food supplements, so the safety and quality of these are now constantly in doubt.

In some circles, the fashion is still to criticize the "government" and the "government regulators" as if they were occupying armies rather than citizen-soldiers. The FDA has nevertheless proved itself an essential part of modern society. Its history demonstrates that regulatory agencies can not only establish effective protections but make high scientific standards the starting point for industry and the basis of modern government policy as well.

PROTECTING
AMERICA'S HEALTH

•

The Challenge

FLOXIN

ONE DAY in the fall of 1992, novelist Diane Ayres, a diminutive dark-haired woman of some sturdiness and intensity, was told by her gynecologist that she had a small cyst developing on one of her ovaries. He said that simply taking birth-control pills for a month could probably dissolve the cyst. She did, and the cyst disappeared. But Diane had developed a urinary tract infection, one so mild that she had not even noticed it. The doctor gave Diane a prescription for an antibiotic. She was to take a pill twice a day for three days. She took one with breakfast the next day. Within an hour she began having hallucinations. She was unable to find her way around her home office. She wanted to turn off her computer but couldn't remember how. Her mouth was dry and she felt a strong tingling in her left arm and hand. She called her husband, Stephen Fried, a writer, in his office at *Philadelphia* magazine. Diane, usually voluble and verbal, in control, was having trouble enunciating her words. Her sentences broke down in the middle, as she was unable to find words to say what she meant. Stephen called the doctor, who told him to get his wife to the emergency room.

Stephen found Diane lost in her own closet, confused and unable to find a white shirt that was an inch from her hand. At the hospital, he sat with her through triage. The diagnosis was that Diane had "acute delirium." Her jaw was sore, and doctors said it was probably from clenching her teeth against seizures she had apparently experienced. Her pupils were fixed and dilated, and she spoke of something "melting" just behind her eyes.

She was given numerous exams, a CT scan, an EEG, an MRI, and a spinal tap. Doctors were looking for the source of the sudden insanity—a tumor, perhaps, a small stroke. Those were ruled out. The poison control center, however, said that her symptoms were consistent with previous

3

reports of severe reactions to the new antibiotic she had taken. This and other antibiotics in the same family seemed to trigger seizures, convulsions, and something called toxic psychosis, a sudden mental disorder caused by a drug, even in the smallest doses.

That was when the couple learned that the antibiotic she had been given, trade-named Floxin, and chemically designated ofloxacin, was a new and very powerful agent that had been prescribed in place of the usual amoxicillin. Free samples of Floxin were floating around doctors' offices and hospital rooms, and salespeople were talking it up as powerful and safe. Some doctors were giving it out without much consideration.

At the hospital, doctors now gave Diane psychiatric drugs to counteract the effects of Floxin on the brain, and said that once the drug was washed out of her system in a few days, things would probably return to normal.

But as the days passed, it became clear that the drug reaction was not going to be temporary. The days rolled into weeks, and Diane continued to have hallucinations, visual distortions, and a constant fogginess that made thinking difficult. Her memory failed frequently, she was unable to find words to express herself, and from time to time she simply went blank. Once, she walked to a nearby bakery to pick up a birthday cake and got lost on the way home. The most terrifying of all symptoms, however, was the intrusion of suicidal thoughts, urges that seemed to come from nowhere, including images of doing violence to herself.

Stephen decided to investigate the drug and its effects and soon found out that other people had had similar devastating experiences, including permanent disability. The early reports on the drug suggested that about 16 percent of patients who took the drug had some kind of serious side effects—nausea and vomiting were typical reactions—just about double the number caused by milder antibiotics. And there was one side effect that other antibiotics did not produce—about 0.6 percent of those who took the drug had sudden psychiatric problems.

Stephen discovered that another woman in Philadelphia, a thirty-year-old lawyer with two children, had had a severe reaction to Floxin as well. Her doctor had also switched from a more routine antibiotic to the new drug, which she took in the morning and then again in the evening before bedtime. She woke up in the middle of the night to find her husband panicky, yelling at her. "My husband thought I was going to die," she said. "I was having a seizure—I was convulsing, my eyes rolled back, I was drooling, and I bit my tongue almost all the way through. When I finally came to, I couldn't remember anything." She didn't recognize her husband,

and, she said, "I was staring into the crib, and I didn't know who my baby was."

Despite further treatment, both Diane and the lawyer continued to have severe mental problems. They had permanent disabilities. By the time Diane was stricken, more than 60 million people had already taken Floxin. How many others had been affected in this way? How often had the symptoms been misdiagnosed, not as a drug reaction but as another illness? Did anyone know? What records had the company kept? What was the Food and Drug Administration doing about it?

The rate of severe side effects from this antibiotic has so far turned out to be one in 10,000. If 60 million people used it, about 6,000 people would have severe, permanent, or possibly fatal reactions to the drug. Is this acceptable? How many deaths from this drug would be acceptable? When do we call a drug too dangerous to be on the market? Since there are dozens of other antibiotics, it would seem at first blush that all 6,000 of the reactions were unnecessary. But bacterial infections do not respond to every drug, and so this drug might have halted some infections that the usual agents (such as amoxicillin) would not have. Still, except in rare need, why use an antibiotic that has such catastrophic side effects in some people?

The company that made the drug was having trouble accounting accurately for the number of people in whom its drug had caused insanity. It preferred to count most such events as something other than a reaction to its drug. The government—that is, the FDA—which wanted to gather an accurate total, by law depends on the company and a few vigilant doctors for its count. So, in such cases, vital matters can remain unclear for a long time.

Granted that our medicines are potent and largely effective for the illnesses for which we use them, but how much collateral damage do they do?

Stephen Fried, after spending five years writing articles and a book on his wife's drug reaction, said, "I am trying to find out if my wife was the victim of a pharmacological foul-up or just a statistically acceptable casualty of 'friendly fire' in the war on disease."

PROTEASE

It was four years ago that Michael Hill was raised from the dead.

Michael is from a hardworking Catholic family in Leominster, Massachusetts. "We were a tough bunch," he said. "We worked hard, double shifts at everything. We didn't talk much about our feelings. My parents fought violently. I grew up learning to keep eating my cereal while my parents screamed at each other."

Tough, yes, but Michael was a child favored by biology. He had extraordinary good looks, a naturally trim and athletic frame, and an easy laugh. He played football, hockey, and baseball, and was a lifeguard during the summers. He earned top grades and attended Boston University, with a double major in biology and psychology, in preparation for a career in medicine.

But in his last year of college, after being pestered by modeling agencies, he decided to see if he liked the work of posing better than the jobs of waiting tables and bartending that he had taken to pay his way. The modeling went well, so he planned to spend a year in the glamour business after he graduated before getting back to medicine.

In the fall of 1985, when he was twenty-two, he got on a plane to New York. Soon, he found himself on television drinking Miller beer, or wearing Musk cologne; he was in catalogs draped with slick clothes, or Calvin Klein underwear. He was a contender in modeling competitions and was courted by each of the top agencies. His looks put one in mind of Gene Kelly smiling—wholesome, masculine, and warm.

Michael slipped easily into the flow, beguiled as he was by the lifestyle and pleased with his quick success. He did not drink excessively or do drugs. He was not sexually promiscuous. He worked hard. Early on in the whirlwind he went to lunch and fell in love for the first time. To his own surprise it was with another man.

Later, he got what felt like a fierce flu. He thought it might be mononucleosis, and he didn't want to think what else it might be. The doctor near his parents' home ran a battery of tests, including one for HIV. "The doctor phoned a couple of days later and told me, over the phone, that I was positive for the virus," said Michael. "I was alone in the house. I went up to my parents' bedroom where the gun and bullets were kept. The only reason I didn't just do it there was the thought of my sister." She was pregnant, and he wanted to see the baby. He returned to New York.

Michael took high doses of AZT, vitamin C, and supplements by the handful. He imbibed all manner of strange concoctions to help his immune system. He drank egg white milkshakes. "I did it all. I got crystals, I chanted, I meditated, I got massages. If anything could be stuffed into a juicer, I did that."

Then one day he felt thirsty, had a sore throat, and couldn't swallow.

He had diarrhea and began dropping weight fast. "I wasn't losing fat," he said. "But my arms thinned out, my face started sinking in." He was weak and fearful. He canceled his next jobs, and got on a plane in Milan to fly to his parents' home on April 11, 1995. His skin had the pallor of the grave and his body was rapidly melting down around his skeleton.

At the local hospital, the doctors said he was suffering from severe malnutrition—he could neither eat nor hold anything in his bowels—and a rampant infection with cytomegalovirus. When they tested his immune system to see how many defensive cells his body was producing (about 800 per milliliter of blood is normal), they could find none. The amount of deadly virus in his blood was more than 200,000 copies per drop of blood—a vast infestation. They said that Michael had a final choice. He could be admitted to the hospital or he could go home. Either way, he would die very soon.

His family had just built a new house. "So I had to ask my mother whether it was all right if I could go home to her new house and die there, because I didn't want to die in the hospital. I wanted to be home. She said it was all right."

As workers in AIDS organizations can testify, the times were grim. As they helped those infected and ill get treatment, housing, meals, and other forms of help, their clients would drop off the rolls at the rate of thirty a month. Volunteers could attend funerals every day. Once someone was diagnosed HIV-positive in those years, the prospect was for about two more years of narrow, painful life.

Michael could not walk or eat. His weight dropped from 173 pounds to about 115. But three days after his hospital visit, he was still alive. He was taken to a doctor in Boston, Jerome Groopman, who had specialized in treating and researching AIDS for years and was aware of all the latest experimental treatments. Just as he was visiting Dr. Groopman, a series of new drugs were being brought to market, drugs called protease inhibitors.

In the years before these drugs appeared, those infected with the virus were desperate. From the beginning of the epidemic in 1981 until 1987, there were no drugs to treat AIDS. Then, for the next eight years, there was essentially only one—AZT, a drug with strong side effects and limited power to hold down the virus.

When AZT had been approved by the FDA in 1987, it was one of the faster approvals on record—six months. But the first protease inhibitor in 1996 was put on the market in forty-two days. And the approval of each AIDS drug since then has been nearly as fast.

So when Michael Hill went to visit Jerome Groopman at the Deaconess Hospital in Boston in 1995, there was good news. Michael, whose life was being measured in days, was given a protease inhibitor called Crixivan as part of a study. He rose suddenly like Lazarus. His immune system cells grew back in large numbers; the number of HIV particles in his blood dropped below the level where any could be detected.

It was happening everywhere. By late 1997, the U.S. death rate from AIDS fell by more than half. Because of a medical breakthrough and rapid action by the companies and the Food and Drug Administration, AIDS for many had rapidly become a chronic, still threatening, but apparently manageable disease.

Michael is back modeling, buoyant and alive.

PENNYROYAL

On a fall day in 1994, Jennifer Bilger walked to her local co-op market to pick up a few items. She and her husband, the writer Burkhard Bilger, had recently moved to Allston—the bohemian, low-rent student mecca a few subway stops up the Charles River from the more famous parts of Boston. As she was passing among the teas, she paused at one called pennyroyal. The couple enjoyed sampling the great variety of teas the market carried, some of them, like pennyroyal, in big "glass canisters and funky-smelling barrels," as her husband described them. "We had no recipes to follow. We knew only that pennyroyal was a member of the mint family, and that when we steeped the pale blue flowers in hot water, they gave off a heady, amber-colored essence."

Pennyroyal is noted as early as 1530 in the *Oxford English Dictionary*, which records its use in the British Isles as a medicinal herb, but its history in the medical literature as a potent herb goes back at least 2,500 years. As it sat in bulk containers in the co-op grocery, however, it was unaccompanied by any notices, cautions, or information. It was just tea. The Bilgers had tried different types of tea, "but we really liked this one. It was the one we settled on, I suppose because it's somewhat minty, but not like peppermint, and very soothing, relaxing. It is a really unusual combination of tastes," said Burkhard.

Both had grown up in Oklahoma, high school sweethearts. They had moved east in search of jobs. They were married only a short while when they decided to try to have children. She was soon pregnant, and both were pleased and full of hope. They bought all the books, sought the advice, and generally immersed themselves in the grand and ancient possibility.

The signs were good at first. Jennifer checked in regularly at their nearby clinic. There she was told things were fine and progressing normally. But after a few weeks, the doctors began to say that Jennifer's hormone levels didn't seem to be going up the way they should in response to a new pregnancy. Nothing to worry about, though, she was told.

Of course, she worried continuously. "I got into the levels," she said. "I began watching them and thinking about them." Jennifer is a singer, and she carried on with her work on *Thumbelina,* a musical play for children. She toted thermoses full of pennyroyal tea to rehearsals to soothe her, and to coat her throat after the stresses of singing.

But week after week, at the clinic, the tension continued, as her body seemed to be turning against the pregnancy. Finally, she noticed some "spotting," flecks of blood in her vaginal discharge. Then she felt powerful, very painful cramps. "I remember laying on the bed, sad, crampy, and hurting." Then came a gush of blood and tissue. She had lost the baby.

Miscarriages occur frequently, perhaps in as many as one out of four first pregnancies. But Jennifer was far along, and she was emotionally wrapped up in it. "I wept off and on for a couple of weeks," she said. "It was a real sense of loss. A pall kind of settled over everything. I began to wonder if it was genetic, and began preparing myself for the worst. Maybe I wouldn't be able to get pregnant. There had been some trouble like that in my family," she continued. "Still, we could always adopt, I thought."

Not long afterward, however, the couple began to think differently about it. One day, Burkhard was sitting in their living room, listening to a song by the rock group Nirvana. The words, he says, were "a kind of sinister nursery rhyme, innocent on the surface, but appalling once decoded."

> *Sit and drink pennyroyal tea,*
> *Distill the life that's inside of me.*
> *Sit and drink pennyroyal tea,*
> *I'm anemic royalty.*

Pennyroyal, as the Bilgers learned, is not just tea. It is a potent herbal drug, used throughout history to treat a variety of conditions, but most often to induce abortions. High doses can cause severe liver damage, convulsions, and even death. A somewhat smaller dose ends pregnancy.

As Burkhard wrote in a review of the book *Eve's Herbs: A History of*

Contraception and Abortion in the West, by John Riddle, a historian at North Carolina State University, it was easy to remain ignorant of pennyroyal because virtually no information is provided with potentially potent herbal treatments. "A thousand, two thousand, even three thousand years ago, Jennifer and I would have known that" pennyroyal could end a pregnancy. "Any midwife in ancient Athens could have told us about the pennyroyal in her garden. And we would have laughed, during a comedy by Aristophanes, to hear Hermes advise the hero to 'add a dose of pennyroyal' to keep his mistress out of trouble."

Herbal remedies, along with vitamins and "dietary supplements," are thought of as harmless, despite their long and sometimes dangerous history in medicine. We have developed a society-wide amnesia about these substances, and the forgetfulness is not entirely accidental. An effort by consumer activists to discover the active agents in herbal remedies has been fought at every turn by the "industry"—that is, the manufacturers of these herbal remedies and dietary supplements. This industry is the direct progeny of the quacks and patent medicine makers of the nineteenth century.

It is difficult to understand why potent drugs such as pennyroyal, known to cause miscarriage and abortion, should be permitted to be sold without even the hint of a warning to consumers. But the answer is not simple. It lies in the story of politics and money that has shaped the rules of medicine in America.

Why is an antibiotic that causes psychosis still on the market? How did the government approve an AIDS drug so quickly? Why is a potent abortifacient not labeled as such? The questions cannot be answered simply. Each question involves history, a specific set of circumstances, and the evolution of the FDA. The story begins more than a century ago, in the era of the robber barons.

•

CHAPTER ONE

Dr. Wiley's Time

IN APRIL 1863, a tall, stringy young fellow named Harvey Washington Wiley, wearing a suit of knobby homespun, strode out of his Indiana farmhouse and set off for college five miles down a dirt road. He had announced his leaving without preliminaries: "Father, I'm going to Hanover College." Though his father was a part-time farmer and needed Harvey at home, he did not object.

Harvey started his hike optimistically. But by the time he reached the outskirts of the village where the college lay, apprehension filled his chest. He imagined himself, the poorly dressed farmer boy, entering the cultured village and "being a butt for all the students and a laughingstock in the eyes of the faculty." But he knew that if he turned back, it would be the last he would see of education. After years of firelight reading and all it had inspired—his parents read aloud such rich tales as *Uncle Tom's Cabin* and a biography of Napoleon Bonaparte—young Wiley had to take the chance. He walked into the town.

He was moving as America did at the time. In the first half of his life, two-thirds of the nation still worked on farms. But the flight from the land had begun. Soon, a majority of Americans would be living on crowded avenues and in city tenements, and by the second half of Wiley's life, America as imagined by the Founding Fathers was disappearing. (Today the category "farmer" is not even included in census forms.)

A new regime was rising, in which the nation was led by men of business and their new, large operations, called combinations at the time—the first sturdy examples of that new kind of organization, the corporation. These were companies with a national reach, great sums of money available for action and investment, a rank of powerful officers, and—another new phenomenon created by business—big bureaucracy.

The commercial market, and new attitudes toward money in particular, freed people of the dominance of social systems that were hereditary and thus largely unchangeable. The new system made possible social movement based on the accumulation of money. With the coming of the capitalist markets and the corporations, average wealth increased across the country, though not in the heartland. Where hundreds of small packing plants existed, now only a few remained in major cities; where thousands of local mills had once ground grain, now a fraction as many operated, though they were much larger. Locally produced foods were now shipped into the great maw of city factories, and returned in cans and jars, watered down, preserved, and cheap.

Machines were being invented and applied in every field, and factories built around these hissing, tapping objects. Workers were lined up to feed and operate them. Out the other side came profit. The *creation* of goods en masse was soon matched by the ability to *move* them. Great distances were shrunk by rapid transport. But at the same time, another kind of distance between people was growing. People who had once made food, clothing, medicines, and simple tools for themselves or their neighbors no longer did. The modern estrangement between the people who create goods and the people who consume them now emerged. The corporations were developing a reputation not only for lack of accountability, but also for ruthlessness in competition and hardness toward their workers. There was a fear that the money-centered values of the great combines and their owners would soon displace personal decency and honor.

For Harvey Wiley and many of his generation, the nation's plunge into modern life was a plunge into deep waters. The coming of freedom in commerce, and advancement in science and technology, was thrilling. But the raw side of the new business seemed a direct challenge to morality.

At the farmers' Grange meetings in the second half of the nineteenth century, the talk was of ruthless companies, falling prices, and power slipping away from the farmers as corporations took greater and greater shares of their markets. The voice of the farmers, originally one of stability, was becoming a national voice of protest.

Wiley would become one of the first and best spokesmen for some ideas that arose at that time to find a solution to the growing crisis of money and morals. He and other progressives believed strongly: First, that progress was essential and desirable. Second, that business was a great engine of progress, along with science and education, and should be greatly encouraged. Third, that business had shown in the nineteenth century it could not well serve two masters—it could not seek profit with a single-minded energy and at the same time take care that citizens were protected from the injustices and injuries that its actions or products might cause. The new kind of business could not, in other words, honestly police itself. Fourth, that because the new corporations had grown to such great size and influence, the policing of businesses should be done by government, the only other organization in society of sufficient weight to confront business successfully if needed. These ideas produced fierce arguments at the time, and still do.

Wiley would become a creator of the first regulatory agency, the FDA, which was intended to confront business directly when it strayed beyond the bounds. Its mission was to provide a simple public service: to ensure that the foods and drugs sold in America were safe and wholesome for consumption. The FDA, as a "government regulatory agency," is now spoken of by some with a hiss or a dismissive smirk. But such negativity is born of a modern prejudice, one that is based largely on a misunderstanding of the FDA's mission and its history.

Wiley ambled off the farm an unlikely figure for fame. He was taller than six feet and quite awkward. Gifted with some oratorical talent, he was still very nervous before groups. He was religiously fervent while intellectually adventurous in ways that could and did offend the pious.

He was from Republican Township, the sixth of seven children who grew up on a farm of 125 acres. Two ravines that cut the farm ran down to a creek, which emptied into the Wabash River, not far from where it joined the mighty Ohio. Young Wiley could hear the shriek of whistles as steamboats came up the river and, on a clear day, could see the black columns of smoke from their stacks. His father, Preston Pritchard Wiley, a lay minister and self-educated man, was not much of a farmer. His mother, Lucinda Maxwell, had had only three months of schooling but on her own had become fully literate despite the extent of her daily chores.

Preston and Lucinda Wiley drank in knowledge the way the thirsty drink water. They looked forward to what the world might be, and their children in it. The Wileys educated each of their children, including their daughters. They spent money for important books, and periodicals that took weeks to arrive. Preston taught himself Greek so that he could study the New Testament in the original. A grandfather of Lucinda's left Kentucky not long after the Revolutionary War because of his anger over the slave trade; he moved to Indiana with the slaves he had acquired and set them free upon arrival.

In the Wiley family, Christianity was vital. There was no activity on

Sunday; even punishments with the switch were held over for Monday morning. Preston brought young Harvey with him to the school where he taught. He set the youngster on the floor and drew a large square on the floor with chalk. Harvey was told to stay within it, and apparently he did (he must have been aware at all times of the alternative). He learned to read inside his chalk prison.

Voting then was oral. When his father shouted out his lone anti-slavery vote in the county in 1840, screams of "Nigger!" were directed toward him. Despite the risk, he was a participant in the Underground Railroad that carried slaves to the North and freedom.

The Wileys' sense of justice was at least as strong as their desire for new knowledge. Again and again, they warned their son of the current in society pulling them back toward pre-democratic days. Wealth and power were going increasingly to men of commerce who were willing to use people like farm animals, working them for profit with just enough to keep them going, and sometimes less than that. This was the beginning of the era of the robber barons. Preston approved of innovation, but never at the cost of justice.

Harvey grew up wearing woolens shorn, spun, and woven from the family's sheep. Virtually everything he ate also came from the farm— eggs, butter, corn, wheat, chicken, and mutton. He even planted the newest crop of the time—sorghum; he fed it into a one-horse mill to squeeze out the sugar. But his reading had made him imagine the world at large, and the place in it that he might fill. He imagined becoming a man of learning and then returning, in some way at some time, to bring his knowledge back to the land. It did not take long for the times to intervene. First there was the Civil War, and then the upheaval of economic disruption that drove families from the land to the cities, and in many instances from new hope to new despair.

Wealth in America was rapidly leaving the hands of a large number of landowners and flying into the hands of a few industrialists, reaching the point before the end of the century when about 60 percent of the wealth was in the hands of one percent of the population. Along with the boom in business, the nation found it would have to undergo what began to be called, euphemistically, "cycles"—crashes at regular intervals. There were full depressions in 1873, 1884, and 1893. Perhaps just as important, business and politics had merged into one entity. The era of the common man envisioned not long before had never arrived. The control of politics, once in the hands of kings and hereditary gentry, rapidly passed to a moneyed class. Political corruption was beyond anything easily imagined today. The United States Senate was referred to as the "millionaire's club," and it resembled a convention of industry representatives. Because of strong party control over state legislatures and election rules, it had become common for wealthy men to pay a fee to the party to get themselves nominated and elected to office. "The Senate, instead of representing geographical areas, came to represent economic units," writes historian Sean Cashman. In Congress, it was lumber rather than Michigan, oil rather than Ohio, silver rather than Nevada. There were no public services to speak of, and protests were crushed by private squads or government troops, or both.

All this was transpiring as intellectual, scientific, and technical progress was advancing so rapidly that there is nothing in any corner of history or any civilization to match it.

For Harvey Wiley the times were more than stimulating. In the summer of 1864, when a call went out for volunteers to fight for the Union, he left college and signed up with the 137th Regiment of Indiana volunteers. During his time in uniform, the man in charge of his life was Sergeant Solomon Hampton, a country doctor by trade and a medic in the Union army. Hampton described the farm boy who came to him as "lean, lank, bowlegged, Chinese-eyed, jaundice-skinned," and full of fun. The two men became good friends, and after Wiley finished his studies at Hanover College in 1865, Wiley's first job was as an apprentice to Dr. Hampton in Kentucky.

Wiley studied medicine "and rode over the hills of Trimble County with the doctor on his calls, now to deliver a baby, now to treat a gunshot wound . . . the two young men found each other congenial company and, when work permitted, loved to match wits over a chess board," writes Oscar Anderson. He earned an M.D. from Indiana Medical College, and soon strung together every connection he could to get into Harvard. He earned his bachelor of science there cum laude in less than two years by prodigious work and continual social enterprise. Then he set off for the obligatory tour abroad. He studied under the most brilliant chemists of the time—those in the German universities. When he returned, he obtained a position as the head of the science department at a university just being formed in Lafayette, Indiana, called Purdue University after its financial benefactor. There Wiley created the first student chemistry labs in the state and became a one-man advance in scientific learning for the region.

He continued his own studies, eagerly carrying out chemical analysis of everything he could lay his hands on—dirt, wood, water, cosmetics.

But most of all he worked on sugar and the creation of its synthetic base, glucose.

He flourished as a teacher, and took on projects for the state government. His reputation grew. In fact, it quickly grew beyond the capacity of some Indianans to tolerate it. The president of Purdue at the time, Emerson White, was the virtual opposite of Wiley. White, a former local high school teacher, had little understanding of the world outside Indiana and none of science. He was a religious bigot and a man singularly lacking in humor. Under White, it was virtually a requirement that professors be Trinitarians, and they could not say, as Wiley had, that *all* beliefs should be tolerated. Worse, Wiley insisted that the word "all" included pantheists and atheists as well as monotheists.

Wiley exhorted his students to absorb an "all-permeating ambition to ameliorate the condition of man." Like a preacher, this scientist called his students to action:

> Wherever there is want, there is your place to supply; wherever ignorance, there is your place to teach; wherever sickness, there is your place to heal; wherever oppression, there is your place to relieve; wherever injustice, there is your place to vindicate; finally, wherever in the battle of life there is need of hands or nerve or brain, there amidst the carnage and desolation in the middle of the sulfurous smoke and the hail of death and the tempest of passion and hate, is your place to stand or fall fighting with your face to the foe.

The moment of truth for Wiley at Purdue came when he procured "a nickel-plated Harvard roadster bicycle, with a high front wheel and a small back wheel." He rode it for some time before receiving a summons to appear before the university's board of trustees. One of the trustees read the charges to him. They had "been greatly pleased with the excellence of his instruction" and with his popularity among his pupils. Still, they were "deeply grieved . . . at his conduct. He has put on a uniform and played baseball with the boys, much to the discredit of the dignity of a professor. But the most grave offense of all has lately come to our attention. Professor Wiley has bought a bicycle. Imagine my feelings and those of other members of the board on seeing one of our members dressed up like a monkey and astride a cartwheel riding along our streets." Eventually, after facing similarly absurd conflicts again, Wiley left.

While in Indiana, Wiley had begun to attend regional and national meetings of the new breed of scientists—chemists. There was nothing like it for excitement; Louis Pasteur in France and Robert Koch in Germany had done the same. Both are now known for their discoveries regarding how human diseases are caused and can be cured, but at the time both worked in industry as well as universities—Pasteur on wines, and Koch on the best method of dyeing cloth. Chemistry there was at the center of both life and commerce. Not long before, the nature of all substances on earth had been laid out in the periodic table, a kind of map to the stuff of the natural world. The basic substances were grouped in families, from the most active and dangerous to the entirely passive. Experiments could now probe almost anything inert or living, and might soon reveal some of their essential features—the key elements in food, those that feed the body, those that poison it.

At one of the many meetings Wiley attended, he met Dr. George B. Loring, the U.S. commissioner of agriculture, who was immediately impressed with him. Loring had got himself in a tangle in Washington when he had fought in public with his chief chemist about the value of sorghum as a replacement for sugarcane. The chemist was a fevered enthusiast for sorghum, though it had not yet been proved an economical source of sugar. Loring, interested but unwilling to devote great amounts of time and resources, fired the chemist. But he could not afford to be seen as an opponent of a new, *American* sugar plant. In 1883 he asked Wiley, who was both a friend of sorghum sugar and a skeptical, accomplished scientist, to come to Washington to be the Agriculture Department's new chief chemist. Wiley went.

At the time, science in America, and the university system that would later support it, was lagging many years behind Europe. The United States had no department of health, no department of science, no method of raising money for research. There was no regulation of commerce or science. Science was seen as a subject interesting only to intellectuals and dreamers; businessmen in America disdained it.

Wiley was undeterred. He took on the sorghum project, which plainly had economic consequences, but he was interested in chemistry as a whole, particularly as it applied to the body, and to health. He regarded the chemistry of food as something like the text of God's instructions for the temple of physical health. In Germany, he had learned a new method to determine the sugar content of foods, and he had applied it in Indiana examining samples of syrup and honey from the local markets; to his surprise, few of them were unadulterated. Most were cut with cheap, laboratory-produced sugar and were not, as they claimed, derived from bees or cane. His report on the widespread cheating in honey and syrup making was one of the first of its kind in America, and had drawn the attention of the leaders of the Agriculture Department in Washington.

Food was beginning to be understood as an accretion of chemicals and nutrients that nature had put together and which were perfectly suited to provide sustenance and maintain health. Wiley and others began to imagine a scientific base for the nation's policies on food and drugs. Scientists could, he imagined, work out what was the best in food ingredients, and what should be avoided. He imagined that both foods and medicines might be tested for their healthfulness, and the government's policy set accordingly.

But commerce, in search of profits, had already started to adulterate some ingredients in food, using chemicals to preserve food or hide its putrescence, and to fake colors and textures. A catalog of the debasement of food had already been published in Britain, and Wiley was worried that the American market was wide open to abuse. He had no authority to stop food companies and drugmakers from carrying on with such dubious practices, but he could surely catalog and publicize them. There were already protests, marches, and lobbying in cities around the country against contaminated and deceitfully labeled food. Now, the groups had gained an ally in Washington.

Federal interference in commerce was a hateful notion in Washington at the time; intrusion upon businesses was not to be countenanced. Only if a business behaved like the devil himself could it bring on national action. The business leaders of the latter part of the nineteenth century were not called robber barons for nothing; the era has been described as the most shameless in American history.

With Wiley's sense of mission, both for science and for fairness in trade, his office soon became the center of the storm over commerce.

CHAPTER TWO

•

Commerce, Commerce, Commerce

HARVEY WILEY was a modern, forward-looking man who saw his position and his moment as a grand opportunity. He was also a businessman who had participated in a few ventures himself, someone who believed commerce must be free to be creative and not be suffocated by government direction or needless laws.

At Harvard, in one of the most inspiring talks Wiley ever heard, Senator W. B. Allison said that a great principle in human affairs was the practical fact that freedom worked. He spoke of the new spirit of progress and knowledge abroad in the land. Whereas governments, churches, and custom had largely suppressed the adventure of inquiry before that time, Allison said that

> Under our system of government, no shackles or fetters are placed upon your investigations. This great truth is recognized, that the State has no concern with the opinions of men. Here science with her bold inquisitive spirit has established her right to investigate all subjects after her own fashion, and according to her own method; . . . our own countrymen are therefore entitled to their share of discovery, invention and improvement.

The argument was for science, but the reference to "invention and improvement" meant that business should be free and unfettered, to allow competition among ideas. Free inquiry and free commerce were sides of the same coin.

But what bothered Wiley, who loved both research and commerce, and participated in both throughout his life, was that in research there was a strong sanction against deceit, while in commerce deceit seemed to be an accepted tactic to achieve profits. There was some disjoint here. Wiley could not understand deception about food and drugs, substances that to him were sacramental. They were nature's chemistry. How could one corrupt what was produced by God and nature, and needed for life by humans?

In a small way, sugar was an example. Chemical laboratories including Wiley's own were now able to create glucose, a pure sugar, cheaply and in quantity. But it carried nothing of the taste from plants. So when food manufacturers in Indiana began to put glucose into food, calling it sugar, Wiley was incensed. Both before and after he left for his posting in Washington, he declared that it was *not* the same. Manufacturers could use the cheaper glucose, but they should also *say so*.

The rise of the business fever that swept the nation between 1850 and 1900 was a crusade as fervent and intolerant as any religious uprising. It was the second great American social experiment, and it eclipsed the founders' first visions of the nation. Where they imagined a tranquil, farm-based republic, America was now a high-contrast, high-energy landscape of machinery and industry, in concert with the restless activity of buying and selling.

"The voice of the people and their government is loud and unanimous for commerce," writes Columbia University professor Samuel Mitchill even in the early years of the nineteenth century. "Their inclination and habits are adapted to trade and traffic. From one end of the continent to the other, the universal roar is Commerce! Commerce! At all events, Commerce!" Visitors were stunned, as historian Gordon Wood observes, to see Americans selling their landed estates to go into trade. The nation was simply obsessed with buying and selling. "It is a passion unconquerable as any with which nature has endowed us," said Henry Clay to Congress in 1812. "You may attempt to regulate—you cannot destroy it."

It "was frightening and bewildering to many—that a whole society should be taken over by moneymaking and the pursuit of individual interest," writes Wood. Even Abraham Lincoln, peering into the future just before he died, lamented what he saw, which he called a new royalty: "Corporations have been enthroned. . . . An era of corruption in high places will follow and the money power will endeavor to prolong its reign by working the prejudices of the people . . . until wealth is aggregated in a few hands . . . and the Republic is destroyed."

When Wiley moved to Washington he found himself stepping into the conflict over what standards if any should mark the boundaries of business behavior. Do citizens need special protection, and if so, what should government do to provide it?

Throughout his long life Wiley never did understand why some of those in business couldn't maintain the fundamental sense of honor that obtained between gentlemen. In commerce, selling goods for less, and giving them the best face, is vital. A few businessmen chose the strategy to sell only quality goods, honestly. But others would never make a dollar without a tactical lie and a corner cut. Wiley insisted that profit gained in such dishonorable ways was not worth having. Why were businesses unable to apply principles that obtained elsewhere in society? Tactics could be creative. Strategies could be developed to capitalize on new methods and new national-scale markets. But why was outright deceit unavoidable? And why would businessmen who when met at the club seemed honorable fellows, sell products that could be hazardous to health? Wiley thought, at first, that exhortations upon their honor, and some censure from colleagues for the worst offenders, would be sufficient to tame the excesses in the new wave of commerce, and bring it back within the bounds of decent behavior.

After the Civil War matters seemed to get steadily worse, and by the end of the century the corruption in the food and drug trade was unlike anything seen at any time in history. There had always been some cheating—short-weighting, watering of wine, cutting of medical powders with inert substances to increase their weight. These had been criminal offenses and were sometimes punished harshly. But the abuses never became so common and widespread as they did in America in the late nineteenth century. New forms of cheating were now possible on a large scale for the first time, at exactly the moment when a food or medicine maker did not have to face his customer directly, given the expanded distribution network. His customer was no longer necessarily his neighbor or even a resident of the same state. Adulteration and deception became easy and very profitable.

Wiley's agricultural chemists laid out the issues involving food, in a report to Congress. In an exhaustive and detailed compendium, the chemists described an array of chemical cheapening ingredients, colorings, and preservatives that were being used to change radically the appearance, smell, and taste of bad food without setting off alarms in the senses. Copper sulfate can make faded vegetables appear green again; sodium benzoate can prevent decayed tomatoes from rotting altogether; stearins can stretch lard; borax can make odorous ham acceptable when canned.

These substances became available just as streams of people left the farm for the city and immigrants crowded the tenements. On the farm, foods that must be stored and their containers are sterilized and set aside.

But such methods were not practical for the new business. Sterilization was difficult on a large scale, and while the woman at home might put up a dozen jars of pickles and accept that three of them might go bad, businesses could not accept such odds. In addition, they had to ship foods many miles while they cooked in the sun, cooled in the shade, and shook with the train and wagon. With sterilization not a viable option, and refrigeration too expensive and not always practical, preservatives became vital for transport. Altering food became the easiest way of saving it. So the chemical parade began.

The chemicals used were not required to be tested for their effects on human health, and were not. There were no penalties for selling chemical-laden food. A new industry grew up making and selling preservatives with names like Freezem, Freezine, Preservaline, and Rosaline. They carried no labels, and food company owners testified in Congress that they used them without ever asking their manufacturers of what they were composed. Most were dilute solutions of formaldehyde, sulfites, borax, salicylic acid, and benzoic acid, among other things. (All are toxic to a degree, and now restricted for human use to some degree; three of them are banned.)

In addition to trying to prevent food from going bad (or disguising the fact that it had), the new arts of chemistry created opportunities for complete fakes. A bit of brown color and a dead bee or a honeycomb dropped into a jar of laboratory-manufactured glucose made a "honey" that was cheap to manufacture. Brown coloring and a pinch of flavoring could also "turn" glucose into cane or maple syrup. A spoonful of hayseeds and some pulped apple skins for color transformed the glucose into what could be called strawberry jam.

Most foods were sold by weight, so a common tactic of merchants over the ages had been to mix cheap ingredients with the real article. This practice now became much more widespread, with the added fillip that chemistry could now aid in the adulteration. In chocolate, chemists found ground-up soap, beans, and peas; to restore the darker color of the original chocolate after adulteration, the makers added red oxide of mercury, a substance lethal in large amounts. To flour was added chalk, clay, or plaster of paris. Bakers made their loaves heftier by adding copper sulfate, a chemical that absorbs and holds water at a great rate.

As it happens, some insects when ground up look a lot like coarse brown sugar, and so arose a new ailment called grocer's itch. In examining brown sugar, researchers often found that a substantial portion of it was the carcasses of lice, together with some living ones, suggesting that the grocers might have gotten their skin condition when they scooped sugar for their customers.

Milk was often diluted with water, threatening children's nutrition, but an even more dangerous practice grew up in the late nineteenth century—the creation of swill milk. Instead of milking cows that had been grazing on the pastures, distilleries cut down on expenses by confining a herd of cows in small stalls with a long sloping trough at their head end. After a distillery had finished using grains and water, the leftover swill was sent red-hot down into the trough. The animals couldn't get much nutrition from it, but got huge amounts of liquid, and when milked gave large quantities of nutrition-stripped milk. One medical review reported that one local set of families who had purchased the weak milk had very high rates of infant mortality, and it was probable that swill milk was the leading cause of infant mortality in the district.

As far as medicines were concerned, the nineteenth century was the grand era of the quack remedy. Though we think of the history of medicine as full of foolish treatments and phony drugs, this era was something apart, when medical fraud was created in America on an entirely new scale.

Medicine had always had its lack of reliable information. There were always suspicions about the medicines used by doctors. But from the earliest times there were strong sanctions against making and selling phony medicine. It was a sin more serious than bread improperly weighed or watered-down wine, because not only were customers cheated, but their lives could be put at risk. Moreover when a proven remedy existed, a fake one could keep a patient from getting his or her needed treatment. Producers of quack remedies were not only lightening consumers' pocketbooks, they were actually committing crimes of assault, manslaughter, and homicide, depending on what the seller knew about his concoction.

Medicine was split into the inadequate but seriously intended treatment by doctors and the predatory commercial medicine that had no basis but the desire for profit. And as it happened, medicine was one of the first fully national markets that used nationwide advertising. Quack medicines, of which there had always been a trickle, suddenly became a flood as tradesmen, not doctors, saw the possibilities for profit. A new category of drugs and health supplements, shaped in England but exploited on the American side of the Atlantic, was created specifically to suit the new methods of business. Though called patent medicines, they were not actually patented, for the most part. Rather, the words "patent" and "proprietary" referred to the secrecy in which their formulas were held. Ingredients were not disclosed to either the doctors who administered the "drugs" or the patients who took them.

This secrecy was a break from the past. In every developed nation, doctors and lawmakers worked to construct a known, stable list of medicines and their ingredients. These were the pharmacopoeias and national formularies. They were put together in an effort to assure citizens that the medicines they were taking were standard mixtures of known ingredients, whether or not they could be said to be effective. The efforts to regularize medicine, to set universal formulas for each known remedy, had advanced from the seventeenth century to the nineteenth, with little difficulty—until now.

The patent medicines were often created in whole or in part from the standard remedies doctors used, made from the same herbs and minerals. Their effects were very similar, though confounded by the multiple ingredients they contained, from half a dozen to forty. They were sold solely on the basis that someone, somewhere, was said to have been cured by them. But the chief difference between these and known drugs was not ingredients, effectiveness, or medicinal usefulness. The difference was one of marketing. It was the packages and the advertising sheets that were the key to the rise of the era of quack medicines.

This was a first for any product. Manufacturers, as America's leading historian of food and drugs, James Harvey Young, writes, patented neither the key medicine in these offerings nor the composition of the entire formula. Instead, the makers patented, trademarked, or copyrighted the distinctive shape of the bottle, the box the medicines came in, the type styles and pictures on the labels, and the advertising associated with it all.

The demand for "secret formula" medicines began in the Colonies with medicines from England. But when, during the Revolution, English patent medicines could not be imported, American businessmen filled English bottles with almost anything that seemed a suitable imitation. Then, when they could not get the bottles, they had glaziers make bottles in the key shapes. The point, of course, was that it was not the medicines that mattered. None of them actually worked against disease. It was all a packaged fantasy, and the package was the vital part.

In addition to working with the shapes of bottles—important partly because illiterate citizens could pick them out without having to read labels—salesmen obtained copyrights on the labels, the promotional literature that came with the bottle, and the posters affixed to fences and buildings. They actively went after trademarks, distinctive symbols on the bottles (Hercules wrestling hydra on Swaim's Panacea, for example), signs, and flyers. The efforts to claim legal jurisdiction for their promotional materials were essentially new in commerce, and far in advance of those for any other product. The medicinal nostrum makers pioneered promotion and marketing as no other business had to that time.

They worked with the names—the Grand Restorative, the Universal Vegetable Pill, Wheeler's Nerve Vitalizer. There were more than fifteen thousand of them. The claims for what they did were relatively modest and narrow in the seventeenth and eighteenth centuries but became florid and aggressive by the nineteenth century. Swaim's, for example, was sold with claims to cure "cancer, scrofula, rheumatism, gout, hepatitis, and syphilis," and the list expanded gradually for decades.

Part of the new effort to encourage business in America in the nineteenth century was a new set of postal laws that had been pressed by selected members of the new business class called lobbyists. These laws led quickly and directly to a new type of marketing by medicine makers— the first direct mail campaigns. Lower postal rates for bulk mailing were inaugurated in the 1840s, and soon pamphlets, letters, simulated newspapers, and other devices hawking cures were sent directly to the public. Not only were patent medicines the first to be marketed and promoted directly to the people, they managed to achieve the first nationwide markets in the young country.

And there was an expanding opportunity for the remedies to be announced to the nation—in newspapers. In the days of Thomas Jefferson, there were about two hundred newspapers, mostly weekly papers, in the Colonies, and none reached much beyond the city in which they were published. Multi-city advertising and writing simply did not exist. While only a handful of papers could manage daily publication in the early decades of the United States, by Lincoln's day, four hundred were issued each morning or afternoon; including weeklies, there were four thousand newspapers in America.

By 1860, free education to the children of the poor and mass literacy were facts of life. The makers of the quack medicines were the first to exploit this new common market. Salesmen and advertising agency specialists sold the remedies. The remedies soon dominated newspapers— patent medicines were the number one advertiser nationwide at the turn of the century—and accounted for a large percentage of the income of many newspapers, often half of a newspaper's entire advertising income. The drugs "flourished in direct ratio to the availability of cheap newspapers and magazines," writes historian of medicine John Duffy. One study of a New England newspaper in 1858 showed that one-quarter of the entire newspaper, and half of all the advertising space, was filled with patent medicine advertisements.

In turn, the majority of business for advertising agencies was patent medicines, and admen themselves bought, sold, and created remedies. George Rowell, a pioneering advertising man, decided to make a remedy to fit advertising needs rather than the other way around. He found a formula for an antidyspepsia remedy that had been around for years and could easily be put into the form of light tablets that could be shipped cheaply in the mail. The name for the remedy was invented from the initials of its chief ingredients—rhubarb, ipecac, peppermint, aloe, nux vomica, and soda: Ripans. He sold it for a nickel and wrote, "No matter what's the matter, one will do you good. . . . They banish pain, induce sleep, prolong life." The remedy faced stiff competition, and did not turn a profit until it had been on the market for several years and achieved a regular clientele of at least fifty thousand.

The market for patent drugs was hugely competitive, but even so, one critic estimated that almost fifty makers of patent medicines in New York City made fortunes over $100,000 in the last two decades of the nineteenth century. In today's dollars, that would be fifty multimillionaires in a single city, in a single trade. More than a dozen of these luminaries amassed million-dollar fortunes even measured in nineteenth-century dollars. Businessmen said that a remedy would not fly unless at least $50,000 was poured into advertising it. One maker said he invested $250,000 before he turned a profit. In 1900 a million dollars in advertising was spent on Lydia E. Pinkham's Vegetable Compound (a nostrum that had little to offer except its 40-proof alcohol content). The numbers only grew in the twentieth century.

As James Harvey Young writes, advertising men thought of medicines as their way into the business, the most important test of ad writing. Claude Hopkins, one of the premier ad writers of the nineteenth century, said that copywriting for medicines was the supreme test of a writer's ability, because "medicines were worthless merchandise until a demand was created."

From a time in the 1700s when there were few American medicines, and the ones that existed were advertised in a perfunctory way, it took relatively few years to reach the near hysteria among competitive drug hawkers in the mid-1800s. In Philadelphia, by 1840, one citizen complained in writing that advertising for patent medicines had reached unruly extremes. It was covering every available surface: "the walls of our inns—the corners of our streets, and our pumps thereof—the wrecks of burnt, dilapidated buildings, with their standing abutments—the fences enclosing vacant lots in all our cities, if not our small villages, and the decks and cabins of our steamboats." In short, the ads were in any visible spot not policed by lot owners, and in many places where the proprietors were willing to allow it, for a price. Ads appeared on rocks in the country, on wagons rumbling through the streets of the city. "There is no relief in all the earth," one man wrote in the 1860s.

There developed something of a war between patent medicine salesmen and doctors. Neither group was particularly good at healing illness, but doctors, while seeking profit, were also attempting to establish a rational basis for medicine. At one point, concern about the medical drugs coming into the port of New York from Europe prompted a year-long investigation by Dr. M. J. Bailey, an inspector appointed by the secretary of agriculture. At the end of the study, in 1846, Bailey testified in Congress: "More than one half of the most important chemical and medicinal preparations . . . come to us so much adulterated, or otherwise deteriorated, as to render them not only worthless as a medicine, but often dangerous." Rhubarb root was a common ingredient in medicines, and in one three-month period, Bailey recalled, he had reviewed seven thousand pounds of the root and found "not one pound of it fit, or safe."

Opium was a vital painkiller, and when medical shipments arrived in New York, they had been cut to one-third natural strength, and had been laced with Spanish anise and other bitter powders to disguise the dilution. Further, a substantial part of all opium shipments was infested with live worms. Massachusetts reported that of all medical drug samples taken between 1882 and 1900 in the state, 37 percent were adulterated. In New York, of the 343 samples of one drug purchased, phenacetin, 315 were diluted with acetanilide, a very hazardous painkiller.

The market in medicines, without any regulation, was essentially the same as the only market today with no regulation—the trade in heroin, cocaine, and other drugs. The supply was unreliable, the purity suspect, the price high and variable, and the corrupted substances sometimes fatal.

In the early 1800s, Britain and other nations had begun to enact laws to protect the purity of food and drugs inside their own borders, but Bailey said that in the United States, where laissez-faire was the rule, "These base deceptions are rapidly multiplying." A congressional committee looking into food and drug problems concluded that America "has become the grand mart and receptacle of all the refuse merchandise . . . not only from European warehouses, but from the whole Eastern world." British member of Parliament Jacob Bell noted that the phrase "good enough for America" had long been used in Britain to describe goods that were "reduced by decay, or ingenuity, to American price."

The early alarms had brought the first law against food and drug adulteration, in June 1848. It was clear there was a substantial problem, and the first logical thing to do at the time was to blame foreigners. Much was made of how foreign foods and medicines had deteriorated before entering the United States. So the first law in this category was one banning adulterated food and medicine from abroad.

Very few bad products came into the United States in the year after passage, because the law required that rejected items would be destroyed or sent back. More than 90,000 pounds of drugs destined for the United States were turned back at the port of New York that year. The law did not mention the domestic problem.

There remained a broad confidence that cheating of the kind done by foreigners did not occur substantially in the United States. "No one can believe that adulteration here would be carried to the extent practiced by foreigners," said Representative Thomas O. Edwards, a doctor and chairman of the House Select Committee, which investigated the food and drug problems. "It is scarcely presumable that all the druggists will be engaged in a traffic so nefarious. The rivalry of business, the pride of the profession, and the higher and nobler motives of humanity, will be equal to the ingenuity and invention of the dishonest, and will effect its exposure."

Though the 1848 law succeeded quickly, it also failed quickly. There was no civil service to guarantee the independence and quality of the inspectors. So, in a short time, the positions became spoils handed out after election. The inspectors were subject to direction from politicians who had a significant interest in what came and went in port. Influence and bribes became part of the system. Moreover, the inspectors were not working with fixed standards. There were no fewer than five different definitions of acceptable drugs in the different pharmacopoeias.

Dr. Edward R. Squibb, the founder of the drug giant of the same name in Brooklyn, was a man with a reputation for honesty. After observing the passage and early success of the 1848 law, then its failure, he began to advocate the appointment of independent, federally appointed inspectors to monitor the drug trade. He said that the forces in the market were simply too far out of balance to bring an honest trade in medicines without intervention. "The magic power of profits," Squibb said, apparently was able to corrupt "a large majority" of the pharmacists and many doctors. He felt sympathy for those who wanted to maintain high standards, and believed they deserved a fair chance to earn a good living.

In trying to guarantee the safety and effectiveness of drugs, independent inspectors and high standards would remain among the most important issues throughout the history of regulation. They would eventually be addressed by the civil service system, which was established to assure that government appointments were both independent of political influence and based on merit. In addition, independent agencies would eventually be given the job of inspection and review.

For drugs made and sold in America, the professional organizations tried by voluntary code to stem the problem of adulterated drugs and patent medicines. When it was founded in 1852 the American Pharmaceutical Association admitted only those pharmacists who would sign a code of ethics saying they would sell only high-quality medicines. But soon it was clear that it was not just foreign drug suppliers who were the problem, and not just a few American drug suppliers either. Far too many druggists depended on the sale of the high-profit patent medicines, along with the sale of genuine medicines, to carry them through. So in 1856 the pharmaceutical association dropped its rule that members could not sell nostrums, and instead said simply that the organization would try to suppress and restrict the sale of quack drugs whenever possible.

Dr. John H. Griscom, a reformer with the New York Academy of Medicine who was seeking some solution to the problem of adulteration, said that, ultimately, the fault for the rise of quack drugs "lies rather with the public which patronizes, and not so much with the tradesman who profits by," the sale of nostrums. It was a bit like suggesting that burglary be considered the fault of burglars only if homeowners had taken strict measure to lock up their valuables. He recommended educating the public about quackery while allowing the professions to monitor themselves.

A tension existed between honest and scientific undertakings in drug manufacture and the lure of profits. Druggist Henry P. Hynson was unhappy about the tendency of learned pharmacists who were then beginning to "push commercialism to the front." He said the trade of pharmacy was both "learned in the sciences and trained in its special art," but nonetheless willing to supply whatever junk the market demanded. Pharmacist William C. Alpers, in speaking of drugmakers of the nineteenth century, asserted that "any idea that druggists who studied pharmacy conducted business for the sole purpose of advancing science or gratifying" some "desire for higher education" was an "absurdity." They were "in business for the sake of profit."

Squibb and a committee of the American Medical Association declared the 1848 law a complete failure by 1863. And no law had even been attempted for the American domestic market.

Ultimately, the adulteration of drugs in the United States was enough to get the navy's Bureau of Medicine and Surgery to completely end its reliance on commercial manufacturers. Businesses simply could not be trusted. The bureau set up its own laboratory for making drugs to be sure they would be both potent and uncontaminated. Fear of bad medicine had already produced one panic, at the end of the war with Mexico in 1848.

In that war, only 9 percent of the deaths were on the battlefield. Eighty-seven percent were caused by disease. Rumors and news reports attributed those deaths to contaminated and adulterated medicines shipped to the troops. The drugs of the time, diluted or not, would have been unable to do much to save the army in Mexico, which was swamped with yellow fever, dysentery, and cholera. But the point was driven home, as it had never been before; that American businessmen were careless even when it came to young men fighting for their country. A report on the adulteration of drugs issued by the House of Representatives said that "the cold-blooded, deliberate, studied, and fatal deception practiced in articles designed for the relief of suffering and disease, can admit of no palliation—can find no excuse."

European nations, for their part, increasingly came to fear American goods and started embargoes against food, in particular, meat, beginning in 1879. Rampant contamination of American products gave European nations an opportunity to create trade barriers that would do wonders for their own farmers and food manufacturers. After a round of trichinosis infections in the United States caused by infected pork, the acting British consul in Philadelphia wrote to his foreign office, with an apparent combination of horror and glee, of the symptoms of one man in Kansas, ill with trichinosis: "Worms were in his flesh by the million, being scraped and squeezed from the pores of his skin. They are felt creeping through his flesh and are literally eating up his substance." Outbreaks of trichinosis in European countries were traced back to American products, perhaps incorrectly. Nevertheless, even in countries without boycotts, the sale of American products dropped drastically.

Wiley wrote of the times: "Various and colorful descriptive terms have been applied to that next-to-last decade of the nineteenth century. However the era may be characterized, one thing is certain," he said. The "eighties brought forth many changes in business life and left many evils that called to high heaven for remedy."

Movements for broad political reform were under way across the nation in the last two decades of the nineteenth century, focused chiefly on the larger economic and labor crises in society. Marches and riots ended badly, in jail and bloodshed. By the 1890s, business had pressed workers and farmers nearly to revolt. In Europe, rioters had already been in the streets; anarchists and terrorists were creating panic, and revolution was again spoken of in loud voices. In the United States, the strikes and violence were also reaching an intense pitch, yet there was no sign of weakening in the determination of business leaders to take every penny of profit and punish every challenge.

There were more than thirty thousand strikes and riots in the last three decades of the nineteenth century in America, and large-scale industrial violence was introduced as employers and the government attacked striking workers. The symbols of the troubles have become a trio of events—the Haymarket riot of 1886 in which innocent protesters were hanged to send a warning to socialists; the Homestead strike of 1892 in which steelworkers protesting cuts in wages faced an army of Pinkerton watchmen who broke the strike and killed seven workers; and the Pullman strike of 1894, in which the U.S. attorney general, himself on the boards of two railroads, began a military intervention on behalf of railroad companies against nonviolent protesters who had complained about wage cuts. The federal troops killed thirty, and the government prosecuted and imprisoned the labor leaders who dared to protest company policies.

The leading political party on the side of change was the Populist party, which rose from the farmers' Grange meetings, where a mix of fundamentalist religion and "rights-of-the-common-man" arguments made a strong brew. At the same time, local action on food and drug reform flourished, separate from and uncomfortable with the national populist rage. Alice Lakey, one of the chief figures of the food and drug reform movement in America at the end of the nineteenth century, said, "Practically all the industries have now been taken from the home. The brewing, the baking, the canning, the preserving are now all done outside." The American woman began to pay less attention to these matters until, Lakey said, "a rude awakening convinced her that what she was feeding her family did not meet the standards of human decency."

This problem for women in nineteenth-century America, writes historian Lorine Goodwin, was one of "magnitude, intensity, urgency and lack of alternative." From a time not long after the Civil War, the deterioration of the quality of food, drink, and drugs was rapid and demoralizing. There is a shortage of hard data with which to establish the swelling of adulterated products. Health departments were just being established; a state chemist to oversee food and drugs was a new occupation. But what few quantitative reports we have suggest the problem was grotesque.

The changes in society were two-sided, of course. While they led to a corruption of food and drug supplies, they also freed some women from the labors of producing foods and drugs, and allowed them to consider the matters of health on a broader intellectual and social level. Women began to spend time in social and political activities, chief of which was the formation of what are called clubs, but which were often deadly serious political and social-action groups. These were started in every major city, in most states, to establish local boards of health. As they succeeded, they began to become investigators who went out to report local problems and take them to the boards for action.

Women's groups gradually became allied city to city and state to state, realizing, as the corporations had, that concentrating local forces was essential to creating influence. The much-ignored network of women's groups of the nineteenth century was not only a women's movement and a consumer movement combined, it was the first attempt to approximate fact-based regulation and policymaking on food and drug matters.

The faith in laissez-faire economics, in which businesses and customers were left to wrestle without government aid or rulings, was beginning to falter. Courts began to find that selling a product carried either an expressed or an implied warrant that the product was not a fake or needlessly dangerous. Food adulteration laws were passed in Illinois in 1874 and 1879; in New York, Michigan, and New Jersey in 1881. Ten more states followed by 1889, and an additional nine by 1895.

Some of the nineteenth-century proposals were virtually identical to those of the present. For example, in Missouri, it was suggested that drugmakers list their ingredients on the labels. Among the common ingredients of medicines at the time were a few that most discerning consumers wanted to avoid, though it was difficult as they were so prevalent: arsenic, cocaine, opium, and alcohol. The drugmakers of the time said that to list these components on their labels would require too much trouble and expense, "without any corresponding benefit to the public." A century before economists discovered the "needless burdens of regulation," Missouri drugmakers already had the argument down.

Few doubted that the slough of American politics needed dredging, and laws of some kind had to be enacted to curb bribery, patronage, and influence peddling, which had become the common mode of government. But at first, that did not extend to the reform of commerce. Samuel Eliot Morison writes of the time: "Lawyers, bankers and industrialists . . . saw no need to regulate business, transportation or finance. 'A tree should be allowed to grow as high as it can,' expressed their *laissez-faire* creed, even if the tree overshadowed and sucked the life out of all bushes and plants in the radius."

Societies throughout history have always imposed social controls on business and economic activity, through civil or religious authority. But during the nineteenth century when unfettered capitalism dominated the scene, the long historical relationship was reversed, and society was ruled by economics with the strong presumption that no controls should govern it. The boldest achievement of the time was the corporation. It freed the energy of human groups to pursue the creation of products and profits unlike anything that might have been imagined. And, for the first time in the history of human commerce, individuals could, with legal sanction, escape responsibility for their actions as businessmen. At first, no countervailing protections for citizens were put in place.

As neither broad reform nor the creation of food and drug purity laws was forthcoming, thoughtful conservative leaders in business and government began to wonder if the entire nation would fall apart in an orgy of selfishness, or worse, begin to turn against the capitalists toward socialism. The conflict became more intense, and as government resistance grew and Congress turned away bills and shut off debate on the matter, the effect was like that of putting a lid on a boiling kettle—the pressure increased.

For Wiley and many in his generation, the sudden advances of humankind posed a problem. In philosophical terms, if the progress of science and commerce was embraced, would that not corrupt traditional human values? After all, it seemed that in some way both the cold rationality of science and the cold calculation of commerce were unable to accommodate the comforting beliefs and rituals, not only of religion, but of the honor that seemed to be the backbone of the genteel social order. Put in practical terms, the questions were, how could the commerce in ideas or in goods be both free and regulated? Would a web of rules and prohibitions suffocate the adventures that seemed to thrive in freedom?

The questions arise in society in many forms, in many venues, and at many times. The answers, like the heart of free inquiry itself, are counterintuitive. The beginning of the solution came at the moment when America passed into that short, vital, and often lamented time called the Progressive Era.

•

CHAPTER THREE

The Progressive Era

HARVEY WILEY had become a figure about Washington, one of those who made the news often and about whom people talked after he left a room. His Harvard and continental intellectual credentials were well established. He had enough bulk to be a presence on the speaker's platform (something of a qualification before the advent of amplified sound), and he came to enjoy bold strokes in rhetoric and life.

He was a member and then president of the elite Cosmos Club in the capital, and had a great store of knowledge, as a curious and educated chemist might, about the details of fine wine and whiskey. He was a publicly modern man—the third person in the District of Columbia ever to own a motorcar. He was also the first in the capital ever to have a motorcar accident (it was the horse cart that had run into him, he said).

His wit was useful and added to his expanding popularity. Before the Appropriations Committee of the House, where budgets are consecrated or sacrificed, a skeptical committee member once asked in a certain tone, what is an "agricultural scientist" anyway?

"He's a man who can make two dollars grow on an appropriations bill where one dollar grew before," Wiley snapped.

By the end of the nineteenth century, one source of hope for reform, the populist movement, had burned itself out. The movement had railed against the coming of the industrial state and the rise of the unholy cities. But the populists were able to do little about the economic injustice that was at the heart of the problem. They built a movement by opposing capitalist greed and the lack of human concerns among those at the helm of the economy and the nation. Despite broad support, the movement broke apart on local issues and was never able to elect a president or gain control of Congress.

It was representatives of the next generation, a group grown tired of the rhetoric and looking for a sensible compromise, who saw the way ahead. They were soon called the progressives, and they asserted that government should answer the grievances of the common man, not the influential man. The movement was almost a cross between populist commoners and the educated but sympathetic among upper-class society. The progressives were angry about the greed and brutality of robber-baron capitalism, but were not opposed to the industrial future. They looked forward to it. As writer William Allen White notes in his autobiography, the progressives were not angry populists who were often "farmers who failed, lawyers and doctors who were not orthodox . . . and neurotics full of hates and evanescent, ebullient enthusiasms." Rather, the progressive movement was "in its heart of hearts, *petit bourgeois.*" It was a movement of "little businessmen, professional men, well-to-do farmers, skilled artisans from the upper brackets of organized labor . . . the successful middle-class, country-town citizens, the farmer whose barn was painted, the well-paid railroad engineer, and the country editor." It was, even more, a movement of women. Several national groups with scores of local chapters agitated for change. They succeeded in getting local and state laws enacted; they laid siege to local boards of health and merged into a national network to press for federal laws. They seized populist issues; as White puts it, they "caught the populists in swimming and stole all of their clothing."

Harvey Wiley was among the professional men who joined the progressive movement, as was the rising Theodore Roosevelt. Both had been Republicans for the first part of their lives, but when their party failed to back reform, both left to speak out independently, as progressives. Separately, both wrote that they wanted an adventurous, aggressive nation, as well as one concerned about fairness for citizens.

Whatever arguments were taking place in parlors across America, the subject of reform was more difficult to raise in Congress and nearly impossible to move off dead center. Corporations and elected politicians were partners, while individual citizens had little standing before the Congress. They had to rabble-rouse to attract essential news coverage. The progress of Roosevelt and Wiley, and ultimately the progressive movement, depended upon the press, the only route to the people that circumvented entrenched power. Two episodes for which these two men were famous serve to describe their boldness and their willingness to take up the case of common citizens in the press.

Roosevelt became commissioner of police in New York City in May 1895. He was facing implacable political problems of corruption and conservatism, and was using progressive tactics—investigations and publicity about just how unjust matters were—to combat them. Police departments at the end of the nineteenth century were prime examples of the corruption that sprang up in every area of life. In New York, the matter was so bald that a schedule of prices for each rank of officer was published (a policeman could be promoted to patrolman for $300 and to captain for $10,000). The prices were steep, but they could be recouped quickly on the beat. In the mid-1890s about two-thirds of the New York City police budget came from bribes.

Within a week after he began his job, Roosevelt forced the resignation of the two most corrupt police officials, and began awarding medals to those who worked at their jobs with a public spirit. He even began to patrol New York City himself, in the middle of the night, to see how his troops were doing.

These famous "midnight rambles" began on a warm night in June 1895, at about two o'clock in the morning, when he left his club on Fifth Avenue and walked east to Third Avenue. He was disguised, more or less, having turned up his collar and pulled a wide-brimmed hat down over his eyes. Joining him was the journalist Jacob Riis, who had planned their tour through the dangerous nighttime streets between Forty-second and Twenty-third Streets on the East Side.

They walked south from Forty-second Street and didn't see a single policeman until they reached Twenty-seventh Street, though the roundsmen were supposed to be posted nearly every block. Farther on, Roosevelt caught six asleep or otherwise occupied, including a policeman who was found "partly concealed by petticoats," as the *Tribune* discreetly described it.

On another night, he found patrolman William Rath in a saloon, eating oysters instead of standing at his post. The newspaper *Excise Herald* reported that the following dialogue took place:

ROOSEVELT: Why aren't you on your post, officer?

RATH (*deliberately swallowing oyster*): What the ———— is it to you?

COUNTER MAN: You got a nerve comin' in here and interferin' with an officer.

ROOSEVELT: I'm Commissioner Roosevelt.

RATH (*reaching for vinegar bottle*): Yes, you are. You're Grover Cleveland and Mayor Strong all in a bunch, you are. Move on, now, or—

COUNTER MAN (*in a horrified whisper*): Shut up, Bill, it's His Nibs, sure, don't you spot his glasses?

ROOSEVELT (*authoritatively*): Go to your post at once. (*Exit patrolman, running*)

"These and subsequent nocturnal jaunts delighted the citizens of New York, who for years had been starved of entertaining municipal news. No such eccentric behavior by a public official had ever been recorded," writes Roosevelt biographer Edmund Morris. In addition, Roosevelt made it clear that the police would no longer enforce the law unequally— that is, working specially for those who could afford the monthly bribe— but would be both tough and fair in all circumstances. The cleanup of the police made him a national figure instantly, and word of his exploits was even reported in London. One writer who followed Roosevelt during a day's work in those years was Bram Stoker, author of *Dracula*. Stoker wrote in his diary, "Must be President some day. A man you can't cajole, can't frighten, can't buy."

Wiley was already a figure in the federal government when Roosevelt came to Washington as assistant secretary of the navy. After Roosevelt led the Rough Riders in Cuba, he talked about the conditions there, and about the bad food and medicines his men had been forced to consume during the campaign, thus placing him squarely in Wiley's camp. Roosevelt's superior, General Nelson Miles, had said that after the 1898 war, the Swift and Armour companies must not be relied on for future provisions. As he said, "There was sent to Porto Rico [*sic*] 337 tons of what was known as, or called, 'refrigerated beef,' which you might call embalmed beef, and there was also sent 198,508 of what was known as 'canned fresh beef,' which was condemned . . . by nearly every officer whose commands used it."

Roosevelt said that some of his men refused to eat the canned beef. He at first thought it was the green recruits who had the problem, and singled out one young red-haired Kentuckian to punish when Roosevelt saw him throw away his rations.

"I can't eat the canned meat," the soldier told Roosevelt.

"If you are a baby," Roosevelt responded, "you had better not have come to the war. Eat it and be a man."

The Kentuckian obeyed orders and immediately vomited.

Later, Roosevelt himself ate some, saying, "I tried to eat some of it myself when I was hungry, and found that I could not." He said it was "slimey, stringy and coarse . . . like a bundle of fibers." After soldiers in great numbers got sick on the meat, the troops abandoned those rations.

Roosevelt's tales of Cuba were welcome fodder for Dr. Wiley's growing campaign to establish minimum standards for food. Over the years Wiley had gained some friends in Congress, and he had put the case to the nation as one of both honest dealing and of concern for a healthy, vigorous life. But Roosevelt's position helped Wiley finally to secure hearings in Congress and, by 1902, funds for a few experiments on food and drug safety.

Wiley's adventure, the counterpart of Roosevelt's midnight rambles, was called the "poison squad" experiment by reporters. Like Roosevelt, he was surprised by the huge, and national, interest the episode raised.

Wiley had coaxed $5,000 out of Congress to study the effect on health of the preservatives that were by then commonly used in foods. It was difficult to create a useful experiment on the subject. He read the literature of chemistry and medicine and found almost nothing relevant. Studying animals wouldn't be much use, because only the grossest kinds of problems could be identified. The animals, after all, could not complain of anything subtler. Wiley spoke to officials at the Imperial Board of Health in Berlin, where such issues were taken very seriously and where some national laws already had been put in place, despite the lack of detailed studies. The officials said they had once conducted an experiment in which two people were given doses of borax to see if that preservative was harmful.

That was the way, Wiley decided. Give a suspect preservative to humans, under controlled conditions, and in amounts that gradually increased. Then he could record any significant changes in their digestive systems as the tests progressed. It would be the first significant study of the effects of commonly used preservative chemicals on people.

Wiley placed small notices in the newspapers to attract a dozen volunteers. To his surprise, scores of candidates came forward. And at the same time, newspaper reporters began to show up, jesting, sneering, and completely absorbed in the whole idea.

Wiley selected young men as the guinea pigs, mostly medical students or scientific hopefuls in the Agriculture Department itself; as he put it, "young, robust fellows" who might be expected to have "maximum resistance to deleterious effects of adulterated foods." He invited them to what he called his "hygienic table," which he had set up in a basement mail room at the department. They would, upon the commencement of the experiment, take all their meals and drink (except water) in that room, which Wiley had fitted out as a dining hall. There were white tablecloths, a good chef (Wiley sometimes stepped in as *chef de cuisine*), and a variety of excellent though simple meals.

The volunteers were not paid, and the work, as he warned them, would be much harder than it seemed. They had to eat at the scheduled mealtimes only. They had to submit to frequent and thorough medical exams, and worst of all, they had to carry with them at all times a satchel with the necessary jars and sampling equipment to collect all the urine and stool they produced, to be analyzed in the department laboratory.

For ten days the men ate meals with no preservatives. Then, the preservative under study would be introduced gradually over many weeks, beginning with small quantities that were certainly equal to or less than that which might be found in the American diet. Borax was studied first, because the department had found that thirty-three of sixty-seven commercial "preservers" sold to food manufacturers included it. It also seemed to be the least likely to cause severe symptoms. Salicylic acid, then sulfurous acids and sulfites, benzoic acid and sodium benzoate, and formaldehyde were tested afterward.

Wiley thought the effects of the preservatives would be mild for most. Going into the trials, he said, "Personally, I have never gone so far as my associates in the pure food congress and other movements relating to injurious substances in food. I have always been of the opinion, and still am . . . that it is entirely sufficient to place upon a food label the nature of any substance which has been added . . . and leave to the consumer himself . . . the determination of whether or not that substance is injurious to him."

The first doses of borax—half a gram each day—were tolerated well by "my boys," as Wiley called them. To help keep morale up, he made sure to be with them for most meals, ingesting the full course of chemicals himself. The doses were now increased, in search of a "limit of toleration." He thought regular indigestion might result at high doses. By the time two to three grams were added per day, appetites in the squad had dropped off sharply. The men rejected food, reporting a constant feeling of fullness. In between meals they had indigestion and stomach pain. Some had bouts of bowel trouble during the day. At four grams, the men had severe headaches as well as abdominal distress, and they had become lethargic and in enough pain so, as Wiley put it, the dose "produced an inability to perform work of any kind." They were flat on their backs. After the period of dosing, the men went back to wholesome foods again and recovered. (More modern testing bore out Wiley's conclusions sufficiently so boric acid is no longer permitted as a preservative.)

Four more preservatives were to be tested in this first round of experiments. Even with scaled-down doses, three of the chemicals produced similar or worse symptoms. No deaths resulted, but Wiley said later that he believed some of the men had permanent impairments of the stomach and bowels from the experience.

These experiments were noteworthy but clearly flawed. For example, there should have been a second group of basement diners who were similar in age and status—a control group who ate the same meals, but who did not get the preservatives. The comparison of the two groups would have been decisive. But this level of sophistication in method was not yet part of scientific practice.

Wiley's experiment came just at the moment when scientists were beginning to understand what was essential in scientific testing. It had been a long time coming. In Egypt four thousand years earlier, life expectancy was about thirty-six years. At the opening of the nineteenth century, it was about thirty-seven years. It was for want of a method, a tool to pry open the secrets of health and disease, and by which remedies could be tested reliably, that the essential mysteries had gone unsolved.

The watershed for medical science and the rough basis for the poison squad experiments had come just after the beginning of the nineteenth century. At that point, translating experience into numbers, into statistics, was just being understood as an impartial and powerful method. It lifted the facts out of human experience and simplified them for all to see. By the 1820s, Paris physician Pierre Louis challenged doctors to stop carrying out their work randomly and instead to collect data and submit it for inspection. One specific target was the excessive bloodletting of a colleague. He suggested that all doctors use the "numerical method" to study disease and its treatment, and draw conclusions from the data, not from personal anecdote. "Without statistics," he declared in one of a series of articles, "therapeutics is nothing more than a jumbled heap of banal and doubtful recipes." His pronouncements began a series of academic debates in France in the 1830s. His opponents pointed out that diseases were not single entities but differed in each individual—in the way people got diseases and in the way the diseases progressed. Numerical study, it was argued, would soon be lost in a maze of individual differences. Opponents held that statistics would only confuse matters.

Experiments using data collection continued sporadically, but they remained unconnected to one another or to any general theory of how disease occurs. In one now-famous eighteenth-century experiment, naval surgeon James Lind tested six different substances for their effects on scurvy. Doctors thought of scurvy as a kind of fever and inflammation, which, in the system established by the second-century Greek physician

Galen and still used in the eighteenth century, had become associated with alkalinity. Thus, the treatments of choice would be acid drugs. Lind tried cider, seawater, vinegar, elixir vitriol (sulfuric acid), citrus juices (lemon and orange), and a mixture called "electuary" made of garlic, myrrh, mustard, cream of tartar, and other items.

The scurvy disappeared only in the sailors who took the citrus juices. Nevertheless, doctors were still not convinced of the experimental methods. Lind himself did not even recommend citrus juice over other anti-scurvy treatments, and the Royal Navy did not single out the proper treatment for another fifty years. Experiments on the effects of digitalis, various laxatives, and treatments for dropsy were carried out, but again their importance was obscured, and they lay useless for 50 to 150 years. Statements from "authoritative" figures, then and now, superseded belief in data.

Wiley understood the scientific method in general, and that impartial testing was at its center. The poison squad experiments were flawed, but they were the first experiments to examine commercial food additives and their effects on health in more than two people. They were, in fact, the beginning of the tradition of science in government policy that has continued and has been refined to this day.

At the time, preservative and coloring chemicals were being pumped into the nation's food supply without any kind of scrutiny. Wiley and his staff, between 1887 and 1902, had already produced a series of detailed reports describing the ways in which food was being adulterated. The reports had shocked the public and members of Congress, which led to the $5,000 allocation. The experiments served notice that food and drug reform could draw wide interest.

So it was that for more than twenty years, Wiley had acted as a sort of chairman and moderator of the national debate on the subject. He conducted investigations, issued reports, and traveled to women's clubs, state food and drug departments, and professional groups. He helped organize annual meetings of scientists and industry representatives to open discussion on what laws might be considered.

Year after year, Wiley served as "the generalissimo of a coalition of state chemists, physicians, pharmacists, women's club members, journalists, manufacturers and members of Congress working to secure such a law," writes James Harvey Young. Wiley's oratory reached out, with grand flourishes, to try to describe the depth of the issue. "What is this great movement for purity of foods and drugs?" he asked. He answered his own question: "Only the application of ethics to digestion and therapeutics. This is the new philosophy. Namely, the morals of metabolism." He outlined this perhaps too lofty idea in practical terms. It was the introduction of science and new technology into business that made the problems fundamental, more than just commercial. With the new knowledge, the very definitions of each food and drug were being challenged. Humans, he said, had been provided by nature with reasonably good instruments to detect bad food—noses, palates, and sensitive digestive organs. But new science and technology had given tradesmen tools to deceive the senses.

The poison squad experiments shocked Wiley enough for him to change his long-held attitude that any and all substances could be added to food provided the labels acknowledged it. He began to doubt the wisdom of allowing all drugs, pesticides, and chemicals on the market, and then waiting to see if there were widespread problems. At the time, chemicals could be pumped into America's food supply virtually without limits—in high or low doses, in any variety, including high or low toxicity. Now that the first concrete results were in, he thought, shouldn't the industry begin to be more careful?

Hesitantly at first, but with increasing vehemence as industry began a counterattack on him and his experiments, Wiley said that preservatives should no longer be allowed in food routinely, but only when they could be shown to be necessary to preserve fresh food. Before the experiments, he had relied on "expert testimony" from scientists and industry representatives, but now, having seen how ill some of his subjects became, he testified in Congress, "I was converted by my own investigations."

The debate in Congress over a national food and drug bill was intensified by the poison squad, along with outbreaks of protest against food companies and indolent local health commissioners (where any health authorities existed). The industry lobbyists made a variety of arguments. The substances used were not as harmful as people supposed; reformers had simply whipped up a panic. Businesses in America had a right to carry on without interference from government. The National Association of Retail Grocers said that it would support a ban on using harmful substances in food if industry could have a say in what "harmful" would mean. Otherwise, they said, the consumer was entitled to no more protection with regard to food than with any other merchandise.

Frank H. Madden of the wholesale grocers group from Chicago told Congress that his own firm, Reid, Murdoch and Company, made cheap jelly from glucose and the skins of apples. This, he said, was perfectly wholesome and palatable, but if labeled for what it was, people just wouldn't buy it. A variant of this argument was used by many industries.

"Such a law," said the Proprietary Association's committee on legislation, "would practically destroy the sale of proprietary remedies in the United States." To disclose that fanciful products were actually as plain as the bottles of powder in any apothecary could be catastrophic. Members of the association asked whether, if such a law were to extend to all consumer products, women would now have to be told that their corsets would not actually give them a "fine, well-developed bust"? Or would doctors be required to tell their patients, in plain English, what was in the medicines they were prescribing?

Representative William Adamson of Georgia said, in a classic statement of pseudo-populist rhetoric, that he did not want to pay for a burgeoning bureaucracy designed to meddle in the business of the people. If the federal government got involved, it would mean putting up with "a pestilential lot of spies, meddlers, and informers." He asserted, "I believe there are millions of old women, white and black, who know more about good victuals and good eating than my friend *Doctor* Wiley and all his apothecary shop." He said regulation of food and drugs by the federal government was not only unconstitutional but silly. "You might just as well get the traditional boy with his sore toe," he said, and have "Congressman [James] Mann [of Illinois] speak about the horrible condition of that sore toe for two hours and say Congress ought to do something to cure that sore toe. It is just as logical and sensible and fully as constitutional."

Perhaps more to the point, Thomas Wilson, the spokesman for the meatpacking industry, said, "We are opposed to, and what we appeal to you gentlemen for protection against, is a bill that will put our business in the hands of theorists, chemists, sociologists, etc., and the management and control taken away from the men who have devoted their lives to the upbuilding and perfecting of this Great American Industry."

One congressional hearing permitted an unusually clear view of how the problem developed for businessmen. Many of the witnesses brought to the hearing were paid by industry to testify against the proposed laws, and others were recruited without payment but told that their business would never be the same if the regulations became law. One such industry witness was Walter H. Williams, of Williams Brothers, a Detroit canner.

Williams was not a public man, and not practiced in the steering of argument. So after his opening statement, when the questions began, he said pretty much what he thought. It was clear that he had no idea which ideology he was supposed to be supporting. When asked whether federal regulations might be a good idea, he recounted his woes from conflicting state laws, and said, sure, absolutely, if they could untangle the mess he was in now.

Then the questioning penetrated one layer deeper. He was asked about some of the products he made and sold. Under questioning about what was in his "Fourteen-ounce Highland Strawberry Preserves," he said he started with sugar, 45 percent. Then he had added 30 percent glucose to reduce any further sugar cost. Then he added apple juice, 15 percent. And finally, strawberries.

"Why do you put it up in that form?" asked one congressman.

"This is a cheap preserve," he said, "as cheap a preserve as can be made. . . ."

"What is the idea of putting the apple juice in?"

"To make it cheap. If it was simply strawberries and sugar together . . . they would have to retail for about 35 cents. This bottle retails for about 10 cents," said Williams.

Asked where he got the apples, he said from discarded apple skins and cores. Including the wormholes? Yes, he said, but not more than you'd expect with canned apples, either.

At one point, it appears that Williams became a little ashamed of the products being dissected, even though his was one of the more reputable firms in the business. He did not use fake coloring, he boasted, he used no preservative, and he actually did include a few real strawberries, unlike some competitors. In the end, he said, "I would just as soon be out of business on them as to be manufacturing them. I believe they should be labeled [as the law suggested and the industry opposed], showing their ingredients and showing the quality of the goods. . . . If we could sell the pure goods, we would be more than pleased. We can make a profit on those which we cannot on these."

It was clear that people often had little idea what they were buying, and that the trade was operating at the level of the lowest common denominator. Without some rules, all were forced to compete with the cheapest and most deceptive dealers, at their level.

"While deodorized eggs and artificial butter sold at cut prices . . . the farmer's market for fresh eggs and real butter suffered," writes historian James Harvey Young. "In a lawless world, the exigencies of competition tended to drive commercial practices toward the level of the most unscrupulous." As one Senate report put it, "faith in commercial integrity" and the "very foundation of trade" were being undermined. The status quo could not hold.

No one in the discussion over food and drugs denied the fact of adulteration. But citizens could not expect any government aid in dealing with the market in those years. Twice the House passed a national pure food act. But each time the Republican leadership in the Senate—particularly Nelson W. Aldrich of Rhode Island, a grocery wholesaler himself, and a man with ties to the baking powder and chemical industries, and two corporation lawyers, Orville H. Pratt of Connecticut, and John C. Spooner of Wisconsin—killed the bill by refusing to bring it to the floor. They were named as among the most corrupt senators.

Harvey Wiley, probably the most generally knowledgeable physician in the nation on such matters, suggested that at least tens of thousands of people died each year from patent medicines and adulterated food. The habit of giving infants patent medicines containing opium could have been the worst of all, and alone may have cost tens of thousands of children's lives over the last two decades of the century.

The last significant law on foods had been passed in 1848, a crackdown on adulterated imports. By 1883, when Wiley became the nation's chief chemist, nothing more had been done. Meanwhile, the British had passed two new laws on food and drugs.

The history of the attempt to pass even a moderate food and drug bill in America became "a capital illustration of the Senate's treasons, stratagems, and spoils," said a 1905 editorial in *The Nation* entitled "The Year of the Food Law."

Then, all at once, after years of failure, the pro-reform coups de grâce were delivered: first, in the form of a series of devastating magazine articles that roused the public, and then in a muckraking novel.

The shocking series of news articles came from, of all places, the *Ladies' Home Journal,* the most popular magazine of the era, with a circulation of nearly a million. The editor, Edward Bok, despised patent medicines and had once written an article in which he called for a boycott of them. When he hired lawyer and writer Mark Sullivan to write the series, Sullivan discovered that one of the most popular alcohol-sodden remedies, Lydia Pinkham's Vegetable Compound, had a long-running scam as its chief sales device. Pinkham's grandmotherly face was on the medicine, and the words invited suffering women to write to her personally, saying that "no man" would ever see the letter. Sullivan discovered that when letters went out in her name, it was not Pinkham corresponding with these women. She had been dead for more than twenty years. (Sullivan photographed the grave, and the picture of it ran next to the Pinkham advertising.)

Sullivan also discovered why newspapers in America had been so silent on the subject of patent medicines. The head of the Proprietary Association, Frank J. Cheney, had devised a clause for those lucrative advertising contracts that said if a new law restricting patent medicines was passed, or if the newspaper ran negative stories on the subject, the contract was automatically canceled and all planned ads withdrawn. Cheney said that before he devised this stratagem, he had to pay out $75,000 per year ($3 million today) in bribes. His expenses dropped to $6,000 after the blackmail scheme began. It was quickly picked up and used across the country by patent medicine makers and was surprisingly effective. In Massachusetts, for example, when legislators debated new rules for patent medicine makers, newspapers simply ignored the subject. The agents of the proprietary industry also took to reminding editors exactly what was at stake by sending them information on just how much the newspapers would stand to lose in advertising revenue if the subject were treated in an unfriendly manner in their columns.

The exposés in the *Ladies' Home Journal,* as well as in half a dozen other popular magazines, kept coming. With the newspapers on the side-lines, the magazines were having a field day informing the public about the unsavory practices of the trade. The biggest hit came in *Collier's,* from a journalist named Samuel Hopkins Adams, who wrote a series of six articles from October 1905 through February 1906.

The patent medicine association realized that these articles could do them considerable damage. Its leaders had learned of the articles and their expected scale as soon as Adams began to interview the manufacturers. Soon, Adams found himself being trailed by two detectives. One weekend as he was leaving New York on a train for a house party in Connecticut, he met the wife of a friend at the station. She was also on her way to the party, and the two sat together. He soon got a message that his trip with the woman might be made public if he continued his investigations. Adams suspected which of the patent medicine companies had paid for the detectives, and as it happened, he knew the mayor in the town where the company was located. He paid the mayor a visit and discovered that the mayor had some useful information about the manufacturer in question. The manufacturer had recently been surprised by police in a roadhouse with another man's wife, and had jumped from a window and broken his leg. The story had not got out, and Adams soon let the manufacturer know he was aware of the incident. The blackmail against Adams was quickly dropped, and the detectives stopped trailing him.

Adams used chemical analysis to discover what was in some of the medicines, and sought out patients to report on the effects they had experienced. For example, Peruna, an industry leader, was a remedy sold for a variety of illnesses, from colds and congestion (called the "catarrh" at the time) to tuberculosis, inflamed appendix, the mumps, and "female complaints." The main secret ingredients in the bottle were alcohol and water, with 28 percent of the mixture pure alcohol. It was especially popular among women of the temperance movement, who had sworn off liquor. Another product he unmasked was called Liquozone. This potion was sold for everything from dandruff to dysentery, and contained 99 percent water and one percent sulfuric acid, to give it a bit of bite. Adams pointed out that the danger here was chiefly that those who took Liquozone believed they were being treated, and so did not go to a doctor until perhaps it was too late.

Adams's greatest efforts and most potent prose were reserved for the many remedies that contained highly addictive substances—opium, cocaine, and one not often mentioned in recent years, acetanilide. These "soothing syrups" were commonly given to squalling infants, for whom the drugs were frequently fatal. The American Medical Association, which in 1906 had just begun to keep data on remedies, found a dozen infant deaths reported in its letters from physicians that year. Acetanilide was a common ingredient in medicines, especially as a "headache powder" and a painkiller. It did relieve pain. But it also caused severe heart disorders and heart attacks in a substantial number of cases—Adams listed in his article the names and addresses of twenty-two people who were killed by the substance.

The articles had an instant impact, and 500,000 copies of each were reprinted by the American Medical Association and sold after the magazine issues had come off the stands. Now, Harvey Wiley again tried to enlist Roosevelt, by then president, in his campaign for a regulatory law. By early 1905, Roosevelt had already heard from a number of groups on the issue, and in particular from another campaigner for food and drug regulations, Robert McDowell Allen of Kentucky, a chemist and a lawyer who administered Kentucky's food laws and had followed Wiley's efforts with admiration. Eventually Allen became the leader of the National Association of State Dairy and Food Departments, which came out in favor of a food and drug law. He organized a group including members of the American Medical Association, to represent the nation's doctors, and Alice Lakey, to speak for the national organization of women's clubs, that met with the president and urged him to act. Roosevelt promised to study the matter, and did. He spoke to Wiley and other notable chemists of the time, as well as to his own personal physician. By November, after Adams's series had started, Roosevelt agreed to support a food and drug bill, and in his State of the Union speech in December 1905, he officially put himself on record in favor of it. Privately, he had promised more than just passive support as well.

Within days of the last Adams piece on patent medicines, an even bigger bombshell hit: Upton Sinclair's novel *The Jungle*, about families struggling to make a living in the meat industry. There were very few pages devoted to the practices of the meat packers, but those passages were so disturbing that some readers were made sick; others said they wept. Even fellow muckraker Lincoln Steffens had warned Sinclair before publication that the material might be too much for its readers, whether it was true or not. Particularly disturbing were the accounts of the workers, sick with tuberculosis, spitting onto the floor, then dragging butchered meat across it. There were tales of meat in storage rooms, rotting and covered with rat droppings, which was then made into sausage, detritus and all. There were even tales of workers who had fallen into the great acidic lard vat and become, after their bones had been fished out, a part of "Durham's Pure Leaf Lard."

Five publishers turned down the book, mostly because of the few sickening pages on sanitary practices. But it was not as if these things were being mentioned in public for the first time. Charles Edward Russell had already written about them, and in Britain Adolphe Smith had written in detail for the medical journal *Lancet* the horrid practices that had grown up in American abattoirs. He was an expert on the practices of the meat trade around the world, but found nothing to compare with the unregulated Americans. In any case, Sinclair resisted taking out the graphic passages to please a publisher, and with donations began to have the book privately printed. But after only a handful of orders for the book were taken, Doubleday, Page agreed to publish it uncensored. Before committing the company, the eponymous Walter H. Page sent proofs of the manuscript to James Keeley, managing editor of the *Chicago Tribune*. Keeley sent back a critical thirty-two-page report that he said was prepared by one of his reporters. He lied; a publicist had prepared the report for the meat packers. By chance, the imposture was discovered, and Doubleday went ahead with publication. The book, when it arrived in bookstores, sold out instantly.

Though the slaughterhouse stories in the novel seemed fantastic, they were later documented in a series of investigations. Sinclair, twenty-five years old at the time of his own investigation, was trying to make a living writing romantic novels. A socialist, on the side he had written articles for socialist newspapers, including one piece about the failed strike of meat packers in Chicago. The editor of one paper suggested his next novel be about "wage slavery," the phrase fashionable on the left at the time to describe the plight of those who work in bad conditions for little pay and few benefits. Sinclair agreed and set off to the area of Chicago called Packingtown, where he lived for seven weeks with the workers. He entered the plants freely by using an ingenious disguise—he simply carried a dinner pail. "So as long as I kept moving," he wrote, "no one would heed me. When I wanted to make careful observations, I would pass again and again through the same room."

Both Sinclair and Doubleday, Page sent copies of the book to the president, who was already primed on the issue after his experiences in Cuba and lobbying by Wiley and the Allen committee. Two "investigations" reporting no irregularities had already been carried out by Agriculture Department employees who themselves would have been embarrassed by a scandal. Now, Roosevelt was getting a hundred letters a day about the issues raised in *The Jungle*.

Finley Peter Dunne wrote of the president's encounter with *The Jungle* in the Irish dialect of his mythical Chicago bartender, Martin Dooley:

> Tiddy was toying with a light breakfast an' idly turnin' over th' pages iv the new book with both hands. Suddenly he rose fr'm th' table, an' cryin': 'I'm Pizened,' began throwin' sausages out iv the window. The ninth wan struck Sinitor Biv'ridge on th' head an' made him a blond. It bounced off, exploded, an' blew a leg off a secret-service agent, an' the scatthred fragmints desthroyed a handsome row iv ol' oak trees.

He described a scene in which Teddy was in hand-to-hand combat with a potted ham. "Potted" ham, it was said, was equal parts plaster of paris, sawdust, rope, and incautious laborer. To what kingdom does canned chicken belong? Dooley answered, "It is a mineral."

Hennessy, taking a drink in Dooley's tavern, and following the news of the meat scandal, said that the penalty for the Armours, Swifts, and other rich men who ran "The Meat Trusts" should be that they be forced to eat their own products.

"I suggested that," said Mr. Dooley, "but Hogan says they'd fall back on th' Consitution. He says th' constitution f'rbids crool an' unusual punishments.' "

Roosevelt invited Sinclair to the White House to plot a strategy to unearth the truth. Roosevelt was skeptical of Sinclair's stories and despised the author's socialist attitude, but agreed to send honest and reliable men to investigate the plants in secret. He chose Charles P. Neill, commissioner of labor, and James Bronson Reynolds, a well-known social worker, for the work, and sent Sinclair to brief them. The two men would travel to Chicago incognito and pay surprise visits to the packers. But the plan was betrayed, and packinghouse workers toiled in three shifts, day and night, to clean the plants. They literally slathered buckets of whitewash on the premises. When Neill and Reynolds arrived in Chicago, reporters were waiting to greet them. The companies had teams ready to give them tours and explain their modern methods.

Even with three weeks' warning and effort, the packers could not prevent Neill and Reynolds from being revolted at the filthy conditions and the total lack of concern from managers. They even witnessed a pig carcass falling off the production line into a latrine. It was hauled up and put, uncleaned, in storage with the others.

Within weeks of the publication of *The Jungle,* the sales of meat fell by half. Where Roosevelt had been unable to get cooperation from packers unwilling to concede anything, he found them suddenly agreeing to some kind of federal inspection.

In the end, Sinclair's socialist message was lost on his readers. As he wrote, "I aimed at the public's heart, and by accident, I hit it in the stomach."

A few months before, after more than twenty-five years of effort, Wiley had despaired of ever getting a law. "Pure Food bills in the Senate had been regularly committed to the Committee on Manufactures," he wrote, "much as an infant would be left to starve in a barren room." But now the president was behind the bill, a great wave of magazines and newspapers had come out for it, and even the mainstream members of the industries to be regulated were asking for some bill that would save their hides from the constant flailing they were receiving. As Senator Weldon Heyburn of Idaho asked, "Has there ever been in the history of this country a more universal demand for action upon the part of Congress than the demand that has gone up from one end of the country to the other in regard to legislation upon the pure-food question?"

The American Medical Association, which had been working mostly out of the public eye, now confronted Senator Aldrich. The AMA, writes historian Sean Cashman, "told the Republican leader . . . in no uncertain terms that its 135,000 member physicians in two thousand counties would urge their patients to lobby the Senate if the Senate did not pass the pure food bill."

The rise of public outrage and the president's efforts to pass legislation were finally enough to overcome the last barrier. "The Senate was in a jam," said Senator Albert Beveridge of Ohio, "and public feeling had become intense. Aldrich came to me one afternoon and said, 'Tell Heyburn if he asks consideration for the Pure Food bill there will be no objection.' " Beveridge passed on the message, but Heyburn didn't believe it. Aldrich had held up the measure year after year, and Heyburn said he wasn't going to be made a fool of again. But Beveridge insisted, and said he would be responsible. So finally, in the afternoon of the same day, Heyburn once again asked the Republican leadership to let a bill be brought to the floor for a vote, where a majority had long been waiting.

From the spring of 1906 until the end of June, when the laws were passed, the brawl in Congress was wild and changeable. The meat law fight came first. The president did not make the Neill-Reynolds report on conditions in Chicago public immediately. He knew he would need a weapon to dislodge the bill from the House Committee on Agriculture, where its chairman, James W. Wadsworth, a cattleman, was suffocating it. Roosevelt told Wadsworth he wouldn't make the damning information public, but he would appreciate it if the bill proposed by Beveridge could be passed out of committee.

The industry offered a compromise measure instead. Roosevelt said it "was so bad that in my opinion, if [the provisions] had been deliberately designed to prevent the remedying of the evils complained of, they could not have been made worse." He released the Neill-Reynolds report, and it had just the impact Roosevelt said it would—it proved the accuracy of charges made in *The Jungle*.

Finally, though, the bitter divide in the House and Senate became a crucial matter of party loyalty. The Republicans feared an irreparable split between the conservatives and reformers (that *did* come later anyway), and the resolution required a personal meeting between House Speaker Joseph Cannon and Roosevelt at the White House. The two agreed to have someone broker a compromise for the sake of the party. They chose Representative Henry C. Adams, who quickly pulled together a group of various interests and hammered out a bill sent back to Congress.

After further changes and last-minute arm-twisting, the final law included these provisions: Federal meat inspectors would be created, paid for by a standing congressional appropriation of $3 million annually (a substantial sum in those days). Cattle, sheep, pigs, and goats would be inspected both before and after slaughter. Diseased or unfit animals, as well as unacceptable parts, would be destroyed in the presence of a federal inspector. Plants would be open to inspectors at any time, day and night, every day. Inspectors would be empowered to check both meat and processed products for "dangerous dyes, chemicals and preservatives." Henceforward the Agriculture Department would define the level of sanitation in meat plants. They would be forbidden to ship uninspected meat, parts, or products across state lines. Interestingly, the punishment for failure to abide by the federal rules was not fine or imprisonment but the withdrawal of all inspectors. The effect of this was that the meat could no longer bear the "government-inspected" stamp, and could not be shipped out of state.

The bill was a breakthrough in that it established that inspection and approval before marketing were essential to safety, just as the Biologics Control Act of 1902 had done, but on a huge, visible scale.

The Food and Drug Act, which followed within days, was quite a different matter. It had been fought over much longer, and it had been a more difficult problem to deal with. It created the nation's first regulatory agency but set it a difficult and vague task. Safety was difficult to determine for the hundreds of substances in question. Moreover, it was not just a question of safety; it was a question of fraud. The drugs were being sold with claims to being cures. The frauds often seemed obvious, but proving them would be another matter. It was unclear how consumers were to be protected on this score before the drugs went to market. The solution was to rely on labeling, to make a bill that outlawed misrepresentation. But in the fight over the bill, the key requirement that patent medicine producers put a list of contents on the label was eliminated. In a nod to at least some standards of honesty, there was a requirement that the product inside a bottle or box not be adulterated or impure, as vague a prohibition as that was.

The law also required that if the company chose to say anything on the label about contents, the statements must be true. The only required disclosure was if a medication contained alcohol, opium, cocaine, morphine, chloroform, marijuana, acetanilide, chloral hydrate, or eucaine, including what amount. Beyond that requirement, the law banned labels that had "any statement, design or device regarding such article, or the ingredient or substances contained therein which shall be false or misleading in any particular." In other words, if a statement was made, it had to be true, but statements of ingredients rarely needed to appear on labels.

But what about claims? If a bottle listed no ingredients but claimed to cure cancer, was the label illegal (or "misbranded," in the technical term of the law)? As it turned out, no. When the question was tested in the courts, such claims were permitted, since the science of the time could neither verify nor disprove them.

The law covered foods in much the way it did drugs. It stated that they could not be "adulterated" or "misbranded"—that is, provide misleading information on the label. Food was counted as adulterated if it was missing a key ingredient (such as flour in bread), or if its inferior quality was masked by coloring, powdering, coating, mixing, or staining. Any food was adulterated if it was "filthy, decomposed or putrid." It was also adulterated if it contained any "poisonous or other added deleterious ingredient which may render such article injurious to health." This would be difficult to define and enforce, but among the items potentially covered here were preservatives such as formaldehyde, borax, and sodium benzoate (perhaps as a result of the poison squad studies).

In addition to the weaknesses in the language, there was the problem of enforcement, for which Congress did not authorize a cent. Nor did it give the government the power simply to determine that the law was violated; it required that the government take each offender to court and prove that each particular food or drug was adulterated or mislabeled, and by what standard it was making the judgment. It did permit the temporary seizure of individual shipments if they appeared to violate the law. But if the government won a case after months or years in court, the final penalty was only a misdemeanor, with a fine that could not exceed $200 for the first offense. Flyers, brochures, newspaper ads, posters, and later radio ads as well were not counted as labeling—and thus a huge loophole was opened up.

In the end, the law *did* succeed in establishing two points: first, that the federal government was the agency that should take on widespread commercial abuses; second, that both patent medicines and regular formulas used by physicians should be counted as drugs (here, the law used the definition similar to that offered by patent drug makers themselves—

"any substance or mixture of substances intended to be used for the cure, mitigation or prevention of disease").

The president signed the bill into law on June 30, 1906. He said that progressives were at war with themselves, but this was a victory for the better half. "Half of them . . . [wishes] to attempt the impossible task of returning to the economic conditions that obtained sixty years ago." The other half, he noted, wishes "to recognize the inevitableness of combinations in business, and meet it with a corresponding increase in governmental power over big business."

For Harvey Wiley, the act was not all he hoped for, but when asked how he felt, he replied with a question: "How does a general feel who wins a great battle and brings a final end to hostilities?"

Roosevelt, like Wiley, made the case in moral terms: "Every new social relation begets a new type of wrongdoing—of sin, to use an old-fashioned word—and many years always elapse before society is able to turn this sin into a crime which can be effectively punished by law." In a key redefinition of the American way of life, he was saying that the government must actively seek fairness on behalf of citizens. This solution came about not only because greed and abuse forced action, but also because there was a new hope created by the advances in science. As historian James Harvey Young writes, there was a sudden interest in the use of science for the public. The world was "gradually awakening to the fact of its own improvability," economist Irving Fisher said. A sense was emerging that there must be a more decent way of doing things, and that discoveries in medicine and science could produce a different world.

Though it was not understood at the time, the change in policy that came with this law was a fundamental one. It was an assertion that it was the job of the government to protect citizens from some kinds of commerce rather than just to protect commerce. It was recognition that business most often had the means to take care of itself regarding government policy, but the average citizen did not. It acknowledged that there are instances, such as the ensuring of a supply of safe and wholesome food and medicine for the nation, in which the government must protect citizens against business. It would not be an easy principle to enforce.

•

CHAPTER FOUR

The Law Succeeds, and Fails

THE PASSAGE of the law was called a triumph for Dr. Wiley and his impromptu army. According to the overenthusiastic editorial writers at the *New York Times*, "the purity and honesty of the food and medicines of the people are guaranteed." The *New York Tribune* wrote, "Complaint may be made that the laws passed do not go far enough or are unsatisfactory in this or that detail. But the all important fact is that they do go a long way, and that they blaze a path for future Congresses to follow." Journalist Samuel Hopkins Adams, who was one of those chiefly responsible for raising the issue of dangerous patent medicines, thought the bill was "a complete and overwhelming rout" of the Proprietary Association. Most medicine makers were pleased that "fakirs" would be put out of business and that the "reputable manufacturer" would benefit.

The laws were the first wave of regulation after decades of avoidance. Other nations had long since passed laws to control deceptive and adulterated commerce, but the American law was unique in that it didn't just make nasty business practices illegal. It established a scientific agency, a small body of researchers and inspectors led by the chief chemist, to report on and, in a limited way, police the dark part of commerce in food and drugs. It seemed that with the law the whole climate of business must change, as a watchdog was now on patrol. But the optimism lasted a very short time. The first lesson of regulation was about to be learned: victory comes not in gaining a law but in making it work.

The Bureau of Chemistry of the Department of Agriculture and Wiley as its chief now had far greater responsibilities. From the first day, Wiley was flooded with requests for information about the new law and how it would work. He did not know; regulations hadn't been written yet. He had no new staff or money even to sample the nation's potentially adulterated or fraudulent goods. Then, too, there was the problem that every line of the law would have to be translated into a specific position of the Department of Agriculture, and each position turned into either advice or action.

There were some successes. The bureau's first campaign in which several inspectors worked together was the "dead-horse" racket in New York City. In those days it was not uncommon for horses to keel over dead in the streets and remain there for some time. One company, based across the Hudson River in Hackensack, sent wagons around the city to collect the corpses and bring them back to New Jersey for rendering into fertilizer. But a substantial portion of the meat of the horses also ended up back in New York as "beef" for human consumption. Inspectors tried to break the ring by going undercover, in two guises. A couple of inspectors, suitably dirty and unkempt, joined the small crowd of homeless people who scavenged a large dump site near the Hackensack plant. From there a watch was set up. Other inspectors hired on as hands at the plant, and one was quickly promoted to driver of one of the dead-horse vans. They soon had their evidence, but on the night before their raid, the company bosses got wind of it from local officials and fled. Though there were no prosecutions, the adventure was counted as a success because the ring was broken up.

Then there was ketchup. The bureau knew, but had a hard time proving, that ketchup was made largely of tomatoes that were "in a high state of decomposition," as they put it. Preservatives helped kill the bacteria, and the vinegar and spices covered the taste and smell. Chemists at the bureau worked out two methods to help identify rotten goods that went into the bottles. Since rotten tomatoes led to a watery product with far fewer solids than normal, the percentage of solids could be measured. In addition, they found that rotten tomatoes characteristically contained a very high count of mold particles.

Unfortunately, the inspectors were not permitted to work unannounced and could not compel employees to testify or to produce documents. But in one key Indiana case, an inspector located the home of a company clerk, whom he persuaded to give the names of a few line workers at the factory. In court, the inspectors, after presenting their forensic chemical evidence, still felt that they probably had not made a strong enough case before the local jury. So the bureau called as a witness an older woman who worked at the sorting belt. She testified that the belts moved far too fast for her to pick out all the rotten fruit. In fact, she said, the belt moved so fast that the field mice had to leap off it to escape.

Sometimes, she said, they failed to escape, and became an extra bit of spice for the batch. Her testimony broke up the courtroom in laughter; the agency got its verdict.

It was the first time in the nation's history that inspectors and scientists—though only a handful—were reviewing the foods and medicines put on the market. But in their spirit and sense of mission, these inspectors became the heart of the new agency, working as detectives on behalf of citizens.

In the field, the inspectors were not always accorded respect as they did their work, but in most places and at most times the citizenry was willing to cooperate to some extent. In one minor case in North Carolina, it was shown that a company was filling its five-ounce cans of oysters with about an ounce of oyster; the rest was liquid and debris. After testimony, the judge instructed the jury that if they found that the cans were light-weighted (and the judge added that there was evidence to that effect), then the jury should find for the government. The bureau's Paul Dunbar said to the local prosecutor that, in light of the judge's comments, the agency would win the case. The prosecutor said, as Dunbar wrote later,

> "You probably have heard of a little unpleasantness we had down here some 60 years ago known as the Civil War. These jurors are not going to convict their neighbors on the say-so of a bunch of Yankees from Washington." Promptly, the jury brought in a not-guilty verdict. His honor called the defendant to the bench and said, "You have heard the verdict of the jury, but I warn you not to let anything like this happen again." The defendant promised earnestly that thereafter his cans would contain five ounces.

In court, where the 1906 law required most of the final decisions to be reached, there was regular activity, and the government won most of its cases. Wiley chose as his first case on quack drugs one that seemed blatant enough: the medicine in the case was toxic and had frequently been fatal. The accused was Robert N. Harper, and his product was a "brain tonic"—sold as a headache cure—called, weirdly enough, Cuforhedake Brane-Fude. It comprised alcohol, caffeine, and a high dose of acetanilide, the lethal pain reliever that had been written up by Samuel Hopkins Adams in *Collier's*, complete with a list of twenty-two fatalities that he had identified. A survey of the literature and interviews with doctors convinced the Agriculture Department that the number of deaths from acetanilide was many times higher than those Adams found in his quick search, and that those who took it regularly became dependent on it.

Harper was a pharmacist and chemist who had worked for the John Wyeth pharmaceutical firm. He went into business for himself making Brane-Fude and sold millions of bottles. He became president of the Retail Drug Association and president of his local chamber of commerce. His potentially lethal packages said that the medication inside was "a most wonderful, certain and harmless relief" and that it had "no . . . poisonous ingredients of any kind."

The law said that medicine labels were illegal if they were "false or misleading in any particular." Wiley decided that the label was misleading, because the ingredients were not "harmless" as stated but could be fatal, and that its claim to be "Brane-Fude" was false, as there was no useful nutritional content in the mixture. The only conceivable "food" ingredient was alcohol, which hardly did the brain any good.

A jury found Harper guilty. But when it came to punishment, the judge, noting Harper's status in the community, gave him a light sentence. It was the first federal conviction under food and drug law, and the meager punishment was a signal heard to the present day. For a variety of social and legal reasons, sentences for violations of federal food and drug laws have been uniformly light, with fines small and prison terms almost unheard of, regardless of the number of deaths and injuries caused. The offenses are essentially counted as commercial transgressions, not threats to individual or public health. Harper was fined $700, the maximum allowable. As Wiley told reporters after the trial, Harper "had made two million on the product . . . and was just $1,999,300 ahead." Harper thought of appealing the conviction but decided it was not worth the expense. It was easier to pay the fine and carry on making and selling the remedy, which he did for years. The system had "worked" but not in the sense it was meant to.

The secret-ingredient medicine industry, which had fought regulation to the end, found that the new law was really not very burdensome after all. Most pleas in court were guilty ones, yet few manufacturers went out of business. A number of medicines were discontinued or their ingredients were changed. These were primarily the medicines that contained narcotics and alcohol—most people would not buy medicines with high levels of either when the ingredients were listed on the label.

On the other end of the spectrum were worthless products sold as cures for disease. They were harmful not in themselves but only in their power to take money from customers under false pretenses, and for the possibility that they would keep patients from getting proper treatment. Prosecution in this relatively benign area led to a crippling Supreme Court decision in 1912.

The case at hand was *Johnson* v. *the United States*. One Dr. Johnson of Kansas City, maker of Dr. Johnson's Mild Combination Treatment for Cancer, declared his remedy could cure almost any cancer painlessly with no help from doctors. One Johnson ad said,

> CANCER CURED AT HOME. I have so perfected my Mild Combination Treatment that patients may use it at their home with practically as good results as though it was applied at my offices. I will gladly furnish to every sufferer positive and indisputable proof that my treatment does cure cancer. I will furnish ample evidence of my integrity, honesty, financial and professional ability. No matter how serious your case may be—no matter how many operations you have had—no matter what treatments you have tried, do not give up hope . . . you can be cured at home.

A federal court judge deciding the case, while not agreeing with Dr. Johnson, nevertheless declared that the Food and Drug Act's requirement that labels could not be "false or misleading in any particular" did not apply to curative claims. Thus, if the ingredients on a label were misstated, prosecution could succeed. But if the ingredients were correct and only the claims for its ability to cure were false, no prosecution could go forward. In the debate in Congress before the law was passed, it was clear that Congress had intended the most outrageous curative claims to be illegal. But the judge did not look to the congressional intent. The government appealed to the United States Supreme Court, only to find a majority, led by Oliver Wendell Holmes, agreeing that curative claims should not be settled in law or in court.

Holmes said that Congress should not attempt to insert itself into the long-running medical debates about what cures and what does not. In dissent, Charles Evans Hughes agreed that neither Congress nor the courts should intervene in uncertain areas. But, he said, not all areas were uncertain. Even allowing "the broadest range to the conflict of medical views there still remains a field in which statements as to the curative properties are downright falsehoods and in no sense expressions of judgment." This included cancer, which no faction suggested was curable. The Supreme Court's decision in the Johnson case was met with disbelief and outrage, and President William Taft quickly drafted a message to

Congress asking for immediate passage of a bill to override the Supreme Court decision.

Later, in the summer of 1912, Congress passed an amendment that was, in name, intended to correct the mistake of the Supreme Court. The amendment said that any medicine whose label claimed cures that were "false and fraudulent" was illegal. But in the real world, proving fraudulent intent by a medicine maker was virtually impossible; his defense could simply be, "Well, *I* believe it!" and the case would be closed. It would await another era to address this problem of the law.

Thus, after twenty-five years of effort, one hundred bills, half a dozen national conferences, and a battery of hearings inside and outside Congress, the first regulation of drugs came down to labels. The law prohibited the shipping across state lines of food and drugs falsely labeled. But if no ingredients were listed on the label, there was no offense. And if claims for cures appeared not on the label but on a flyer packaged with it, there was no offense. The law still permitted, as muckrakers vehemently pointed out, that the human population of the United States be guinea pigs for all experiments with medicinal drugs. No testing was required before the drugs were sold, and if the federal government was concerned about any drug, it had to *prove* in court that the drug was harmful to a substantial number of people before removing it from the market. If the danger was subtle, a cumulative effect over a long period, or if it affected, say, only one in a thousand people, the damage would likely continue indefinitely.

As we can see now, the 1906 law did not follow the greatest principle of government—that laws must channel natural instincts, not oppose them. (Paying taxes in week-by-week amounts before you get your hands on the money is a method that works. Paying taxes by writing a huge check at the end of the year does not work well.) Setting boundaries that prevent the production of poisons and frauds before they become market winners can work; trying to clean up the mess after the damage has been done ultimately cannot be effective. The law depended on Wiley's crew's identifying problems, then persuading manufacturers to correct their abuses, and if they would not, the Wiley watchdogs were forced to take the culprits to court. Not very efficient, as it turned out.

And of course, after the enactment of the law, the interests that were opposed to the regulation in the first place did not go away. They were not a group of poor accused criminals; they had resources, which often included a bank of well-paid lawyers and lobbyists. In fact, these particular sets of accused happened to be the wealthiest, best-connected, and most aggressive people in society. Wiley came to realize that changing the practices of the worst of this group was not likely without a true ferocity on the part of federal employees.

Wiley's technical decisions after the law was enacted were almost all correct, and his grasp of the logic behind the law was quite good. But he now had to make crucial policy choices that required the skills of a politician, which he did not possess. Politicians are not, at heart, either technicians or moralists; the essence of action for the politician is the crafting of fair-appearing compromises and the leading forward of skittish factions. Roosevelt now found Wiley, often correct technically and morally, to be clumsy in the political ring.

Some significant trouble of this sort occurred regarding corn syrup. After the law was in place, syrups and sugars could not be faked by using glucose. But since glucose is chemically constructed from corn, one manufacturer, an offshoot of the Standard Oil Company, had the idea that glucose could be sold as such if it was called corn syrup. It sounded natural; moreover, it avoided the word "glucose," which people associated with unwholesome glues. Wiley opposed the suggested usage, because the word "syrup" meant a product taken directly from the plant as sap or juice, as maple syrup was drawn from maple trees. The new phrase, he said, was simply being used to get people to buy what they otherwise would not. Corn Products Refining Company, manufacturers of Karo syrup, began a strong campaign. Lobbyists went to Congress and generated masses of letters to the Agriculture Department, Congress, and the president. The secretary of agriculture, James Wilson, flip-flopped a couple of times before the campaign hit its stride, and in the end Roosevelt had to make the decision. Three secretaries of Roosevelt's cabinet were present in December 1907 when the president held up a vial of the syrup and cursed both the manufacturers and Wiley. Roosevelt decided for the manufacturers. He said, "You must make the manufacturers call a spade a spade, but don't make them call it a damn shovel."

Then there was the French vinegar affair. In May 1908 the French company Cessat of Bordeaux had shipped some vinegar to the United States. The bottle had a trademark that pictured an anchor, a rope, and some bunches of grapes, among other things. In French, it stated that the contents of the bottle were not wine vinegar, made from grapes that kept fermenting past their prime as wine, but rather were distilled vinegar, created chemically from things other than grapes. Wiley held up the product's entry into the United States because of the apparent deception. The French agreed to print "distilled, colored with caramel" in English on the label, and to cut out the bunches of grapes, though not the vine leaves. Wiley wanted the grapevine removed also, and refused to let the shipments in.

The intercession of the French ambassador with the State Department, then with the president, ended the matter. The president was angry, and called Wiley and all other relevant officials on the carpet. The officials "must make adequate explanation or else be considered liable to punishment for useless, illegal and improper interference with shipments of foods from a friendly nation. . . . This pure food law is, if well administered, one of the best laws on the statute book; and I will tolerate neither having it administered with weak or corrupt favoritism towards dishonest or deleterious business, nor a nagging, vexatious, foolish or corrupt spirit towards honest business." The vinegar was cleared into American ports.

Wiley's inability to divert or accommodate the businesses that showed up at his door was worrisome to Roosevelt. Wiley's direct superior, Secretary Wilson, had disagreed with Wiley often and felt overshadowed by the educated and famous food and drug crusader. So, with the agreement of Roosevelt, Wilson acted to put a check on Wiley by appointing a sort of shadow chief of the Bureau of Chemistry, a chemist who would be second in command at the bureau and serve as chief when Wiley was out of town, but report directly to the secretary of agriculture rather than to Wiley.

This plan was announced to Wiley in a particularly rude fashion one winter morning. Wilson appeared in Wiley's office in the company of a young man who had just arrived from Michigan, whom the secretary introduced as "Dr. F. L. Dunlap, your associate."

"Mr. Secretary, my what?" sputtered Wiley.

"Your associate. I have appointed an associate in the Bureau of Chemistry who will be entirely independent of the chief and who will report directly to me. During the absence of the chief he will be acting chief of the bureau."

Wiley later wrote that he was "astounded and dumbfounded at this action. He handed me at the same time a letter in which he established this office and described the duties of the officer." The new "associate" would help undermine Wiley in a series of conflicts.

The fight over preservatives was one of the longest-running battles of the era. It had started even before Wiley joined the government in 1883, and had produced his publicity victory in the famous poison squad experiments. Now it would help unhorse Wiley. He was inclined to prevent the use of preservatives in food until data proved them safe. He felt the law had given him a mandate to err on the side of consumers and safety rather than businesses and profit. Wiley concluded that sodium benzoate should be phased out of general use and permitted only where it was clearly needed—where food was likely to spoil without aid, such as food shipped to remote locations. He had issued a ruling in 1907 to permit the use of benzoates temporarily, but at no greater than .10 percent concentration. Then, he tried to phase out their use completely.

This alarmed the industry, and lobbyists sought and obtained another debate and hearing on the issue, despite the fact that the law did not allow for additional hearings for special pleadings. At the new hearing the canners said that they feared being left behind unfairly. "If you exclude benzoate of soda from catsup, and there is somebody who can make it without," said one of the manufacturers, "whereas the great majority cannot, then you create a great monopoly in this country."

Some manufacturers had sided with Wiley and had proved that benzoate was not necessary to preserve ketchup. It is not easy without chemical preservatives, but they had done it. Historically, only three other ways had been found to keep food from spoiling—drying it, heating it, or refrigerating it. But a handful of innovative companies, aware that consumers disliked having chemicals added to their food, had worked out methods to avoid their use. Chief among these was H. J. Heinz. Heinz found that if ketchup was made with very fresh fruit, under sterile conditions and with secure bottling, there was no need for sodium benzoate. They hoped to take advantage of their efforts commercially, and pressed to have other manufacturers come up to their standards. But the other manufacturers did not want to be bound by tougher standards. They felt there was little evidence of any problems with sodium benzoate, so why force manufacturers to stop using it? Their worst fear was that some manufacturers would meet the standard and others would fail. The necessary care and cleanliness to make ketchup without preservatives required controls at each stage—fresh tomatoes, very clean machinery, sterilized bottles, and the exclusion of air at several steps.

The manufacturers who wanted to keep their preservatives pressed ahead. Representative James Sherman of New York, himself a canner and soon to be vice president, took the case directly to the president, arguing that a ruling against preservatives would destroy "Republican business." Though it was not clear at the time, the canners and bottlers who wanted to use preservatives might have been in the minority of the trade and made the cheapest mass-market goods. Wiley, Wilson, who supported Wiley on this issue, and Sherman, who spoke for the industry, met with the president in the Cabinet Room at the White House. The more innovative manufacturers who did without preservatives, such as Heinz, were excluded from the meeting.

Sherman argued that eliminating preservatives would put many out of business and cause others to lose hundreds of thousands of dollars.

Roosevelt then asked Secretary Wilson, "Mr. Wilson, do you think the addition of benzoate of soda to foods is injurious?"

"Yes," Wilson answered.

Roosevelt then asked Wiley the same question.

"I do not think, I know. I have tried it on healthy young men and it made them ill."

Likewise, Agriculture's chief attorney McCabe and chemist Dunlap agreed.

"Then," Wiley recalled Roosevelt saying, as he whacked the table with his fist, "gentlemen, if this drug is injurious you shall not put it in foods!"

For a moment, Wiley seemed to have won. But as he himself noted bitterly afterward, he did not keep his mouth shut and walk away with that.

Sherman raised another topic. "Mr. President, there was another matter that we spoke to you about yesterday and that is not included in what you have just said about the use of benzoate. I refer to the use of saccharin in foods. My firm last year saved $4,000 by sweetening canned corn with saccharin instead of sugar. We want a decision from you on this question."

Wiley burst in before the president could reply or ask a question. "Everyone who ate that sweet corn was deceived," Wiley said. "He thought he was eating sugar, when in point of fact he was eating a coal tar product totally devoid of food value and extremely injurious to health."

As Wiley recalled, "turning to me in sudden anger, the president changed from Dr. Jekyll to Mr. Hyde, and said, referring to his friend and personal physician, 'Dr. Rixey gives it to me every day. . . . Anybody who says saccharin is injurious is an idiot.' This remark broke up the meeting. Had he only extended his royal Excalibur, I should have arisen as Sir Idiot. That distinction has not departed from me to this day. The thing which hurts most is that . . . I fear I deserved it."

From that moment on, Roosevelt's caution about Wiley turned to an active distrust. Not long afterward, Roosevelt wrote:

The trouble with Dr. Wiley is, that to my personal knowledge, he has been guilty of such grave errors of judgment in matters of such great importance as to make it quite impossible to accept his say-so in a matter without a very uneasy feeling that I may be doing far-reaching damage to worse than no purpose. I tested him personally in reference to corn syrup, the use of saccharine [*sic*], and the importation of French vinegar. In each case he made a ruling which was nonsensical, the kind of ruling which, if we allowed it to stand and to be followed by similar rulings, would certainly have meant the upsetting of the whole pure-food law. These instances gave me a great distrust of Wiley's good judgment. On the other hand, I have such confidence in his integrity and zeal that I am anxious to back him up to the limit of my power wherever I can be sure that doing so won't do damage instead of good.

The day after the meeting over sodium benzoate and saccharin, the president agreed to Sherman's request to appoint an "expert" panel of scientists, one, of course, that could effectively neutralize Wiley. (In passing the 1906 law, Congress had considered but dropped the idea of having an independent board of scientists.) The industry took the cue and began at the same time a nationwide campaign against Wiley, getting newspapers and magazines to run attack articles based on its arguments. Wiley was stung. He declared that the "expert panel" was plainly illegal, which it may well have been, and simply a capitulation to commercial interests.

The first action of the new board was to redo the poison squad experiments on sodium benzoate. This time, the work was done in secret, keeping Wiley in the dark, although industry scientists were invited to consult with Ira Remsen, a distinguished chemist from Johns Hopkins and the most prominent member of the board. Board members later testified that it was clear at the time that their mission was to try to give industry a hearing and some opportunity to continue using preservatives and other new chemicals; in other words, the panel's charge was biased. The panel took for its design of the new "poison squad" experiments a near duplicate of the experiments Wiley had done. And the raw results of the new study were similar as well. But the symptoms the Remsen board saw were ascribed to other factors. Did the subject have a mild cold? Wasn't losing a pound and a half during the experiment within the normal range of adding and losing weight? The Remsen board was looking only for *extreme* symptoms. Thus, though the results were actually alike in many ways, the Remsen report was completely different from Wiley's: it reinterpreted the symptoms of those in the study as ones unconnected with the preservative, and declared that sodium benzoate was not notably harmful, even when taken in large quantities. If Wiley had been quick to find symptoms associated with the preservative, this board had veered widely in the other direction.

The board permitted preservatives such as sodium benzoate to be used indefinitely. There would be no phaseout of the substance, as Wiley had decreed. The manufacturers had won the political tussle. It is ironic that sodium benzoate was the substance fought over; after all, in Wiley's first poison squad experiments four of the six preservatives tested were found to be far more hazardous. All six are now known to be toxic to some degree, and three of them are banned from food. But it was the manufacturers who picked the field of battle.

When he read the Remsen report Wiley's first impulse was to resign. It was plain to all now, he felt, that special interests had simply intervened and canceled out the legally established work of his bureau. The law required Wiley's bureau and the secretary to make a judgment, which would then be tested in court, where the final determination was to rest. But now the process had been subverted, and Wiley's opinion never reached the court or a public airing. After reflection, Wiley became newly energized and decided to fight on a bit longer. He organized his many supporters, and soon a bill was introduced in Congress to declare the Remsen board illegal.

Of course, the fight had been not so much over data as over policy. Should the department err on the side of safety and the consumers? Or should it err on the side of business freedom until practices were proved to be dangerous? This question has remained the single most important one in the history of food and drug regulation—in fact, in the history of all government regulation. How should science be used in making policy judgments? The answer has been many decades in formulation. For the industry, it was a struggle over the best way to do business in America. Though industrialists had said the elimination of preservatives would beggar them, this was not true and they knew it. Now, they were infuriated at these uppity regulators and the extra expenses their demands would require.

Years later, two of the most ardent foes of Wiley and his attempts to restrict sodium benzoate confessed that after a time they realized they were wrong and Wiley right. They had been to Congress many times, they had fought battles in court half a dozen times, and they were key forces in marshaling opposition to Wiley. But in the end, Walter H.

Williams, head of the Detroit company, and Elliot Grosvenor, leader of years of lobbying efforts against the restriction of preservatives, dropped their advocacy of preservatives. Williams even wrote to Wiley saying his company had dropped the use of sodium benzoate. Williams said chemical preservatives proved

> entirely unnecessary in such food products as ketchup, sweet pickles, preserves, etc. Not only did [the company] find that a preservative such as benzoate is unnecessary. But we were convinced that permission to use it allowed food manufacturers to be very careless in their methods of manufacture. . . . At the time we all believed we were absolutely and honestly right in our contention, but most of us have since found we were wrong, and that working under proper factory methods and conditions we can comply with all regulations called for by the national food and drugs act and turn out much better products than under the slip-shod methods generally used before the passage of the act. . . . When I look back over the changes that have come to the food industry during the past twenty-five years and see the great changes for the better that have come to our methods and our products, I wonder why we were all so blindly asleep as we were, and why, much sooner than we did, we did not welcome and follow your teaching.

Whatever strength the 1906 law might have had in theory largely buckled under continued political pressure and challenges in court. The problems were inevitable. The 1906 law was built on the idea that false claims must be prosecuted, rather than addressing the real issues of whether food additives and drugs put on the market were safe and worked as they claimed. What Wiley should have done from the beginning, and should have asked for in the 1906 law, he realized only years after the law was in place and he had been attempting to administer it. The model for a law, he said, should have been the simple and direct law on vaccines, passed to little notice in 1902.

It had been created during a small crisis in the new field of vaccines. The principle that a tiny dose of a disease-causing agent could coax the body into making its own robust defense against the disease had only been proved at the end of the nineteenth century. There were no vaccine companies, no industry, only a handful of scientists and public health workers studying the issue. It had been shown by 1894 that animals that got diphtheria produced inside their bodies a strong antitoxin to the disease. It was a potent defensive weapon created by the body itself, and if it was taken from the body of the animal, it could be used to prevent or even cure diphtheria in humans as well. Public health laboratories in New York perfected the technique of extracting and purifying the anti-diphtheria substance from horses that had mild cases of the disease, and soon other public health labs and a few commercial companies copied their methods and used the new antitoxin on patients between 1896 and 1901.

It was the U.S. Hygienic Laboratory, the forerunner of the National Institutes of Health, that had done the initial work, and its chief, Joseph Kinyoun, warned that the work of making antitoxins was very complex and potentially dangerous. In a letter, he warned about premature commercialization and copying of the sensitive techniques. He said labs around the country might well "commence to prepare the serum as a business enterprise, and there will, without a doubt, be many worthless articles called anti-toxin thrown upon the market. All the serum for sale should be made or tested by competent persons. The testing, in fact, should be done by disinterested parties."

There was no regulation, no way to prevent companies from making antitoxin carelessly or selling false versions of the medicine. There was discussion of criminal prosecution should trouble occur, but it was unclear on what basis a lab or company would be prosecuted.

Kinyoun's fears were realized beginning in October 1901. Careless errors were made in the manufacture of one batch of antitoxin in St. Louis. (One horse from which the medicine had been drawn had another disease, tetanus, and lab workers failed to destroy all the flasks contaminated with it.) Five children in St. Louis died when given the contaminated antitoxin. A similar incident involving contaminated smallpox vaccine killed nine children in Camden, New Jersey. There were reports of hundreds more cases and other deaths. So early in 1902 a bill was quietly introduced in Congress, and with little discussion and no publicity, the Biologics Act was passed and signed into law by President Roosevelt that year.

The law created a simple solution to the problem of deadly medicines. It established licenses for those who wanted to make and sell vaccines and antitoxins. Federal scientists from the Public Health Service would inspect (sometimes unannounced) the licensees and certify that they were preparing the medicines properly before sale was permitted. Licenses expired and were renewed annually, with scrutiny guaranteed at least once a year. Failures could mean revocation of licenses, and some companies did fail. The program was an immediate success, praised by both manufacturers and public health officials.

The final act in Wiley's long tenure was a skirmish over grain. The bureau's inspectors had begun to find grain that was musty, spoiled, and decayed, and to which sulfur had been applied to halt the rot. He announced that he would soon apply the food law to prosecute grain dealers selling such products. In March 1912 the Grain Dealers National Association was meeting in Washington, and Secretary Wilson took the opportunity to declare that he would not permit any seizures and prosecutions on this issue. It was new territory, and the Agriculture Department was not prepared to enter it, despite what Wiley had said. At that meeting, President Taft took the opportunity to bolster his support with farms and businesses. He said that while he wanted misbranding and adulteration to stop, he wanted to assure the farmers of America that he would not let government action destroy legitimate businesses. There would be no action before the election.

Wiley's wife was pregnant, and due in May with their first child. He had been up to the new farm in Virginia and loved it. In reviewing his career it seemed that this might be the best time to leave. He had won vindication at least in principle from Congress and the White House, but it was still clear that protection of the consumer was just not a major concern of the Republican party. Even a vindicated Wiley would not be able to lead a consumer movement from his government chair. The battles would go on and on, and he was tired of them. Numerous businesses had offered him substantial sums to come work for them; he would not consider them. He had resolved never to profit commercially from his advocacy of pure food and drugs. He had an offer to make a speaking tour of the country, and an offer of a regular column in *Good Housekeeping* on food, nutrition, and sanitation. The column and the speaking engagements attracted him. Though they did not pay hugely, they seemed to him a final position from which to aid the public brigade for food and drug reform.

Thus, within ten days of the Taft and Wilson statements on grain, Wiley submitted his resignation. Wiley "may at times have seemed a little harsh and pedagogical to those injuriously affected by a strict enforcement of the pure food law," wrote the *New York Tribune* in bidding him farewell, "but the great mass of the people applauded his unyielding insistence on honesty in the preparation and labeling of food as an admirable exhibition of official virtue." As the election campaign wore on that year, Taft courted him, but finally Wiley determined to break his lifelong bond with the Republican party, just as Roosevelt was resolving to do, and for the same reasons. The mantle of reform had shifted, permanently, from the Republicans to the Democrats in that year, in part at least because of the food and drug campaigns.

There had been great hope in the beginning, especially in the heart of Harvey Wiley. But by 1930, Wiley was bitter about what had happened to him and to his bureau. Even twenty years after passage of the law, when the agency was well established, it had only 295 employees to cover the food and drug problems of a nation of 100 million people. The agency's annual budget was less than the amount needed to produce the Agriculture Department newsletter. And a single problem of the farming business (for example, an appearance of the corn borer) was attacked quickly and relatively effectively with more people and money than those used in an entire year's work in the bureau's policing of food and drug problems. Wiley had seen a law enacted, and gained the assertion of principle by Congress and several presidents. But in the end, he felt the plan had not worked. As he lay dying, the law's importance was deflating steadily as businesses found paths around it, products multiplied, and new fields of commerce continued to open up over which the law had no jurisdiction.

•

CHAPTER FIVE

Capitalism in Crisis

THE OPPORTUNITY for change would not come again until the nation
had been through the mud and barbed wire of the First World War,
then got high on the sudden prosperity of the 1920s, and paid for it with
the dark days of depression.

Walter G. Campbell had become head of the bureau in 1921. He had
been hired by Wiley himself as soon as the 1906 law had been passed,
when Campbell was still a bright-eyed young lawyer from Kentucky. He
had a smooth and confident style, which today would put one in mind of
actor Ben Kingsley, who can simultaneously look modest, unassuming,
and sharp as a needle. Campbell kept a crease in his trousers, made a
point of courtesy, and had a keen eye for the heart of issues. In those days,
a man could be, and often was, judged by his poker playing, a standard
off-hours occupation. In the bureau, Campbell was counted as one of its
two best. He had a poker face and gave the continuous impression of
being "an unusually lucky player," the certain sign that luck wasn't the
issue. In these games, of course, it was the chemists who were perennial
losers, as they tried to handle cards like a mathematical problem rather
than the psychological and social one that it is.

Campbell, who went by the nickname "Walt," had been at the bureau
long enough to observe the bombardment from every artillery piece in
industry and politics. He had been picked by Wiley as the bureau's first
head inspector and had been there for meeting after meeting with the
president, each of which was followed by hope and then by despair.
Campbell had carried on as the Progressive Era ended and the bureau
became steadily more hobbled by small budgets, adverse court rulings, and the renewed boldness of business. He was there when Wiley
resigned.

After the First World War, America was disrupted by the worst inflation in memory, race riots, widespread strikes, and the beginning of the Red Scare. Two Communist parties were founded in the United States, and at the same time, radicals in labor unions were purged. Bombs were exploded in assassination attempts. The federal government arrested thousands using plainly illegal warrants as it went after all "communists" across the country. The police killed dozens of radicals and scores of blacks in a wave of attacks. Though it now seems impossible, in various states, half a dozen candidates for office who had won election fairly were simply ejected from their legislatures and prevented from taking office because of their suspected radicalism. The nation, which was fundamentally conservative, was having an immune reaction, ruthlessly purging itself of all leftish fevers.

So, in the 1920s, the Republicans, who were now clearly the country's business party, began what they called the "return to normalcy." What they did not understand was that there *was* no more normalcy. Society had changed irrevocably, and stability would have to be created, not returned to. Though conservatives count it as the greatest decade of prosperity in the nation's history, that was true only for the top layer of society. Unemployment at the time was high. The incomes of large segments of the working population rose little or not at all. And while economists were still dreaming eighteenth-century Adam Smith–like dreams, the economy actually bore almost no relation to that lost world.

By the end of the 1920s, a series of huge industrial oligarchies had displaced individual owners. Two-thirds of the industrial wealth in America had slipped from ownership by single individuals to ownership by huge corporations. In 1929 only two hundred corporations controlled half of all American industry. In personal terms, a few tenths of one percent of the people at the top were extraordinarily wealthy compared to the rest of society. At the peak of "prosperity," 71 percent of families in America had incomes of less than $2,500, and more than 80 percent had no savings whatsoever. Herbert Hoover said it best: "The only problem with capitalism is capitalists. They're too damn greedy."

With the American economy on the brink of collapse in late 1928, Hoover, as president, surrounded by prosperous friends and still expecting some "trickle down," declared, "We shall soon with the help of God be in sight of the day when poverty will be banished from this nation." Those holding the sacks of cash were determined not to give an inch. Mogul Andrew Mellon said he saw "nothing in the present situation that is either menacing or warrants pessimism." According to Charles

Schwab, "never before has American business been as firmly entrenched in prosperity as it is today."

The administration continued to support banks and stock market speculators, and said that credit should continue to be available to them, for "after all, what is credit but confidence?" At the same time, Hoover demonstrated no confidence in workers. Patrick J. Hurley, secretary of war, referred to unemployment relief not as credit but as "a gratuity" that he would not consider giving because it would demean those who received it.

This pure capitalist fantasy ended with the beginning of the depression. For the nation, the experience was overwhelming, and was likened to a civil war. As Robert and Helen Lynd write in *Middletown*, "The great knife of the depression cut down impartially through the entire population cleaving open lives and hopes of rich as well as poor. The experience had been more nearly universal than any prolonged . . . event in the city's history; it has approached in its elemental shock the primary experiences of birth and death."

What Campbell faced when he looked out from the parapet of his little bureau was utterly different from what Wiley had seen when he had climbed the tower almost thirty years before. Wiley had begun when, in essence, there were *no* food and drug regulations. There was also little hope that medicine would actually turn back the tide of human disease. There was no great sense that science would join with business. Progress was still an entirely fragmentary matter.

But now Campbell saw businesses that were not simple individual enterprises but, instead, giant social institutions. He saw that they were learning to take advantage of knowledge. Campbell's agency had little power, and so most of what he tried to do was done by alerting businesses to their violations, then negotiating with company leaders to stop the worst abuses. Wiley, in old age, complained bitterly about this to Campbell, saying it was not the job of the government, nor was it anywhere in the law that the bureau should conduct elementary school for companies. It would be a waste of resources, he said, and signal a lack of seriousness about the job to be done.

But Campbell and the bureau, since 1927 officially named the Food and Drug Administration, were adrift in a rising sea. Half the products he was looking at did not even exist when the 1906 law was written, and he had very little authority to regulate much of the other half. Cosmetics were one example. There had been virtually no market for them at the end of the nineteenth century; there were only simple powders, creams, and scents. But now there was a substantial market and it was filled with chemicals, some of which were dangerous to human tissue. That was not mentioned in the 1906 law. And what about pesticides? A large number of new ones were coming into use, they were being applied to crops, and they were showing up later in processed food. But the law didn't even provide for the government to get a good look at the new substances being injected into and onto food, much less control them. Campbell was feeling overwhelmed and was hoping to get by as far as he could with diplomacy and a few prosecutions, while he tried to determine how to plug the leaking dike.

The facts were, to modern eyes, startling. Anyone could concoct a medicine in his kitchen and sell it, with no testing required as long as it didn't contain narcotics or one of a few listed poisons. (Potentially fatal ingredients used in medicine were not counted as poisons at the time, only those so toxic that they killed *immediately*.) If the new kitchen concoction turned out to be damaging or fatal to some customers, the maker was not required to pull it off the market, either. If the number of dead and ill increased to the point that it was obvious to society at large, the maker still could not be stopped so long as he said his intention was to cure ills. At most, the FDA could begin a court action that, if contested, could last for some years and result in a minuscule fine. At the end of it all, the maker could give his concoction a new name and start all over again.

Such was the mass of loopholes referred to as "food and drug law." The trade in patent medicines alone by the early 1930s was $350 million, far larger than when Wiley tried to pass a law to curtail it in 1906. The basic notion remained: damage first, review later.

By the end of the 1920s, there was no longer a question of whether there would be regulations on businesses, as there had been in 1906. Even through the conservative Republican presidential retrenchment from Warren Harding to Hoover, from 1920 to 1932, the whole phalanx of business interests was asking for and receiving government regulation. Most of it was not consumer-oriented, but it was regulation nonetheless, and it aided not only business in general but particular businesses in America. Regulation was used to stop the decline of farm products and raw materials; high tariffs were set, and the banking industry and money supply were aided with new rules.

After the 1929 collapse, the country would have to consider establishing laws and regulations to stabilize the out-of-control economy. The depression would bring not only trouble but also remarkable improvisations in politics to deal with it. When Franklin D. Roosevelt was inaugurated as president on March 4, 1933, he said, "This nation asks for action, and action now." He said he might have to take and use powers granted to a president only during wartime. That statement was greeted with an outburst of cheers.

The nation's income was half what it had been four years earlier, and a quarter of the nation's workers had no employment. The president had declared the morning of his inauguration that all banks in America should close down. He froze the nation's supply of gold. And he called the Congress of the United States into emergency session.

During the three days when the banks were shut down and the economy frozen, Roosevelt pulled out his notes, called together his advisors, and created a new banking system—deliberately not tearing down the present system even though its denizens had viciously attacked him and demonstrated their brazen greed during the past few years, to the point that if Roosevelt had declared their arrest and incarceration in March 1933, it would have raised little surprise and few laments.

Four days after the inauguration, Roosevelt and his team had finished the first of his emergency laws, the one to rebuild and regulate the healthy banks and take over the hopeless ones. The next day it passed Congress in forty minutes, and the Senate waited impatiently as the House finished and sent over the only copy of the bill. Senator Huey Long of Louisiana tried to start a debate but was quickly shouted down by the lawmakers, who were nearly a mob. The bill was passed by seven-thirty in the evening, carried to the White House, and signed within the hour. It was but the first of a series of emergency acts, including fifteen major laws pressed through in the first one hundred days of Roosevelt's administration.

Part of the Roosevelt team, in fact an intellectual leader of it, was Rexford G. Tugwell, a professor of economics at Columbia University who was as shrewd a tactician as any to be found in a university job. He was a small, debonair man, good looking enough to earn constant comment in news stories about him. Officially, he was second in command at the Department of Agriculture, but he was part of Roosevelt's transition team and one of the key advisors who helped shape the campaign of the one hundred days.

Issues of food and drugs were not among the pressing economic emergencies, but Tugwell believed they had a different sort of importance. He said the welfare of citizens is nowhere more directly exposed to greed and ruthlessness than in these trades, and that there was no better example of the trouble with free markets than the sale of food and drugs. A "pure" market in these areas would permit the killing of citizens first, with investigations to follow, and action last, and people were simply not protected.

Before the inauguration Tugwell said, "One of the first problems I shall meet . . . will be the Pure Food and Drugs administration which has been perverted by the attempt to protect business interests." He had been told the current leadership at the administration was corrupt. The head of the nation's leading consumer group had promised to get him the evidence. Tugwell had read some of the reports of the outrageous products on the market and their deadly or fraudulent effects, and assumed the trouble was with the agency. If the information from consumer groups "pans out," he said, "we'll blow them out of the water." He meant to torpedo the agency. "I have long wanted this chance, and shall make the best use I can of it, though I realize how much risk I shall run in doing it." He added with some determination, "I'll do the best I can for the consumer regardless of the politics; I won't compromise on this."

Tugwell fired his first rocket in early March 1933 when he penciled a note to Walter Campbell. Tugwell was irritated by a letter that had come in to his office asking about lead arsenate, a poison being used to spray fruit trees. A routine reply was drafted. Tugwell was supposed to sign it and send it out in the name of the Department of Agriculture. Instead, he wrote in the margin words to the effect that, if lead arsenate is a poison, why are we taking the side of the sprayers? He sent the comment and the unsigned letter to Walter Campbell.

So the first communication Campbell received from a New Dealer in a hopeful new administration was, as one friend called it, "a kick in the teeth." Of course he would like to ban poisonous sprays (as well as pull the plug on dangerous medicines and toxic cosmetics and all other forms of cruelty in the food and drug trade), but the law wouldn't allow it. It had been created to give business a wide berth. Even Harvey Wiley had worked hard to assert and demonstrate that businesses should be free and regulation must be limited.

We can imagine Campbell's frustration and anger at the Tugwell note. Campbell had the jurisdiction, so he had to take the blame. But the agency could not make rules or declare what was safe. It could only propose, and then face hearing after hearing, and finally court action, often only to be back again at the start.

Campbell got the note from Tugwell after regular working hours one night, as he and several others chatted in his office. Now he told them he would march over to Tugwell's office first thing in the morning and tell him a thing or two. But one of the cooler heads in the office, Benjamin White, realized that the note, while irritating, was a declaration from Tugwell that he was on the side of tough enforcement. These agency men had worked so many years without backing that they almost failed to recognize it when it arrived.

As the scales fell from his eyes, Campbell said, "White is right. That's the way I'll approach Tugwell." And so, no longer angry and defensive, Campbell marched over to the office of the assistant secretary of agriculture the next morning with a pitch in mind. He described for Tugwell the weakness of the 1906 law, the few positive amendments that had been gained in the past quarter century, and also the many "ripper" amendments by Republicans in the Coolidge and Hoover years that were attempts to further gut the Food and Drug Act.

With his recitation of law and history, Campbell convinced Tugwell. In turn, Tugwell headed for the White House that morning. He knew that Roosevelt often drew parallels between his career and that of the cousin he so admired, Theodore. So Tugwell reminded him that it was "Uncle Teddy" who created the first food and drug law, and that it was now in disrepair. It would be fitting for the president to take up the issue again.

By noon, Tugwell had called Campbell to say the president had approved a major revision in the food and drug laws. Two legislative writers were recruited, and the drafting of an entirely new law began.

When young men and women arrive in Washington to work in Congress, it has long been traditional to tell them "sausage" stories. That is, they hear tales of the unseen deals, favors, prejudices, and backroom fights that demonstrate making law is an ugly business, like making sausage. But as the young workers gain seasoning in Washington, they come to realize that it is more than just the unseemly combining of offal to produce the edible.

Work began on the new food and drug law in 1933, with the politics and business interests similar to that in 1906, with one notable exception. There was a new entity in American polity—the professional consumer-interest group. Several had just been established, they were growing rapidly, and they were already influential. The most prominent of the type was called Consumers' Research (the ancestor of today's Consumers Union and its revered publication *Consumer Reports*).

The news that a bill was being drafted passed within hours to industry and others in Washington, and the queries came in fast and heavy. As the drafting took months, and opinions were solicited from industry and citizens, the various businesses affected became increasingly nervous and began to plan an aggressive campaign.

When the text was officially released, well-choreographed screams of protest filled the press and the hallways of Congress. The food and drug industries were not actually unified against the bill, but the oxen likely to be gored squalled first and loudest, and gave the impression that all of industry was revolted. Those in the food and drug world who saw merit in having a new law represented less organized interests, and it would take time for their voices to be heard.

The bill itself was intended simply to extend the previous law: It would prohibit misstatements and claims on advertising beyond the label. And ingredients would have to be listed on the bottle. These items do not seem very radical until you realize that all the secret-formula makers depended on their freedom to make claims without factual backing, and they relied on unrestricted collateral advertising for their products. If they had to list all ingredients, and make no claims to cure an array of diseases, they had very little indeed. To make matters worse, in the new law there was a list of illnesses for which *no drug,* whether a secret formula or a prescription, would be allowed to claim it was a cure. There was no cure for cancer or for diabetes. Instead, the medicines for these illnesses would have to state that they were palliative treatments, or say nothing specific. The law did not ban any drugs per se. But it was perceived as a ban, because many manufacturers knew from experience that if they either disclosed their ingredients or toned down their claims, their "medicines" would not sell.

There was also one truly new element in the bill: any proposed new drugs would have to be submitted along with accompanying information showing they were safe. For the first time, companies would have to justify themselves and their products to the government *before* sale.

The attack on the bill was carried out largely under the generalship of the two trade groups of secret-formula drug makers, the Proprietary Association and the Institute of Medicine Manufacturers. They used the full range of weapons immediately and intensely because they feared the bill might pass quickly along with other New Deal bills designed to produce economic recovery in the nation. They arranged for hundreds of letters to be sent to members of Congress, and to a variety of other government agencies as well, condemning the new food and drug proposal. Employees of the drugmakers were recruited into writing batches of letters to their representatives, which produced an array of missives with identical wording in each congressional office. The language on one form letter said the new bill "will put thousands of men and women out of work. It will close dozens of manufacturing plants and hundreds of stores. . . . It will help none. . . ."

One letter sent by a group calling itself the Minute Men and employed by the trade groups read:

> MR. RETAILER . . . Do you know:
> 1. There are pending in Congress new Food Drug and Cosmetic Bills that are likely to put you out of business?
> 2. Do you know it will be impossible for your customers to buy many of your fastest sellers without a physician's prescription?
> 3. Do you know that many of your fastest moving items will be forced off the market altogether?
> . . .
> 5. Do you know these pending bills give government officials absolute domination over manufacturers' business and your business . . . ?

The letter went on to recommend that the retailers protest to Congress, get each of their employees to write, and let suppliers and landlords know that they might not be able to do business with the retailers anymore if the law were to be passed.

One company representative sent to a newspaper a letter from a manufacturer that read:

> You are about to lose a substantial amount of advertising revenue from food, cosmetic and drug manufacturers. . . . You need to bring all the personal pressure you can upon your Senators and Representatives. You need to enlighten and thereby arouse your public against this bill that is calculated to greatly restrict personal rights.
>
> If this bill should become law, we will be forced to cancel immediately every line of Creomulsion [a cough syrup advertised as a cure for pneumonia]. . . . We would be only one of the many drug, cosmetic, and food advertisers who will be forced to liquidate in this manner.

The news coverage of the bill was extremely thin, and what there was tended to the negative. The pressure on newspapers was intense. One St. Louis editor wrote to Tugwell saying that opponents of the bill had created the "hottest heat he had felt in a quarter of a century" of political commentary. How much this pressure produced the scant or negative reporting is not known, but in a poll of Washington correspondents following the activities on Capitol Hill, 49 percent said their own newspaper was covering the issue unfairly. An additional 34 percent declined to say whether it was fair or not, and only 23 percent counted their paper's coverage fair. This result is remarkable considering the source—these reporters had both loyalty to their papers and a better-than-average idea of which stories on their beat were being distorted.

In going after consumers themselves, the most famous of all secret-formula medicines—Lydia E. Pinkham's Vegetable Compound (containing no vegetables, but 18 percent alcohol)—gave "pink slips" to its customers. These slips said that a bill in Congress would make it "very hard for you to purchase Lydia E. Pinkham's Vegetable Compound or any other medicine which you are now in the habit of using and which you know helps you. We are trying to stop this bill from becoming a law. . . . Please sign your name and address to the enclosed letter and mail it in the enclosed envelope immediately. Destroy this colored slip after mailing letter."

The drugmakers referred to the proposed changes as the "Tugwell bill," though he had nothing to do with the actual provisions. But Tugwell was an academic, and worse, as a drug trade writer noted, "The world knows that he has visited Russia." Though he had come back saying the Soviet system was a failure, his economic papers did advocate a "regulated" capitalism. He believed it would be the only system that could take into account both the needs of businesses and citizens. The drugmakers wrote that the bill would "Sovietize" drug sales in America and produce "a virtual dictatorship over the trade." The attacks on Tugwell became so frequent and extreme that soon lampoons appeared as well, with one suggesting that Tugwell's plan "is to abandon both the silver and gold standards . . . and issue aspirin tablets from the Federal mint."

Opponents said the bill would do nothing less than cancel the "sacred right" of self-medication. This cry, too, became so widespread that spoofs of it began to appear. One article in *The Nation* said:

This measure frankly challenges the sacred right of freeborn Americans to advertise and sell horse liniment as a remedy for tuberculosis . . . [challenges] his God-given right to advertise and sell extract of horsetail weed as a cure for diabetes. This is precisely the sort of constitutional question which stirs men to the very depths of their pocketbooks.

The patent-formula makers lit fires of objection across the country, and worked as hard on their colleagues as on consumers and legislators, to convince all that the proposed law was a radical and dangerous departure. Lawyers for one of the patent medicine journals delivered the opinion that, if the bill passed, "no manufacturer can possibly continue in business except by the grace of the officials in Washington." There was some truth in this. Colored water would no longer pass as a cancer cure; horse liniment would not be acceptable as a cure for tuberculosis; and alcoholic concoctions would not pass as cures for collapsed uteri.

Dr. James Beal, speaking for the secret-formula makers at a drug trade conference, said that anytime the government failed to endorse a remedy under the new law, it would be death for that cure. Remember too, he said, that there was still disagreement among dermatologists about whether talcum powder causes irritation, and whether starch and fatty oils are harmful to their users. These, too, might be banned, he suggested.

The scare was thorough. Old and poor Emma Carlisle of Whitakers, North Carolina, wrote a letter to her congressman saying she feared the new law. "If anyone has sick headache, would it be a violation of the law to make a cup of thyme tea for relief? The poor can't have a Doctor for every minor scratch." One journal warned its readers in 1934 that "the FDA is a group of people prejudiced in the interests of the public."

The groups that banded together for the earlier law came together again for this campaign, notably women's clubs, scientists, state health officials, pharmacists, public health groups, and a handful of companies that felt a law would give them a competitive advantage. And now, there were also the professional consumer advocates.

The activists had been working even before the first New Deal bill was proposed. Muckraking books exposed the frauds and hazards in the food and drug trades, beginning with a pair of books—*The Tragedy of Waste* in 1925 and *Your Money's Worth*, the first consumer manifesto, published in 1927. The first, written by economist Stuart Chase, argued that a good deal of the economy was producing wasteful goods and advertising that worked only to promote otherwise indistinguishable soaps, tooth powders, and worthless patent medicines. Chase then joined with F. J. Schlink, a mechanical engineer who had become fascinated with the peculiarities of the marketplace, to write *Your Money's Worth.* The books sold surprisingly well and were followed by an even greater blockbuster, *100,000,000 Guinea Pigs,* written by Schlink and a colleague, Arthur Kallet, at the fledgling Consumers' Research group.

The group was founded in 1929, and by the time *Guinea Pigs* was published in 1933, the group had already grown to 45,000 members and was expanding rapidly. *Guinea Pigs* went through twenty-seven printings in its first year and continued to sell well for several more years. The book was, as historian James Harvey Young puts it, "a mixture of technological analysis and fiery tract." It stated facts; it named actual brands and listed their crimes and frauds openly.

The authors took on the best-known names, including Listerine, which at the time was not just sold as mouthwash. This is one example of a product that succeeded under both lax and, later, tougher law, the difference being that dangerous and dishonest marketing was dropped, and a new approach was found to replace it. Listerine was advertised to the public as an agent that could prevent disease, including tuberculosis. Listerine "kills 200,000,000 germs in 15 seconds," one ad claimed. But as Kallet and Schlink pointed out, it could kill some common bacteria but could not help prevent or cure colds, coughs, or any serious infection, such as tuberculosis. The bacteria killed were not those that cause sickness. Besides, 200 million is a minuscule number among bacteria.

"Almost no advertising intended to influence the general public is honest," said Kallet and Schlink, "in the sense that a decent scientist understands honesty." They wrote of the current rules: "In the eyes of the law we are all guinea pigs and any scoundrel who takes it in his head to enter the drug or food business can experiment on us." They said the law had failed consumers, and the authors suggested that the bastion of integrity that was supposed to protect those who ingested food and medicine—the manufacturers—was now no more than an advertising posture.

The exposés in these books were investigated by Campbell. Pragmatically, he did not want the debate to be about principles or theories or legal matters. Rather, he thought evidence of suffering and injustice was the heart of his case for a law. Lobbyists could speak to congressmen about the health of businesses and about the principle of letting the market operate. It sounded sensible. But no congressman would be able to listen to stories of cures gone wrong, and injured people, and not come away saying to himself, Something is wrong here.

Campbell interviewed staff and had them provide him with the most poignant cases from among their records and knowledge, and when he went to testify about the food and drug bill, he created an exhibit of them. Why do we need to reconsider the law? Because of these, he said. He showed more than a dozen actual boxes and bottles of products of different types that were causing suffering and were currently beyond the reach of the law, and gave their case histories.

One reporter quickly dubbed the effective exhibit the "Chamber of Horrors," and it had an effect similar to that of the poison squad experiments earlier—because they were factual and dramatic. Eleanor Roosevelt heard about it and made a special, well-publicized trip to the FDA offices to view the full display. Soon, versions of the display were sent out to women's clubs for discussions, and when FDA officials went out to speak, they toted the horrors with them.

Among the cases in the exhibit was one dealing with a cosmetic called Lash Lure, a mascara made with synthetic aniline dye. The story told was that of a midwestern woman, Mrs. J. W. Musser, who was the entertainment committee chairwoman at the local PTA. She was being honored one May evening for her work—there was to be a banquet and her picture would appear in the state PTA magazine—so a few hours beforehand, she went to Byrd's beauty shop to get her hair done, and there the attendant convinced her that it would be nice if she had her brows and lashes touched up at the same time. She did, with Lash Lure.

Two hours later, her eyes were stinging and tearing, and she went to the pharmacy to get something with which to wash them out. The skin of her face was also red and swelling, and she got an ointment for that as well. Nothing helped. She was in pain, but as she was guest of honor, she felt she had to appear at the banquet. She went, but by 9 p.m. she had to go home. By the next morning she could not open her eyes. She went to the doctor, then the hospital. Her face was swollen and pus was draining from her eyes. Several ulcers had developed beneath her lids and were eating away at her eyeballs. After eight operations and months of care she left the hospital permanently blind.

Publicly, the company that made Lash Lure admitted it was familiar with some injuries claimed by its customers, but said most injuries were exaggerated. While a few did have bad reactions to the product, for many others it was effective and nontoxic. The company changed the preparation's name several times but kept it on the market. The number of injuries from the dye in Lash Lure is not known, but one company selling a similar product had in its records notes showing 370 cases of blindness or death from infections after ulceration. The cases were settled out of court. It was estimated that for Lash Lure, about one of every hundred women who got the treatment had massive swelling of the lids and ulceration of the eyeballs. Of those, most recovered a portion of their sight.

During the congressional hearings on the bill, lobbyists were pressing the point that products like those in the Chamber of Horrors were rare or already off the market. They were not representative of what was going on in business.

Mrs. Alvin Barber, president of the American Association of University Women, decided to counter that argument when she testified at congressional hearings. During a break in the hearings, she found four shops within six blocks of the hearing room that were applying and selling Lash Lure. The congressmen were impressed by her testimony, and a delegation of them asked to be taken over to see the full Chamber of Horrors exhibit at the FDA headquarters.

Among the "horrors" was an item called Crazy Water Crystals. It was said to bring people back to life after all other treatments had failed. "It cures ailments brought on by constipation, high blood pressure, rheumatism, arthritis, liver and kidney troubles, auto-intoxication, bad complexion, excess acidity. . . ." In a national radio ad costing hundreds of thousands of dollars for a single airing, the company said of the crystals that "millions [were] drinking their way to health in the simple, natural way."

One of the testimonials read: "Crazy Crystals pulled me out of the Grave." Another one read: "I was a sufferer from arthritis and inflammation of the bladder for several years. After hearing so much about Crazy Water Crystals I decided to try one more thing. I now have no bladder trouble, my arthritis is gone and I eat anything I want."

The mystery crystals were actually 98 percent sodium sulfate (also known as Glauber's salt, an age-old laxative). In the drugstore, one could purchase Glauber's salt for five to fifty cents per pound. The Crazy Water Crystal Company sold its product for six to thirty times that much. The salts, dissolved in liquid and taken in small quantities, were a good laxative. In larger quantities, they could cause stomach rupture and peritonitis. As one Iowa doctor wrote, the crazy crystals are "wonderfully effective in rupturing the appendix. I had one [appendectomy] where the solution ran out of the abdomen . . . and recrystalized on the sheets." In one survey in Philadelphia not long after the salts became popular, 437 out of 481 deaths due to peritonitis had come from consumption of laxatives. At the Mayo Clinic, the rate of deaths from peritonitis due to laxative consumption was reported at about 95 percent.

In 1922 the Crazy Water Crystals Company made the claims on its label to cure everything from arthritis to kidney disease. The maker was prosecuted under the 1906 law (as amended in 1912) and fined $100. He quickly moved the claims to the back of the package but kept them on the label. Federal drug inspectors again seized a few of the company's interstate shipments. The government was going to destroy them, and in order to get back fifteen cases of the salts, the maker admitted in writing that the claims made on the label were false and fraudulent, and agreed not to put them on the label anymore. He didn't. But advertising that was *not* part of the label was not regulated by the food and drug law. Hence the ads of the National Broadcasting Company, as well as a new sales tactic by the company: along with their shipments, salesmen delivered a stack of flyers containing their claims, to be handed out to customers. The company went ahead, now clear of the law. Its attorney, Thomas B. Love, a former secretary of the Treasury, asked the government to stop telling people about the previous seizures and the admission of fraud by his client, as his client "is no longer violating any law or even the proprieties."

Less hazardous but perhaps more blatant were the medicines that contained nothing at all but water. Mountain Valley Mineral Water claimed to be effective in treating rheumatism, cystitis, nephritis, cardiac diseases, and diabetes mellitus. On analysis, its composition was found to be the same as the tap water where it was manufactured, in Atlanta.

The drugmakers found the Chamber of Horrors exhibit so abhorrent that they began a strong campaign against the exhibit itself. First they denounced the accuracy of the displays. In the *Drug Trade News,* the organ of the United Medicine Manufacturers of America, for example, the chamber exhibit was called "dirty business. . . . In this Chamber of Horrors the Department has a group of products represented as helpful for diabetes, cancer, tuberculosis, and other diseases of the human system. . . . Not one of these products has had any appreciable volume of sales. No responsible manufacturer makes them. Neither the Proprietary Association nor the United States Medicine Manufacturers would accept for membership within their ranks any manufacturer producing such products. . . ." This rebuttal backfired badly. As it happened, a number of the products in the chamber *were* made by members of the Proprietary Association and the United States Medicine Manufacturers.

Those members who did not make exactly these products made very similar ones for the same markets. Among the most distressing was one called Habitina. The nation now had hundreds of thousands of morphine and opium addicts who were hooked on patent medicines. Habitina was sold by Delta Chemical Company of St. Louis as a way to break the addiction. ("MORPHINE and other drug habits are positively cured by Habitina. For hypodermic or internal use. Sample sent to any drug habitué FREE by mail, in plain wrapper. Regular price $2.00.") Each bottle of the cure contained eight grains of morphine and four grains of heroin, along with alcohol and caffeine, with flavors to disguise it all. One doctor reported that a patient of his had a habit of taking six grains of morphine a day until she sent away for the cure, after which she found herself taking sixteen grains of morphine and eight grains of heroin daily. Of the eight patients whose experiences the company submitted as testimonial cases, four had died of overdoses before the trial. The article in the *Journal of the American Medical Association*, in an uncharacteristic burst of emotion, asked, "Why can such things be?"

The bureau eventually prosecuted the two proprietors of the Delta Company, more or less successfully. They had made about $500,000 in the six years they sold their remedy. They were sent to jail briefly, then released after paying a $7,000 fine.

After the secret-formula makers failed to discredit the Chamber of Horrors list with a barrage of deceitful publicity, they began threatening FDA officials with prosecution if they used the exhibit in any way that would support new food and drug laws. A decade earlier, a law had been enacted that prevented federal officials from lobbying on behalf of legislation. The FDA's public effort on behalf of a law it had drafted was certainly lobbying on its own behalf. After consultation with the attorney general, it canceled the traveling horror show exhibits. Speeches by FDA staff members on the need for legislation were halted. One final shout escaped the agency before the FDA became publicly mute: Ruth deForest Lamb, publicity officer for the FDA, managed to publish a book, *The American Chamber of Horrors,* a print version of the road show.

In Congress, the bill was introduced and championed by Senator Royal S. Copeland, chairman of the powerful Senate Commerce Committee. He was an odd spokesman for the measure in a number of ways. He was a practicing homeopathic doctor who took substantial sums of money as a consultant to makers of medicines. Nevertheless, his spirited pressure for a new drug law seemed genuine. His admiration of the FDA and his belief in its work came early, when he was New York City commissioner of health during a deadly outbreak of botulism from improperly preserved olives; the FDA traced the offending olives back to their manufacturer, and carried out the microbiology not only to explain the outbreak but to set new standards that saved the collapsing industry. And later, when a crank millionaire cornered the market in contaminated ergot and tried to force the FDA to approve it, Copeland held lengthy hearings on the case. The hearings demonstrated that the FDA was doing its job and was a cadre of honest government employees whose limitations were largely due to low budgets and periodic assaults from entrepreneurs.

There was room enough for doubt about Senator Copeland's understanding, however, when he repeatedly cut backroom deals that weakened the new bill. Consumer groups suspected he was a mole. Primarily he was just a fellow who loved to get along, the very spirit of compromise in the Senate—maybe too much so. He loved the meeting of minds that would lead to a law, and seemed to have little sense of when compromise was warranted. After he introduced into the Senate the first FDA-written version of the new food and drug law, called S. 1944, he met with members of the industry alone and was quickly and politely scalped. He allowed industry to strike the single best provision of the bill, the requirement that drugs should be proved safe before being allowed on the market.

The new version of his bill gradually lost the support of the American Medical Association, the Consumers' Research group, and the American Pharmaceutical Association. Eventually, five new versions were written. Some passed one house but not the other. Eventually one passed both houses of Congress, was agreed to by a conference committee of the two houses, and was killed by a Republican maneuver in the House of Representatives just before it could be sent for the president's signature. Representative Clarence Lea of California killed the bill; he was close to fruit growers there, and they were incensed about the FDA's attempts to cut back on the chemicals used to preserve fruit for drying and shipping.

By 1937 the bill's prospects looked dim. Consumer and professional groups started arguing for a totally new law. The impatience with Congress began to show, as one state after another began to enact laws that were modeled on the Copeland bill. Finally, the legislative drama came to an end much the way it had ended in 1906. A crisis was the deciding factor.

With food and drugs there are constant crises: rashes of death and debility flare up almost annually. A dozen had occurred since the 1906 law and passed nearly without comment. For example, the use of dinitrophenol as a quick weight-loss agent produced a wave of toxic reactions beginning in 1933, including nine reported deaths, some two hundred cases of cataracts and blindness, and numerous other injuries, including liver and kidney damage, bleeding sores on the skin, and potentially fatal blood disorders. Medical statisticians use the rule of thumb that the ratio of reported cases to actual cases is ordinarily somewhere between one to 10 and one to 100. For dinitrophenol, that suggests a hundred deaths and thousands of cases of cataracts during that period. One journal noted that the epidemic of cataracts in young women was likely the largest on record. Yet the deaths and injuries from dinitrophenol did not lead to a great outcry or a new law.

What seems required to make a new law is the presence of two circumstances when a crisis occurs—a bill must *already be present* in Congress, and legislators and significant elements of the public must already be *educated and paying attention* when the crisis hits. Some say the crisis must also involve children.

At the end of the summer of 1937 the Massengill Company of Bristol, Tennessee, was selling a drug called sulfanilamide. It was a new drug in the first great family of antibiotics, which had been awaited for decades by scientists. It was a true antibiotic in that it attacked and killed the bacteria that were causing disease. It was effective against several bugs, and as these sulfa drugs came on the market, doctors and patients snapped them up instantly. They were used most often to treat infections of venereal diseases and the streptococcal infections of childhood sore throats. Salesmen for Massengill reported back to headquarters that patients and doctors were happy with the pills and tablets they got, but would be far more pleased if they could get the bad-tasting medicine in a more palatable liquid form. Such comments suggested that the first company to make such a product would take over the market, at least for a time.

The chief chemist at Massengill was Harold C. Watkins, who had

89

remained employed there even though he had been caught selling a fraudulent nostrum a few years before. Watkins tried one solvent after another and finally found that diethylene glycol, a sweetish but largely tasteless fluid, seemed to do the job. He put in seventy-five grains per ounce; above that figure, the sulfa drug precipitated out on cooling. The concoction was checked for flavor and fragrance, and then manufactured in a few batches, totaling 240 gallons. The liquid, Elixir Sulfanilamide, was put in bottles of four ounces each and shipped to druggists beginning on September 4, 1937.

The first city in which the drugs passed from druggist to doctor to patient was Tulsa, Oklahoma. By October 11, Dr. James Stephenson sent an urgent telegram to the offices of the American Medical Association in Chicago, asking for the composition of the Massengill product, as six of his patients had died immediately after taking it. The AMA sent back a telegram saying it did not know, but that it had not certified any liquid form of sulfa drug. The AMA also telegraphed the Massengill plant, asking for samples. The company agreed to send them, provided the AMA kept the ingredients secret. The AMA quickly did a few laboratory tests and determined that diethylene glycol was a highly toxic substance.

Meanwhile, a doctor in New York who had heard about the new liquid and the possibility of deaths in Tulsa had called the FDA in Washington on October 14. An FDA inspector arrived in Tulsa on October 16. He found that the number of victims in Dr. Stephenson's practice was now ten. Nine of them were children being treated for strep throat, and one was an adult being treated for gonorrhea. Stephenson had written twenty other prescriptions for the Massengill drug, so the number of cases might rise.

The FDA inspector attended the autopsy of one of the victims. The man on the table had been admitted to a Tulsa hospital very weak, nauseated, and with abdominal pain. He had not been able to urinate for more than a day. His kidneys had failed, then recovered for a time, then failed again. On the table, the examining doctors found that his kidneys were hugely bloated, purple, and full of blocked passages, completely dysfunctional. It was apparent to those present that he would have been in excruciating pain for hours or days before his death. Not everyone had the same reaction, however: one man had swallowed seven ounces of the drug, felt a little ill, and stopped using it, without further symptoms; in another case, a child died within three hours of taking two ounces of the liquid.

When FDA inspectors reached Massengill's Tennessee plant, they found that Tulsa would not be the only site of the problems. Two hundred forty gallons of "elixir" had been shipped across the country, from California to Virginia. That day, federal agents interviewed chemist Watkins and the head of the company, Samuel Massengill. The men described what they had done, and said they had not conducted safety tests of the mixture before sending it out. None was required, was it? After hearing of the "problems," however, Watkins had himself taken four ounces of the drug as a test, and said he felt fine. He had also given it to some guinea pigs and they were fine, too. (The next day Watkins fell ill and sent a telegraph to the AMA asking if there was an antidote to diethylene glycol poisoning. None, they replied. But within a week, Watkins had recovered.)

In Washington, Walter Campbell held a press conference at which he said that fourteen people had died after taking the Massengill product. He said it was not clear what the problem was, but it might be the diethylene glycol. He also said that the FDA could not legally investigate or prosecute the matter unless it could be shown that there was something wrong with the label on the bottles sold. He had, however, begun a national investigation, as his agency was the only one with *any* possible jurisdiction. The law had no prohibition per se of dangerous drugs. (Campbell was fortunate in that the medicine was labeled an "elixir," which technically is a liquid containing alcohol, so he went ahead with his investigation in hopes that the technicality would be sufficient cause to investigate.)

The full field force of the FDA in the United States, 239 inspectors, began to search out the druggists and doctors who had received the shipments. Local health agents joined the search. Massengill proved to be trouble, though. At the beginning of the crisis, on October 15, the FDA had asked the company to recall from doctors, druggists, and distributors whatever was left of the shipments. The company sent out a notice that all should send back the preparation, but said nothing about the reason for the return or the emergency nature of the recall. The recall was largely ignored. It wasn't until October 19 that the company was told it had to send out a second notice, indicating that the drug was life-threatening.

The FDA inspectors had to reach all salesmen and distributors of the bottles, get their lists of deliveries, and follow those another step or two to the final point of sale, a druggist or a doctor's office. Then they had to enlist the doctor's cooperation in finding patients at risk. That was because while the drug was usually dispensed by prescription, some druggists sold it directly without keeping records. And some doctors, fearing trouble, refused to help. One Texas physician had to be jailed before he would identify the patients who had been given the syrup. In South Carolina, a doctor who had received a shipment flatly denied giving it to a Negro patient of his who had died. To check, the FDA inspector visited the victim's family; they were sure he *had* taken it. They also said he had just been buried, and that local custom was to place personal effects on top of the grave of a dead family member. The FDA man drove to the cemetery, where he found on the grave a small bag in which there was a four-ounce bottle of Elixir Sulfanilamide with three ounces missing.

By the end of November, 107 deaths had been reported, most of them children. Not counted in the statistics was Watkins, the chemist who had caused it all, who committed suicide. It is unclear how many more victims there were, but the FDA investigators drastically kept the number of deaths down by recovering, within four weeks, more than 90 percent of the original shipment. About six gallons, apparently, accounted for all the deaths.

In December, when it was clear the episode was over, the question of prosecution arose. Samuel Massengill himself wrote to the AMA, staking out the company's position. The deaths were regrettable, he said, "but I have violated no law." He also began circulating a letter to doctors on the "Facts About Elixir Sulfanilamide." It stated there was no error in manufacturing and that the drug had been extensively tested before shipping, with no indication that it could cause any harm. The cause of the deaths was unknown but might be due to diethylene glycol. (Ultimately a prosecution for mislabeling took place, and the company was fined $26,000, or about $240 per death. It was the largest fine ever levied by the FDA to that time.)

The AMA, pushing for a new law, issued a statement noting that the death toll from ill people taking useless quack medications was far higher than 107. The all-but-interred proposed law on food and drugs rose Lazarus-like as the mail poured in to Congress. The disaster came unexpectedly and affected mostly children, just when the merits of regulation were being debated. The proposed law was revived and readied for passage. Then, at the last minute, Representative Lea, the House commerce chairman who had last killed the bill, picked up the phone to call the FDA. He was under great pressure and was ready to let the bill be voted on, but he had a final question: Would the bill under consideration have prevented the elixir tragedy? Campbell's answer was no. The provision requiring safety tests before marketing new products had been stricken early on. The provision was now restored, and Roosevelt signed the Food, Drug and Cosmetic Act on June 15, 1938. It has provided the framework for drug creation and sales in the United States since that time.

The crisis had been a modern one. It was not about crank products and false claims, but rather technical knowledge and potent modern medicines, about checking potent substances *before* selling them.

The law was passed at a key moment in the nation's life, as it recovered from economic catastrophe. And it came at a time when the drug industry was just beginning to realize that the nature of its business in the future was not to stamp out millions of identical bottles of chemicals, but rather to fashion drugs that could attack the underlying bases of disease. The sudden appearance of the sulfa drugs, and one or two earlier hopeful treatments that had emerged from university scientists (such as the treatment called salvarsan for syphilis), helped executives realize that for the creation of new drugs, they should look more to high-level university labs than to the poke of the patent hawker.

Few companies had staffs of research scientists yet, or spent much money studying the nature of disease and treatment; still, the idea was in the air. The 1938 law made it clear that companies could not survive without scientists and laboratories, without knowing something substantial about the drugs they were selling and about human illness itself. They would have to, at least, produce scientific tests of safety for the FDA. In the 1920s the top two hundred drug companies in the United States had only a few thousand scientists on staff, and most of those concerned themselves with the processing of chemicals. But by the 1940s, there were 58,000 scientists in the industry engaged specifically in research.

The 1938 law was a landmark in civil governance, not just for the United States, as it turned out, but for democratic governments around the world. In the years to come, each nation of the developed world would adopt its central principles. It was the first law to require the checking of drugs before they went to market. And it put into law the notion that the scientific approach—not the commercial, not the anecdotal, not the approach based on authoritative opinion—would be the standard for modern society. This would mean additional work for those trying to create and sell drugs, as they would have to prove them worthwhile. But it

immediately offered some protection to citizens in a field prone to predatory practices. And though it was unforeseen, this step toward a rational
basis for medicines also gave a great boost to the drug-making industry.
In fact, it is, as we will see, one of the key factors that *created* the modern
pharmaceutical industry and the modern use of medicines.

•

CHAPTER SIX

The Birth of the Modern Pharmaceutical Trade

THE REVOLUTION in medicine took place between that summer afternoon in 1938 and an October day in 1951. Between those dates the pharmaceutical industry went from a handful of chemical companies with no interest in research and no medical staffs to a huge machine that discovered, developed, and marketed drugs of real use in treating disease. Though it is now said that this was a great leap forward in American business, the businesses were, of course, dragged to this discovery by their boot heels. It was a sudden conjunction of several forces that created modern medicines and transformed the companies that make them. The last push toward the modern era came in the emergency of wartime, when military orders fused together a coalition of government, university, and industry scientists who then made history. While the wartime project that made the atomic bomb is more famous, it could be argued that the wartime project that made penicillin was more important.

"The quarter century following the enactment of the Food, Drug and Cosmetic Act of 1938," writes James Harvey Young, "witnessed a revolution in the drugs which doctors prescribed for patients. So vast was it in scope, so significant in repercussions, this revolution ranks as one of the major events in medical history." The conditions for the development of those drugs had been coalescing. The science had matured, beginning with the germ theory and then the testing of drugs against the germs. The patent laws had changed to make possible the profitable control of a drug by the company that owned it. The industry, which previously had no real interest in research or medicine, began to see things differently with the advent of sulfa drugs and when the 1938 law forced them to test their drugs. They had to create departments made up of physicians and scientists. Business had ignored and disdained science, and until at least 1941 the pharmaceutical companies largely ignored the idea that science and innovation were important to progress, and even at first, to their shame, refused to participate in the great public project to make penicillin.

The development of the "germ theory" near the end of the nineteenth century made it clear that all the worst diseases of mankind were due to microscopic, living organisms passed from one person to the next—pneumonia, tuberculosis, influenza, diarrhea, diphtheria, cholera. Initially, progress was made with simple steps. Between 1880 and 1920 washing with soap and water, diverting sewage to provide clean drinking water, and disposing of contaminated food raised life expectancy from the plateau where it rested for millennia (fewer than forty years on average) to a new high of more than fifty-four years. The next wave, the creation of active chemical and biological agents to attack disease directly, would be harder to achieve, depending as it did on the cooperation of academic scientists, commercial drug executives, and medical practitioners, three groups that had never been willing to share so much as a carriage ride in America.

The social and business structure that would carry medicine from the laboratory to the citizens had not yet been built. The pharmaceutical businesses as we now know them did not exist. As we've seen, the companies simply regurgitated old nostrums by the thousands. At that time, government, which now has grand, multi-billion-dollar institutions to study disease and medicine, as well as agencies to supply the old and poor with services, financed no medical research and offered no help for ill people.

In America, scholarship historically had been confined largely to the general arts, not science. In 1861 no doctorates in science were awarded. In 1890 only 164 were given. Scholars were going to the Continent to study; five hundred Americans enrolled in German universities in that year. Harvard philosopher Josiah Royce said that German scholarship was "our master and our guide . . . the air was full of suggestion. . . . One went to Germany still a doubter as to the possibility of the theoretic life; one returned an idealist, devoted for the time being to pure learning for learning's sake, determined to contribute his *scherflein* [small donation] to the massive store of human knowledge, burning for a chance to help build the American university."

The young American scientists who studied in Europe returned enthralled with the idea of pure research that was not so much a profession as a calling. And as they returned to the States, they soon came to despise the businessmen in charge of drugs and medicine, as well as the staff drudges who called themselves scientists. They saw that business had little or no interest in knowledge or discovery. Businessmen's concern was money, and they operated a cutthroat trade in potions and notions, all dependent not on knowledge but on advertising.

The split between science and business was one of the key factors that had halted medical progress in the United States. Representative of this was a war between the pharmacologists in universities and those who worked for industry. John Jacob Abel of Johns Hopkins University, the leading American pharmacologist before the Second World War, could hardly hide his disdain when asked about doing pharmacological work for industry. "I personally would not think of working on a problem suggested to me by any firm, anywhere." The first code of ethics of the American Medical Association, written in 1847, counted the patenting and advertising of medicines to the public as unethical. The leading society for scientists in pharmacology at the time, the American Society for Pharmacology and Experimental Therapeutics, founded in 1908, had made clear that no connections with industry would be permitted. Two articles of their bylaws read: "No one shall be admitted to membership who is in the permanent employ of any drug firm." And: "Entrance into the permanent employ of a drug firm shall constitute forfeiture of membership." The prohibition, though challenged periodically, was retained by the academic society until 1941.

Scientists outside and even inside drug companies felt that some of what industry was attempting to do was simply sinful. The American Medical Association spoke out strongly against patenting medicines. Edward R. Squibb said, "I do not myself think that anything should be patented by either physician or pharmacist; I am sure that the patient would not be benefited thereby." Patenting automobiles was one thing, but decent citizens surely would not withhold lifesaving medicines in order to profit from suffering. It would be like patenting bread and exacting a crippling price for it, ensuring that some would not get any. At the time these arguments seemed both strong and obvious. But if companies devoted themselves to producing, in rapid fashion, new and potentially lifesaving drugs, ones that scientists might *not* discover on their own for many decades, then perhaps profit and patent might actually be harnessed as forces for good. It would take a struggle of several decades, the intervention of two world wars, and other remarkable events to place this new possibility before America and the world.

With intellectual development slow in America, and open hostility between the men of intellect and the men of money, America simply watched as Europe advanced into the modern world with its industrial chemists and universities forging new alliances. Still, even in Europe, discoveries were coming more slowly than expected. The next great advance after Paul Ehrlich's salvarsan did not come for twenty-five years. It was another derivative of the coal-tar dye industry, sulfanilamide, in this case a red dye that had actually been created years earlier (in 1908) by German chemists seeking substances with which to dye leather. Gerhardt Domagk at Farbenindustrie rediscovered the chemical in the early 1930s and tested it as a drug. It was successful in animals, and Domagk eventually treated his own daughter with it experimentally. She had a severe strep infection in a wound on her arm, and the arm was about to be amputated when the drug rescued her.

But Farben delayed getting the drug to market for three years. The company had a business difficulty. It had patented a drug it called prontosil containing some useless side molecules on a vital, germ-killing molecule. Unfortunately, this vital heart of prontosil was a compound called sulfanilamide that one of Farben's own scientists had discovered years earlier, patented, and then let the patent run out because he never found its germ-killing properties. Now, the Farben scientists had a clumsier molecule with sulfanilamide, which had proved wonderful at killing germs. So the company kept the matter quiet for a time and patented prontosil, knowing full well that once it announced the value of prontosil, bright chemists from other companies would soon discover that the real germ killer was the lesser molecule sulfanilamide, whose patent had expired.

The company wanted to go to market, but if it did, it would be giving away the keys to a larger kingdom of profit. After some three years of public deception and private argument within the company, while patients were denied treatment, the company leaders finally allowed their scientists to write up a report on the success of prontosil in animal and human tests against infectious disease.

It was published in an out-of-the-way journal, but French scientist Ernst Fourneau at Pasteur Institute read it with excitement and wrote asking for a sample of the drug to study, a routine request among university scholars. The reply was oddly ambiguous. Fourneau understood the importance of the research, and he prepared his whole lab to follow up. He traveled to Germany to talk to the leaders of Farbenindustrie and take back a sample. He was confronted by a stunning coldness and a request for money. The samples would be forthcoming only if some profitable arrangement for sale of the drug in France could be made. But in France, there were no patents at all under law, so there was little Fourneau could do. Besides, he felt the attitude of the company was an outrage against both man and science. People were dying because a treatment was being withheld.

Angry, he returned to Paris prepared to make his own prontosil regardless of Farben's wishes. Work at Pasteur soon showed that the curious red dye was not a new substance, and the reason for the German attitude became clear. Prontosil was not active—by itself. It was a large molecule that the body had to break down before using a smaller part, the active agent called sulfanilamide. A search of patent records showed the French that while the Farben company held a patent on prontosil, the patents on the all-important sulfanilamide molecule had expired. Gleefully, the French set about breaking the unethical German silence on sulfanilamide and delivering it to the world markets. In less than a year, the new drug had been distributed to doctors and hospitals in Europe and America, and proved itself powerfully effective in treating strep infections, gonorrhea, and meningitis. It was not an ideal drug, with severe and sometimes fatal side effects in one of twenty patients, but it was confirmation that systematic chemistry could confront diseases directly.

The search for new drugs clearly would not be easy, and it was not certain that companies could actually do the work profitably, as the Germans found when they tried to hide a vital treatment until they could devise a profitable alternative. The creators of sulfanilamide profited far less than they had hoped because of patent problems. Farbenindustrie reaped little profit from the several years of research on sulfa drugs, while those who "poached" on the territory, such as the French, probably made out better, funding far less research. And there was the case of American Cyanamid's Lederle Laboratories, which produced a pneumonia vaccine at great expense, and built a plant to manufacture it, only to find eight months later that a different drug, sulfapyridine, could effectively treat the disease. Their investment of millions was lost and the vaccine plant made obsolete.

Unlike in previous centuries, lifesaving medicines could now be made, almost at will, with some research. And they could instantly reach vast markets.

Randolph Major, chief of the fledgling Merck research laboratory in New Jersey, hired its first serious academic research scientist, Max Tishler of Harvard, in 1937. At the time, Merck, like the other American firms, had not produced a single useful drug of its own. The plan at the company was to begin with vitamins. Years of successful experiments on scurvy and another vitamin-deficiency disease had been obscured, but by the middle 1930s, three separate "food factors" that must be present to prevent disease had been found; they were dubbed vitamins A, B, and C. Diseases caused by vitamin deficiency were not among the leading health problems, but vitamins could still be profitable. Merck scientists synthesized vitamin B_1, which helps eliminate beriberi, the deficiency disease most common in Asia, and in the late 1930s, it accounted for 10 percent of the company's profit. Vitamins grew more lucrative when, with a boost from publicity, people began to believe that they needed to take vitamins regularly for general health. (They don't, but the fear of not having them still drives large sales of these substances.) To take advantage of this popular perception, vitamins were added to bread and flour and the bakery goods sold as "enriched." It was assumed that more of these "vitamins" would be discovered, so it was Merck's plan to "isolate every vitamin . . . determine their structures if it hasn't already been done, and make them available."

But competition remained a problem. Companies willing to invest in research needed assurance they would get some control over their market, so substantial profits would result. That would be possible only with some rules and some encouragement set out by the government.

Government regulation had laid the necessary base for weeding out fraud and false advertising. Regulation had made research not only a standard but essential for every company making drugs. And now the embryonic industry would be formed, tested, and ultimately shaped by the next challenge, one of the greatest chemical inventions of mankind—penicillin. It would be both model and prod. Before, European universities led the world in medicine; after, American companies and universities would dominate. The shape of the industry moved from chemical assembly lines to genuinely intellectual domains that were mining nature for products.

It is often written that Sir Alexander Fleming discovered penicillin in 1928. He had many dishes of germs growing in his London lab as part of an experiment when one day a few particles of a kind of soil mold, one of the many species of penicillium, blew in through the window, settled on the dishes, and quickly killed the germs in little circles around the spot where each landed. When he came to the lab the next day, his curiosity drove him to find out what had killed the bacteria, and he discovered penicillin. Actually, the windows to his labs couldn't open because filing cabinets were in the way, and the effect of penicillium on bacteria had already been discovered at least nine times in recorded scientific studies. In each case, the power of the mold to exude a substance that killed germs had been observed, and the mold had even been tried directly on patients with infections. Each time the work failed because the mold was too finicky to control.

In fact, the 1928 penicillin episode ended when Fleming could not grow enough of the mold or extract enough of the key substance in a form that didn't deteriorate. He lacked the time and funding to press forward, and he set aside the work. Others failed in their pursuit over the next dozen years until Howard W. Florey was appointed to head the pathology department at Oxford. Florey's team was bigger and better funded, as well as better versed in the art of handling mold. After five years of dogged work, Florey and a refugee scientist from Germany, Ernst Chain, together had finally produced enough stable chemical from penicillium to test on mice. Eight mice were given injections to cause strep infection, which quickly took hold in all the animals. Four of the animals were then given varying doses of the penicillium extract, while others were left untreated. The scientists stayed late into the night as the mice began to succumb to the infection; the researchers left the lab at 3:30 a.m., by which time all the untreated mice were dead and the treated mice alive. The next morning Chain came into the lab first, and saw that the treated animals were still chasing about in their cages. Lab workers said that his first reaction was not to shout but to dance. The researchers knew what they had—this substance had killed strep in this experiment, but they knew it could kill several other bacteria as well, each one of which was fatal to humans in great numbers each year. The date of this experiment that changed human history was May 25, 1940.

Quickly, the scientists used the rest of the substance they had produced to conduct similar experiments on rats and cats as well as mice. Their paper on penicillin was published in the medical journal *Lancet* on August 24. Their elation soon sank, however, as they began to solicit support for making the new drug in commercial quantities. The British drug firms ICI and Boots had each been approached and offered a chance to make and market penicillin if they would just invest in developing the chemical from an extract of mold to a clinical drug. Both turned down the chance. England was at war, after all. But America wasn't. The Oxford group worked day and night to make new batches of their brew.

Surely they could induce an American company to join with them in production of what must be the most promising drug ever to come out of a laboratory, or even out of nature.

Florey and his colleague Norman Heatley packed up some mold and broth, secreted it inside their luggage, and boarded a Pan American Clipper for the United States. They arrived in New York on July 2, 1941, with the humidity up and the temperature at about 94°F. They feared the finicky mold would perish in their suitcases. But it survived, and they carried it and a sales pitch from company to company. Eastman Kodak, Johnson & Johnson, and Distillation Products each turned down chances at penicillin research and development. So did Connaught in Canada. All companies were aware of the experiments with penicillin; its huge potential had already been reported in the *New York Times*. But they worried that the quantities produced so far were too small and had been grown on the surface of little dishes; it would literally take acres of these little dishes to make anything like a commercial quantity. They were also aware that the sulfa drugs had begun to encounter resistance by microbes; what would happen if a company invested millions of dollars only to find the drug's power fading a year after it went to market? The penicillin produced by the British was chemically unstable and could break down into useless constituents if handled improperly. The penicillin might turn out to be toxic to people once it was tried in large numbers; sulfa drugs had shown some of that, too. And, of course, it was unclear whether any of the process used to make penicillin could be patented effectively, because the penicillium mold was a product of nature.

Florey and Heatley got a completely different reception from U.S. government scientists. They were essentially academics who had learned much in the practical world of the government's agricultural experiment stations. They were unencumbered by worries about profiting from discovery, and they were aware that the war in Europe meant casualties on a scale even greater than during the previous war. Penicillin, if it was as powerful and safe as it appeared, could raise wounded soldiers from their pallets by the thousands. In the Civil War, as many as half of all those wounded died.

The government researchers were excited, adventurous, and ready to go. On the same day that Florey spoke to Percy Wells, director of the Agriculture Department's Eastern Regional Research Laboratory, Wells sent a telegram to the department's scientists in Illinois, where a new research center was starting up. Wells asked whether the lab would be interested in turning over a large portion of their time and effort to "pilot scale production of bacteriostatic material from Fleming's penicillium. Can you arrange immediately . . . ?" The answer came the next morning: "Pan setup and organisms available. Details of proposed work of course unknown and suggest they [the British scientists] visit Peoria for discussion. Laboratory in position to cooperate immediately." As it happened, the American government scientists were far more skilled than the British in the art of growing microorganisms taken out of the soil. They threw themselves into the task and within four months had got the mold producing twelve times as much penicillin as it had in Oxford. By the time they were finished with the program, they had increased the yield of penicillin 120 times, and increased its therapeutic potential as well.

In short order, America was at war in both the Atlantic and Pacific, and the mission to scale up the production of penicillin and test it extensively in humans soon became a matter of war priority. The war agency that was spearheading scientific research was the Office of Scientific Research and Development, the agency that would become best known for the Manhattan Project, which produced the atomic bomb. It also tackled penicillin. Dr. Alfred Newton Richards of the University of Pennsylvania was given the job of leading the wartime medical research. In the two months before the United States declared war, Richards had met twice with drug company leaders in a renewed effort to get them committed to making penicillin. They refused, and he came away frustrated and disappointed. In December, when he tried again, he had results in hand from the agriculture lab in Peoria—twelvefold greater production. Three of the four company leaders still balked, but George Merck, ahead of the curve on the potential of science to business, agreed, and then set out to convince the others, especially the difficult leader of Squibb. Eventually, Richards got a commitment, though not the enthusiasm he wanted. The government started the funding, and the companies agreed to pick up a majority of the subsequent costs. Heatley, who had been working in Peoria, now spent six months in Rahway, New Jersey, where Merck was located. By March 14, 1942, there was enough penicillin in America to try pure and potent doses on patients, secretly.

The first American penicillin patient was Anne Miller, the wife of the athletic director at Yale University. She had had a miscarriage and became grossly infected with streptococcus internally. She spent four weeks delirious, with fevers that peaked at more than 106 degrees. She was given a hysterectomy in the hope that enough of the infection would be removed with the womb to turn the situation around. That failed. Her blood was now seething with multiplying bacteria. Near death, she was given a dose of penicillin one afternoon. By four the next morning, her temperature was normal. By Monday, there were no bacteria to be found in her body. She walked out of the hospital healthy.

The government's program roped in more companies and independent laboratories, and by D-Day there was enough penicillin for all the needs of the troops at Normandy, and then some. The program to create practical penicillin remained rocky until after the war. Richards was less than enthusiastic about the skills, and worse, the attitudes of the companies, which he said were largely "noncommittal." In wartime, he found that more than offensive. In one case, Squibb had started cutting corners in the manufacture and ended up giving dangerous phlebitis—blood clots—to all the wounded soldiers treated with that batch of penicillin. "It is damn near criminal of them to have shortcut a process without finding out what the shortcut would do," Richards said.

But by the time the war was over, with the development of penicillin, the atom bomb, and radar, to mention only three advances, scientific research had risen from obscurity to heroism. Tishler wrote later that the "logic of survival in modern warfare had dragged science from the periphery of our society right into the maelstrom at the center." Senator Claude Pepper of Florida, in a bit more sour tone, said, "It took a war of catastrophic dimensions to jar enough money out of the national pocket to enable medical research men to conduct their work on an adequate scale." At the end of the war, Vannevar Bush, head of the Office of Scientific Research and Development, wrote a manifesto on the matter at Franklin Roosevelt's request: "Basic research is the pacemaker of technological progress. Basic research leads to new knowledge. It provides scientific capital. It creates the fund from which the practical applications of knowledge must be drawn. New products and new processes do not appear full-grown. They are founded on new principles and new conceptions, which in turn are painstakingly developed by research in the purest realms of science." Then, this was news. It was the beginning of the faith. Prodded by government and regulation, corporations, which had dragged their heels, were now ready to at least consider risky research as a routine part of their march into the future.

Since then the interaction of business, universities, and government has continued to produce new medical treatments (despite the myth that business is solely responsible for medical progress and that it should be left without interference from a meddlesome government).

The new belief in research transformed the world of medicine and pharmaceuticals. The junk medicine that made up the majority of all medical products began to vanish. Because of the new regulations, the advent of penicillin and the new "research and develop" strategy, by the 1950s, for example, Smith, Kline had dropped 14,940 of its 15,000 products—setting aside the dubious substances—and brought to market only sixty products, with which it was more successful.

The number of proprietary medicine makers, the secret-formula companies, was drastically reduced. The end of the war thinned their ranks to the point that only five companies controlled 40 percent of the market. The few proprietary medicines that were useful—aspirin, laxatives, cough remedies, antacids, antiseptics for small wounds, liniments, and vitamins—were now fought over like dinner scraps. Even the head of the formerly aggressive Proprietary Association acknowledged that in the new day and age, the evidence to support the value of secret-formula medicines now looked "extremely spotty." He urged that someone should begin testing remedies to see if they were actually useful!

Now, drug companies began carrying out massive searches for new, potent substances, very like the sifting of thousands of samples of coal tar for good dyes. There were exciting finds. The best varieties of penicillium mold, the ones that produced the most potent drugs, were found casually—one in the New Jersey dirt and one in a sad-looking melon in an Illinois marketplace. In 1951, Bristol-Myers sent envelopes to its stockholders with the instructions that, if they wished to help, they could take a sample of soil from wherever they happened to be, "moist but not wet and free from large stones." They should "mail the soil sample to Bristol Laboratories in this envelope." The company also issued plastic bags and tubes to salesmen and vacationing employees to send in the samples.

More new and truly effective drugs were invented between 1935 and 1955 than in all of previous human history. By the early 1950s, 90 percent of the prescriptions filled by patients were for drugs that did not even exist in 1938. And with the drugs came sharp drops in suffering and death.

"Look back, those who can do so," said the aging British scientist Henry H. Dale in 1950,

> to the beginning of this century and recall the state of medicinal treatment fifty years ago. . . . The idea that a remedy could directly remove, or neutralize, the cause of an illness was still a startling innovation . . . neither physician nor patient had yet learned to expect a medication which would go thus to the root of the trouble. Compare such a position with that today, when we have become so accustomed to the

effective and radical treatment of diseases which till recently were beyond the reach of remedy. [It is] a greater advance in this century than in all the centuries that went before it.

Henry Gadsden told Congress that when he joined Merck in 1937,

You could count the basic medicines on the fingers of your two hands. Morphine, quinine, digitalis, insulin, codeine, aspirin, arsenicals, nitroglycerin, mercurials, and a few biologicals [none of which had been developed by the pharmaceutical industry]. Our own Sharp and Dohme catalog did not carry a single exclusive prescription medicine. We had a broad range of fluids, ointments, and extracts, as did other firms, but we placed heavy emphasis on biological medicines as well. Most of our products were sold without a prescription. And 43 percent of the prescription medicines were compounded by the pharmacist, as compared to 1.2 percent today [1950s].

From the time just before the first use of sulfa drugs to the time a variety of antibiotics were available to the public, life expectancy increased dramatically, from fifty-some years in the 1920s to sixty-eight years by 1950, and seventy-one years by 1960. By that time, the infectious diseases that had been the top three killers of humankind had been erased as primary causes of death, all by antibiotics newly discovered. For example, the death rate for tuberculosis dropped 99 percent between 1920 and 1978—from 113 deaths per 100,000 population to only one per 100,000. Deaths from dysentery, whooping cough, diphtheria, and measles dropped to near zero. Deaths from flu and pneumonia dropped 87 percent. What replaced them are the diseases of long-lived people: heart disease, cancer, and stroke.

It was made clear during this time that the method of science—testing ideas and substances by experiment—was the single most successful and important approach to human health. And the venue of successful medicine had changed from the Old World to the New. Until 1950 all of the major new drugs that began the revolution were created in Europe and Canada—salvarsan for syphilis, insulin for diabetes, sulfa for a few infectious diseases, and penicillin. And now would come the demonstration that government could be effective and could accomplish much that profit motives could not.

The regulations and the government shepherding of the drug business did what the free market failed for at least sixty years to do—it weeded out the brutal, the stupid, and the needless that prevented the pharmaceutical industry from becoming a great engine of discovery and sales. The tough markets had prevented companies from carrying out expensive and detailed research. The laying down of the scientific standard came first, and the creation of the modern pharmaceutical industry followed. A scientific standard, administered by some body outside industry itself, was the essential ingredient. Companies could create real drugs, which would gain the federal seal of approval.

The companies also used the 1938 law to devise the concept of prescription drugs. They would be available only through doctors, at a price the companies themselves could set. The competitive edge shifted from cheapness and advertising aggressiveness to research and testing of drugs. Such a powerful combination of interests—greed, skill, and deep biological understanding—produced one of society's greatest social advances. It was a heady mixture, and the new pharmaceutical industry quickly became both exceedingly proud and profitable.

•

CHAPTER SEVEN

New Drugs, New Problems

THE STORY of one drug, chloramphenicol, and one doctor who used it, is a good illustration of the new system of medical drugs created in the 1950s, and which is essentially still in place today. It happened in an era of confidence and in a booming new American enterprise. It was a story of success but carried inside it a tragedy and hundreds to thousands of needless deaths. The event unfolded so slowly that it never achieved a peak moment, never made the front page or triggered investigations.

Dr. Albe Watkins was a conscientious general practitioner in a suburb near Los Angeles in 1952, the beginning of the era of confidence in medicine and its attendant business. As Thomas Maeder tells the story in the most complete account of chloramphenicol, Watkins had grown up in small-town Missouri, where doctors had to take second jobs to make ends meet. By age forty-two, he had a thriving practice in California, where he and his wife had moved to help ease her severe asthma. Watkins saw thirty or more patients in a fourteen- to eighteen-hour day. He was an average doctor, "not a particularly smart fellow," as he said himself, but interested and willing to work. His practice was aided by the arrival of antibiotics, in particular the "broad-spectrum" antibiotics that could kill so many different germs.

It all began to unravel for him on New Year's Day 1951. His eight-year-old son, James, told his parents that he was having some trouble urinating; when he could go, there was blood in the toilet. Watkins immediately thought of the worst possibilities, including a kidney tumor. He took his son to a nearby urologist, who hospitalized the boy for tests. A small obstruction was found in the urethra, and it had to be removed to prevent major damage to the kidney. Later, the boy needed a second surgery and had a tube inserted in his urethra for a time. Quickly, James recovered. But after the surgery, the doctor had given James an antibiotic, just in case, to prevent infection (an inappropriate prescription). The doctor prescribed chloramphenicol, the most popular of the new broad-spectrum antibiotics, made by Parke-Davis. A second dose was given when a catheter was inserted in James's urethra. James did well for a year, but eventually an infection developed and he ran up a fever of 104 degrees.

Dr. Watkins was a bit wary because he remembered what happened when Streptomycin came on the market a few years before. It was also promoted as a miracle drug, powerful and without side effects; it later turned out that it caused permanent deafness in some patients. As Maeder describes it, Watkins asked a Parke-Davis detail man about chloramphenicol's side effects, and he said he knew of none at all. That was not true—there had already been two or three deaths linked to it in his own sales area. Later, another doctor in the same area told Watkins, "If he told you he didn't know anything about it, then he's a liar, because I told him about one case myself. He knew." But at the time, Watkins accepted what the salesman told him. He gave his son another dose of chloramphenicol. From what is now known, it seems clear that the first doses sensitized the boy's system, and the third dose triggered the catastrophic reaction that now took place.

James became slow, lethargic, and pale. When bruises began to appear on his body, the boy insisted to his parents that he had not been playing rough. Then one evening he was playing a board game with his father when a piece fell on the floor and rolled under the couch. James dropped down to his knees and searched. When he got up, he had two large, dark bruises on his knees. Watkins recognized the instant, massive bruising as a strong sign of a blood disorder. James was taken to several blood specialists, the best Watkins could find, and the verdict was unanimous—James had a rare illness called aplastic anemia, in which the body's blood-forming elements are destroyed. Because blood-clotting factors are also compromised, patients bruise at barely a touch, and wounds can bleed and swell hugely. It is most often fatal. One of the doctors shocked the Watkins family when he said he had seen four other cases like it that apparently had been caused by chloramphenicol.

James grew progressively weaker. He endured fifty or sixty blood transfusions, and finally, as Maeder reports, the boy quietly told his father one day as they looked out the window at the children playing that he knew he would never be able to play again, and he thought it would be better if he died soon. He did, writhing in fits of pain, a few months later, in May 1952.

James never needed chloramphenicol—another less toxic drug would have sufficed. Before all the problems associated with this drug were known, it was seen simply as a powerful antibiotic, and doctors became confident and complacent in its use. Yes, it was the only good treatment for typhus and typhoid fever, and it could kill a variety of different bacteria, but would it kill the one a given patient had? Only a culture would tell. And what about side effects? Its potential effectiveness said nothing about its side effects.

The drug was on the market for at least two years before the first reports of trouble began to circulate widely. Parke-Davis continued to market the drug aggressively and denied problems. It was fighting fiercely for a drug that, all by itself, had turned a midlevel company selling mostly vitamins into the biggest drug company in the world. In a single year, the company's sales rose more than 30 percent, and in 1951 it sold more than $135 million worth of drugs, more than any of its rivals.

What Albe Watkins discovered about the drug after his son died was that quite a few doctors already knew of its potentially fatal side effects. Some reports had already been passed to the Food and Drug Administration, and the Parke-Davis Company had been alerted. One doctor had reported twelve cases to the company. Watkins himself wrote to the company and got a reply from its medical director, who said there was no evidence to connect aplastic anemia to chloramphenicol. Watkins was distraught over the death of his son, especially because he himself had administered the fatal dose. He decided to drive across the country with his wife and his surviving children, visiting doctors along the way, both to alert them and to collect more reports, which he would give to the FDA on his arrival in Washington, D.C.

"We would drive all day in the car, going three or four hundred miles at a stretch," Maeder quotes Watkins as saying, "with the boys playing games in the back seat. Then we'd stop at night, and while my wife was finding a place to stay and getting the boys settled and finding somewhere to eat, I'd get on the telephone. I would just go through the yellow-page listings of doctors, and call them one after another. . . ." He told them he was a doctor, had lost a son to aplastic anemia caused by chloramphenicol, and wondered whether they had seen any reactions to the drug in their own practice.

It was a grief-driven and random exercise, but when he arrived in Washington to meet with the FDA's Dr. Henry Welch, chief of the division of antibiotics, he was able to tell him of forty-some additional cases of severe reactions to the drug. Welch said the agency itself had identified fifty cases, including thirty-six deaths, and the number was rising daily.

We now know that Parke-Davis was aware of serious problems with the drug. Chemists had warned the company that one component, which was a chemical formation called a nitrobenzene radical present in TNT, seemed to have a peculiar affinity for, and toxic effect on, the bone marrow, where blood is made. The drug came on the market in early 1949, and in an article published that year assessing the wonderful therapeutic properties of chloramphenicol, Dr. Joseph Smadel also noted that the drug would have to be closely watched because of this potentially toxic feature. In November the first three cases of blood disorders caused by the drug were reported at a medical meeting in Chicago. The reports of cases from that time on never stopped, though from 1949 to 1952 most appeared at meetings and in out-of-the-way journals.

At the same time, the company was pressing ahead with its promotion of the drug, the "greatest drug since penicillin," as one wide-eyed magazine writer put it. The company advertising spoke of the outstanding effectiveness and the lack of side effects. The ads did not mention the blood disorders until the FDA forced Parke-Davis to put in a few lines of fine print on the subject in 1952. It also required a letter be sent to all physicians in the United States letting them know of the problem. However, this letter, entitled "chloramphenicol from a hematologist's point of view," said that there had been a few reports of blood problems with the drug, but that they were unproved and extremely rare in any case. If problems existed, the letter said, they were probably caused by the peculiarities of some patients. (The FDA requirements extended only to the United States. The company continued advertising the drug with broad claims and no warnings outside of the country for more than a decade afterward.) The letter was followed by a pronouncement from the company medical director, J. P. Gray, stating, "We know of no instance in which aplastic anemia has been proved to have been caused by chloramphenicol." The statements and letters and the news coverage they generated temporarily cut the sales of the drug to about one-sixth of the 1951 sales, but then sales bounded back over the next few years and by 1958 were at the highest levels ever. The company worked to achieve this result by pressing to discredit the bad news about the drug with strong pitches by detail men.

Company executives gave those salesmen specific lines and arguments to deliver to doctors as often as possible. Some of these sales instructions, obtained by Maeder, say that the message should be positive about the product and suggest that its success and the great scrutiny the drug was being put under were the reasons it appeared to have problems. Here are some of the lines from 1952:

Suggested Details
Chloramphenicol

Doctor, I am glad you asked me about the Chloramphenicol "situation." Needless to say, we of Parke-Davis are also concerned. We are particularly concerned about the increasing tendency for newspapers and magazines to "practice" medicine. . . .

Chloramphenicol is among the most important products that have run the gauntlet of newspaper evaluation. Perhaps the dramatic qualities of the antibiotic, itself, have contributed to this condition. A relatively few articles, however, have accused chloramphenicol of being associated with certain blood dyscrasias [blood cell abnormalities]. On the other hand, intensive investigation by the Food and Drug Administration, carried on with the assistance of a special committee of specialists appointed by the National Research Council, resulted in unqualified sanction of continued use of chloramphenicol for all conditions in which it had previously been used. . . . [This is false. Both the FDA and the NRC determined that blood disorders are caused by chloramphenicol, and both recommended restrictions on its use, and education of doctors about the possibility of misuse.]

Up through October, 1952, 59 published papers, reporting experience involving more than 1,700 patients, have presented data in which thorough blood studies had been made on each patient before, during and following therapeutic courses of chloramphenicol. Doctor, is it not significant, that in not one of these 1,700 patients was there any evidence of blood dyscrasia following administration of the antibiotic? . . . Before terminating this interview, may I re-emphasize a fact which has not changed with the developments of the past year? Chloramphenicol continues to be the outstanding wide-spectrum antibiotic because of its well-tolerated nature and its high degree of effectiveness. . . . [It is not only true that no deaths would be expected among 1,700 patients who took the drug—it would take about 20,000 patients to turn up a case of aplastic anemia—but more important, even the busiest doctor would not expect to see a severe reaction to the drug in any given year's practice. The attendant blood problems thus had the feel of pure abstraction to most doctors, while they had seen penicillin reactions and had seen cures in difficult cases with chloramphenicol.]

This drug represented a new challenge for the FDA: The drug was very effective. It saved lives. But in a small percentage of cases it was also fatal, and in many cases needlessly so. What could be done?

When Watkins arrived in Washington, the number of cases was becoming alarming. The FDA's Welch was a strong personality, a highly social man, and he gave Watkins the impression of sympathy and great concern. The FDA commissioner at the time was George P. Larrick, a longtime FDA employee and a cautious man. On June 26, 1952, Welch and Commissioner Larrick ordered all sixteen FDA field offices in the United States to drop what they were doing, and inspectors, chemists, and other office staff were to go out to every hospital, medical school, and clinic to determine if there were still unreported cases of blood disorders linked to chloramphenicol. They were to work nights, Saturdays, and Sundays and report to Washington every day. The investigation began on a Friday; by Tuesday, about two hundred more cases had been uncovered.

That day Larrick called Parke-Davis executive vice president Homer Fritsch. He told Fritsch about the FDA sweep. He also said that fifteen blood specialists and other doctors had asked the FDA to restrict the sale of the drug. They suggested that, at least until more was known, it should be used only in cases where other drugs could not be substituted, such as in the treatment of typhoid. But instead of taking that step, Larrick said he would first take a gentler, less public one. Antibiotics had to be certified officially as uncontaminated and potent before being cleared for sale, and the commissioner suggested that certification of chloramphenicol be delayed for a time. This meant no new supply would go to market, but that the drug already in the marketplace could be sold. There would be no condemnation associated with a total recall.

"We are wondering if you could see your way clear to going along with us," Larrick asked Fritsch.

The next day company officials called to say they were already preparing ads that would run in the next two issues of the *Journal of the American Medical Association,* and were rewriting their promotional material to doctors to include a few sentences about the possibility of a problem.

FDA officials objected. A few lines in a promotional brochure would not satisfy them. The commissioner wanted a personal letter sent to each physician. Parke-Davis agreed. Certification was stopped; advertising appeared with some information about the blood disorders added at the bottom; personal letters were sent. But on the key point, whether the drug would be restricted to necessary uses, the company said it had no information about this possibility, apparently deciding to ignore the commissioner's request. The FDA let this, the most important step, slide and did not press the company on it.

By the third week in July, the FDA had 410 cases recorded. Larrick now called the president of Parke-Davis, Harry Loynd, on July 18, not to talk about further restrictions but instead to say that the FDA was going to ask the National Research Council of the National Academy of Sciences to appoint an expert panel to review the evidence and make recommendations. Parke-Davis was invited to attend and make arguments. To accommodate the company further, the FDA determined that the meetings would be held behind closed doors, that the names of those participating would be withheld from reporters, and that all the evidence being considered would be secret. The meeting was held on August 6, 1952, and FDA officials soon learned why secrecy does not work in public policymaking.

The committee of experts concluded that there was a link between the drug and the blood disorders, though the group could not be sure how often the problem would occur. The drug was important, the committee said, because it appeared to be the best treatment for typhoid, some types of meningitis, some urinary tract infections, and some infections with staphylococcal bacteria. They felt that the only reasonable course was to keep the drug on the market, but try to get doctors to prescribe it wisely, only when truly needed. There was some doubt that doctors could be educated or trusted on the topic. It was decided that one way to establish the seriousness of the situation would be to ask doctors to carry out blood studies whenever the drug was used. That way, at least indications of trouble could be spotted early. (As it happens, the blood studies were useless, because once the problem is detected, it is too late; besides, doctors largely ignored the request.)

The statement finally issued by the FDA began in backhanded fashion. It said that the FDA had decided to

permit continued distribution of the antibiotic drug chloramphenicol under revised labeling that will caution physicians explicitly against its indiscriminate use. . . . The administration has weighed the value of the drug for causing harm and has decided that it should continue to be available for careful use by the medical profession in those serious and sometimes fatal diseases in which its use was necessary.

But it was nevertheless a shock to the industry to see the agency come to life. Industry newsletters suggested that the FDA announcement amounted to the agency's taking on new regulatory powers that might not be legal. In the trade, there was fear that the FDA would insert itself into business as never before.

The same day the FDA issued its statement, Parke-Davis made its own announcement, and that was the one that set the tone for the next ten years of action on the drug. It began

> The decision of the Food and Drug Administration, clearing chloram-phenicol with no restrictions on the number of diseases in which it can be administered, brought this comment today from Harry J. Loynd, President of Parke-Davis & Company, manufacturers of the world-famous antibiotic. "The FDA decision certainly reflects new credit on the research scientists who discovered and perfected chloramphenicol, and the clinical investigators who made exhaustive tests before chlor-amphenicol was first made available to the medical profession. . . . This antibiotic . . . has now successfully passed three intensive investi-gations, originally by Parke-Davis & Company, and more recently by the Food and Drug Administration and the . . . National Research Council. Physicians may continue to prescribe chloramphenicol for the treatment of any disease as they see fit."

The step and counterstep in the case of chloramphenicol carried on for many more years. The FDA again and again was unable to bring itself to restrict the use of the drug, and even worse, was unable to make any decision on its own. The agency called on the national academy's National Research Council three times over a decade so that the agency could avoid taking a position. When asked why the FDA acted as it did on chloramphenicol, Deputy Commissioner Winton Rankin, even years later, said he did not know what else could have been done. Larrick testi-fied before Congress that if doctors couldn't sort out what to do on their own then, "I'm at a loss." The truth, of course, is that both the FDA and Parke-Davis were to blame. Regulation had failed.

One would like to believe that finally, as Tom Maeder writes, after a thousand deaths and dozens of lawsuits, innumerable FDA studies and changes in the drug's label, multiple congressional hearings and endless news articles, physicians had finally understood and adopted different prescribing patterns for chloramphenicol. In fact, the use fell in the 1970s only after Parke-Davis's patent expired and the company dropped it from its roster of high-promotion items.

•

CHAPTER EIGHT

The Industry Ascendant

THE LITTLE agency of food and drugs had been modestly growing and exploring its mission for almost fifty years. By mid-century, the American law was the most advanced among nations, and it seemed as if steady progress was in store as the medical revolution began to move through society. But matters were quickly becoming a bit too complex for the FDA. Its leaders found they couldn't keep pace with the booming new market in medical drugs. The agency was headed for a stumble of some proportions.

In society at large, optimism was the tone of the time. The Yanks had steered through both world wars with no destruction at home, only construction. Economic boom followed victory. The machinery of the new pharmaceutical industry was part of it, and it rolled into the second half of the century on wheels of confidence.

Politically, it was an era of conservatism and boosterism. There was renewed prosperity, demands for "loyalty" again. The agenda of workers was set aside, labor rules were reversed, minimum wage plans blocked, and an expansion of social security halted. Republicans and southern Democrats were in open revolt against the new attempts to secure civil rights. American bravado and commerce spread rapidly. As a new Red Scare began, "loyalty boards" were established and public employees were dragged before them. A person might be removed from office "if reasonable grounds exist for believing that the person involved is disloyal," and more than 2,200 government workers lost their jobs because of this "security" worry. The new conservatism, as it had after the First World War, served to remove power from the regulatory agencies or pack them with administrators who did not believe in their original mission.

The glow of success in medical drugs continued for some years, though the signs of trouble were tucked away, quietly, in the files of the drug companies. They included information on the phenomena called "side effects," unintended and sometimes even fatal consequences of taking ordinary medicines. They were at first hidden in the glare of the bright lights that spelled "miracle drugs," a phrase that became common in the press of the era. It was during this time that doctors and public health professionals began to learn that the new business-science of drugs, which the FDA was to oversee, was more complex than it had seemed.

The leaders at the FDA fell in with the changes as they occurred because they seemed sensible. The agency was now overseeing a flow of safer and more effective drugs. Companies could speak the language of science and medicine for the first time.

There was something comforting in dealing with drug companies that now devoted great sums to research and were actually engaged in shepherding useful drugs from lab to market, as the FDA had been preaching for decades. It was now the FDA that had too few scientists and medical experts, and too little ability to pursue properly the issues of advancing science.

The trouble was, the FDA officers didn't understand the new medical market. Dr. John Nestor, one of the first of a new cadre of medical officers to come in the 1960s, and a man who served the agency for decades, said that insiders who wanted more progress called the former inspectors who led the FDA in the 1950s the "rat-turd counters." The old leadership did not seem to have any sense of where the future lay, or how to get there, so they began the new era with a series of strategic and tactical errors.

It didn't help that early in the era a disruptive dispute of a kind that harkened back to the past occurred over beets. The agency had a new commissioner now, appointed in 1951 after Walter Campbell retired, Texan Charles Crawford, who had a background in agriculture. Campbell had spotted his talent for legal language and put him to work as an advisor in the office of the commissioner. He became known for writing regulatory language that industry could not circumvent. But by early in the 1950s his tough language had gotten him and the agency in trouble.

At the time, a company in New York made canned beets in two varieties: ordinary-sized beets and miniature beets that were sweeter, more costly to make, and referred to as "baby beets." At some point the New York company started cutting up regular beets and selling them as gourmet "baby beets." The FDA demurred, and Crawford in particular found the company's circumvention of the language of the law utterly dishonest. He ordered the company to correct their labeling. Unfortunately, the company was headquartered in the congressional district of Representative John Taber, a member of the powerful House Appropriations Committee, the committee that controls the spending of the federal agencies. Taber asked the FDA to permit the company some looseness in the description of the product. Crawford said no. Taber retaliated by calling in favors on the committee and threatened the agency with significant budget cuts. Crawford was stubborn, and a bit naïve as well, and he told his staff that he thought Taber was bluffing. "Right will prevail," he told the staff. "They're not going to cut our appropriation, because that's not right." They did, of course. Between 1951 and 1954, 15 percent of the FDA budget was cut, and 20 percent of the agency's inspectors and scientists were fired. By 1955, the agency had fewer enforcement personnel than it had in 1941. The Supreme Court struck another blow by declaring that FDA inspectors were not entitled to inspect companies if the companies did not agree.

Crawford determined then that his job was to fall on his sword to try to save the agency. He wrote in detail to his bosses of the agency's weakened and demoralized state, and asked the Department of Health, Education and Welfare to set up an independent panel to investigate. He knew that anyone who took a look at the work of the agency and the outrageous behavior of some of the companies would conclude that the FDA could no longer do the job it was ordered to do under law. He pointed out that the FDA was inspecting about 96,000 manufacturing and processing plants in the United States, but the work force was such that inspectors made it to each plant about once every twelve years. After the citizens' panel was created, Crawford submitted his resignation, and it was accepted. He died of leukemia shortly afterward.

In its report, the citizen panel said: "The Food and Drug Administration now has insufficient funds, staff and facilities to meet its essential responsibility of protecting the public health. . . ." But these were politically conservative times. After Crawford left, the pharmaceutical industry flexed its political muscle and was able to influence who his successor would be.

Their choice was George P. Larrick, who had begun his career in the agency in 1923 as a food inspector. He was a genial man, one who wanted very much to be liked, to get along. He believed in the mission of the drug industry, and had preached cooperation and harmony between the regulators and the companies as he rose through the ranks. When it was time to change commissioners in 1954 and the secretary of health, education and welfare, Oveta Hobby, began to consider who should be named, she was subject to a sudden deluge of mail, phone calls, and visits from the drug industry. Most important, President Eisenhower's close friend and political operative in Minnesota, James Bradshaw Mintener, a former lawyer for the food giant Pillsbury Mills, pressed Eisenhower personally on behalf of Larrick.

Larrick himself testified in Congress that he was not a political person—"I regard myself as a political eunuch"—and that he felt those in the drug industry were basically honest and public-spirited. His deputy commissioner, Winton B. Rankin, in reflecting on the era and the boss he admired, once commented on Larrick's closeness to industry. "George Larrick's fundamental objective, I'm satisfied, was to give the American public the best protection he could in the food and drug field. Now, in order to administer a regulatory law, the regulator has to have a constituency; he has to have somebody that will back him before Congress," Rankin said. "If you don't have a constituency, then the first time your regulations begin to pinch, the industry will run up to Congress or run to the political arm of the Administration [in the White House], and get your decisions overruled. So Larrick had to have a constituency in order to administer effectively."

Rankin went on bluntly. "Who was Larrick's constituency? It was regulated industry. That was the principal reed he had to lean on." He needed them; he courted them. When the job of commissioner was open, "he won out largely because the drug industry came to his support. . . . he had a very warm spot in his heart for the responsible members of the drug industry. And that no doubt led to the close relationships [with industry that he had]." Other FDA officials said that under Larrick, the atmosphere was easy; inspectors in some offices were routinely accepting favors such as meals from the companies being inspected. At headquarters, drug company officials were able to simply walk into the building, find the desk of the medical officer reviewing the company's drug application, and wade in with questions and arguments about the evidence. At the same time, if a consumer came to the agency asking for data on the safety of a drug, even one already approved and on the market, he was denied access completely. Secrecy was the rule, and not because the law required it; it was simply a policy of the FDA that whatever data drug companies wanted kept secret was kept secret.

Theodore G. Klumpp, a former FDA official and head of Winthrop Laboratories, said that during the 1950s "the regulated industries had felt their relationship with FDA was beginning to approach what it should be in a free society and in accord with the best traditions of the Republic."

This goes far in explaining the behavior of the agency in the case of chloramphenicol.

This was the shape of the system as it evolved:

First, there was research. Companies searched madly for substances that could have strong biological effects. Or the companies could simply buy a discovery from a university, or borrow the work of a government laboratory. (A majority of drugs do not originate from company research.) Second, the companies patented what looked promising. That meant not only the essential compound, but the methods of manufacturing and every other unclaimed bit of newness about a drug as well. Third, the company had to test the chemical compound for safety, and to prove its special advantages. Fourth, the company had to submit its proof to the FDA. Fifth, if all else seemed on track, the company would build a sales effort and market each drug as if it were penicillin.

The companies lobbied, and succeeded in changing a variety of laws to make this formula work. Patent law was made tame, so it would be easier for them to gain and hold control of the essence of a new drug. The companies also created, through lobbying, the prescription drug system, in which doctors controlled medical drug use rather than patients. This meant that advertising and promotion need not be aimed at the entire American population, a costly and largely ineffective proposition. Instead, companies were able to set out to convince doctors, not the public, of their products' special merits. (In 1930 about 95 percent of drug company advertising was aimed at the public. By 1972, perhaps as much as 90 percent was aimed at doctors.) Additionally, to lock up prescription monopolies, the companies succeeded in getting laws passed that made it illegal for a pharmacist to substitute a generic drug for the brand-name drugs they offered. They also succeeded in making it illegal to advertise the prices of drugs. Customers, and doctors for that matter, soon had no idea what drugs cost.

The companies hired salesmen by the thousand to present to doctors, in person, all the details about their drugs. These detail men presented what they said were factual assessments of the drugs, though they weren't always, and represented the sharp end of an excessively large promotional spear.

In dealing with doctors, one key to promotion has been to assure the sense of "newness" of each drug as it comes out (even if a drug is a near copy of ten others already available). The chief ruse for accomplishing this is the naming. Each drug must have a catchy name, easily remembered by doctors, necessary because most of the drugs were very similar, even interchangeable. It took quite a while for those outside the industry to understand this, and the FDA was possibly the last to understand. Solomon Garb, a pharmacologist at Albany Medical College, testified before Congress with some sense of frustration, first, and wonder, second. "It is becoming exceedingly difficult for physicians to keep things clear," he grumbled. To explain the feeling doctors had, he said, imagine that "drug manufacturers took over the manufacture of baked beans. They would all stop using the word 'beans' and each would give the product a new, coined name," he said. "Some might use anagrams of beans, like Sneabs or Nabes, and others might call them Lo Cals, or Hi Pros. Picture the confusion in the grocery store if beans were no longer named beans, but if each maker gave a completely new name to his product. Further, try to imagine what would happen if there were 300 to 500 additional new names of this type in the grocery store every year. This is approximately what is happening in medicine."

Under the new system, doctors' offices were now flooded with mail from drug companies. An army of woodpeckers from drug companies rattled their doors. From a time when doctors were approached with some restraint by a handful of representatives who themselves were likely to be doctors and pharmacists, now the companies began to recruit lay salesmen by the thousands. Every doctor had to be visited personally. Dr. Harry Dowling, an expert in infectious diseases and a key AMA official, said that one doctor reported receiving 3,636 packages and letters for 604 drugs in 1962. This was in addition to scores of visits by detail men, not to mention additional incentives such as offers of gifts, trips, and tickets.

As one experienced salesman has written, one of the keys to any physician's office is to the "sample closet," a small storage room in which row upon row of boxes and bottles of medicines line the shelves—all free, all highly pitched, all ready for use by the doctor. Even forty years ago it was written that "approximately three-quarters of a billion dollars is spent every year by some sixty drug companies in order to reach, cajole, pamper, outwit, and sell one of America's smallest markets—the 180,000 physicians. And it is not too much to say that perhaps no other group in the country is so insistently sought after, chased, wooed, pressured and downright importuned as this small group of doctors who are de facto wholesalers of the drug business." Already in 1949 doctors were feeling the pinch, when an editorial in the *Journal of the American Medical Association* entitled "Too Many Drugs?" was lamenting the large number of new drugs, each of which appeared to be only slightly different from the last.

Pierre Garai, a senior executive for the advertising firm of Lennen and Newell in New York, was asked to give his advertising man's perspective of the industry in an academic journal article. What he wrote was blunt and eloquent. He said that the single most striking thing about the new pharmaceutical business was its enormous expenditure on promotion. He noted that it was true, as drug executives said, that the companies were doing much research to find treatments for human disease. But that paled by comparison with their promotion of their finds. He noted the interesting fact that all the products emptiest of substance—soap, gum, candy, and soda, for example—were the ones upon which the most was spent for promotion. For these products to succeed it was necessary to put as much as 10 to 12 percent of every sales dollar back into advertising. But pharmaceutical companies spent far more on advertising drugs than was spent on consumer items, 30 percent above the next highest category.

As economist Seymour Harris wrote with some reserve, "According to some experts, it would be expected that advertising for drugs would be relatively small compared to other industries since the demand for product should be determined by the incidence of disease." But that would be an analysis based on the public health need for drugs, not on a company's need to produce revenues. That is the key: the present system is dominated not by research and development but by promotion, in order to sustain both research *and* high profits.

About 6 percent of the money taken in from the sale of drugs was directed into new research. About *four times* that amount was put back into advertising. Harris wrote in late 1963 that the advertising of drugs was beyond that of any other product in America, and added up to

a well-nigh stupefying concentration of promotion weight on the individual physician. Does it increase the industry's cost of doing business? Substantially. Is it reflected in the cost of prescription drugs? Of course. . . . Why all this drum-beating? The answer is quite simple. One, the drug companies cannot compete effectively without it. Two, it works. . . . Effective promotions, heavy promotion, sustained promotion has carried the day. The physicians have been sold. So has the country.

Garai wrote in 1963:

No manufacturer of drugs can afford to restrict his production to genuinely significant pharmaceutical innovations. There simply aren't enough of these to go around in any given fiscal year, or for that matter, in any dozen fiscal years. It should therefore surprise no one that we find slight modifications of existing products marketed by the bushel, a veritable blizzard of parity products slugging it out . . . [with] a steady outpouring of new chemical entities whose advantages, to say the least, remain to be established.

With regard to social conscience among drugmakers, he said it is "naïve to expect any commercial enterprise in our society to devote itself to the common weal. Inevitably, business considerations dominate. The drug companies, protestations notwithstanding, are no exception." He was saying that it remains to the larger society to place additional safeguards if they are needed; self-regulation is a foolish hope.

Dr. A. Dale Console, a former medical director of E.R. Squibb and Sons, in testifying before Congress, said that once development of a drug began at a company, it was difficult to stop even if it became apparent that the drug was not going to be very useful, or it was going to duplicate something already on the market. The drug would nevertheless be the subject of a large public relations and advertising campaign, even to the detriment of better drugs coming along. In Congress, Console was asked about this process: "Is there much of this type of research that you are talking about that really produces nothing worthwhile, and is not intended to?"

Console replied,

I think more than half is in that category, and I should point out that with many of these products, it is clear *while they are on the drawing board* that they promise no utility; they promise sales. It is not a question of pursuing them because something may come of it. It is quite clear that there is no point in pursuing this; that you won't end up with a product that has any real value; but it is pursued simply because there is profit in it. [emphasis added]

The companies spent a lot of time talking about the many research failures they had experienced for every success. This, they pleaded, required higher prices for the more successful drugs. Yes, Console said, it is true that there are many failures for each success, but "the problem arises out of the fact that they market so many of their failures."

In this system, the flow of drugs was restricted, information about them was limited, and prices were set at very high levels. Sales were unlike anything seen in the history of sales, and there was a kind of wild *joie de vendre,* as one advertising man put it. Princeton University economist Jesse F. Markham, an industry consultant, acknowledged after analyzing pharmaceutical industry prices and practices in the early 1960s, that the result of the "patent, produce, and promote" plan in America was remarkable. The companies did not behave as if there was a competitive market in drugs, he said.

Concerned doctors at the time wanted to know the details of every drug and every treatment, and they gradually became alarmed at the flood of drugs and the scarcity of information available about them. The powerful new drugs were wonderful, certainly, but they were also potentially dangerous. And, as the companies pressed to get the drugs to market and into patients' bodies, the doctors felt they were quickly losing control. They did little complaining in public lest they seem to be losing their grip just as they were gaining a new respect in society. But when prodded, some of them were clear: Pediatrician Lawson Wilkins asked, "How in the world can any physician be expected to keep up with the new pharmacy?" Dr. Dale Friend at Harvard Medical School gave a rhetorical answer in a medical journal: "It is utterly impossible for the practicing physician to have enough information to select the drugs he uses in the treatment of patients wisely. It is obvious that among the nearly 8,000 preparations now available there are many agents that are unwanted, useless, undesirable, of limited value, or actually harmful. This huge number of preparations has served to increase the cost of medical care and the cost of drugs and has placed a severe burden on the physician and pharmacist." Dr. Harry Dowling wrote: "In many fields there are too many drugs that differ so little that they are practically the same. Instead of 24 antihistaminic drugs, we would be better off with five or six and still have enough for vigorous competition. And there are hundreds of mixtures of drugs that have no excuse for being."

Dowling, after grumbling about the problems for doctors and the needless drugs, got to the heart of the matter:

> Any attempt to increase the demand for a drug beyond a certain point means that the drug will be given when it isn't needed. Demands for soaps, perfumes and automobiles can be expanded indefinitely, if people can pay for them; demand for antibiotics, sedatives, and diuretics has a ceiling that is determined by the number of patients who need them. Any attempt to push above that ceiling not only costs more money, but also results in poor medical care.

By poor medical care, he meant that patients would be taking extra risks, that there would be more side effects, disorders, and deaths caused by the drugs. In other words, oversupply and overpromotion in medicine is a serious matter. It does not conform to the nature of illness, or the practice of medicine, or the desire of consumers, but purely to the needs of industrial marketing departments.

The "purchase, patent, promote" system created a steady flow of new drugs from their discoverers, through companies, to the public. Most thoughtful observers began to feel the flow of new drugs was simply too great. Dowling, tracking drugs in the decade from 1959 to 1968, found that the number of new drugs being disgorged into the market every year was between 200 and 400. But among them, the truly new and useful drugs held steady at a low, relatively stable level—an average of 3 new drugs per year. Today, the World Health Organization maintains a list of important drugs that numbers about 300 out of the 10,000 to 20,000 offered by drug companies.

Another effect of the system, ironically, was the difficulty of obtaining useful information about drugs. There have always been a few independent groups willing to do the work necessary to describe in detail what's good and bad about each of the 10,000 or more medical drugs available on the market. To catalog the full list, locate scientific papers about each, review what is available in the public record about dangerous side effects, and put it all together in readable, well-balanced summaries is a vital but extremely difficult task. And until the early 1950s the American Medical Association had been a key source of information about the problems and relative value of drugs, an efficient watchdog. The AMA had published lists of fraudulent and useless drugs, and often gave critical evaluations of the others. Its committees of top experts spoke always for reining in unscrupulous companies. The AMA lobbied Congress for the 1906 and 1938 laws.

But just at this moment in the early 1950s, when doctoring was becoming more complicated and the new drugs were pouring in the door, the AMA suddenly changed its approach. In the rain of profit that came with the research-based drug system after World War II, the AMA found itself at odds with the drug companies just when the association could least afford it. Companies were steering their drug advertising away from the AMA's scientific journals, and the association was in trouble financially. A group of the more conservative leaders staged an internal coup and succeeded in winning back the advertising revenues of the drug companies for its publications by making the AMA a more pharmaceutical-friendly place, an uncritical industry ally. The group closed its test laboratories and canceled its "seal of acceptance" program that doctors relied on to tell them what was useful and what was not. The group stopped visiting drug plants to see which were well run. And the group stopped its campaign to get doctors to prescribe drugs by their generic rather than brand names. (Surveys showed that the AMA's advice on drugs was probably the single most important and acceptable advice doctors used.)

After the turnaround, the AMA's advertising revenues represented more than half the entire income of the association. The doctors' association was now participating in, and profiting from, the commercialization of medicine, rather than examining it critically.

All of this produced an eerie landscape in which doctors had little unbiased information about drug treatment. Surveys conducted in the 1950s and 1960s found that between half and three-quarters of all doctors counted on pharmaceutical companies as their primary source of information. Floating on a tide of new drugs, and dependent on the drug-makers for steering, the doctors were losing their way. In one study of seventy-six community hospitals, involving 85,000 patients' charts, it was found that about half the time antibiotics were misprescribed—most often given when they were not needed. In another study, it was determined that one-third of surgery patients were inappropriately prescribed antibiotics. In studies that assessed doctors' performances more generally, the results were equally dismal. A staff of doctors followed the work of eighty-eight physicians in one North Carolina community, reviewing everything each physician did during three days of practice. It was found that the doctors gave the right diagnosis and treatment 43 percent of the time in cases of high blood pressure, 33 percent for respiratory infections, 17 percent for emotional problems, and 15 percent for anemia. They found doctors prescribing antibiotics for viral illnesses, administering combination drugs for anemia that had little or no effect, treating nonexistent organic conditions with drugs when the patients' problems were emotional, and often giving the wrong dose or wrong schedule when prescribing drugs. A study of doctors in Canada used the same method and determined that unsatisfactory performance ranged from 15 to 85 percent, depending on the disorder.

These troubles rarely surfaced in the public consciousness. Optimism reigned. Treatment was the rage. Thanks to some of the new drugs, doctors had effective weapons against many of the common scourges of mankind. It was as if Prometheus had stolen the fire of the gods, as Stuart

Levy writes, and both citizens and doctors were soon using it like holy water or a talisman. There were reports that antibiotics had cured cancer, and had vanquished viral diseases as well as bacterial ones, even though antibiotics have no biological effect whatsoever on viruses.

Eventually, though, questions were raised about the foundations of the medical drug miracle, and whether it was time to examine the whole enterprise a little more closely.

•

CHAPTER NINE

The Grand Bargain

IT BEGAN with a sore throat on a winter day in 1951. It was irritating enough to send Walton Hamilton, a Washington attorney, to his doctor that day; he was told he had a streptococcal throat infection and was given a prescription for chloramphenicol. When he went to the drugstore, the pharmacist told him the antibiotic would cost fifty cents per pill, $10 for a five-day supply ($100 in current dollars)—a lot of money for a simple sore throat. Hamilton had worked as a consultant for the antitrust division of the Justice Department in the New Deal era and was now a partner in the powerful Washington law firm of Arnold, Fortas & Porter. As Richard Harris writes, Hamilton called his doctor because he suspected doctors had no idea what the cost of medicine was. He was right. His doctor said at least two other antibiotics would be fine, and that he would check the price and call back. He did. "I'm sorry, but they're all the same price," he told Hamilton.

"Exactly the same?" the lawyer asked.

"To the penny."

"I presume they are all made by the same company, then."

"No," the doctor said. "They're made by three different companies."

Hamilton knew about price-fixing issues. He was also married to an economist one step closer to those issues, Irene Till, of the Federal Trade Commission (FTC). He smelled a rat. Harris notes that Hamilton talked it over with his wife, who was equally surprised at both the high prices and the "coincidence" that the prices were identical.

That experience led, ultimately, to a moment in 1957 when Till was working for the Senate subcommittee on antitrust and monopoly issues. She had moved there after her former FTC boss, John M. Blair, had become the chief economist for the committee, under the chairman, Senator Estes Kefauver of Tennessee. Kefauver had held hearings on the steel industry; then he focused on the auto industry. When Kefauver needed advice on what topic should be considered next, Blair asked Till for her opinion. She answered without hesitation, "Drugs."

Blair was not sure it was a good topic. The economics of it were complex, the industry was new and no one had studied it, no good industry numbers were available, and the industry was riding a popular high because of the success of antibiotics. And, of course, the drug industry had enormous cash reserves, and could retaliate forcefully and effectively if they did not like the bent of the hearings. But through the years, Till and others had been saving documents and accumulating data, because they knew the day of reckoning for the drug industry would come.

Blair was not convinced until one afternoon when he was looking at FTC reports on about two dozen different industries. Until that time drug companies had been listed under the chemical industry. But now, someone at FTC had broken them out separately, and it stood out. The pharmaceutical industry was not only the biggest profit maker, but the levels of profits were *double* the industry average, 19 percent of investment, after taxes. Blair called Till and together they looked at the numbers. "My God, just look at those profits!" he said to her. She allowed that she had never seen any numbers like it in her years as an economist. The decision to go ahead with an investigation of the drug business was taken that day.

The topic of drug profits was not within the bailiwick of the Food and Drug Administration. The FDA does not have any authority to regulate drug prices, or any of the economics of the industry. Similarly, it doesn't have any authority to regulate the behavior of doctors in the practice of medicine. Its authority centers on the products themselves: whether they are safe, whether they work, whether they are advertised honestly.

But though the hearings began with drug prices, they would wend their way around to issues of medicine as well. Kefauver was someone who, once digging into a subject, would dig till he hit bottom. He was a peculiar and slyly brilliant man, and a populist intellectual. He had a soft drawl, wore a coonskin cap occasionally while campaigning, and talked a lot about the conditions at home for the folks. He had become famous and popular, even a national figure, when he held hearings in 1950–51, among the first televised, on organized crime. He broke open connections between organized crime and politics in a number of cities. However, he managed to alienate party officials on both sides by demonstrating that crime was completely bipartisan. In 1954, even though he was standing for reelection, he took controversial positions on three issues, each of which was believed to be enough to sink him in Tennessee. He was one of those who initiated the petition to censure Senator Joseph McCarthy at the end of McCarthy's bold and uncompromising campaign to rout Reds and their sympathizers from government. Kefauver also refused to sign the Southern Manifesto against civil rights for Negroes (the only southerner to refuse). And possibly worst of all, when the Democrats offered a bill to make membership in the Communist party illegal, his was the only "no" vote. "It had to be done," he said in a simple explanation to his staff, who were sure it was the end for them. "The bill is unconstitutional." His three positions, though, were perceived at home as reflecting a completely honest concern for citizens. So, against all odds and predictions, he won reelection.

Now Kefauver would be probing medicines and how effectively they were regulated. It was a major turning point in the history of regulation, and the consequences of it would reverberate through the next forty years of medical politics.

Just as during the two previous crises that led to new drug laws, muckraking journalism was alive and well. After the decision in Congress to go ahead with hearings, but before they began in 1959, John Lear, science editor of *Saturday Review* magazine, became interested in drug issues. The magazine was then a popular review of news, issues, and culture, a bit more sophisticated than *Time* and *Newsweek*. Lear's interest was piqued when a woman wrote to him asking for an explanation of antibiotics, and expressing her confusion about what to use. He wrote back tartly suggesting she ask her doctor. She wrote again, saying that she had asked her doctor and found that *he* was quite confused, hence her first letter. When Lear spoke to a few prominent doctors he was surprised to discover that the confusion extended up to the most airy intellectual heights of medicine. The doctors told him there were too many drugs and that they were overpromoted. When the doctors refused to let their names be used in any stories, Lear knew he was on to something.

His series of stories began with one that reviewed a single advertisement for an antibiotic, Sigmamycin from Chas. Pfizer. The headline said, "Every day, everywhere, more and more physicians find Sigmamycin the antibiotic therapy of choice." Beneath that was an array of business cards of eight doctors around the country, complete with addresses, telephone numbers, and office hours. The doctor who brought the ad to Lear's attention said he thought the doctors' cards, and implied endorsements, were fake. Lear wrote to the doctors, but his letters were returned. He sent telegrams and was told there were no such addresses. He telephoned and found there were no such phone numbers. In his subsequent article, in January 1959, "Taking the Miracle Out of Miracle Drugs," Lear described the general overpromotion and misuse of antibiotics. Kefauver later said the series was largely responsible for moving the committee to investigate the broad issues of drugs, rather than limit the hearings to prices and profits. It was an important choice.

For years, academic doctors and even reputable company officials had said there should be some limits to the profits of drug companies. Several ideas had been suggested, like caps on profits and rules that would require companies to limit their monopolies on a drug to three years after approval and marketing. The proposition that companies could set their prices as high as the market would bear—the market being their sick and dying fellow citizens—made many uncomfortable. But the issue was never confronted until the Kefauver hearings.

Since 1945 the companies had been essentially on their own, borrowing science from the universities and government labs as fast as they could, then creating products and filling the market with them with little intervention from the public agencies. But by the end of the 1950s, a restlessness had developed. A series of bad drugs had been marketed, and now talk of reform had gone from unconnected discourse to a steady, insistent murmur. The dissatisfaction with many elements of post–World War II society was coming into the open. Concern over nuclear bombs and their frightening offshoots, including the spooky and apparently ever-present new factor in life, radiation, reinforced that technology had not been all good.

While John Kennedy was no breakaway rebel, his administration, and Lyndon Johnson's following it, emphasized health—that is, the public's health rather than the improvement of the health industry. Medical care programs for those who could not afford them—Medicare was the term finally used—had been an issue that dissolved after Franklin Roosevelt's era through the Eisenhower years. Now it began to gain shape and weight again. There was an uneasiness about allowing the business professional to run things, an attitude that had characterized the booming 1950s.

The public hearings on the drug industry began, according to their best chronicler, Richard Harris, at seven minutes after ten on the morning of December 7, 1959, with a discussion on the new category of steroid drugs. These drugs come from a large family of hormone molecules that the body uses to produce strong effects when needed. Adrenaline and the sex hormones estrogen and testosterone are steroids. In this case, the kind of steroids discussed were those that were newly found to be effective in two very different illnesses—arthritis and allergies.

It was eventually discovered that such steroid shots could not be given regularly in any but the worst cases, because the steroids had some severe side effects. But the path had been opened with the first of the drugs, cortisone, and from 1949 on one drug company after another threw itself into manic research to create all the molecular relatives (hydrocortisone, prednisone, prednisolone, methylprednisolone) that might have a similar effect.

At the Kefauver committee hearings, the leadoff witness was Francis C. Brown, president of Schering Corporation. Industry observers were pleased. Brown was counted as knowledgeable in the ways of Washington and a good speaker. What they had not counted on was that the committee had put together information that, no matter what Brown did, was going to be eye-opening.

After a statement by Brown about the greatness of the pharmaceutical industry, the committee passed out copies of charts and numbers on the Schering steroid product prednisolone. The company, of course, had refused to tell the committee how much it cost to make the drug, or how much it spent on promotion. But tracking through data from the FTC and from subpoenaed sales records, committee investigators had been able to calculate key figures the company had expected to keep secret. Investigators determined that the total cost of making the chemical and bottling, labeling, and packaging the medication could not have cost the company more than about a cent and a half per tablet. Schering sold prednisolone to druggists for 17.9 cents per tablet. Druggists in turn sold it for 29.8 cents per tablet.

Brown was asked by a committee staff member, Paul R. Dixon, "Do you consider it reasonable to charge 17.9 cents for a tablet when your cost certainly must be less than 1.6 cents?"

Brown took some time to reply, then said there were many factors to consider in setting a price. There were costs such as promotion, research, sales, and so on. Kefauver challenged him immediately. "Let's get this very clear," Kefauver said in slow, deceptively soft tones. "You buy this material from Upjohn. . . . All you do is put it in a capsule, add your brand name to it, and sell it. . . . We have a reliable concern that will tablet it for $2 [per thousand tablets] . . . so that your maximum cost per bottle of one hundred, which must include some research and some profit, is $1.57. Yet [you] sell it for $17.90. How do you justify that?"

Brown replied he didn't think the $1.57 figure was accurate. (It wasn't; it was too high.) But he said, for the sake of argument, he would accept it. He again offered as justification the high cost of research and promotion, only this time he put them in even more vague terms. There were high costs for the "distribution system," and for "educational," "pioneering," and "trailblazing" work. John Blair of the committee staff pressed him again on the cost of research. He noted that the company itself had put the total cost of research at 8.5 percent of its gross income. Taking that figure and deducting it from the 17.9 cents per tablet, Blair pointed out that the markup would still be 16.4 cents.

Kefauver decided to put the matter in the simplest terms, and asked Blair to calculate the markup from 1.5 cents to 17.9 cents per tablet. It was 1,118 percent. As Harris reports, the moment this figure was spoken reporters began to scribble furiously. It was still early in the day; they could make the afternoon papers.

Blair followed up with another chart, this one showing that from 1955 to 1958 Schering's profits, after taxes, had varied between 23 and 47 percent of net worth. In the five and a half years since becoming a private corporation, Schering's total net profit had exceeded the purchase price of the firm by about $3 million. "Everybody wants Schering or any other company to make a reasonable profit," Kefauver said to Brown. Then he told him about people he had spoken to who couldn't afford the medicine. "There are these people who have to have these medicines, and many of them can't get the medicines. . . . I just meant that as a matter of public policy, it seemed that during some of this time you might reduce the price of your medicines a little bit rather than trying to garner back more than the corporation cost in five years."

Brown replied, "There were a great many uncertainties hanging over our company. . . ." He could muster nothing better. He soon fell into blubbering defensiveness, calling the 1,118 percent figure a "headline item." The company had to make high profits on some drugs, he said, to compensate for losses on others.

Kefauver took him up on that immediately: "Now, just where is the big bargain that you have on some other drugs?" He proceeded quickly to some other Schering profit figures. On estradiol, used for menopausal problems, the company bought the drug in bulk from Roussel, a French firm, for about 11 cents a bottle. Schering sold it for $8.40, a markup of 7,079 percent, Kefauver pointed out. Brown again talked about research, and Kefauver shot back, "You did no research on this drug. You bought a finished product from Roussel. All you did was put it in a tablet, put it out under your name, and sell it at a markup of 7,079 percent."

"What am I expected to say?" Brown responded. "I have repeated a number of times we are engaged in an overall operation."

Another chart produced by the committee staff showed that the four largest companies making prednisone and prednisolone (Schering, Merck, Upjohn, and Pfizer) charged exactly the same prices for them, and that these prices hadn't changed a penny since 1956 when they were introduced. Brown said that the competitive situation required such prices. Kefauver found that puzzling. "I have never understood this kind of a competitive system. How is it, if you really want to be competitive, you don't lower your price to get more of the business?"

"Senator," Brown said, "we can't put two sick people in every bed where there is only one person sick."

At this point, Harris reports, one representative of the drug industry had had enough. He got up and left the room, saying later, "I never expected to hear anyone in the business testify that drug prices were high because the number of sick people was limited."

A grand bargain was being exposed for the first time, with all its peculiarities and consequences. And it was making news. When Brown returned to his hotel room the evening of the hearing he found on the front page of the *Washington Evening Star* the headline "Senators Find 1,118% Markup." At breakfast the next morning, Brown saw the *New York Times* front-page headline, "Senate Panel Cites Markups on Drugs Ranging to 7,079 Per Cent." The *Chicago Tribune,* far to the right politically, declared that what was really important was that the United States had developed new drugs and the Russians hadn't. The *St. Louis Post-Dispatch* picked up on the comments by industry that drugs were not overpriced, but very cheap, because they were saving lives. Of course, bread and water were also essential to life, said the *Post-Dispatch,* but were not priced accordingly. "In other words, the drug industry ought to be able to charge as much for a life-saving drug as the life it saves is worth. . . ." This, the editorial said politely, was poppycock. "The yardstick of a fair price is the cost."

What was being explained in the Kefauver hearings, in excruciating detail, was just how the medical drug industry discovered, developed, promoted, and sold its products. And that the price of drugs had nothing to do with the cost of business.

The hearings continued for nearly a year and featured about 150 witnesses. Four major classes of drugs were analyzed in some detail. The pattern across the board was the same—discovery and patents were followed by massive promotion and huge markups. Prices in the United

States turned out to be three to four times what the same companies charged for the same bottles of pills in other countries, even though there must have been an additional cost to transport them. Investigating the claim that patents were essential to give corporations the incentive to do research and discover drugs, the committee staff found that countries that *refused* to permit patents created just as many new drugs as those that *granted* patents. The only difference was the predictable one—the price of drugs in countries allowing patents was 18 to 255 percent higher.

The hearings confirmed that many pharmaceutical ads were misleading and based on little or no evidence. It was shown again that doctors were unprepared to deal with the promotional blitz and had few defenses against the information that came their way through it. Dr. Dale Console, now retired from years of service at Squibb, recalled that when he was trained, it was said to be vital to puzzle out the cause of a fever. Fevers, like many symptoms, had many different sources and could lead to very different outcomes. But promotion tended to emphasize simplicity instead. He recalled one campaign in which he received a clinical thermometer and a sample of a drug from a drug company in the same package. "The invitation is delightfully tempting," he said. "Too many physicians, pressed for time, would like to believe that medicine can be practiced with a thermometer and a bottle of pills." The temptation for doctors is unlike that in other fields of endeavor, he reflected. "If an automobile does not have a motor, no amount of advertising can make it appear to have one. On the other hand, with a little luck, proper timing, and a good promotion program, a bag of asafetida with a unique chemical side chain can be made to look like a wonder drug. The illusion may not last, but it frequently lasts long enough. By the time the doctor learns what the company knew at the beginning, it has two new products to take the place of the old one."

During the hearing, just how much promotional weight was applied to doctors was enumerated. Walter L. Griffith, director of promotion for Parke-Davis, had given the following figures to the American College of Apothecaries in 1959: the prescription drug industry had turned out "3,790,908,000 pages of paid journal advertising" and "741,213,700 direct-mail impressions," while its detail men had made between 18 million and 20 million calls on physicians and pharmacists all in one year. After reviewing the record, Kefauver concluded that the promotional effort had essentially one purpose—to plant trade names firmly in the minds of doctors.

And where was the FDA in all of this? If the agency were an official arm of the drug industry, it could not have been more quiet, puzzled, and embarrassed. And the FDA had advance warning of what was coming; Kefauver, Till, and Blair were in the entourage from Capitol Hill that previewed the hearing for the FDA leadership.

Some years later Deputy Commissioner Winton Rankin said he and other officers of the agency had no idea how far out of touch with the pharmaceutical revolution the agency had gotten. "The agency didn't know how much catching up needed to be done." It has been highly unusual for a member of the Senate to visit a regulatory agency, rather than simply calling up officials of the agency and demanding their presence. But Kefauver was a courtly man. He told the assembled FDA leadership that he was interested in legislation that would deal with the problems of prescription drugs. But, Rankin reported, "Larrick didn't want to have a darn thing to do with Kefauver's bill. He saw it as just a lot of trouble for Food and Drug that was not going to help the agency." He added, "We didn't believe we were going to get any legislation through Mr. Kefauver." The attitude was not belligerent toward the senator exactly, he said, "ah, perhaps tolerant would be the word? 'Let's humor the gentleman and he'll go away eventually when he finds out he can't get any law!' " He, Commissioner Larrick, and the others in top jobs there began the hearings thinking the subject of drug prices and industry promotion practices were isolated. As he put it, "Fine, Mr. Kefauver, you've got an interesting investigation, but what's it got to do with the FDA?" Later, as it became apparent that Kefauver *was* having some considerable impact on the Hill, Rankin said, there was still no impulse to help him.

One subject raised during the senator's visit to the FDA was the all-important one of brand names. Kefauver thought there was a chance that if the FDA were given the power to name drugs, the agency could assign sensible, memorable names to the generic chemicals, and cut short the branding of drugs. At the very least, the agency could stop the practice of allowing generics to be given difficult-to-remember names. FDA officials smirked at the idea. Rankin said the FDA officials did not understand the importance of names at all. His explanation was that the agency, "for more than fifty years, had gone on the strong belief that it didn't have anything to do with prices [or, presumably, names associated with them]. It was just concerned with the quality, the purity, and truthful labeling of foods and drugs." In addition, he "saw no reason why the agency should be saddled with this extra duty and it obviously would have been a very time-consuming duty."

Another change suggested by Kefauver was that authoritative information to doctors about the relative quality and drawbacks of all drugs should not come only from the companies but from some impartial source as well—the FDA. Again, agency officials did not object, exactly, but failed to understand the proposal. "We opposed that," Rankin said. "It was our view that the package insert [written by the companies] could serve adequately. . . ."

It was also proposed that the FDA could more easily exercise authority over the drug companies if each one was licensed, and the license was subject to review or revocation, as is usual in most other areas of commerce. But again, Rankin said, "We did not support that. . . ." He said it was "too drastic a remedy." Even when it was suggested that the FDA determine by scientific tests, or at least review of scientific tests, which drugs were effective and which were not, FDA officials were at first divided. Some saw that putting medicine and regulation on a firmly rational footing would be a significant social advance, but others worried that such an action would challenge not only the largely useless products that constituted a substantial part of the market, but also those people whose judgments then reigned.

Kefauver came away from the meetings at the FDA without illusions about the position of Larrick and his deputies. He believed that regulatory agencies were often run for, if not by, those they are supposed to be regulating. Just then, as if on cue, one of the most egregious sorts of conflict of interest was brewing inside the FDA.

According to Rankin, the first indication of trouble came in a *Saturday Review* article by Lear, who mentioned without details that Dr. Henry Welch, chief of the antibiotics division, had taken substantial amounts of money from drug companies for "extracurricular" work. After the article appeared in the fall of 1959, before the Kefauver hearings began, Deputy FDA Commissioner John Harvey questioned Welch about the payments. Welch refused to talk. Harvey, surprised and disturbed, solicited the help of Rankin and Robert Roe, head of scientific affairs and Welch's immediate superior. The three told Larrick that if Welch wouldn't even say what he'd done, they felt he could no longer remain with the agency. Surprisingly, Larrick responded that Welch was a friend and that he would do nothing wrong.

So a short time later it was not news within the agency when Welch's corruption was itemized in public at a congressional hearing. Rankin was present when Kefauver listed the details. Welch had received at least (the true total was not known) $287,000 from drug companies from 1953 to

1960. That was more than his total FDA salary for the period. Welch had accepted myriad industry suggestions about how to decide difficult issues. A committee of the FDA said his judgment as an FDA official had not been influenced by money. But Rankin said frankly, "I don't believe it. I think that was not a correct finding. I don't think a man can go about acquiring the kind of money that he was acquiring . . . without having it influence his official judgment." Welch was removed from the FDA after the Kefauver revelations. Larrick was not.

Meanwhile, Dr. Barbara Moulton, a medical officer at the FDA for five years, had become increasingly disturbed by how heavily weighted the drug review process was toward the companies. She had to face repeated meetings with, and criticisms from, industry executives. In fact, she said, the officers of the companies had more influence with the top FDA officials than the agency's own medical officers. She recalled before the committee one moment when after a review of the company data, she had serious worries about the safety of a tranquilizing drug. But as she was explaining this to *four* representatives of the company, her superior showed up, sat down, and told the industry reps that the agency would release the drug without any proof of safety over longtime use and before the company's pharmacological studies were finished.

On another occasion, when she was concerned about the addictive properties of another tranquilizer, she asked the company involved to consider sending out a warning to doctors. This time, another of her superiors told her the request was inappropriate. He told her, "I will not have my policy of friendliness with the industry interfered with." Moulton was demoted and eventually forced out.

The Kefauver hearings ran their course through 1960 and into 1961. Dr. Walter Modell, editor of the journal *Clinical Pharmacology and Therapeutics,* said that drugs were being released without rigorous testing, and the resulting damage to patients was far too frequent. Twenty-four drugs had been approved and then had to be recalled. There was, he said, "a short-sighted view of all the effects; faulty experiments; premature publication; too-vigorous promotion; exaggerated claims and careless use—in brief, a break in the scientific approach."

Kefauver wanted to force the FDA through legislation to hew closer to the scientific approach, to require that the generic names of drugs appear on every label, even if a brand name was also there. This would clarify for both doctors and patients just what the medication was, and would tend to level the commercial playing field. He would require manufacturers to include warnings about the known hazardous side effects of their drugs on labels or package inserts. He wanted to make sure that each company making drugs for public consumption had a license, and that the license would be reviewed periodically. He also included in his proposed bill a provision that the FDA should consider the effectiveness of a drug as well as its safety in deciding whether it should be permitted on the market. The logic was simple, and agreed to, in principle, by all parties—if two drugs had similar side effects, but one worked effectively and the other failed to alleviate the illness, they were not comparable. One could be permitted on the market because it had a benefit along with a risk.

The secretary of health, education and welfare at the time, Abraham Ribicoff, suggested the proposed reforms would advance human protections greatly.

Richard Nixon was given the job of attacking the Kefauver bill for the Republicans, and he objected to the bill on the grounds that it would continue the erosion of individual (read: business) liberties and turn more power over to the centralized national bureaucracy. Ribicoff and Nixon were both correct. But the bill would also give an additional measure of protection to citizens from harm that had been demonstrated to be real for some tens of thousands in the case of chloramphenicol and other problem drugs of the 1950s. While supporters and opponents lined up more or less predictably, the AMA took the position that allowing the FDA to use stricter scientific standards would rob doctors of their authority. One *Newsweek* columnist virtually stated their position: "It is a dangerous legal precedent to allow any bureaucrat to keep off the market something that, even though harmless, is in his opinion 'ineffective.' This is trying to protect the patient against the judgment of his doctor, trying to protect the consumer against his own judgment. Efficacy can be determined only by freedom of trial, and in no other way."

This argument creates the image of a bureaucrat's interfering with a doctor's efforts to get important drugs to the patient. It suggests that scientific studies are not important, and only "freedom of trial" can determine whether a drug works. Such trials do not exist. Doctors dispensing drugs are not researchers. The columnist was suggesting that there should be no judgment made, *except by companies,* as to whether a drug should go on the market. At the moment the columnist was writing, what was happening with antibiotics exemplified the problem and made clear why scientific standards needed to be established. The National Academy of Sciences and other expert groups had concluded more than once that antibiotics don't work to cure viral illnesses such as colds and flu, and that drugs sold for that purpose should be pulled from the market. There was simply no case to be made for the continued use of penicillin to treat colds.

But doctors had been using penicillin that way for years. Accordingly, companies had been making and selling hundreds of preparations, some of them over-the-counter cold preparations, some of them prescription drugs; doctors had prescribed them, and patients had spent money on them. Where was the harm in letting doctors give these drugs to patients, columnists asked, even if they *are* useless? They make the patient feel that the doctor is doing something, which has a beneficial effect.

But, of course, all drugs are only *relatively* safe. The danger of giving antibiotics is, first, that antibiotics do have side effects. In a handful of cases every year, patients are killed or severely injured by taking ordinary, "safe" antibiotics. No one should take an antibiotic needlessly. Second, widespread use of antibiotics when they are not needed allows various disease germs to become resistant, so the drugs will not work when they *are* needed. The number of disease germs that are gaining the power to resist many different antibiotics has been rising steadily. For instance, while cancer treatments have given additional life to many patients, the anti-cancer drugs leave the patients vulnerable to infection. The patients then take antibiotics to save themselves. But currently 15 percent of these cancer patients die because of germs that have become resistant to antibiotics.

There is social and cultural damage done as well by the attitude of the laissez-faire doctors, columnists, and companies. It breeds contempt for the underlying science. Moreover, without a citizen-protection agency to evaluate information and make some choices based on the data, that authority is given to those who have both a vested interest and an extensive record of bad judgments—drug companies that profit from drug sales.

Companies were stunned by the Kefauver hearings and the rising criticism of company practices. Dr. Louis Lasagna of the University of Rochester, who had campaigned for better data and more scientific tests of drugs, described the point of view of the drug companies at this time:

> Most people—in and out of the medical profession—were not unhappy about the state of affairs at that time. The drug industry, certainly, was riding high, as were the men in the sales and advertising professions who directed drug promotion. Doctors and their patients had available to them a large number of new drugs that could add comfort to the lives of many and were indeed life-saving.

Suddenly, this apparently peaceful and prosperous scene was shattered by a series of attacks—from journalists such as John Lear of the *Saturday Review*, and from the well-publicized efforts of congressional groups, including the Blatnik, Kefauver, Celler and Harris committees. The drug industry, which had come to think of itself as both successful and respected, found its officials accused of everything from overpricing to fraud. The FDA and certain clinical investigators were criticized sharply for ineptitude or dishonesty, or both. The practical physician, long accustomed to the praises of society, was portrayed as an uncritical dupe.

By March 1962, Kefauver had made a tremendous impression with his hearing but was losing the battle for votes to reform the medical industry. His worst defeat came from the Kennedy White House. Because of some previous bad blood between Kefauver and Kennedy, and differences over some provisions of the bill, there was little desire to throw the great prize of presidential support to Kefauver. Rather, health officials were ordered to write their own bill and set it in motion.

Richard Harris interviewed one top White House official who said, "Estes is disliked in a lot of quarters because he's such a lone wolf—and, what's worse, a reformer. . . . [The President] doesn't want to get involved in anything controversial, and just about everything that Kefauver puts his hand to is controversial." So, in his "consumer message" of 1962, the president mentioned as being worthy of action measures that were in Kefauver's drug bill, but he did not mention drug company prices, the bill itself, or Kefauver. Within a short time, the bill was set aside in Senate committees, and it appeared to be permanently interred. Four of the senators from the South who hated Kefauver for his civil rights stance—Sam Ervin, James Eastland, John McClellan, and J. Bennett Johnston—gave the funeral orations.

The industry was now admitting to members of the Kennedy administration, privately, that some reforms might be necessary. As is the practice among smarter industry lobbyists, once it is clear that reform has been killed, the industry works avidly to seek a "stopper" bill—that is, one that looks like reform but really changes nothing. The object is to appear to have responded to the call for reform. Apropos, lawyers for the drug industry, chiefly Lloyd Cutler, drew up an industry-friendly bill and gave it to Senator Eastland, the powerful chairman of the Judiciary Committee, the parent committee to Senator Kefauver's antitrust subcommittee. Eastland was sympathetic but said Kefauver would take him apart if he took a bill so obviously industry-bent to the floor. So instead, when the White House called Eastland asking for action on the drug bill, he cleverly said he was ready to deal. He scheduled a meeting in a conference room of the Judiciary Committee for the negotiations. Kefauver was not invited or informed.

Present were the staff members of Senator Eastland's committee, three lobbyists for industry, one rep from the Department of Health, Education and Welfare, Jerome Sonosky, and Food and Drug Administration lawyer Theodore Ellenbogen. Sonosky and Ellenbogen, completely outgunned, were representing the Kennedy administration. They soon found themselves talking only to Lloyd Cutler.

The group started with the thin gruel of the industry's counter-Kefauver bill, not the Kefauver legislation. When Sonosky looked at the language drafted by the industry, he realized that whatever assurances the companies had made in public about being cooperative, in this bill the industry had compromised on nothing. "Not an inch!" Sonosky said. At the end of the day of "negotiation," Sonosky reported that he and Ellenbogen had fought fiercely and come out thinking that the bill represented no progress, but at least it would not be a step backward in drug laws. Reform seemed dead, if not yet interred. The Kefauver bill was crumpled and was sailing toward the wastebasket when the situation suddenly changed. A drug called thalidomide deflected the bill, and history.

•

CHAPTER TEN

Thalidomide

THE SOURCE of thalidomide and other drug disasters was a subsidiary of the Vick Chemical Company, the well-known producer of Vick's cough drops and Vick's VapoRub. The company had long been a fierce opponent of regulation. Its products had not been medical drugs for the most part. In fact, Vick had little knowledge of medicine, no top-rank scientists, and no laboratory dedicated to medical research. But it did own large production plants and a national promotion and distribution network that might be made to carry drugs as well as cough drops. As a result of this combination of inexperience and boldness, Vick and its subsidiary, Richardson-Merrell, Inc., muffed its first few products as it tried to join in the profits of the pharmaceutical revolution. And in no small way, either.

Researchers at the time had discovered a strong link between high levels of cholesterol in the blood and the onset of heart disease. Just how these two things were related was not known, but many assumed that taking in high levels of cholesterol in the diet led directly to disease. Richardson-Merrell decided to try to make and sell a substance that would lower cholesterol in the blood. The result was the company's first major drug, MER-29. Chemically, it was called triparanol. Richardson-Merrell would later call it the "first safe agent to inhibit body-produced cholesterol. . . . [and] the first to lower excess cholesterol levels in both tissue and serum, *irrespective of diet.*" The company eventually would suggest that people who liked high-cholesterol foods could eat them without worry, as long as they took MER-29 regularly, like vitamins, for life. The company estimated that if it could persuade consumers to use the drug this way, it could make $4.25 billion a year (in 1950s dollars).

Researchers at the company gave the drug to twenty-seven rats and three monkeys, then immediately put it into the hands of physicians to try out on their patients. The FDA pharmacologist E. I. Goldenthal was assigned to review the case, and after looking at the skimpy data, opposed letting the drug on the market. He said there wasn't any proof it worked, but there was a significant risk to patients. "There is little margin of safety," he wrote to his supervisor, medical officer Frank J. Talbot. "This compound is producing toxic effects [including eye damage, liver changes, loss of sexual function, and suspected deaths] at relatively low doses." He said the company needed to carry out careful trials over several years before the answers to the questions of its safety and effectiveness could be answered.

Talbot overruled Goldenthal. At the time, medical officers could approve a drug essentially on their own authority. To turn one down, however, required the unanimous support of the medical officer, the lawyers, the chief of the drug branch, the chief medical director, and the commissioner. This was because the 1938 law said a drug was automatically approved unless the FDA, for good reasons, stopped it. Thus, the legal burden was on the FDA. In this case, Talbot said he decided to let the drug on the market on the basis of speculation: "My thinking was that here was a drug purporting to lower cholesterol. We were dealing with a highly lethal disease state. . . . This drug might be helpful in dealing with the No. 1 killer of men."

He was led to the belief that it might be effective, he said later, by a paper he heard presented at a medical meeting. It suggested that MER-29 was among the more effective drugs to lower cholesterol. So, within nine weeks of getting the application, Talbot approved the drug. As it turned out, and he later acknowledged, the paper he heard presented at the meeting was wrong. The author withdrew the data and it was never published. Deputy Commissioner John Harvey also said later it was clear that the drug should never have been approved. But the FDA in those times was working very hard to get along, and there had been much fussing about how much data a government agency could require from a private company.

The drug went to market in April 1960. There were protests from some doctors, and criticism from perhaps the only independent, thoughtful voice in medicine, *The Medical Letter*. By June came reports that in studies done by university scientists the drug caused cataracts in animals. The first report of cataracts in humans came in August 1961. A second came in October from the Mayo Clinic. In addition, studies sent to the FDA showed that numerous stillborn litters were produced when doses were increased in animal studies. Doctors within the agency began to pressure Commissioner Larrick to take the drug off the market.

At first Larrick feared he did not have the authority to do that; it was not easy under the 1938 law. The agency could take a drug off the market only if there was proof of a serious hazard, and he felt the warning signs did not amount to proof. Instead Larrick negotiated with the company for some weeks, with the result that side effects seen in animal tests would now be described on the label. Larrick also got the company to send a letter warning doctors to be on the lookout for similar effects in people. By January 1962, a survey of MER-29 users showed cataracts were appearing at about three times the normal rate in patients using the drug. MER-29 remained on the market.

That winter an FDA inspector not involved in the drug business, Thomas M. Rice, shared a ride from a Cincinnati suburb into the city with another man not involved in the drug case, Larson Jordan, who worked for the telephone company. During the ride Jordan said that his wife had worked at Richardson-Merrell in the scientific labs, but quit in disgust when she learned how much cheating was going on at the company. Rice asked if he could chat with Jordan's wife about her experiences.

On February 27 he forwarded a report to FDA headquarters on his talks with Mrs. Jordan. Within days, two FDA investigators, John Nestor and E. I. Goldenthal—both of whom had suspicions about MER-29— were dispatched to the company's Cincinnati plant. They found that the data showing how safe the drug was had been faked. Monkeys were never given doses that were reported in some cases, and in other cases the doses were smaller than reported. The experiment was said to have lasted sixteen months; in fact it went on for seven months. The animals developed blood disorders and ovarian trouble, resulting in drastically reduced litter sizes; the company scientists reported they were all healthy.

With the evidence of felonies in hand, Larrick was able to convince Richardson-Merrell executives to voluntarily remove the drug from the market. Meanwhile, Merrell had acquired another potential blockbuster drug, one it called MER-32, thalidomide.

Merrell did not invent thalidomide. The company bought it from a German company, Chemie Grünenthal. In Germany it was easy to bring untested drugs to the market, as regulations were primitive. On the basis of a handful of lab reports and testimonials, the drug not only went to market there in 1957 but was sold as a nonprescription, over-the-counter product.

The drug had some attractive commercial properties. From the data the company sent out, it appeared to be a strong sedative that was also remarkably safe. Sedatives have a great variety of uses, from bringing on calm and sleep to reducing the nausea associated with pregnancy. With this one, Grünenthal felt it could solve a serious problem that had developed with drugs already on the market as sedatives. Barbiturates and their relatives were very effective, but they were also very dangerous; they became the method of choice for thousands of suicides each year. What was needed was a drug that could calm people without danger. When Chemie Grünenthal's scientists said they had found a drug that was almost as powerful as a barbiturate but with no noticeable side effects, company executives were elated.

It was soon on sale in England, from Distillers Limited, because no serious confirmation of the drug's effectiveness or safety was required. In the United States, the first company to take the drug seriously was Smith, Kline and French, which began testing it. The company had a professional staff and had taken the mandate of the new era of scientific drugs seriously. They *wanted* to know whether the drug worked and whether it had side effects. Their results were at odds with Grünenthal's glowing reports. They found that it was not comparable to barbiturates in its sedative effects, but more like a mild tranquilizer such as Miltown. Moreover, this effect was achieved only at high doses. In any case, they saw a flawed drug that didn't live up to its producers' claims. The company declined to buy the American license. Grünenthal then approached Lederle. It, too, declined the drug. Finally, Grünenthal found the eager Vick Chemical Company and its subsidiary, Richardson-Merrell.

As we look back now, thanks in part to a team of reporters from the *Sunday Times* of London, it is clear that the marketing of thalidomide can be attributed to a series of failures that included weak regulations in Germany and England, irresponsible promotion by the German drugmaker, and inexperience and market aggression on the part of Merrell. The investigators demonstrated that the greatest failure probably took place in Germany, at the Grünenthal laboratory of Dr. Heinrich Mueckter in the town of Stolberg-am-Rhein.

Mueckter, who joined the firm after a stint in the German army's virus-research program, was not trained in drug research. He worked under Wilhelm Kunz, a pharmacist with no research or medical training, whose job it was to find a breakthrough drug for Grünenthal. Kunz and Mueckter tried out many new chemicals and found thalidomide by 1954.

Some of their earliest tests on rodents were startling, or so they reported. The drug appeared to put the animals in a state of calmness, if not sleep, at a low dose. When the researchers checked the drug's toxicity, they could not find any, they said. Subsequent tests of the drug's toxicity have shown greatly varying results, but all later tests have found some significant toxic effects. Still, it was Grünenthal's original data that was broadcast widely and was the basis for the claim made around the world from 1955 to 1962 that the drug was a "completely safe" sedative.

The company had begun experiments on humans in 1955 by sending the drug to a number of doctors in Germany. The *Times* investigators reported that in December of that year the company called together all those who had tried it and prepared reports of their experience. This sort of casual collection of data would now be unacceptable, as it had no blinded studies and no controlled experiments; there were "studies" in which some doctors kept precise numbers and some did not, in which some gave one dose and some another, in which some gave the pill for a day and others regularly for some weeks (though none gave it over a longer term).

In that December meeting the doctors, who had been paid by the company to carry out the tests, reported that the drug was an effective sedative but also produced an array of consistent and dangerous side effects. They found that taking the drug left an unpleasantly strong grogginess and "hangover" in many patients the next morning. Several doctors reported more dangerous signs—dizziness, nervousness, wakefulness, and giddiness—all indications that the drug was attacking the nerves in some patients.

Some of the doctors who tested the drug told the company they didn't want to use it anymore, that the company needed to conduct more experiments before releasing it. Others, like Dr. Herman Jung, a paid consultant, described it in glowing terms: "We have a substance that, at the correct dose level, has no undesirable side effects. I believe that [thalidomide] is a satisfactory drug and that with the necessary promotion it will succeed in the pharmaceutical market." In papers afterward, the company reported the positive information and completely ignored the negative. It reported its confidence in the drug to officials, who quickly permitted it on the market without need of a prescription.

It went on sale October 1, 1957, under the brand name Contergan in Germany. In other countries the name varied slightly, and in Sweden it was sold, literally, as the "Babysitter" drug, to be used by children as an aid to their harried mothers. Massive promotion began in Europe and

Africa. More than twenty nations began use of the drug between 1958 and 1960.

The first negative report came to Chemie Grünenthal in December 1958 from Dr. Gustav Smaltz of Frankfurt. He reported neurological symptoms of giddiness and loss of balance in his patients taking the drug, the *Times* investigators reported. The company wrote back to him, "We feel obliged to say that this is the first time such side effects have been reported to us. . . ." This was false, of course. Throughout 1958 and 1959, as the drug's sales quadrupled, the reports sent to the company about side effects increased.

Some of what was reported was familiar by now, and some was not, including symptoms called peripheral neuropathy. This is a disorder that signals serious poisoning of the nerves. It usually appears first in the hands or feet, with a tingling sensation and a feeling of numbness or cold. It progresses to cramps, weakness, and a loss of strength such that patients find it difficult to walk because they cannot judge the position of their feet at any moment. The symptoms may recede, but in some cases the damage is irreversible.

One Swiss company distributing the drug wrote to Grünenthal that twenty doctors had reported symptoms in their patients of hangover, dizziness, and trembling of the hands. One doctor, the Swiss company reported, gave the drug to his wife and said later, "Once and never again. This is a terrible drug." Grünenthal was still not listening. Even after this and other reports, company officers wrote to a doctor worried about the peripheral neuropathy his patient developed after taking the drug: "Happily we can tell you that such disadvantageous effects have not been brought to our notice." In the company's promotions for the beginning of 1960, it told doctors and patients buying the over-the-counter package that the drug was "non-toxic" and "completely harmless even for infants."

When Grünenthal found Richardson-Merrell in 1958, it met a kindred spirit—financially aggressive, inexperienced in drug work, and not too concerned with medical issues. Richardson-Merrell was willing to bring the drug to market in the United States without *any* testing. The company signed the licensing papers that year, and on February 2, 1959, according to the *Times* team, one Richardson-Merrell executive reviewing the situation noted, "We have no specific human safety data. We will have to collect them partly for our own information and partly to satisfy the Food and Drug Administration." Nine days later, the company was giving the drug to patients, including pregnant women, without testing even in animals.

Because testing was still a matter of some discretion for companies, as the law did not specify what was needed, many companies took differing approaches. Ironically, just at the time thalidomide was making its way to the market through Richardson-Merrell, another American company, Hoffmann-LaRoche, was working on a different type of sedative, Librium. It was a sedative that was effective, and had mild side effects. Hoffmann-LaRoche did the tests to prove it. In fact, it went a step further. Since the drug was likely to be used by women, even pregnant women, the company tested to determine if it might cause birth defects. It didn't. The birth defect testing was done a year before thalidomide came into Richardson-Merrell's hands.

When Richardson-Merrell executives decided to sell their drug not only as a general sedative, but specifically to treat the nausea of early pregnancy, they found themselves without any information on how the drug might affect women and fetuses. Rather than conduct appropriate tests, however, they decided to take the public relations approach—they would have a doctor write an article declaring that the drug worked well in pregnancy. When an editor at the *Journal of Obstetrics and Gynecology* received the proposal for an article, he told the company that it would be necessary at least to find out if the drug crossed the placental barrier into the fetus before suggesting the drug was safe. The FDA also asked for this information. But the company hadn't done the necessary testing and had no idea. It was not, as it was later alleged, that such testing could not be done. In fact, as the *Times* report showed, Richardson-Merrell itself had done such tests on MER-29 and included a warning against its use by pregnant women. It is not known why the company avoided such a test or warning in the case of thalidomide.

After the company started distributing the drug to doctors for "testing" in patients, the results of the animal studies began to come back. Unlike the Grünenthal data that showed the drug harmless, Richardson-Merrell's animals were dying rapidly. Of eleven mice, six died. Then twenty-two out of thirty male rats tested died the same day. Fearing that rats were oversensitive to the drug, they gave it to a dog. Two hours later, the dog began having seizures and vomited. It became calm for a time, and then went through a period of severe agitation. The next morning it was found dead.

Nevertheless, the company had a schedule to keep if it was to put this drug on the market by early 1961. So the company continued to press its "testing" campaign in humans. The drug was sent out in what would have been the largest human drug trial ever conducted in the United

States. Two and a half million tablets were sent out to 1,267 doctors, who in turn gave them to about 20,000 patients. (Previously the largest experiments had involved about 5,000 patients and 200 doctors.) The results from such a huge experiment would have been extraordinary, and probably could have yielded information in very fine detail about the action of the drug, except that the company didn't actually collect the data. The marketing department, not the medical department, ran the "trial." The salesmen were instructed that when they gave the drug to a doctor for "testing" they were not to offer placebo look-alikes as well, which would have been needed if a doctor wanted to run a carefully controlled test. The salesmen were also told not to offer consent forms that doctors needed to fill in when giving patients experimental drugs.

The company's internal documents, quoted in the *Times* investigation, make clear the marketing emphasis. The "Objective of the Job" brochure given to salesmen said they were to "contact teaching hospitals . . . for the purpose of selling them on Kevadon [Richardson-Merrell's trade name for the drug] and providing them with a clinical supply." The salesmen were duly loaded up with data about their competition, the barbiturates, and how dangerous they were, including figures for accidental overdoses and suicides. "Bear in mind," the salesmen were told, "that these are not basic clinical research studies. We have firmly established the safety, dosage and usefulness of Kevadon both by foreign and US laboratory and clinical studies. The program is designed to get widespread confirmation of its usefulness. . . ." They were told that doctors should be assured that they "need not report results if they don't want to."

To give one example from later court documents of how doctors reacted, Dr. Roy Nulsen, an obstetrician in Cincinnati, was a friend of one Richardson-Merrell executive, so he agreed to give his patients the drug. He had done similar "testing" before and was familiar with the routine. He didn't keep a record of how many pills he dispensed or to whom. He testified that "the girls in the office" filled out questionnaires on how the patients were doing. After a time the company asked him to write up a report for a medical journal on his success with the use of thalidomide in pregnant women. He agreed. As it happened, Nulsen did not actually write the article but let the medical director of Richardson-Merrell, Dr. Raymond C. Pogge, write it. Nulsen merely signed it. He later testified that the data on the mothers and babies he treated was not actually written down, but rather communicated to Pogge "by telephone . . . or it may have been that we had lunch together, or it may have been when we played golf." Pogge wrote that the drug was known to be safe for the fetus, but that it was not actually known whether it crossed the placental barrier or not. The journal that had raised the question accepted this answer.

The company had not yet spoken to the FDA, nor did law require them to. Under the 1938 law, doctors could experiment on patients with new drugs, in any numbers and with any chemical, so long as they called the work an experiment. There was also no requirement that patients give their consent to be part of the experiment. They were simply given the drug.

The application to officially market thalidomide in the United States was sent to the FDA in September 1960, seven months after the company began to distribute the drug to doctors. The application was handed to Dr. Frances Oldham Kelsey as her first drug approval. Kelsey, forty-eight, was a thin and shy woman, a mother of two, soft-spoken but self-confident nonetheless. She had the proper training for the job—she had an M.D., and a Ph.D. in pharmacology from the University of Chicago. It had been decided that, since she was new to the job, she should be given a simple, straightforward kind of case. This was just a sleeping pill, one that was already on the market in other countries, where there didn't seem to be any problem. Of course Grünenthal and Richardson-Merrell had simply decided not to report problems, the *Times* found, and doctors on their own, chiefly in Germany, had not yet made a loud-enough cry to reach the ears of those at the FDA.

But Kelsey did not like what she saw in the application before her. "I must say I was shocked at the caliber of work that would go into these applications in support of safety," she recollected. The Kevadon application made large claims, most of them unsupported. "The claims were just glowing, too good to be true," she said. The reports from clinics were short of data; as she noted, "they were really more testimonials than scientific studies." The application was filled with pseudoscientific jargon that was beside the point, raising in FDA reviewers' minds a question as to whether the Richardson-Merrell scientists knew what they were talking about. The application relied heavily on citations from foreign drug studies, which on inspection were themselves lacking key information. There were no long-term studies, such as use for a year. The animal data was sketchy. Under the law, Kelsey had sixty days to tell Richardson-Merrell if she objected to the marketing of the drug.

Kelsey consulted with several colleagues on it and then asked the company for more information. That quickly brought the company's fire, in the person of Dr. Joseph Murray, a fierce advocate who had no compunctions about calling, writing, and visiting FDA personnel to lobby for his company, or about calling Kelsey's superiors to get her to act in Richardson-Merrell's favor. The pressure didn't work. Kelsey was able to raise enough serious questions about the shoddy scientific work to delay the application as the true data from Germany and Britain was beginning to surface.

In February 1961, FDA researchers combing the world's medical literature found a letter from a doctor in the December 31, 1960, issue of the *British Medical Journal*. It described peripheral neuropathy in patients taking thalidomide. Kelsey wondered if the loss of sensation in these patients was enough by itself to hold up the approval. She was told it was, and then a colleague, Dr. John Archer, suggested to Kelsey that the nerve damage might mean much more—the possibility of birth defects. Drugs that attack nerves, as this one clearly did, often caused birth defects. This possibility was raised verbally and in writing with Richardson-Merrell at least twice during 1961. Kelsey asked the company for proof that the drug was safe in pregnancy. The company had none.

The pressure from Richardson-Merrell increased. It sent doctors who had some "experience" with the drug to talk to the FDA. One of those who lobbied to get thalidomide to the market was Dr. Louis Lasagna, who had once been a critic of poor medical studies but had since begun selling his services to drug company clients.

Ralph Smith, head of the FDA division of new drugs, backed up Kelsey and her colleagues. The company executives were furious, but they would have to find out more about the drug. Murray and another Richardson-Merrell executive flew to Britain and Germany for briefings by scientists from the British licensee, Distillers Limited, and Grünenthal itself. They were informed that thalidomide *did* have real toxicity, and that in experiments mice were routinely killed by it. They were told that the drug caused peripheral neuropathy. They were also told that there were only thirty-four reported cases, and that the nerve damage was reversible. These statements were false; at the time, Grünenthal had more than four hundred reports of nerve damage in its files, the *Times* investigators found, and evidence of numerous cases in which the damage was not reversible but appeared permanent and debilitating.

When Kelsey and Richardson-Merrell executives met again, she listened to their recitation of the rarity and reversibility of the effects. Kelsey said she now had a report from a doctor in California of a case in which the damage had not been reversed after the patient stopped taking the drug. She told them what should have been clear to all from the beginning: the drug was not lifesaving, and not greatly more useful than other drugs on the market. Thus, she said, it would be "highly unexcusable" to put out a drug with such potentially serious side effects.

The company, now many months past its planned rollout in March 1961, demanded to know when the FDA expected to approve the drug. Smith called the company to inform them that there was no way to know when or if the drug would be approved, and that in the meantime a warning must be put on packages being sent to doctors for testing, saying that pregnant women should not be given the drug. By this time, Richardson-Merrell executives had called, written, or met with Kelsey more than fifty times that were recorded, and they were now threatening to go to the commissioner to have her reassigned.

By the fall of 1961, however, Grünenthal had already begun quietly to settle lawsuits brought by European patients who had taken thalidomide. By this time, doctors had reported the births of numerous deformed babies directly to the company, and though Grünenthal withheld that information, it did send notices to Richardson-Merrell and other licensees documenting that peripheral neuropathy was being reported in greater numbers of patients. Grünenthal did not give numbers, but by that date it had 2,400 cases on record and was estimating that at least 4,000 had occurred. German doctors now criticizing the company said the figure was nearer 40,000. Grünenthal urged licensees in Europe and other developed nations to stop using the word "non-toxic" with regard to the drug. Drugs sold in Africa, however, continued to carry the label "completely harmless."

The real horror was still making its way slowly to the fore. The first "thalidomide baby" was apparently born in Germany sometime in 1957. The syndrome was one sometimes seen naturally, and carried the name phocomelia—meaning "seal limbs." These grossly deformed babies had many problems, but the signature defect was the absence of long bones in the arms and legs, which meant that the hands and feet or just the fingers and toes of the infants sprang directly from the trunk. It was a hideous deformity to expectant parents. In the disorder, it was also common for the baby to be born with no bowel opening, no ear openings, and segmented intestines. Of course, many of those with the disorder died and were never counted as thalidomide babies.

The occurrence of phocomelia in Germany up to the time of thalidomide was estimated to be about one case in 100,000 births, meaning that most doctors never saw it. But by 1961, the rate had risen to about one in every 500 births—200 times greater than normally, and very noticeable to doctors. Reports that this side effect was occurring began in the spring of 1961, and were passed on to the company headquarters of Distillers and Grünenthal, one by one, for months.

The companies had kept it quiet until finally, at a conference of pediatricians in Germany, Dr. Widukind Lenz of Hamburg, who had repeatedly reported occurrences of the syndrome to Grünenthal, and who found himself followed by detectives and harassed by lawyers, finally decided to tell other doctors. The number of cases of phocomelia, he said, had rocketed in Germany. He said he had found eight cases himself, and estimated that more than forty more had occurred in Hamburg alone in September and October 1961. The only common factor he had found in the new cases was thalidomide. In checking back through the records, he found that, from 1930 to 1955 in Hamburg, among the more than 210,000 recorded births, only one case of phocomelia had been reported.

On November 18, 1961, the news finally broke in public. A reporter for *Welt am Sonntag* reported on Lenz's paper and statistics under the headline "Malformations from Tablets—Alarming Suspicion of Physicians on Globally Distributed Drug." By November 27, Grünenthal had pulled the drug off the market, blaming the sensationalism of the press. "Because press reports have undermined the basis of scientific discussion . . . we have decided to withdraw Contergan from the market immediately." Richardson-Merrell heard the news two days later, on November 29. Murray called Kelsey and told her the drug had been withdrawn in Germany. Kelsey asked why. Birth defects, he said. He added that he hoped the association was coincidental.

The German and British companies did not admit there was a problem with the drug. They took the position that it was purely speculation, and those who were carrying on the speculation were to blame, such as the "half-wit" (the German company used the word) Lenz. Scientists in several countries now began to investigate the phenomenon, and soon the evidence against the drug was documented in many journal articles reporting not only large numbers of cases of phocomelia in babies whose mothers had taken the drug, but also numerous detailed studies of animals in which birth abnormalities were observed. None of this was made public in the United States. The FDA knew, however, and a cable describing the birth defect epidemic was sent to the State Department.

Commissioner Larrick was frozen. He made no announcement. He did not move to have all the pills rounded up as other commissioners had in other crises. Was the company right in saying there was really no connection between the drug and the deformed babies? Did he have the authority to act? After all, the agency hadn't approved the drug. Finally, he decided to ask Richardson-Merrell what it wanted to do. The company, he was told, wanted to send a letter to doctors. And so it did:

> Dear Doctor,
> We have received information from abroad on the occurrence of congenital malformations in the offspring of a few mothers who had taken thalidomide . . . early in pregnancies. It is impossible at this time to determine whether, in fact, there is any causal relationship. However, until definitive information is available to us, as a precaution, we are adding the following contraindication to the use of Kevadon: Kevadon should not be administered to pregnant women or to premenopausal women who may become pregnant. We are actively following this matter and you will be advised when it is finally determined whether or not this precautionary step was necessary.

The letter sent in December reached only about 10 percent of the doctors who had been giving thalidomide to patients in the Richardson-Merrell "clinical trials." Letters to other investigators and other doctors did not go out until several months later, March 1962. Kelsey gradually became alarmed as she learned that the company was not taking the situation seriously. By April she convinced FDA officials to at least get a list of doctors who had been in the "clinical trials." The company did not have one; it sent to the FDA a list of about 1,000 of the more than 1,200 who actually had been in the program. Two hundred forty-one of the doctors were obstetricians. Kelsey was working to convince her boss and Commissioner Larrick that the evidence against the drug was far stronger than the company said, and the agency must act. By May it had still not done so.

By that time, the fraud committed by Richardson-Merrell executives in the case of MER-29 was known, and in a confidential memo that circulated within the FDA, agency officials were warned to take no statement by a Richardson-Merrell official at face value—every assertion needed to be checked. Larrick still did not act on thalidomide.

American newspapers were slow to pick up the story, as it was unfolding largely in Germany. But the press had some help from outraged players in the drama. John Blair, who had seen the Kefauver bill nearly expire, was now ready to pounce. He collected what details he could about thalidomide and the deformed babies, including the fact that thalidomide was nearly put on the market in the United States but for the objections of Kelsey. Blair passed this information to Bernard Nossiter at the *Washington Post,* who in turn passed it on to a *Post* editor. The editor was impressed enough to give it not to the regular medical writer but instead to Morton Mintz, a city reporter with the capacity for outrage.

Mintz broke the thalidomide story in America on July 15, 1962, under the headline "Heroine of FDA Keeps Bad Drug Off Market." Soon after, the cases in America of babies deformed by thalidomide began to be reported. Ironically, one of the worst cases in America occurred in the obstetrical practice of Dr. Roy Nulsen, the doctor in Cincinnati who had obliged the company by signing his name to a journal article promoting the use of thalidomide in pregnant women. He would testify that he did not deliver any thalidomide babies, but it was shown that he had given the drug to more than eighty pregnant women, and delivered three thalidomide babies without recognizing the syndrome. There would have been two more thalidomide babies, except that they expired just before birth.

After Mintz's story, Larrick decided he had enough evidence to send out FDA investigators to retrieve the thalidomide pills distributed in America. By August, the FDA had still been unable to collect them all because of the poor record-keeping by the company and the doctors who were dispensing the drug. More than half of the doctors had no record of how many pills they either received or gave out. Investigators had found, in addition to more than 2.5 million identifiable tablets, that Richardson-Merrell had distributed some tens of thousands of *unlabeled* tablets, as well as liquids and powders containing the drug. It was found that several hundred of the doctors in the "clinical trial" made no reports to the company about their use of thalidomide, and about one-third of the doctors involved made no attempt to talk to the patients who had taken the drug, or to retrieve the pills from them. There was now public outrage.

Hubert Humphrey, chairman of the Senate subcommittee on reorganization, called Larrick to testify. Senator Jacob Javits questioned him.

JAVITS: You have the power to order a withdrawal?
LARRICK: I think we do, yes.
JAVITS: And in this case did you actually order it?
LARRICK: No.

JAVITS: Was it withdrawn [by the company] as quickly as you would have ordered it withdrawn . . . ?

LARRICK: I think the firm proceeded with reasonable diligence to get the drug off the market. I do not think any firm, to date, can do as good a job of getting a drug completely off the market as we can. And in spite of the fact that they tried very hard, we have . . . still found some drug on the market.

Later that day President Kennedy said at a press conference that the new, gutted version of Kefauver's bill was too weak. "I hope the members of Congress will adopt the more careful provisions contained in the administration bill. . . . The administration bill, for example, unlike the Senate Judiciary bill, will allow for the immediate removal from the market of a new drug where there is an immediate hazard to public health, which cannot be done now." The president asked doctors and the public to turn in their thalidomide pills or destroy them. Not long after, he awarded Kelsey a medal at a White House ceremony. Larrick, ultimately, was permitted to retire.

The number of grossly deformed babies born because of thalidomide treatment is now counted conservatively at about 8,000, most of them occurring in Germany and other European countries. Another several thousand infants, perhaps 5,000 to 7,000, died of their deformities before birth. Although no accurate count is possible, the FDA said that 17 thalidomide babies had been born in the United States, and an additional 9 cases were probable. In addition, 10 to 20 more might have been born but died early. Altogether, there were about 40 cases. If the drug had made it to the American market by its target date, it has been estimated that an additional 10,000 babies might have been born grossly deformed from the drug.

The question of what a company should be required to do before bringing a drug to market was now a public issue. The subject of drug regulation was now suddenly flooded with the light of interest. What had been behind the scenes was now on the front page. The congressional debates over drug regulation, which had cooled down to mere embers, were now fanned back into flames.

The two hang-tailed agents from the Department of Health, Education and Welfare, Sonosky and Ellenbogen, who had been steamrolled by Senator Eastland and the drug industry lobbyists as the Kefauver bill had been gutted with changes to become an "Eastland" version of the bill, were now asked to quickly draft a new drug reform act. They started with a version of the bill referred to as the "Harris version" for Representative Oren Harris of Arkansas, a co-sponsor of it. From shortly after lunch until nearly 3 a.m., the two men redrafted the bill, aiming to strengthen it by adding bits of the Kefauver bill and making a few revisions of their own. They were up again in a few hours, and worked until 9 a.m., when Sonosky took their draft to Theodore Sorensen, a key presidential advisor.

After going over the new bill, the two climbed into a limousine and rode to the Capitol. There Sorensen made it clear to Senator Eastland that this was a bill the president wanted passed. The bill was now fairly close to the Kefauver bill, minus the revision of patent law. Eastland was being forced now to eat the version of the bill he had produced. But given the new climate created by thalidomide, he felt he had no choice. Sonosky then went back to the Health, Education and Welfare Department, where Assistant Secretary Wilbur Cohen was waiting with another request—to produce a report that would explain the new bill and its amendments. When that was done, Cohen and Sonosky went to the Oval Office, where Kennedy told them that the bill must be put through quickly: the American people expected action, and it had to be taken. The work went on, as the new version of the bill was sent up to Capitol Hill, where it was now shorthanded as "The President's amendments."

Among the many meetings that followed was one in which Senators Everett Dirksen and Roman Hruska tried to leave out a number of the new changes. They had worked assiduously to kill the Kefauver bill and to defend the drug industry. But just as Dirksen tried to adjourn the meeting without considering all the amendments, the newly emboldened Sonosky stood and said, "No, gentlemen, this doesn't take care of thalidomide. And it doesn't take care of the President's other amendments either. We have *not* finished, gentlemen." Sonosky was only an adviser, and the senators were astonished at his outburst. Hruska let his sense of guilt get the better of him, and said, "Do you mean to say that we aren't interested in deformed babies?"

"I didn't say that . . . ," Sonosky started.

"Yes, you did!" Hruska barked. "You were looking directly at me!"

"I'm sorry, Senator, but I wasn't." Sonosky turned to Dirksen. "Was I?"

Dirksen didn't answer, and Hruska tried again. "All right, were you accusing me of not caring about deformed babies?"

"Well, Senator," Sonosky said, "If the shoe fits . . ."

Eastland adjourned the tense meeting at that point and said the discussions would continue the next day. Now, clearly, it was the backers of industry who were under pressure. When Kelsey was given a gold medal for distinguished service and the new bill was making its way through the halls of the Capitol, one editorial writer noted, "Washington is performing an act of contrition for bureaucratic fumbling and an almost total disinclination . . . to press for higher ground than expediency in their decisions."

The industry worked at every meeting to modify the zeal of the reformers. A key question was: What standard should be met when deciding safety? Lloyd Cutler and other company representatives argued that the evidence could be "substantial," while the administration argued that the standard should be a "preponderance" of the evidence. Substantial evidence was far weaker, because any good evidence could be considered substantial. The administration was arguing instead for a standard that would make it clear that a majority of the studies had to reflect a common agreement before a drug could move forward. The impasse was broken when John Blair, the Kefauver committee counsel and economist, said he would be willing to accept "substantial" evidence as long as Cutler was willing to stipulate that the evidence had to consist of "adequate and well-controlled" scientific experiments carried out by "experts qualified by scientific training." As Sonosky said later, "I just couldn't believe it when Blair pulled that off. It gives us all kinds of power—especially the word 'adequate'—to make sure drugs do what is claimed for them."

Few drug applications of the time could have met the standard, because few companies had done truly scientific studies. So the standard was an historical step forward. The FDA and pharmaceutical industry together would have to create from these words a working, day-to-day standard that was the highest ever put into effect. The standard that medicines would be held to now was a seriously scientific one, the first important instance in lawmaking when that was the case.

Behind this advance were not only years of pressure to improve the state of medicine but, of course, thalidomide. The furor it caused pushed reforms into law. It is now clear that alert and intelligent analysis of the drug by a team at the FDA, not just a knee-jerk reaction, was what stopped a worse disaster. The lesson of thalidomide is that a good scientific standard, used before market, and based on scientific data rather than impressions or authoritative assurances, is essential for safety.

The new law would give force to higher standards, and it made many traditionalists nervous. As the bill approached passage, some conservatives in the medical profession and in industry began to make threats. A poll was taken among drug company executives and the heads of other firms that were dependent on the drug companies for their business. That group said businesses would have to cut back expansion plans, and might move out of the United States altogether. They said the cost of drugs would go up, and the development of new drugs would slow down. It was slightly embarrassing that the anger was confined to a minority of businesses. The results were sent to the members of the congressional committees considering the new drug bill.

Some of the changes proposed in the new law were "radical, even revolutionary, and changed the basic philosophy of the food and drug laws," said Dr. Theodore G. Klumpp, former medical director of the FDA. He was referring to the proposed provision that, in emergencies such as those caused by sulfanilamide and thalidomide, the Department of Health, Education and Welfare could declare an emergency and take a drug off the market temporarily. This would be an interference with the rights of businessmen and doctors to ply their trade, Klumpp contended. He suggested hearings be held and the government be required to go to court before any drastic action be taken against a drug. The government should not be the arbiter of "conflicting views" of a drug, thalidomide included. What Klumpp was arguing for was a company's right to continue making profits from a drug until the last possible moment the public would allow.

The Pharmaceutical Manufacturers Association's L. T. Coggeshall, head of a committee to review the proposed new law, said that in the present climate of strict regulation, scientists would no longer want to go into drug company research. Of course, top scientists never did have an interest in industrial work in America, and the low number of top-quality scientists in the field had for years been a source of problems to companies developing important drugs. But in an unusual admission, he added that the new rules would pose no serious problems for companies that already had high standards of research.

In the first week of October 1962, Congress passed the law now called the Kefauver-Harris amendments to the nation's food and drug laws. The votes in both the House and the Senate were unanimous. President Kennedy signed the bill into law on October 10.

For the FDA, the events of the few preceding years were stunning. The modern pharmaceutical revolution, in which they had participated directly through the 1940s, had been seized from them, transformed through public events and debates, and now handed back to them. It was Kefauver himself who, just at the moment of triumph when the bills were passing in Congress, gave the FDA a final poke in the ribs. He said from the floor, "At the outset of the investigation we were actually discouraged by top officials of the Food and Drug Administration. Not only had they no remedies for most of the problems with which we were beginning to be concerned; they did not even recognize them as problems."

After World War II the drug companies had recognized the commercial value of research and high scientific standards, and began courting the best scientists. In the government, the National Institutes of Health was building a first-rate research establishment. But at first, the Food and Drug Administration languished; there was no sense of urgency, no sense of the new mission of science and medicine that was so evident elsewhere in universities, industry, literature, and film. In the 1950s there were no top FDA officials with medical training; all the leaders were former inspectors—a cadre that had its own pride and ethic that stretched back to the days of the horse cart capers in New York, but was not ready for the new world of potent drugs and fast money. The FDA did have a medical department with a handful of M.D.s in it, but they kept up their private practice and manned their FDA desks only part-time.

When a company submitted its application to put a drug on the market, there were no rules. The companies had no particular scientific or medical guidance from the FDA about what evidence was required to show a drug safe and effective. Drugs were often given to humans before they were tested on animals; there were no rules against it, and for a long time the FDA did not object. When things went wrong with the drugs, the FDA was often the last to know, and the slowest to act when it did know. There was a fear within the FDA of acting against the companies' wishes. So the agency made some special effort to work, like cleaner fish on the sides of the companies, without disturbing the great-toothed creatures. Even when reports of seriously toxic drugs were given to the FDA, they were not made public by the agency because the companies requested it. In one case, scientists from NIH starting tests of a heart drug asked the FDA for information in its files about how toxic the drug was; the FDA refused to send it over. Moreover, in the 1950s and early 1960s the FDA was not a brilliant keeper of records. It did not know all the drugs on the market, or what was happening with them.

For example, Efocaine, an anesthetic introduced in 1952, was found too toxic to keep on the market, and its manufacturer pulled it. The FDA wasn't aware of its disappearance. In the medical literature there were at least twenty-eight papers describing cases of severe side effects from Efocaine, but in the FDA files there was only one. When investigators later examined the tests on which the drug was approved, they found only a single, small test on animals. And that test had mixed results.

In sum, during the 1950s and early 1960s the drug companies were occasionally policing themselves in the new pharmaceutical market, while the FDA was struggling to catch up. After the Kefauver hearings, thalidomide, and the new law, the FDA was now seen as a potential serious force, one that could protect the public in an emergency, one that had to be a better policeman of the activities of the aggressive drug companies. The pressure had not let up. Immediately after the Kefauver hearings, there had been hearings conducted by Hubert Humphrey.

Humphrey summarized the state of disarray he found at the FDA:

The more we have examined the handling of drugs by the Food and Drug Administration, the more we have been surprised, shocked and disappointed. . . . Often testing has been going on in a manner which should have sent shivers down the spine of the medical profession . . . drugs intended for use by victims of chronic disease—day after day, year after year—were released by the FDA even before, I repeat, *before* chronic toxicity tests had been completed on animals . . . shocking reports of injuries and deaths to test patients, as received by drug companies, have often gone unreported to the FDA, or have been downgraded by skillfully-contrived half-truths, or have been reported accurately to the FDA, but virtually ignored. . . . Drugs have been approved which the FDA now admits should never have been approved. Drugs have been kept on the market long after the FDA admits they should have been eliminated.

Representative L. H. Fountain of North Carolina also became vitally interested in the pharmaceutical business and its regulation—his hearings ran off and on for a decade.

The thalidomide case was the impetus for imposing tougher regulations on companies. As the secretary of Health, Education and Welfare wrote to the medical editor of the *New York Times,*

It is unfortunately true, as the thalidomide incident so well illustrates that the drug industry does not now always adhere to high standards, either in planning or in investigation, selecting the investigators, or providing the investigators with full information about the hazards that may be expected in conducting the clinical trial. . . . The proposed regulations would change this. And they would have made it impossible for Richardson-Merrell to distribute millions of tablets to physicians who made no pretense of being investigators. They would have required the development of a rational plan of investigation and its conduct on a sound scientific basis.

Simply put, the 1962 bill covered each of several fundamentals, and laid out a rational system for the testing of drugs about to be introduced into America's medicine cabinets. The previous law said that new drugs could be sold to citizens at will, unless the FDA objected within sixty days of being notified of the pending marketing. The power rested with the companies and the burden with the FDA. Business came first, health second. The new law reversed that. Companies wanting to sell new drugs would now have to demonstrate that they could be used safely, and that they worked for the stated purposes.

While the law of 1938 had said that drugs must be safe before being given broadly to patients, there was one great loophole, which Richardson-Merrell had exploited to the extreme. It was that a company might give some samples of the drug to patients for experimental purposes. They gave thalidomide to 20,000 patients "experimentally." The 1938 law did not require that patients know what they were getting, or that doctors keep track of what they were giving, or that companies keep track, for that matter. The 1962 law stated that experiments on humans could not be done at will and without records. The FDA must be notified before experiments were conducted, doctors and companies had to keep records, and patients had to be asked for and give consent before being subjected to an experimental treatment.

But the most important words in the bill were some stiff phrases in section 505(d)7. If the long view is taken, the words in this section might be counted as among the great statements in American law. Beyond the laws that establish democratic government itself, the rules for maintaining a safe and just society must be established. And here, centuries of thought and experiment come to bear. Nations had long wrestled with charlatans, frauds, and criminals who pressed useless and dangerous substances on customers. But the final arbiter was an "expert," not empirical scientific evidence. The old standard allowed "experienced" doctors to declare what was safe and what worked. The new law was a direct threat to that authority, and the AMA's house of delegates unsuccessfully demanded outright repeal of the new law, at least as far as it suggested that a drug's effectiveness could be determined by scientific tests.

For the first time, experts were in second place and investigations themselves were central. And those investigations had to be "adequate," meaning large and numerous enough studies. They had to be "well controlled," meaning that testimonials and unverifiable results would no longer suffice. "Controlled" meant studies that included comparisons of patients who took the treatment with those who did not. The word "well" in front of it meant that not just any two groups could be compared, but that the two groups must be otherwise comparable.

The full meaning of this change—this carefully worded change—in the nation's law would not define itself for some time. Making the change would require a series of rippling disruptions that would continue for decades; the displacements are still taking place across government and society. Scientific tests are not always as popular as they seem, but it was because the "adequate and well-controlled investigations" were finally laid into law, after centuries of disputation, that medical progress was made.

Unfortunately, when Congress took this forward step, getting serious about science and testing to protect the public, it did what it had often done before: it voted to give the agency new duties and responsibilities while failing to provide the money to allow the agency to carry them out. The error would cause years of dissension and trouble, and would not be remedied for three decades.

•

CHAPTER ELEVEN

Science Meets Policy

JUST ELEVEN days after Lyndon Johnson became president in November 1963, he took the time to speak to the heads of the regulatory agencies of the government. Johnson understood the touch of political pressure of the kind often felt at the FDA, and he let them know he understood: "I know the pressures that you feel and the duties you must discharge. When those pressures are honorable, respect them; when they are not, reject them. . . . Let the venal and the self-seeking and the tawdry and the tainted fear to enter your building and fear even more to knock on your door," he said.

Johnson took some pride in selecting top-tier intellectuals and performers for his appointees. He picked the respected John Gardner, head of the Carnegie Foundation (and later founder of Common Cause), to run the Department of Health, Education and Welfare. Gardner, in turn, chose as Larrick's replacement Dr. James Goddard at the Centers for Disease Control in Atlanta, the chief representative of the progressive attitude among health officers of the federal government. The CDC had been shaped into a highly efficient and professional team; its officers were the disease detectives who attacked epidemics by working both the lab and the street. They were not entangled in the social turmoil of the times; they were working on *missions*. Analytical, professional, and somehow innocent, they thought it could all be done. Goddard wanted to be surgeon general, and was about to put his case to members of Congress and the administration to reorganize the Public Health Service to bring research and health organizations closer together. But he was persuaded to accept the leadership of the FDA instead.

It was a striking appointment, and demarcates the entire early history of the FDA from the decade and a half of reform to come. Goddard was the first outsider ever to be named commissioner. He was also the first M.D., and the first professional public health officer to lead the agency.

He was a lean man with a brush crew cut and a blunt, boyish style that later came to be called the Right Stuff. He wore heavy, black-frame half-glasses favored by doctors (often left dangling around the neck on a chain). Goddard also shot from the hip and was blunt, close to crude in the way he talked about what needed to be done. He spared few feelings at the FDA, and this ultimately caused problems. But he arrived with a mandate from Gardner to change the agency.

Goddard started his job in January 1966. In the commissioner's office, he found "*this thing,*" as he called it—a towering bundle of tall, silver, twisting strands, a sort of sculpture crowned with a big plaque. It declared that the pharmaceutical manufacturers of America were grateful for the work of George Larrick, commissioner. "Get that damn thing out of here!" he said.

Goddard did not know a great deal about the agency, but he knew it was time for change. He wanted a corps of professionals at the FDA who knew their stuff and were open public advocates as well. Following the industry's lead would no longer do. For six years, the agency had been under interrogation in Congress, and it was found wanting in terms of independence and integrity. "Look," he told anyone who would ask about his relations with industry, "there are three elements here. The pharmaceutical industry works to develop drugs, we decide whether they're safe and effective, and the practicing physician has to exercise his judgment in using them." That's it, he added. "We can't be working for the industry. Our job is skepticism and test."

Larrick had been fearful of industry's money, expertise, and political power. But he underestimated the FDA's potential clout. Late in his term, he became involved in a fight over a substance called Orabilex, a liquid ingested by patients who were about to be x-rayed, to increase the contrast in pictures of gallbladders. The FDA, quite inefficient in those days at tracking deaths and injuries from products, estimated Orabilex caused twenty-five deaths; university physicians said the number was much higher, perhaps a hundred. The FDA had looked only cursorily at the data submitted by the manufacturer, E. Fougera and Company of Long Island; articles in scientific journals that appeared to be written by disinterested scientists were in fact written by company employees. The agency now asked the company to send out warnings to doctors, but did not have the product withdrawn from the market. In 1964, two years after the agency learned of the hazards of Orabilex, the FDA finally scheduled a meeting with White House officials to discuss a ban. The company learned of the meeting and pulled the drug from the market itself.

Goddard began his tenure by staying late each night, working his way through applications for new drugs. He questioned old hands at the FDA. A few months later he chose a speech at the Pharmaceutical Manufacturers Association meeting—the most visible platform he could for sending the drug industry a message.

"I am very uneasy . . . ," he told the company executives. "I will be quite candid with you . . . the pharmaceutical industry as you and I know it today may be altered significantly, altered beyond your present fear. . . . If this sounds alarming it is because, frankly, I *am* alarmed."

He talked about investigational new drug (IND) applications, which announced a company's intention to begin human experiments with a new drug—the first step in obtaining approval.

I can say I have been shocked at the quality of many submissions to our IND staff. The hand of the amateur is evident too often for my comfort. So-called research and so-called studies are submitted by the cartonful and our medical officers are supposed to take all this very seriously. I cannot, however. As their chief I have told them that unprofessional INDs should be cancelled immediately. If the sponsoring company is imprudent enough to waste stockholders' money on low quality work, then that company must bear the consequence of such waste. The Food and Drug Administration will not waste public money reviewing it.

He also said there was dishonesty in the applications. He cited such abuses as withholding unfavorable data, failing to choose doctors unconnected to a company to conduct tests, and planting favorable articles in journals before full testing of a drug.

Now Goddard turned to the most important issue—the new drug applications (NDA). The NDA is a company's application for final approval and marketing of a drug after animal and human tests have been conducted. These applications should contain the most conclusive data proving a new drug is safe and effective. Goddard said he was "shocked at the materials that come in to us. I have been shocked at clear attempts to slip something by us. I am deeply disturbed at the constant, direct, personal pressure some industry representatives have placed upon our people. Gentlemen, the NDA situation needs your attention—and now."

He offered as an example an application for a new cancer treatment. The company, which he did not name in his speech, suggested in its application that the product was not being recommended for children yet because of a "lack of clinical experience in this age group." In fact, there was clinical experience with this age group showing the drug was ineffective. As for adults, the drug was used on 127 patients and in only five did the patients' tumors shrink. Since shrinkage sometimes occurs spontaneously, this is a very poor result. The company suggested marketing the drug with no mention of children, and a label that read: "Although the drug has been used in patients with a variety of solid tumors, and has been effective in a few of these, no specific recommendations for such use can be made at present."

Goddard was incensed. He said that if he were practicing medicine and read the label, he would think the drug worth a try. But minor shrinkage in less than 5 percent of patients, Goddard said to the executives, "is no basis for offering the drug for the treatment of every cancer patient."

He cited another case of a drug that could be useful but only if handled with great care. The FDA suggested a label that said "WARNING— DANGEROUS DRUG" as well as "Unparalleled potency." Instead the company proposed a label describing the drug as "unusually effective" with "unparalleled potency." Goddard scolded the executives: "The effect was clearly promotional rather than precautionary. This is the language of advertising, not the language of danger. This is not in the spirit of science." He commented on the hyperbolic and emotional language in advertising aimed at doctors, calling it irresponsible. He said that every time a company was caught producing misleading advertising, pressure to bring new and even tighter federal control built up. "I am asking you to join us in correcting abuses and in seeking not what will just 'get by,' but what is excellent in the science of drugs."

Over the next few months, Goddard met with one industry group after another and delivered similar speeches, each making clear it was time the industry raised its standards and ended deceitful practices. He waged a similar campaign within the agency. He met with department chiefs as well as those working under them, and made it clear that standards would now be higher. The law was to be taken seriously and enforced. For him, "the traditional way" was unacceptable. Though he made as many people angry with his approach as he made hopeful, he kept the lines of communication open. When Robert McCleery, who was in charge of policing the honesty and accuracy of drug advertising, could get no cooperation from his superiors in pursuing companies he thought were running deceitful ads, a conversation with Goddard resulted in a series of enforcement actions against misleading ads; companies found guilty of the practice were forced to write to every physician to acknowledge the deceit, and run a new, corrected ad. In the next two years, companies were ordered to correct ads and rerun them twenty-two times.

Goddard took the language of the 1962 law literally. It said that not only would drugs approved in the future have to be shown safe and effective, but drugs currently on the market would now have to pass scientific muster. That was difficult, because most of the drugs then on the market had never been properly tested for safety or effectiveness. Reviews of the medical literature suggested that only about one study in five was controlled *at all* by the use of comparison groups, never mind controlled in a way that would pass scientific scrutiny. Requiring such a high standard for new drugs was one thing, but for those already being sold, such a standard would probably mean removing 80 to 90 percent of all drugs from the market. That meant confronting a phalanx of lawyers trying to protect company assets, many large dogs guarding many bones. But that was exactly what Goddard did.

Since the time of Hippocrates, there had been a desire to see rational science organize and classify drugs as to their usefulness or worthlessness. The sophistication of marketing practices in the nineteenth century compounded the problem. The American food and drug laws of 1906 and 1938 had helped eliminate some of the most poisonous drugs from the market. But there were 4,000 drugs on the market in 1962 that would have to be reviewed (allowing for different ways of delivering and dosing drugs, the total of *different* drugs was about 2,820 made by 2,340 companies). The drugs included some of the most popular and profitable drugs made by American companies, which accounted for a huge profit.

Larrick had taken no action in this area. When Goddard took office, he discovered that was due largely to the opposition of one man, Dr. Joseph F. Sadusk, Jr. Sadusk was a slim, severe-looking man who wore frameless glasses and slicked his receding hair straight back against his head. He was the director of the FDA medical review bureau, as well as a professor at George Washington University, and he was quintessentially a man of the medical establishment. He made it clear that he was an opponent of a strictly scientific review of drugs—he valued the opinions of doctors over clinical trials and statistics. When one drug was tested in a clinical trial without proper controls, making it very difficult to determine if the drug was effective, he told the medical staff at the FDA that he did not believe statistical evaluations were all that necessary. After all, at medical schools he had been at, statisticians were not members of the department. He also said he was not happy with the 1962 law, that forcing drug companies to show their drugs worked was not necessarily a good idea.

To Goddard's amazement, he had a chief of drugs who did not believe in the scientific testing of drugs. He met with Sadusk to discuss why the review of existing drugs had not taken place. As Goddard describes the encounter, he asked:

"Why is this, Joe?"
"Well, Jim, you have to understand that only a doctor in his office, with his patient, can determine what's good and what's not," Sadusk replied.
"Joe, surely you don't believe that."
"Absolutely, I do."
"Well, then, I'll give you till Monday to think this over. If you can't do this job, then I'm going to have to relieve you of your position."

Sadusk resigned.

Goddard and his deputy, Dr. Herbert Ley of the Harvard School of Public Health, now turned to the problem of how to conduct the review with very limited resources. A colleague pointed out to Goddard that the National Academy of Sciences, the most distinguished body of scientific and medical scholars in America, had a charter requiring the academy to assist government agencies with scientific tasks. The academy and its study arm, the National Research Council, routinely brought panels of top scientists to Washington to review technical subjects.

Goddard bullied the head of the academy, Frederick Seitz, into co-operation with offers of additional manpower. Goddard had already convinced the surgeon general to provide eleven Public Health Service physicians—young doctors doing their training with the service—to act as staff aides to do the footwork. It was a brilliant stroke. A contract was signed in June 1966 between the FDA and the academy, and the work began that summer, with more than 180 doctors and scientists brought to Washington for the first meetings. The committees did not insist on strict standards of evidence but required some substantial evidence that each drug worked. (The study was known as the Drug Efficacy Study of the National Academy of Sciences, National Research Council.)

There were, ultimately, thirty different committees of experts set up by the academy, each one to review a class of drugs—antibiotics, pain relievers, heart drugs, and so on. And each committee member received thousands of pages of material on the drugs under review—cartons full of articles from scientific journals as well as information submitted by drug companies.

The companies were given two months to submit information, but the time was extended. About 85 percent of the four thousand piles of data submitted by companies and drawn together by the panels were for prescription drugs, about two-thirds of them single-chemical drugs with a specific purpose. Another 20 percent had two active ingredients. And about 5 percent had as many as a dozen active chemicals. Anachronistically, many of the drugs had a long list of different possible uses. That meant that almost half the drugs had to be reviewed by more than one committee, as each committee was devoted to consideration of drugs by disease or body system.

The panel members read the material, met, and determined if each drug was (1) effective, (2) probably effective, (3) possibly effective, and (4) ineffective. Inclusion in the third category allowed a drug to be pulled off the market. The last category spoke for itself. As the work went on, however, the scientists found that two other categories better fit many drugs. One was "effective, but. . . ." This was used when a drug was effective to treat a condition, but more effective and safer drugs had superseded it. The category "ineffective as a fixed combination" was filled mostly with medications in which two or three antibiotics had been combined. This was a particularly strange, irrational category of drugs. A single organism that gets out of control causes infectious disease. For each organism, ideally, a drug can be found to kill it. Adding a second drug not intended for that organism made no sense. Doctors in the past had, and patients even now have, the general feeling that drugs are like weaponry—the more firepower against germs the better. But it is not true. Frequently, the two drugs interfere with one another. Two drugs, each with side effects, represent an increased hazard with no added benefit. Initially, doctors often prescribed these combinations for colds and flu—viral infections unaffected by antibiotics. The peculiarity of this category in the scientific landscape was made clear by the position of the American Medical Association. Its own scientific panels, composed of experts in infectious disease and treatment, had denounced all combination drugs, but at the same time the AMA's political and business leadership testified in Washington staunchly in favor of letting companies make them and doctors prescribe them.

The FDA-academy review took about three years. When it was finished, Duke Trexler, the director of the study at the academy, wrote, "a large amount of information on drugs that constitute more than 80 percent of the current market has been reviewed and cast into a body of informed opinion."

Before the great drug review was finished, Goddard's candor and brusqueness—"I have no tact," as he put it—cut short his tenure. Earlier, he may or may not have made a remark to a reporter at a meeting to the effect that children might be better off smoking marijuana than drinking alcohol. This was a common enough observation among doctors, but it produced a plethora of press coverage and congressional hearings, even after the source of the story, United Press, issued a retraction, and other reporters at the meeting said they did not hear him say it. But it fed into the growing impression that Goddard could be trouble. When he had wanted to be surgeon general, he had remarked about philanthropist Mary Lasker, who could have been a key supporter in his efforts to move up, that he was uncomfortable with getting her support in return for following some of her wishes. He said he wasn't sure he wanted to be one of "Mary's little lambs." That didn't help him either.

Another remark that damaged him was actually a very sensible one. In a speech he said that, sooner or later, the corner drugstore would probably close down. The pharmacists, for all their training, were just pouring pills from one bottle into another. They shouldn't be in the store, he said; they should be in doctors' offices giving advice to patients about drugs. It sounded as if he wanted to close the corner drugstores. Willard Simmons, head of the National Association of Retail Druggists and an influential man, was close to Vice President Hubert Humphrey, and his organization donated large sums to political campaigns. He was deeply offended and let the vice president know. Humphrey, a former pharmacist, understood his ire. Before that, at gatherings, Goddard said, "Hubert would come and put his arm over my shoulder and say to the photographer, 'Here, take a picture.' After that, Hubert'd be on the opposite side of the room." When Goddard asked a Humphrey aide what the problem was, he was reminded of his remark about pharmacists; the retail druggists were donating $100,000 to the 1968 Johnson-Humphrey campaign and had expressed their wish that a new FDA commissioner be appointed. By the end of the summer preceding the election, Goddard offered to resign and the White House accepted.

Goddard leaked to reporters the name of his preferred successor so that he could ensure his man would get the job. Dr. Herbert L. Ley, Jr., who had replaced Joe Sadusk as director of the bureau of drugs, became the new commissioner.

Ley was a quiet and confident man, a public health professional who had worked at the Harvard School of Public Health, where Goddard had also trained. He was straightforward, scientific, and not as political or as ambitious as Goddard. He assumed his job near the end of the Johnson-Humphrey administration, at a time when the Vietnam War and other social issues had produced a steady level of political turmoil. When Richard Nixon won the presidency, Ley continued about his job in a methodical manner, and for some months didn't set off any political alarms. He continued to raise the standards. He succeeded in establishing scientific procedures to ensure the equivalence of prescription and much cheaper generic versions of the same drug.

But politics soon intervened. A drug called Panalba, made by Upjohn, was a combination antibiotic that made no sense. Tetracycline was the key ingredient, and if a doctor decided that a certain dose of the drug would best attack the infection of a patient, what was the point of adding novobiocin? In fact, studies had shown that tetracycline was relatively safe and just as effective, while novobiocin caused adverse side effects in about one in five users. While most of the side effects were merely irritating, some of them were serious, including liver damage and blood disorders. The FDA had records of twelve deaths due to Panalba, and experts estimated there were many more. The company had learned of problems early in the marketing, but carried on. Panalba was heavily promoted and represented 12 percent of Upjohn's business at the end of the 1960s. About 23,000 doctors were prescribing it annually, and the drug was pulling in about $1.5 million per month.

The experts assembled by the National Academy of Sciences concluded, unanimously, that the drug should be taken off the market. The academy wrote that Panalba had "no place in rational therapeutics." Then, in March 1969, an FDA inspector looking in Upjohn's files found that the company had done its own research—at least several studies—and had not told the FDA about them. These studies showed that novobiocin *counteracted* the effect of tetracycline, and therefore the combination was clearly less potent than tetracycline alone, though the promotion for Panalba said the opposite. The company had known for ten years that some patients would get sicker, and some would die, if they took this drug.

Upjohn appealed to doctors who had prescribed the drug, and many said that no scientists and bureaucrats should challenge their medical experience, the only real measure, in their view, of whether a drug works. Buoyed by those doctors and the support of the AMA, the company held a special board meeting and, after considering the number of deaths caused and the amount of profit earned, voted to ignore the warnings and to fight in the courts to keep the drug on the market. They also decided to conduct a political campaign within the government to get the FDA over-ruled.

On April 30, 1969, Ley sent a memo to Secretary of Health, Educa-tion and Welfare Robert Finch, telling him that the agency was about to remove Panalba from the market and order the company to send a "Dear doctor" letter around the country alerting physicians to the drug's haz-ards. When Upjohn learned of the FDA's plans, it worked feverishly to head off the decision. Acting as a go-between, Representative Garry E. Brown, who represented the district in Michigan where Upjohn is located, arranged a meeting in which the president of Upjohn, its Wash-ington counsel, Finch, and Undersecretary John G. Veneman would be present. After the meeting, Veneman called FDA Deputy Commissioner Winton Rankin on May 5 and "suggested" a new course of action on Panalba—there was to be no publicity, no Dear doctor letter. The drug would remain on the market, and a hearing would be held to review the evidence.

Ley was incensed and ready to put himself and the agency on the line. The next morning Ley fired off a memo to Secretary Finch's office, in which he said in part, "The basic question before us is whether the Gov-ernment is prepared to move promptly and effectively to stop the use of a hazardous drug when the available facts and the national drug law show clearly Panalba represents serious hazards to patients who take it which are not balanced by any benefit to be expected." The implicit message in the letter was that when public hearings were held, Ley or one of his col-leagues would be forced to say that Finch kept a killer drug on the market. There were two congressional hearings scheduled at which this might happen—one before Senator Gaylord Nelson and one before Represen-tative L. H. Fountain. The revelation would be extremely damaging to Finch.

Three days later Robert Mardian, the general counsel at HEW, called the FDA with the message that the matter should be kept quiet and that a hearing must be held. At ten-thirty the same morning, the key staff member for the Fountain committee, W. Donald Gray, was at the FDA preparing for hearings. He requested the FDA's files on antibiotic com-bination drugs, and asked what the agency was planning to do with Panalba.

"I knew they would have preferred it if I stonewalled," Ley said, using a favored term of the Nixon years, "but he was threatening me with a subpoena." Moreover, Ley said he saw no reason to lie. He told Gray that, weeks before, the FDA had sent its recommendation to Finch to ban Panalba. To Gray it appeared that the FDA was ready to act on a dangerous drug and that the secretary's office was stalling. Ley told Gray that the files on the antibiotics could be shipped to the committee in an hour for whatever part they might play in a hearing. But Ley was wrong—it could not be done in an hour, Gray was informed later that day; Secretary Finch had an apparently new "unwritten policy" that requests from congressional committees about "potentially explosive situations" were to be referred to the secretary's office first. Gray asked whether that new policy meant that President Nixon was invoking "executive privilege" to retain the documents.

With that retort it became clear to all concerned that any hesitation now would look like a cover-up. So shortly after lunch that day, Finch cleared the release of the documents, agreed to ban Panalba, and Ley was a dead man. He was fired at the end of 1969, after only a year and a half in office. His name appeared on the famous Nixon "enemies" list— a singular honor for a civil servant at the FDA.

The Panalba case eventually went to the Supreme Court, where the FDA's authority to ban Panalba was upheld.

When the efficacy study of older drugs (of which Panalba was one) was delivered to the FDA, it was announced that about 7 percent of the drugs reviewed were completely ineffective for every claim they made. Another 50 percent of drugs were judged effective to some degree on some claims and ineffective on others. These findings represented a significant blow to the drug companies.

The challenge from the companies, of course, was immediate and fierce. A number of unnamed industry spokesmen appeared in news reports. "The FDA is beyond its authority," said one. The FDA's judgment was "an authoritarian determination of what is good for medicine." The majority of the companies argued that there should be legally binding hearings (which they hoped might take a few years) on each drug, and that a physician had the "right" to prescribe anything he wanted. It was about the "rights" of drug companies and doctors (in the form of the Pharmaceutical Manufacturers Association and the AMA) versus the "rights" of patients as represented by the FDA, public health groups, and consumer advocates.

As a result of the Drug Efficacy Study, some three hundred drugs disappeared from the American market, including the now-defunct category of "combination antibiotics." It was a significant victory for the FDA and for the effort to establish science as a basis of policy.

•

CHAPTER TWELVE

Partisan Politics

THOSE WHO were present during the next troubled era of the FDA between 1970 and 1980 speak of infuriating disruption and satisfying progress, and they tend to speak, even decades later, with rising emotion: "There were some vicious actions by the higher-ups within the FDA to clear out the whistle-blowers," said one, "who, we can see now, in retrospect, were absolutely right on the facts. . . . The industry pressure was huge, and they got through many drugs that just didn't have the evidence to support them at all." Another FDA insider of the same era saw things differently. Speaking of the same events he said, "We had some people in the agency who were simply obstructionists. They disliked companies and just would block anything out of pure personal animus. I think some of them were just not sane; they were so extreme. They just didn't know what they were doing."

What is certain is that there were political intrusions from above, severe personality conflicts among officials, and management crises that became embarrassingly public. Nevertheless, both FDA officers and drug company officers had found that the new scientific standards set down in the 1962 law called for a revolution in thinking and behavior across medicine and medical science. Until then medicines were not being carefully tested for their efficacy or safety. Medical experiments now had to be universal and routine. Researchers in universities and at companies, as well as medical reviewers at the FDA, soon realized they had to learn how to work effectively, day by day, on a wide variety of drugs. Careful clinical trials hadn't even been described in textbooks and academic papers until the 1940s and early 1950s. The learning process would not be easy.

In fact, it took more than two decades before the letter of the 1962 law was being observed. Modern medicines are new chemicals: complicated, powerful compounds that can be dangerous when placed in proximity to living things. Human bodies are complicated and unpredictable. So scientists learned the hard way, after the misleadingly simple example of penicillin, that a new pill will not usually yield tidy, countable results. Thus, the history of the FDA from the early 1960s to the early 1980s was the story of a long adjustment to the simple command to go forth and test. Despite the FDA's insistence on seeing test results, companies often challenged the agency's right to require specific tests. In essence, as the courts reinforced the law in one ruling after another, the parties in the scrum—the FDA, the company officials and researchers, and academic medical researchers—had to invent the art of clinical trials as they went forward. And the rules for conducting medical experiments that had been articulated in the 1960s were quite different from those that were articulated in the 1970s.

Conflict and countervailing trends were widespread in society during the period. The social reforms of the 1960s still had momentum, but a conservative backlash began with the election of Richard Nixon in 1968. The nation seemed to be stepping forward and backward at the same time. The civil rights movement erupted from nonviolence into the worst riots in America in a century; Vietnam had become an entanglement and then an unpopular and unwinnable war. Resistance to the draft spread rapidly from campus to campus, and by 1967 in Martin Luther King, Jr.'s march on Washington, the movements of the left merged into one broad force. The environmental crimes of large corporations became daily news fare. The Survey Research Center at the University of Michigan, which tracks American attitudes and behavior, noted that when Americans were asked, in 1964, "Is the government run by a few big interests looking out for themselves?" 26 percent had answered yes. By 1972, the figure was 53 percent. The 1970s were a time of disillusionment and reaction. These forces directly affected the FDA.

There were attempts across the government to rein in the bureaucracies and make them steer closer to the path of Republican conservatives. The Nixon administration set a precedent by making the job of FDA commissioner not a career government job or a post for an expert or a manager, but a political appointment. Nixon, though more moderate in some respects than the leaders of the hard right, shared with Barry Goldwater and Ronald Reagan the anger that holds together the radical conservatives. It was not so much an ideology as a bundle of fears and dislikes, a series of reactions to the state of the modern world. They did not offer positive programs that would aid the nation; rather, they saw everywhere demons that had to be banished.

And so it was in the FDA. The Nixon administration began by actually counting the number of Republicans and Democrats at the agency and vowing to change the balance, to "take political control." This attitude on the part of the administration showed itself periodically in nasty, partisan acts, enemies lists, and loyalty tests for government workers. This was true for a pair of officials in the Department of Health, Education and Welfare—Deputy Undersecretary Fred Malek, a West Pointer with rough edges, and Alan May, a devoted conservative, head of the Office of Special Projects.

They were Republican officials joining an organization that had been run by Democrats for the greater part of the previous forty years, and it was to be expected that most who worked there would be Democratic-leaning. For the most part, people with social concerns who consider public service careers tend to be Democrats. Still, in Washington, a new leader, whatever his policies, can usually command allegiance from all federal workers. For the most zealous of the Nixon crew, however, this traditional approach was too weak. They wanted to appoint large numbers of conservatives to federal government jobs, not only at the top but several layers deep. Malek and May, who believed it was important to seize political control of the federal work force, were unhappy to find they had few jobs available to offer the Nixon loyalists ready to take over government.

May was twenty-eight years old, a recent law school graduate, a Vietnam veteran, and a part of the Nixon campaign apparatus. In 1969 he was appointed to the Office of Special Projects, which was in charge of HEW political appointees. He was collecting the résumés of job seekers and matching them with jobs in the new administration. The government bureaucracy, however, had largely been put beyond the reach of partisan politics much earlier in American political history by the creation of the civil service system. Of the 110,000 positions at HEW, only about 200 could soon be opened up for Nixon loyalists. The rest were career employees who took merit exams and moved up accordingly. The FDA was a nonpolitical agency. Only three officials there could be cashiered and replaced by the president and his staff. Democrats in previous years had managed to place their people in the few open jobs, and sometimes had managed to create a few new career civil service positions in which to place their loyalists as well. May found this situation intolerable and declared that the merit system had been "raped" by the Democrats. His solution was a direct attack on the civil service system. In 1969 he began "Operation Talent Search" to find worthy conservative Republicans to place in jobs, and then devised a number of tactics, some of them illegal according to a later government report, to replace career workers with his choices.

His approach had the now fully ironic feel of the Nixon years in Washington—he was stupid enough to write out in detail the illegal tactics he was using and to publish them in a "secret" book. It is a good measure of just how much May understood about government and politics that he expected the multiple copies of this book, handed out at meetings, then collected at the end, to remain secret.

The book came to be called the "Malek manual," after the man who used it most effectively. In the section on separating career employees from their jobs, in what was called "The Responsiveness Program," was the following advice:

- Transfer the victims to remote geographic areas, or subject areas in which they have no interest or expertise, or if necessary some make-work job.
- Do not demote them, but instead, praise them and say they are very much needed at the new job, in order to avoid civil service hearings when the employee protests.
- Make the transfer suddenly and without notice, lest the victim have a chance to muster support from fellow employees or superiors.
- When asked about the reason for the transfer, lie. Do not refer to any campaign to clear out career employees for their political replacements.

So it was that, without notice, on December 9, 1969, Commissioner Ley and five other FDA employees—Deputy Commissioner Rankin, Associate Commissioner for Compliance Kenneth Kirk, and three officers in the public information office—were informed they were being "transferred." Rankin and Kirk between them had almost seventy years of service in the FDA, in both Republican and Democratic administrations. They were to be gone by the next day. There was no accusation that they had done something wrong.

Kirk, who was sixty-one, chose to retire. Rankin accepted the transfer but soon found that the job he was given was indeed a make-work job, so he retired as well. Ley was offered a job he was totally unsuited for. But news reports made it clear, based on administration sources, that he had been fired, not reassigned. He, too, decided to retire. When asked about Ley's "transfer," keeping strictly to the advice of May's manual, Malek lied about it. He said the transfer had nothing to do with Ley's politics or performance, that he was needed in the new, phantom job. Malek was following the manual.

One of the three public information officers in question, Thomas F. Williams, wrote an eloquent epitaph for himself. He wrote Malek that he had recently received one of the highest ratings in the department for his work, and he was proud of it:

> Career civil service employees should not be tried and found guilty in the dark, judged by the criteria of partisan politics, and deprived of the rights they have earned through their professional competence in a non-political arena. Career civil servants should not be punished by the rules of a game they are not allowed to play. They do not share the spoils of partisan victory, and it is not intended that they suffer the penalties of partisan defeat. I know that the career Civil Service employee is not universally held in high regard. The press often depicts us as a group of blundering idiots. The Congress often sees us in a similar light. The Democrats think we are not Democratic enough, and the Republicans think we are not Republican enough. But I submit that we are a valuable, indeed the essential, resource of government. We give the programs sense and continuity despite the twists and turns of changing political fortune. We are the natural allies of each new Administration as it sets about its task of implementing the will of the electorate.

A number of idealistic medical officers who had been hired at the FDA in the wake of the Kefauver hearings, attracted by the mission of the agency in protecting the public's health, were now in for a scorching.

The man chosen by the Nixon administration to run the FDA after the internal conflicts had already begun was Dr. Charles C. Edwards, a Republican, of course, and a man with a background of conservative employment. He was a lean and aggressively pragmatic man who had begun his career as a surgeon. He worked at the Mayo Clinic, then successfully managed programs for the American Medical Association, operated safe houses for the Central Intelligence Agency in Washington, and was eventually recruited at a top salary by the business-management firm of Booz-Allen Hamilton, to help lead their team that advised health-industry companies.

Edwards was a man who moved easily among people, spotted key ones, and cultivated them. His sense of management, of medicine, and of government was based on relations between people: Whom do you know? To whom can you talk? In short, he was a medical politician. When he got the call from the office of the Secretary of Health, Education and Welfare, he was pleased. He flew to Washington that day to meet with Finch and Malek. Edwards recalled being asked, what do you know about the FDA? "I said, 'Not a hell of a lot.'"

He was told they needed an answer quickly. Edwards, swift on his feet, said he would give an answer quickly, but he needed, right now, an office, a telephone, and a secretary. He wanted to call friends and contacts to check out the current situation at the FDA. He needed to know something about the crew that was so much in a hurry to hire him. By the end of the day, he agreed to head the FDA, taking a large pay cut.

Edwards resettled in Washington and slyly moved into an office in the HEW building, saying nothing about taking over the FDA. He began by studying the FDA in CIA fashion, sitting in an office and gathering information without alerting the subjects of his inquiry. Edwards took office on the same day Ley left.

The agency now had a rising profile, and showed up more and more often on the agenda in the HEW, at the White House, and in public debate. The Republican plan for the FDA had been to erase the legacies of Goddard and Ley and find someone who would understand "the needs of business," as Edwards described it. Edwards enjoyed relations with business executives. He owed his appointment to his friendly relations with Foster McGaugh, who worked at Booz-Allen and was a key donor and fund-raiser for Nixon. When Nixon won, McGaugh recommended Edwards to White House advisors. But he may not have been the business pushover the administration had expected.

The agency Edwards walked into, still struggling with its transformation, aspired to the ranks of public health agencies like the Centers for Disease Control and the National Institutes of Health, except that it couldn't yet match the scientific standards of those agencies, and it was still regularly targeted by aggressive businesses whose products it regulated. Companies wanted the agency to cooperate in their medical marketing, and consumer groups wanted the agency to refuse.

The FDA reflected the at-war-with-itself nature of American society. It is a nation built on conflicting myths—freedom of business enterprises, and protection of the rights of the common man from predation by the businesses. And the FDA scientists were left with the dirty work—they had to apply new knowledge to the marketplace, whether it hurt or helped business.

The agency had a mandate in law to regulate a very large portion of the products in the American market, under an array of different laws. Within the agency, it was hoped that Congress would provide additional funds for a few more medical reviewers and a few other trained experts so that work could be done with increased speed and accuracy, meeting the objections of both sides. The money, however, was not forthcoming. In 1965 just fourteen medical officers reviewed 2,500 applications. The situation had not improved much by the time Commissioner Edwards arrived.

He decided to turn the agency away from its public health orientation and deal with "the real world." He said it was necessary to understand what the drug companies were doing and why. He felt his predecessors were "hard-liners" who gave companies little slack. Edwards knew how to speak more softly, how to negotiate without going public. But those who thought he was going to be an industry shill were wrong. He felt that industry's best move was to acknowledge the validity of some of the criticism. It was a bit like Teddy Roosevelt's strategy to save the capitalists by giving a whipping to the worst among them. Edwards noted in a speech before the Pharmaceutical Manufacturers Association that the consumer movement troubling businesses was the fault of businesses themselves. "It is in large part the direct result of past injustices to the consumer, inadequate products, and false and misleading promotions." The movement "is bringing heavy pressure to bear on both industry and government. This, too, is here to stay, make no mistake about it."

He took the same position on drug effectiveness as Goddard and Ley had. He stood behind the results of the National Academy study. He worked with the academy to define for companies what a good "controlled experiment" was, one that would effectively prove whether a drug worked or didn't. He signaled that he understood the pressures on businesses, and would seek solutions that made sense for them, but he also made clear he thought big companies should be responsible on health issues and could absorb an occasional loss. "They make a lot of money," he said. "They can take a hit." He thought most companies were responsible most of the time.

Knowing the terrain and the objectives of those moving through it are essential to modern management; Edwards wanted to understand those companies he was regulating. He did not read and absorb regulations; piles of paper put him off. He wanted to know who the players were and what was on their minds. He courted the chiefs of drug companies. He felt it was important to talk to them one-on-one. Unless you understood their concerns, you couldn't push them toward greater drug safety and effectiveness. Personal connections were essential; if you wanted to take a product off the market, knowing the man who would have to take the hit would smooth the way. And when you needed some consideration at budget time, it was essential to know someone in Congress on the Appropriations Committee. He worked to make the acquaintance of several key members.

He brought in talented and intelligent people at the top and in the bureaus of the agency. Early in his administration, he asked a small group of informed outsiders to give their opinions in a report analyzing the FDA, at least the issues he cared about. Dr. Roy E. Ritts from the Mayo Clinic and four others delivered to Edwards a scathing indictment, not of the staff of FDA, nor their dedication, but of the organizational chaos. Laboratories were "so poorly managed that scientists seemed unable to describe their work coherently." The labs had extremely old equipment, much of it broken down and unsafe, that is "a disgrace to the agency and the committee can only express alarm that FDA scientists are asked to work under such circumstances." The committee suggested extending the use of outside advisory committees to obtain the latest scientific information when relevant. And it made clear there was no way the agency could operate properly in its current state of total financial neglect. Edwards managed to get the report a good ride in the press, including on the front page of the *New York Times,* which would make his pitches to his superiors and to Congress much easier.

To stiffen management, Edwards imported a whole squadron of people from Booz-Allen, including his deputy commissioner, Sherwin Gardner, and Dr. Henry Simmons, who became czar in the bureau of drugs. Edwards found a top manager from a food company, Virgil Wodicka, to run the bureau of food and pesticides. And in the legal department, he hired the most powerful food and drug industry lawyer in Washington, Peter Barton Hutt of Covington & Burling. It did not escape the notice of consumer advocates that every member of this new team came from industry and not one from among consumer groups or knowledgeable university people.

Some of Edwards's candidates for FDA jobs could not be hired after industry passed along negative reviews to HEW. Many of the career employees at the FDA felt that the consumer protection mission of the agency was becoming compromised. They greatly distrusted drug companies and their emissaries—with good cause based on what they had seen historically—and were disturbed that industry could veto new hires. These lifers were also subjected to relentless pressure to overlook problems with drugs—company representatives could still call and visit FDA medical reviewers and their superiors, even without appointments.

Edwards felt the backlog of drug applications called for action. But Simmons, chief of drugs, and Dr. George Leong, a political appointee inserted into the hierarchy, were unaware that Goddard had eliminated the backlog; it was the drug companies themselves that had created the new backlog by successfully lobbying to get Congress to halt the recruitment of additional Public Health Service doctors. The new FDA officials had assumed incorrectly that a backlog had been caused by the sluggishness of overcautious reviewers.

Leong wrote that he thought "the primary role of the Bureau of Drugs in the Food and Drug Administration is to assure the American public of the availability of safe and efficacious new drugs without undue time delays prior to their release for marketing." This was the view of conservative Republicans and of the drug industry, but the food and drug law itself did not speak about how quickly drugs were to be approved, and the courts had found that the original intent of the food and drug law was quite different. One federal court summarized the purpose of the law as "the protection of the public from products not proven to be safe and effective for their alleged uses and the safeguarding of the public health by enforcement of certain standards of purity and effectiveness." The Supreme Court, in *Weinberger* v. *Hynson,* stated that the law "requires the commissioner to disapprove any application when there is a lack of 'substantial evidence' that the applicant's drug is effective. . . . Evidence may be accepted only if it consists of 'adequate and well-controlled' investigations, by experts qualified by scientific training and experience to evaluate the effectiveness of the drug involved. . . . The legislative history of the act indicates that the test was to be a rigorous one." The Supreme Court declared plainly, "clinical impressions of practicing physicians and poorly controlled experiments do not constitute an adequate basis for establishing efficacy."

Edwards and his team felt strong pressure from industry. One of the attacks on "activist" FDA reviewers came from Dr. Milton Mendlowitz, a researcher who worked for Pfizer Pharmaceuticals. He wrote to complain that he wanted to increase the allowable dosage of a drug just being given to humans for the first time. The FDA asked him why. Mendlowitz exploded, saying that the FDA was "hampering our efforts to study the

effects of this drug." He wrote that the FDA decision to delay his "investigations" while it investigated further was unconscionable. "Such restrictions on a clinical investigator are, in my opinion, most undesirable unless
they can be supported by incontrovertible evidence." Mendlowitz and
Pfizer had got it exactly backward: the burden of proof was on the doctor
who wanted to, in effect, experiment on humans, not on the FDA, which
was overseeing them. When Dr. Richard Crout, second in command of
the drug division, was shown a copy of the Mendlowitz complaint, he
said he thought it was legitimate. When it was pointed out that the letter
reversed the burden of proof laid down in the law, Crout then said he
didn't agree with the author of the letter. Matters were plainly complicated.

Mendlowitz's kind of arrogance and wrongheadedness suffused all
relations between the drug companies and the FDA during the 1970s.
The chafing between the agency's toughest reviewers and industry executives soon turned to outright anger and loud disputes. And in the agency
itself, when philosophical differences soon caused personal antagonism,
the new management team would try to tame or remove the dissidents
beneath them.

Dr. John Nestor, a cardiologist with a specialty in pediatric disorders,
was among the consumer advocates at the FDA, as well as one of the
strongest personalities on the medical staff. He had joined the FDA
in 1961. One of his formative experiences there was dealing with
Richardson-Merrell, visiting the company's labs and helping uncover
their fraud on MER-29. He had also once suffered severe swelling and
burns as a severe reaction to a new antibiotic. The company that manufactured the drug knew of its potential risk but was not required by the
FDA to warn doctors or the public.

Nestor felt that the FDA and industry were natural adversaries because the "medical and commercial philosophies collide" when new
drugs are reviewed. "You've got to make a choice as to whether you're
going to operate under the business and commercial ethic and make a
profit for stockholders, or whether you're going to operate under the scientific ethic and make decisions in favor of the patient. You can't be on
both sides," he said. He was once quoted in a magazine article saying, "I
have never found an honest drug company—although I haven't dealt
with all of them. Even those who would like to be honest find out that they
are at a competitive disadvantage and can't afford to be." Nestor had just
seen a commissioner fired for political reasons, and three prospective
employees turned away because they were vetoed by industry. He said,

"For fifty years the food and drug industry has had this agency in its pocket, and it has it in its pocket today worse than it ever did. . . . I don't think you have to destroy the capitalistic system to make the drug companies responsible. I think the first thing we ought to do is start enforcing the food and drug law, which has never properly been enforced."

Dr. Richard Dunham, another FDA officer, was charged with deliberately criticizing drug applications without giving any guide as to how to fix them. Dunham said that giving such help was: "The game of schlemiel—to tell drug companies what to do to get approved. It's not up to us to tell them all the details of what should be done. They're the applicant. We're the critic. The game of schlemiel on the part of applicants is the number one game: you lead me by the hand. The number one game of the agency should be 'gotcha.' You tried to slip one past and I knew where to look for your trick."

Nestor (and others like him) was committed to giving strongly skeptical reviews of new drug applications, and had found more than enough sloppy work and fudging of conclusions by drug companies to keep his skepticism alight. He was actively hostile to company representatives, berating them and refusing to help them improve their work. He also took on colleagues at the FDA who he thought were getting in his way or being too soft on the industry. One co-worker who changed something Nestor had written came in for a tongue-lashing, as did a woman who had talked to company representatives behind his back. In spite of his outbursts, Nestor had many supporters because of his strong point of view, his honesty, and his first-rate work as a reviewer.

Part of Nestor's duties was to review heart and kidney drugs—cardio-renal drugs—and he worked under Dr. John Winkler and Winkler's assistant, Richard Dunham. This group was considered the center of both the "anti-industry" bias and of personal friction within the agency. So, not long after Edwards's new managers were in place, they determined to break up the group. Henry Simmons and his assistants Crout and Leong followed the Malek-May model. Nestor and Winkler were transferred out of the division because they were "needed" elsewhere, and Dunham was demoted by paperwork sleight of hand. Sometime later, several further actions against the "consumer activist" reviewers were taken, including abrupt transfers—eleven of them between 1972 and 1974, all on the flimsiest of grounds. Simmons and his assistants lied about the reasons for the abrupt transfers and withheld damning memos from a later investigation, a department investigation showed. To justify their actions, the managers said, first, the "activists" were disruptive, whatever their opinions; second, an adversarial attitude toward industry was never helpful regardless of the toughness of the standard being enforced; third, the strictest scientific standard that the law had set down should not be considered as gospel.

Action taken against a reviewer was rarely the result of a manufacturer's complaint. In one egregious case, however, Dr. Robert Knox was removed from reviewing the drug fenfluramine when he was critical of its manufacturer, A.H. Robins. The company had sent emissaries to the agency to complain about Knox's "objectivity," and agency officials accommodated them. Morale was low and sinking.

In the midst of the troubles, Edwards had moved up a rank within government to assistant secretary of health, education and welfare, still overseeing the FDA, but handing over the commissioner's job to Alexander Mackay Schmidt, dean of medicine at the University of Illinois, in the summer of 1973. And the dissension inside the FDA broke into a public free-for-all when Senator Edward Kennedy held surprise hearings in August 1974, just a few days after Nixon had resigned the presidency. The hearings seemed almost of a piece with the Watergate affair because they centered mostly on the testimony of the eleven FDA officers who had been punished by management in partisan actions.

Congressional hearings are the nation's best political theater. What otherwise might be scattered newspaper stories, brief broadcast segments, and an occasional speech on an issue of vital importance are brought together with great visibility on a single stage. But given the timing, the Kennedy hearings began virtually unnoticed. FDA officials were alerted that there would be a hearing but not told who the witnesses were, and they were deliberately misled about what the subject was. Kennedy's staff feared that if the FDA leadership had advance notice of such things, retaliation and purges would have begun immediately.

The agency was advocating reform, trying to implement scientific standards, but for the most part the companies were not cooperating. The FDA leadership was trying to force compliance but shied away from confrontation. The FDA medical reviewers, who had to face off with the industry reps whose sloppy studies they were supposed to review, had reached a point of open rebellion. They had been punished unfairly as a result, and went to Congress with their stories, en masse.

The hearings began when Kennedy introduced the eleven FDA medical officers and cited their extraordinary academic credentials, describing how they had been pressured, browbeaten, and finally removed from their jobs because they found legitimate, scientific reasons for why one or another drug application should not be approved. As the *Evening Star* noted the day after the first hearing, the revelations were "enough to chill the blood."

For some time the leadership had been spreading the falsehood that since thalidomide, reviewers were timid about approving drugs for fear of allowing a bad one to be brought to market. Kennedy's first round of questions was intended to demolish that notion. All the doctors said in response that no superior had ever criticized them when they recommended approval of a drug. Each of the eleven also testified that they had been overruled on occasion when they found serious defects. The industry as well as their own bosses had pressured them.

The FDA leadership was caught flatfooted. They were pilloried in medical journals and in public because other countries had drugs that Americans did not. They had announced their intention of turning the FDA into a modern, professional organization, getting along with industry while looking at drug applications with a skeptical eye. But the fact is that they had intervened on behalf of businesses. They had overridden the letter of the law to allow drugs on the market that were not strictly proved safe and effective.

From the 1960s onward, the FDA was trying to establish very high standards, not yet contemplated in other nations, while still carrying on business day to day. The transition was rough and the internal fights were played out in public, as is the accepted if much-rued practice in the United States. By the end of the turmoil, officials had been censured, the new standards were largely in effect, better management practices were in place, and openness to the public was established, at least as a principle.

Prior to the Kennedy hearings, in 1972, one enterprising physician, Dr. William Wardell, then at the University of Rochester, noticed something he found disturbing about the new regime in drug science in America. He had spent time working in Australia and in England, and one day he mentioned to his colleagues that some drugs there were not sold in the United States. His colleagues scoffed. They said American medicine led the world in training, pharmaceutical invention and manufacture, and, most important, standards. If some drug was not for sale in America, then it either didn't work or was unsafe.

Wardell was bothered by those assumptions and decided to do some research. He found that out of 180 new drugs that appeared in Britain and America from 1962 to 1971, forty-three were introduced in Britain first and thirty-nine were introduced in the United States first or simultaneously. That was not much of a gap. But the journal article he wrote on the subject in 1971 gave rise to major controversy about a so-called drug lag. Was the FDA needlessly holding up good drugs?

In fact, the question Wardell raised modestly was far from simple. Ninety-five percent of the new drugs put on the market are "me too" drugs—that is, drugs almost identical to a half dozen already on the market. These are drugs that need not be rushed under any circumstances. Of course, every reasonable person wants to bring a useful drug to market as soon as possible, but safety must come first. Quick approval can kill people. *All* countries have drug lags. Different drugs are tested first in each country. More drugs have had to be recalled from the market in Britain after they injured or killed patients than have been recalled for safety reasons in America. In one study, twenty hazardous drugs were recalled in Britain while in the same period only ten had to be recalled in the United States.

Wardell was unable to pinpoint the reason for the later approvals in the United States. It is, after all, the companies that decide where to market a drug first and when to apply for that approval. Drug company executives say many things govern their choices, including where their facilities are located and where money is cheapest. Also, it is clear that sometimes, when a company is aware that a new drug has significant safety problems, it holds the drug back from the United States but offers it for sale elsewhere, a dubious bit of behavior that makes conclusions about drug lag more difficult to make. At the same time, the FDA's lack of trained medical staff in this period, and the reluctance of Congress to provide the resources for the needed review staff, guaranteed some delay.

It is ironic that the so-called drug lag first became an issue during the FDA term of Edwards, the professional manager. It became an enduring issue, one that eventually came as near as any ever did to ending the scientific standard of drug review and even the life of the FDA itself as a serious regulatory agency. From 1938 on, of course, there had always been grumbling about the FDA by companies eager to put their drugs on the market. But with the new law in place, companies were required to submit much more information, and the FDA, with no additional resources, began to take longer to plow through it. In truth, some drugs were approved quickly and some were not. FDA standards were now higher, but the agency's speed was little different from that of drug agencies in other nations.

One drug, propanolol, a beta blocker, was delayed for an extended time, not because of sluggishness at the FDA, but because of fierce fights over the standards. (This drug got Wardell to investigate the pace of approvals in the United States.) The company simply hadn't done the scientific studies necessary to get the drug approved. Some FDA medical officers refused to pass it without that evidence; others urged them to give the company a break because the drug appeared to be important. But outside the FDA, where no one knew of the fight over evidence, it appeared simply that a small bunch of bureaucrats were holding up a medicine that *everyone knew* (based on the doctors' grapevine and sketchy studies) was an excellent treatment.

The issue was finally resolved when one of Edwards's key supervisors, Crout, decided to approve the drug. "We didn't have the evidence," Crout says now, "but we approved it anyway." He felt the issue had become an embarrassment. When the drug was later proved by substantial studies to be effective, the FDA had a black eye on drug lag, but its delay had been correct in principle. The seed of a great deal more trouble had been planted.

Even though the question Wardell had initially posed was reasonable, the response it drew was hardly that. In his paper, Wardell did not blame regulations for "drug lag." While the FDA and Dr. Sidney Wolfe of the then-nascent gadfly organization Health Research Group said that "drug lag" was a poor measure to use, since it measured mostly unimportant drugs, and didn't take into account the drugs that were approved elsewhere but should not have been, critics quickly snapped up the concept and used it to drub government and declare the need for "regulatory reform." Not so long before, President Kennedy had said there was a "missile gap," with America supposedly trailing the Soviet Union in the production of nuclear warheads. The "drug lag" took on a similar mythic connotation.

Conservatives who were fierce opponents of regulation said the FDA bureaucracy was grudging and slow in its review of drugs. They said it held drugs off the market for years, costing companies millions of dollars and allowing thousands of Americans to suffer and die while waiting for the drugs they desperately needed. It was said to be proof that government bureaucracy and the onerous regulations passed in 1962 had damaged the ability of American companies to compete in the international drug market. An interesting question had been inflated into a corrosive myth.

Conservative economist Sam Peltzman of the University of Chicago now produced a couple of papers that electrified both the right and the free market advocates, and are quoted even today in spite of the errors in them. The key paper is awkward and poorly written, but its message emerges gradually from a fog of verbiage. Peltzman began by saying that the purpose of the 1962 Kefauver-Harris amendments was essentially to prevent the rare thalidomide-type catastrophes in medicine. He said that to achieve protection from such tragedies, the new regulations required drug companies to carry out "extra" tests of safety. He claimed these tests had broad, unintended consequences—delaying the approval of not only the rare harmful drugs, but lifesaving treatments as well. If lifesaving drugs were withheld for "extra" testing, he maintained, people must be dying while they wait for these drugs to be certified safe by the government. Thus, to decide whether the regulations are beneficial or harmful, we should simply count the total harm of thalidomide that was averted by regulation, and count the total harm caused by holding back other vital drugs, and compare the two.

He asked whether "it is worth delaying the introduction of all new drugs to weed out the occasional thalidomides." He got the thalidomide numbers and historical facts wrong, but ultimately, he concluded that the horrible effects of drugs like thalidomide were regrettable but acceptable, hardly enough to justify drug regulation. Companies should be left unfettered in bringing their new products to market. The bottom line for Peltzman was:

Adding the [1962] amendments' prospective benefits in improved drug safety to the benefits from reduced waste on ineffective drugs does not give anything approaching the sum of the costs the amendments have imposed by forcing consumers to forgo benefits from effective new drugs. It would require an extremely large valuation of the nonquantifiable benefits of reduced mortality—say, several million dollars per life saved—for the amendments to appear as a break-even proposition.

There are questionable assumptions in Peltzman's paper, even in his central thesis. He assumes that the 1962 regulations prevent only rare, well-publicized tragedies. He sees no other benefits from the law and the high standard of scientific testing required before drugs go to market. His conclusion seems unusual in light of the debate that led to the 1962 law. From the train of historical cases it was clear that careful testing was vital to the process of science and medicine. Peltzman was dismissing the hardest won advances in medical science, simply assuming that the data submitted by drug companies to the FDA before 1962, without well-controlled studies, was sufficient to determine all the important things about a drug. But that is exactly what was disproved between 1938 and 1962.

As evidence of the terrible effects of regulation, Peltzman pointed to the number of drugs approved before the new law and after—315 in 1959 to about 80 in 1966.

But the facts don't fit the tidy conclusion. First, the number of drugs produced by companies and approved by the FDA began dropping sometime between 1956 and 1959, depending on the source. Second, the effects of the 1962 law could not be felt until 1966 at the very earliest, but for the most part after 1970. Third, drug companies had mined out the chief scientific discoveries of the 1940s and early 1950s; a decline of new drugs was inevitable, according to the testimony of drug company leaders of the 1950s. Fourth, the very advance in scientific methods and knowledge that was embodied in the 1962 law was being recognized in both medical science and industry. Companies had been making multiple copies of every drug, and scientists were beginning to conclude that not all these copies were of equal value or even safe. Companies began backing away from some of these copycats, and from the plethora of useless combination-of-ingredients drugs.

So clearly, it was not just regulation that led to the decline in the number of new and approved drugs. (In Europe, there was a similar dramatic drop in the introduction of new drugs during this period, though no equivalent law was passed.) More important, the dozens of drugs per year that had been coming to market in the 1950s, but now were not, constituted largely junk, and *none* were important treatments. The number of drugs approved before and after the new standard was established in 1962 that represented actual advances in treatment remained steady throughout the period. About two or three truly useful new drugs were approved annually from 1960 on (four out of 306 in 1960). That small number was the base then, and remains the base today, though some would charitably say a dozen useful drugs appear each year. The fact remains that the vast bulk of drugs are produced for commercial reasons, not out of medical necessity.

Today, 10,000 to 15,000 drugs are on the market, and the World Health Organization considers that a properly equipped pharmacy needs only 350 of them.

For the most part, Charles Edwards stayed above the fray. His bias tended toward industry, but, above all, he tried to be an "honest broker" and a good manager. Despite the eruptions within the agency and the drug lag debate, there were solid accomplishments.

One of his old friends in Georgetown from his CIA days, Florence Mahoney, introduced him to key members of Congress, which helped him to increase the budget of the agency, doubling it in two years, a rare feat in Washington. He brought in managers who rearranged the FDA's methods of planning, to the point that it became a model in some ways for other agencies. To open up the agency to public inquiry, expert advisory committee meetings were held in public. In 1970 the first set of practical guidelines on what constitutes an "adequate and well-controlled" clinical experiment were laid down, a landmark in medical research, and the courts had backed up the FDA in making these new guidelines.

The commissioner now kept an open calendar of his meetings, and the docket was open for requests. Committees of experts had been appointed before, but now there was a *system* for expert advice. Expert panels were established in each area of disease or body function, each had scheduled meetings, and the public could easily learn when and where they were to be held. From a handful of occasional groups in 1969, the number of regular advisory committees grew to sixty-six by 1974. These groups were excellent at bringing fresh data to the agency, and because of their involvement, the FDA no longer had to stand alone in defending their decisions. In the words of Washington politics, it provided the FDA leadership "cover" for decisions. Meetings with industry executives were now regularly scheduled. Meetings with consumer advocates occurred for the first time on an official, if less frequent, basis.

Outside the agency, an array of new laws was passed on the swells of the consumer movement. The Freedom of Information Act took effect in 1967, giving citizens new access to government meetings and records; the Advisory Committee Act of 1972 set down rules for expert committees, ensuring that they were held in the open for the most part, with consumer representatives attending. The Sunshine in Government Act required more openness as well.

In other words, American governmental agencies were now expected to carry on their work in daylight, with a set of administrative rules. Such rules, published in the *Federal Register,* made clear what was expected of them. This was a vast improvement over the days when agencies confronted companies in court in order to establish the rules (or at least what the limits were). That solution often produced vague rulings and did not encourage communication between the regulator and the regulated. The volume of rules and explanations grew exponentially. The idea was to make agencies accountable and to give the regulated a chance to know where they stood. The downside was "hundreds of thousands of pages, literally tons of documents burdening the American businessman," rich fodder for the foes of so-called big government.

It has been estimated that before 1969, 90 percent of FDA files were secret. Carolyn Morgan helped change that.

Morgan had a family and did not want any more children. She wrote to the Department of Health, Education and Welfare for information and data so that she could determine which contraceptive was most effective and safe. At first, she was denied the data by the FDA's Office of Information for Public Services. Then a second denial came from the office of Roger Egeberg, assistant secretary of health, education and welfare. An assistant to Egeberg said that the question she asked would require the FDA to divulge trade secrets, interagency communications, medical files, and much other information protected under the law. This was true, she was told, because the information she needed was buried within about 1,900 files that were not public. To extract them would cost about $12,600 in labor. There would also be a copying cost. If Morgan persisted, the department might comply, but she would have to send an upfront payment of $5,000 to cover initial costs. Egeberg's officer suggested she be satisfied with the printed labels for each of eight contraceptive pills, together with advisory committee reports and a bibliography of about 4,000 citations on the topic. Instead, Morgan filed suit. Over the next few years Morgan had another baby, lost her suit in court, but saw the enactment of new legislation that would help her get the information she needed. Ultimately, that case and other cases prompted Peter Hutt, just appointed by Edwards as FDA's new top legal man, to establish rules that made 90 percent of the FDA's data open.

The Freedom of Information Act was passed in 1966. It was revised and toughened in 1974 after agencies failed to adhere to its provisions. It was a landmark in representative government and declared that, among other things, government agencies were required to give to citizens copies of all the rules relating to agency work, and in specific decisions, documents showing how and why each decision was made. It gave citizens true access to the workings of government; now they not only could complain to their representatives, they could act themselves by using an agency's own information and its own appeals procedures.

The new FDA rules opening up its files produced a sudden wave of requests. Thousands of them in 1975 made the agency spend about $1 million to respond (for which it received only about $78,000 in fees). The number of inquiries soon grew to an average of about 45,000 per year. Congress had appropriated no new funds to cover the substantial new FDA responsibilities.

The consumer movement had blossomed. Ralph Nader's *Unsafe at Any Speed*, together with his court victories and his new advocacy organization, Public Citizen, convinced Americans that business managers cared less for customer safety than for profits. In the 1960s and 1970s, Congress created ten new federal regulatory agencies (each of which borrowed something from the FDA), including the Environmental Protection Agency, the Occupational Safety and Health Administration, and the National Highway Traffic Safety Administration. It was the third wave of reform of capitalism, after the Progressive Era and the New Deal.

At the same time, a new variety of nongovernmental consumer group, more bold and focused than Consumers Union, had been fueled by sixties activism. In one year during Edwards's term, 1971, two such effective organizations were created that have become major figures in the regulatory landscape. They both have small budgets and use more volunteers than paid workers. One is the Center for Science in the Public Interest, based in Washington, D.C., a group that concentrates on food and nutrition issues. It was created by microbiologist Michael Jacobson, chemist Albert Fritsch, and meteorologist James Sullivan. The second group, Dr. Wolfe's Health Research Group, was an offshoot of Ralph Nader's advocacy group, and was created almost on the spot one day by Wolfe. Wolfe is a dark-haired, dark-browed, and buoyant man who is always on the edge of deadly seriousness. His father had been an inspector for the Labor Department who investigated businesses for child labor violations, filthy conditions, and the like. His mother taught in an inner-city school, with the aim of convincing the students they had a chance to get to Harvard. Both government and personal intervention made sense to him: How else would abuses be fixed? He was a young physician, trained at Case Western Reserve University in Cleveland, where he studied under Dr. Benjamin Spock. Spock preached that it was essential to think of patients as people, with continuing lives and day-to-day concerns, rather than just as technical medical problems. Spock required students to visit families in the ghettos, to see how they lived and what their backgrounds were. Wolfe earned his M.D. after work at Cleveland Metropolitan Hospital, and went to the National Institutes of Health to begin a career in research. Now his rearing in a home where social concern was vital would come into play.

Wolfe received a call one day at NIH from someone with whom he had done his residency at Cleveland Metropolitan Hospital. The man was now an epidemic intelligence officer at the CDC in Atlanta. He asked Wolfe if he was aware that some of the bottles of intravenous fluids people were given in hospitals were contaminated. Massive infections had been reported in 350 patients, nine of whom were dead. Wolfe recalled reading a short item about it in the CDC's weekly report. But his friend told Wolfe that the drug company that made the IV fluid bottles, Abbott, had convinced the FDA and CDC to keep the bottles on the market while the investigation of the problem continued, arguing that a recall would cause a shortage of IV fluid. Wolfe's friend felt the problem was caused by a very unusual bacterium, so it seemed to him certain that the Abbott IV bottles were the source.

Sparked by his former colleague, Wolfe decided to do a bit of research. He called other companies that made IV fluids to discover if enough was in the pipeline to serve hospitals' needs. It was work the FDA should have done but did not. It turned out that other companies had large stockpiles. So the potentially fatal IV bottles did not have to be given to patients. "The company had bluffed the FDA and CDC," Wolfe said. He called up Ralph Nader, whom he had advised on medical issues. "Ralph, I really would like your help in getting these things off the market immediately," he said. Nader advised writing a formal letter to Edwards documenting the case. And, simultaneously, he suggested giving the letter to reporters. Wolfe followed his advice and the media took it from there.

Edwards realized a blunder had been made. He stepped back and dealt with it in his usual person-to-person style. He picked up the phone and called the CEO of Abbott, and the next day the CEO and his full retinue of aides were in Edwards's office. He approached them as if they were partners in a bind. It took ten more days to sort out all the manufacturing and distribution details, but then the Abbott bottles were pulled from the market. They were held off the market for three months while the company corrected the problem and demonstrated that to the FDA (it involved changing from a screw top with a defective plastic liner to a bung-style stopper on the bottles).

Wolfe demonstrated the enormous potential effectiveness of public interest advocates, people who work to solve public problems with fact-gathering and no motive of personal gain. Citizens had protection, and government and industry were kept on their toes. Wolfe was now asked to tackle a host of issues. When a majority of his time was absorbed in the public health work and not in his laboratory science he quit NIH and has been the center of Public Citizens' Health Research Group ever since. During that time Wolfe has remained perhaps the most educated and effective watchdog on medicine and the FDA.

Since the founding of the Health Research Group and the Center for Science in the Public Interest, a number of other groups have grown up to challenge the siege engines of money and influence that are camped around the Capitol. They were formed with a curious naïveté that almost suggested that incantations could change behavior. Of course, they knew that the incantation had to appear in the newspaper, after which the simplest information could have an enormous impact. This effect has been called the "third force." As theorists have often said, in mature capitalist societies, someone must speak for the value of morals and human life against the stark, strict consideration of profits.

Edwards's style, of course, was establishmentarian. He did not always put himself on the line for the public interest. One such case dated back to 1879, when Dr. Joseph Lawrence, while researching chemicals that could kill germs, created a relatively simple mouthwash that was effective in killing some bacteria during surgery. He decided to sell the substance, which he called Listerine, to suggest a connection, nonexistent, with Joseph Lister's pioneering work in antisepsis. The company Lawrence worked for (eventually Warner-Lambert) decided that since the public knew germs caused disease, and Listerine could kill some germs, the best advertising approach was to assure customers that Listerine killed the germs that cause disease—colds and sore throats. The claim, which was first advertised in 1921, was completely false, as laboratory tests proved. For one thing, viruses, not bacteria, cause colds. Listerine has no effect on viruses, nor does it kill the bacteria that cause most sore throats. Listerine does not shorten the duration of these maladies either.

When these fraudulent claims for Listerine persisted during Edwards's reign, Caspar Weinberger, who was secretary of HEW at the time, called him and said there was some interest in the department for working with the Federal Trade Commission to put an end to them. Edwards met with the FTC toward that end. Soon, Edwards was made aware of the fact that the head of Warner-Lambert, Elmer Boechst, was not only a substantial financial backer of Richard Nixon but also a personal friend. "At any rate, we were told to back off that one" by the White House, Edwards said. "It wasn't a major issue. We backed off it. But in the process Elmer . . . became a very good friend of mine." Later, Listerine began arriving, by the case, at his home, Edwards said.

Alongside the rise of consumerism, a major change was going on in journalism. There was a time when all newspaper writers were generalists, but after the Second World War newspapers began assigning their reporters to specialized beats such as atomic energy. That meant the reporters had to study the subjects they were writing about and spend a great deal of time in the company of scientists. They did, and their stories began to appear prominently with increasing frequency in their papers. With the Kefauver hearings and the thalidomide story, the science of medicine received similar treatment, and some reporters made the subject a full-time job. Morton Mintz had been at it for years at the *Washington Post*, since his reporting on thalidomide and his 1964 book on the drug industry. He was a figure of legend who produced some trembling within the agency and at drug companies. Other reporters, including William Hines and Judith Randall, now began to pursue the issues when their news organizations permitted them to.

Citizens themselves, and the gadflies who had decided to act in their behalf, now demanded inclusion in the FDA's decision-making. It was an important stage in the evolution of the agency. After the first attempts to open the agency, citizens and citizen-advocacy groups took advantage of the opening and created a role for themselves, permanently, in the agency's affairs.

Charles Edwards was commissioner for a bit more than three years, and afterward as assistant secretary of health, education and welfare for another two years, directly in charge of the FDA, he had effectively extended his reign over the agency. Though his years were among the most troubled in the agency's history, they were also a time of substantial forward movement.

Edwards had chosen Dr. Alexander M. Schmidt as his successor, in large part, not surprisingly, because of his reputation as a manager. But a managerial nightmare, the Kennedy hearings, occurred on Schmidt's watch, and he became obsessed with them. He spent a great part of his energy while commissioner fighting the charges made during the hearings, carrying out an in-house investigation for more than a year, and then producing a sadly one-sided report on the events, finding his top officials blameless and pointedly failing to include the testimony of those transferred or dismissed during them. It was soon rejected by all sides.

The agency was beginning to be a business-style hierarchy of managers with goals and strategies. Though it would never go away, the internal feud over how tough the FDA should be in drug review had quieted. Companies now had large teams of scientists and goals of their own in medical discovery. FDA approval had become the mark of seriousness in making and selling safe and useful medicine. The companies' scientists, working on credible clinical trials with both FDA staff and university scientists, now depended on this symbiosis and forward movement of knowledge for their own progress. Conservatives in time would again threaten the new equilibrium, but there was no going back.

CHAPTER THIRTEEN

•

The Limits of Policy

THE LAST major public decision of the Food and Drug Administration in the 1960s, just before its transformation into a more modern administrative agency, was on the sweetener cyclamate. It was the last decision of an era, as Barbara Troetel writes, because it was made without public comment, public hearings, and extensive media coverage until the decision to remove the sweetener from most products was a *fait accompli*. The agency was moving forward, both in sophistication and openness. When, a few years later, another sweetener, saccharin, became suspect, it was an entirely different matter.

The saccharin issue emerged just as Donald Kennedy, twelfth commissioner of Food and Drug, was preparing to come to Washington in 1977. Kennedy's appointment during the administration of Jimmy Carter was unexpected—he was not an M.D., not a policy man, not a man knowledgeable about the drug industry or the agency that regulates it. He was a neurophysiologist who happened to be helping out a friend of his in Washington. Sidney Wolfe, making the best of it, said Kennedy was a good choice since he had no medical training and therefore was not taught in his formative years that drugs and drugmakers are good. The Pharmaceutical Manufacturers Association said that he "isn't our candidate for the job . . . but absolutely everything we've been able to find out about him is good."

Kennedy has said that the most dramatic issue he faced while commissioner was also his first. He had not yet even left for Washington when Deputy Commissioner Sherwin Gardner called to say the FDA had just gotten the results of a study the United States and Canada had co-sponsored, and it showed that beyond any reasonable doubt, saccharin caused cancer, at least in animals.

Kennedy had a certain naïveté about Washington when he arrived at the FDA, but he would learn under fire. Soon he was standing before television cameras and 120 reporters, talking through the politically charged debate over saccharin, which would eventually erode some of America's trust in the science behind scientific regulation. The matter had last been addressed decisively when Teddy Roosevelt dismissed Harvey Wiley's objection to it. By 1977, the scientific data indicated otherwise. The first studies naming saccharin as a cause of cancer were published in 1972 and 1973, and debate began then, with calls for its ban. With more incriminating data mounting, the FDA alerted the public; it also offered industry a substantial amount of time to assemble evidence of saccharin's usefulness to human health. But by March 1977, the FDA announced it was planning a partial ban on the use of saccharin in America, based on data that showed it caused cancer in animals. Even then, months were allowed for public comment and debate before the agency would make a final decision.

In the brief cyclamate flap, it had been noted by Coca-Cola president Fred Dickson, "You'd have to drink 550 Frescas a day to get as much cyclamate as the rats. . . . You'd drown before you'd get cancer." But Coca-Cola went along with the ban. Now, as the debate over saccharin was renewed, the argument ridiculing the rat tests became dominant. The industry had honed its skills.

Part of the campaign to keep saccharin on the market was a barrage of advertising and bought commentary that suggested dire health consequences from the loss of saccharin. Problems with obesity would increase, and diabetics, even though they could get saccharin at the drugstore, would probably suffer more catastrophic cases of sugar toxicity, including blindness, kidney disease, heart attacks, and the loss of their extremities. (The additional health problems did not materialize in Canada or elsewhere when saccharin was removed from foods and beverages.) It is worth noting that saccharin was made chemically and cost the soda companies six cents a gallon. Sugar cost them a dollar a gallon.

One of the more lucid public discussions of saccharin illustrates how difficult the issue was to deal with. It took place at a policy forum sponsored by the American Enterprise Institute in 1977, and was moderated by former ABC News chief John Charles Daly. Daly opened with a clear statement of the problem: saccharin was to be banned, based on a variety of evidence, but centrally, a Canadian study that showed saccharin fed to rats caused bladder cancer. He mentioned the Delaney amendment of 1958, which stated, "No additive shall be deemed safe if it is found to induce cancer when ingested by man or animal." He said that the FDA's suggestion of a ban was not reliant on the Delaney clause alone. The

FDA would probably have acted against saccharin in any case because of other requirements in the law that said any additive put in food must be found safe in general, not just on the question of cancer. And, after all, saccharin was not a vital, lifesaving drug.

Daly noted that about 70 percent of saccharin was consumed in soft drinks, and another 20 percent in food, toothpaste, mouthwash, and lipstick, for example. He reminded the audience of the know-nothing position, expressed brilliantly by Representative Andrew Jacobs of Indiana, who suggested putting a label on food with saccharin: "WARNING: The Canadians have determined that saccharin is dangerous to your rat's health."

The discussion began with Sherwin Gardner explaining that the tests of saccharin were not strange, massive feedings, but ordinary procedure. They included heavy feedings to see if the trigger mechanism for cancer was set off, and lighter feedings to assess what dose caused cancer in animals. Then Representative James G. Martin of North Carolina said he felt that, despite lab tests, "the best available scientific evidence" showed that saccharin in normal human use is safe. He thought his constituents depended on diet products to lose weight or at least keep from gaining it, and saccharin was important for them.

Dr. Frank J. Rauscher of the American Cancer Society said his group was not opposed to the ban but was concerned that a ban might be worse for the public health than keeping the substance on the market. He said studies showed that saccharin did not help in losing weight, but he was unsure of whether it helped in preventing weight gain. Excess weight, he continued, could contribute both to heart disease and, according to some studies, to cancer. In fact, studies never showed that saccharin helped people to maintain their weight. Still, Rauscher concluded, saccharin wasn't an obvious hazard.

"If saccharin were really a preventive drug," Sidney Wolfe argued, "if it were shown that it really did prevent weight gain, or cause weight loss in people, that would be fine. But I think there is no such evidence and there may well not ever be any."

But for some, saccharin has value of another sort. It makes people who take it *feel good*. People like having Diet Coke, diet TV dinners, diet desserts, even if they don't cause weight loss. Drinking a Diet Coke, which has no calories, makes you feel as if you are being prudent. In this way, saccharin was producing a modest positive feeling, several times a day, for millions of people. Here was a likable product. If saccharin had just been banned from the market, like cyclamate, life would have gone on. But in the public discussion, saccharin started to seem benign. We all take some risks, right?

Martin, in support of his constituents, was soon proposing to the TV audience a bill removing the decision from the FDA's jurisdiction and, in effect, exonerating saccharin.

Daly pointed out that eight European studies showed no harm from saccharin despite years of use. Rauscher noted that the studies could not have shown a hazard even if it was there—most cancers take twenty to thirty years to develop, and widespread saccharin use was just approaching those numbers. Other objections to the studies were raised. Hypotheses and numerical interpretations were tossed around. Wolfe made the problem explicit. "If saccharin were a chemical that caused a two-, or three-, or four-, or five-fold increase in cancer, the epidemiological methods [such as] looking at human consumption would work." But the risk from saccharin was subtler. So those making policy needed to rely on chemical and animal tests. Wolfe reminded the group that such tests had found chemicals that caused human cancer before, such as vinyl chloride and estrogen, as was proved in tragic human outcomes later.

Daly eventually redirected the discussion. "Let's come back home," he said, "Hubert Horatio Humphrey, himself a victim of cancer of the bladder, I believe opposes the saccharin ban. He argues eloquently, as he always does, that the issue is one of reasonableness—science is not so advanced that it can always provide absolute answers."

Now Martin suggested that if saccharin were banned, the reaction of citizens and some members of Congress might be more extreme, to propose laws to redesign animal tests by law, and maybe redesign the FDA itself.

William Hines, then a reporter for the *Chicago-Sun Times,* finally said the recent debate "seemed to produce a sense in the public that anything can cause cancer—given enough of it, water will cause cancer. Also, because the idea of a human being drinking 800 cans of soft drinks a day is grotesque, there is somehow widespread disbelief in the validity of animal tests." The discussion had hit rock bottom, though Hines's words reflect the point of view of many Americans today.

Such a discussion about health hazards and public policy makes clear that in all but the most dramatic cases, scientific evidence is difficult to get across to Congress or the public while a countervailing public relations campaign is in progress. Ultimately, in this case, Martin's view prevailed. Congress passed a law preventing the FDA from banning saccharin.

(Paradoxically, a Canadian ban on saccharin resulted in additional choices for Canadians. Even though the idea of regulation suggests restriction, in fact, as in the creation of the pharmaceutical industry itself, regulation created new choices. In Canada, the soft-drink industry made quick adjustments to offer "regular sugar," "low-sugar," and "no-sugar" versions of soft drinks. The low-sugar versions cut calories from 140 calories per can in regular soda to between 5 and 60 calories. The no-sugar version let Canadians add packaged saccharin or sugar to their sodas if they wanted to sweeten them.)

For Donald Kennedy, the decision by Congress let him off the hook. The FDA had proposed taking saccharin out of food but allowing it for sale in packets if people wanted to use it themselves. *Time* magazine "said it was a 'club-footed end-run around the Delaney Clause' by the FDA," Kennedy remembered. "I thought that was pretty colorful." Kennedy testified before the congressional conference committee, the last stop before final passage of the act. He told the members of the committee that their action would lay down an exception to the law. "If they wanted to do it, they would be establishing a principle that didn't strike me as all that unreasonable: namely, that there shouldn't be any weak carcinogens in the food supply unless people like them a lot."

Wolfe was not happy that Kennedy had not made a stronger case against saccharin by, for example, properly explaining why animal studies are done and why high doses are given. (It would take studies of five thousand or more animals over two years to approximate the same effect achieved with high doses in a much smaller sample over a much shorter period.)

Americans had entered the age of risk assessment. It was now possible to calculate what the hazards of a substance or action might be to society; a similar accounting of its benefit could be made as well. The notion was revolutionary. Such calculations were not even conceivable before the 1970s. The determinations remained problematic in the next two decades, but America's most prestigious body of scientists, the National Academy of Sciences, eventually recommended that the FDA have more options than merely to ban or permit a product; it should be able to rank risks of hazards.

Statistical calculations of risk represented a great advance, except for those who rely on methods other than scholarly assessment, such as lobbying, to determine whether products should be marketed. Companies confronted with a risk assessment that *some* people would die from their product were left with no option but to diminish the science in laymen's eyes, as they did in the debate over saccharin.

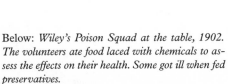

Above: *Mrs. Winslow's Soothing Syrup was opium packaged for children. The ad suggests giving it for teething, but it was sold to women to calm their children in any circumstances. Estimates of the deaths in America from remedies such as this one range from tens of thousands to hundreds of thousands.*

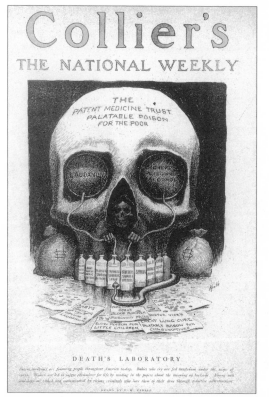

Left: Collier's *ran a journalistic campaign against adulterated food and drugs. This cover is from a 1905 issue.*

Opposite page: *Dr. Johnson's Mild Combination Treatment for Cancer, here advertised in a 1908 Kansas City newspaper, was a fraud. Such treatments were not harmful in themselves, but rather in their power to take money from customers under false pretenses and to keep patients from getting proper treatment. In 1911, the U.S. Supreme Court ruled that the 1906 law applied to food and drug ingredients and composition, but not to the therapeutic claims made for them, which the court said could still be subject to debate. Congress retaliated soon after the Supreme Court decision and passed a law intended to override the justices' opinion.*

Above: *Theodore Roosevelt coined the term muck-raking to describe journalism like that in Col-lier's. This illustration of the concept appeared in the* Utica (N.Y.) Saturday Globe *in 1906, and shows Roosevelt holding his nose while trying to deal with the scandal over unsanitary conditions in the meat packing industry. The Meat Inspection Act was passed in 1906, as a companion to the Pure Food and Drug Act.*

Right: *A fertile field for the muckrake: sausage making in a Chicago packing house before the 1906 law required rudimentary sanitary practices.*

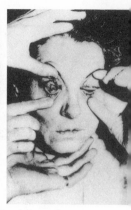

Above: Unregulated cosmetics like Lash Lure caused hundreds of cases of blindness and mutilation, such as the one pictured here in which a woman was blinded after a beauty shop treatment with "mascara." The photo at top left shows the victim before her injuries.

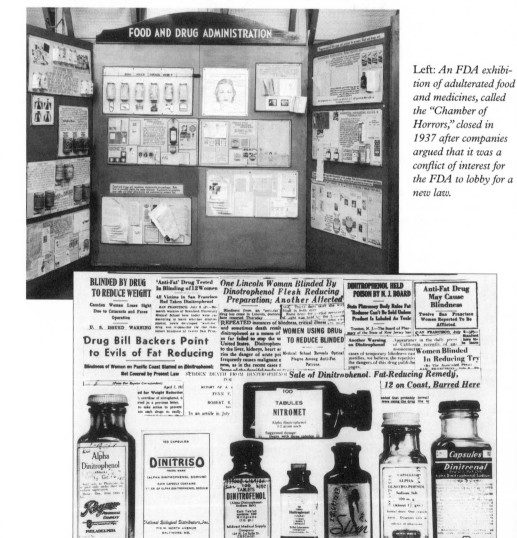

Left: An FDA exhibition of adulterated food and medicines, called the "Chamber of Horrors," closed in 1937 after companies argued that it was a conflict of interest for the FDA to lobby for a new law.

Above: *FDR and Rexford Tugwell, on Roosevelt's left at the microphone, who supervised the writing of the 1938 Food, Drug and Cosmetic Act.*

Right: *George P. Larrick, when he was a chief inspector (he was later commissioner), who helped assemble the "Chamber of Horrors" exhibit.*

Opposite page: *Dinitrophenol, a weight-loss drug that caused an epidemic of cataracts and blindness across the United States as well as a number of deaths. Recently, it has been sold illegally on the Internet.*

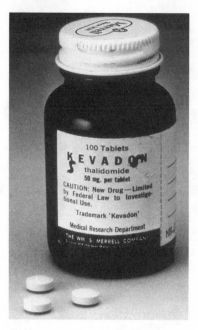

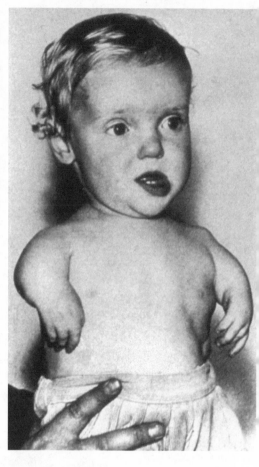

Above: *Kevadon, also known as thalido-mide. It was sold chiefly outside the United States as a sedative despite a lack of testing to determine if it was safe. It caused birth defects when taken in the early months of pregnancy, and led to thousands of cases of premature death and, most famously, a fetal disability in which limbs were stunted. The FDA refused to approve it without better safety data.*

Frances O. Kelsey, the FDA medical officer who stopped thalidomide from reaching the American market in 1962. The drug was approved for marketing in Germany, England, and other countries, but Dr. Kelsey noticed that the safety data was defective, and she asked the manufacturer to provide more information. That pause for questions was itself enough to avoid many thousands of deaths and deformities in the United States.

Opposite page: *A baby with phocomelia, or seal limbs, the result of thalidomide taken by its mother. About 35 children died or were born severely deformed in the United States; about 14,000 deaths and deformities occurred in other countries.*

Right: *Senator Estes Kefauver, chairman of the Senate Subcommittee on Antitrust and Monopoly, led hearings into the practices of the pharmaceutical industry from 1959 to 1962. The hearings were scheduled originally because figures showed that drug companies were reaping excessive profits, far beyond other industries, but the issues covered also included drug safety and excessive drug promotion.*

President Kennedy signs the 1962 Kefauver-Harris Amendments to the U.S. Food, Drug and Cosmetic Act. In the group behind him are Dr. Frances Kelsey (second from left) and Sen. Estes Kefauver (behind Kennedy, with his hand on Kennedy's chair). The amendments set higher scientific standards for safety and effectiveness that all new drugs must now meet.

The 1962 amendments to food and drug law required that worthless drugs be removed from the market. The FDA forced companies to submit evidence that their drugs worked as claimed. Some drug companies buried the FDA in a blizzard of paper in an effort to prevent or delay the removal of the drugs. Here a Squibb employee is surrounded by paper submissions to the FDA.

The Food and Drug Administration building in Rockville, Maryland. Denizens of the building laugh at this photo because it makes their workplace look stylish, when in fact it is a boxy mass of long, dreary hallways and cramped offices.

Jimmy Carter was a hybrid—he had strong democratic tendencies, but some fierce anti-government attitudes as well. He appointed to the top jobs in government a wide array of people from eastern establishment sophisticates (Cyrus Vance to the State Department and Harold Brown to Defense) to rural figures (Bert Lance at the Bureau of the Budget and Griffin Bell as attorney general). He named the outspoken liberal Joseph Califano to head the Department of Health, Education and Welfare, just as the nation was becoming more conservative.

By the summer of 1979, Commissioner Kennedy felt he had put in his time under fire, and he left when a chance came to be a top leader at Stanford University and return to sunny California. And by now, it was clear that FDA commissioners no longer were expected to stay on through elections and leadership changes. As Kennedy left five months before the elections of 1980, Califano chose Jere Goyan as Kennedy's successor. He is a pharmacist by training—the first one to head the FDA—and was an administrator at the University of California at San Francisco. His intellectual credentials suggested that he would critically review the FDA's role in society. He was a bearded, off-the-cuff professional, a bit hippie-like, a man who actually said what was on his mind.

In one of his first press conferences as commissioner, he said frankly "our society has become overmedicated. We have become too casual about the use of drugs, and I'm referring to legitimate prescription and nonprescription drugs, not illicit drugs. . . . Too many people are taking too many drugs without proper understanding of their potential harmful effects . . . I'm a therapeutic nihilist. My philosophy is the fewer drugs people take, the better off they are." He added, "I have a strong belief in the patient's right to know. My philosophy on this makes doctors and some of my colleagues uneasy, but in the best interests of the public health, it should be mandated."

He believed drug companies tend to emphasize the selling of drugs, not conveying information about them. He believed as well that doctors are inattentive and often give the wrong drug at the wrong time in the wrong amounts, without regard to cost. At one meeting of doctors he said bluntly, "I staunchly refuse to accept the notion that any physician, merely because he graduated from medical school and is currently a card-carrying member of his or her county medical society, is great, or good, or even tolerably competent. Too much of drug therapy has been atrociously irrational."

It is not difficult to imagine why he was unpopular with doctors, pharmacists, and drug companies, and why he appealed to consumers as well as reporters. When he took over the job, his priority was to get drug information directly into the hands of patients. He wanted to have included in most drug packages a statement about what the drug was for specifically, what the most serious risks were, and what signs to watch for if something went wrong. Because two classes of drugs had developed—prescription drugs and over-the-counter drugs—an odd imbalance had occurred. Patients picking up a package from a drugstore shelf got both instructions and information about hazards. But those who went in to pick up a prescription drug from behind the counter got nothing if the pharmacist didn't take the time to explain.

It had been known for some time that most doctors gave information about drugs to patients intermittently, inaccurately, and partially, if at all. Studies make it clear that doctors passed on information about serious side effects of drugs only about a third of the time. The same was true of pharmacists: key information was given to patients less than half the time. Often very little information was given to the patient who was taking the most potent and potentially toxic drugs. Now Goyan proposed that each prescription bottle should contain a sheet of paper containing the necessary information for the consumer. This would be a clear safeguard against doctors and pharmacists who did a poor job.

The AMA, the pharmacists, and the drug companies vehemently opposed the plan. Opposition did not deter Goyan. Before he became FDA commissioner, as dean of the UCSF school of pharmacy, he radically changed the curriculum, eliminating about a quarter of the established courses and requiring instead a year of experience in clinics for would-be pharmacists. The job of reform, he said, was about as easy as "moving a cemetery." But the package-information proposal became law and was in operation by January 1980.

Goyan also turned his attention to the labeling of processed and packaged foods. Some was already required, but it was sporadic and largely unintelligible, intentionally so. Companies were reluctant to compare the health value of one product against another. Too many would look bad from the start: too much fat, too much sugar, too much salt. Goyan deemed it important that consumers be told the key information about the foods they were buying, including the number of calories, the amount of fat, and vitamin content. His proposal to label processed and packaged foods also drew vehement opposition, and did not become regulation by election day.

By the time Goyan ended his term on inauguration day 1981, many of the essential components of a complete scientific regulatory agency had been assembled. First, and most important, the agency could review products for safety and effectiveness *before* they went to market. A scientific base had been built—it required by law "well-controlled scientific studies" as the absolute standard. It had been placed squarely among agencies of the public health whose job was not to serve industry but to serve citizens. The agency was thoroughly professional, and was open to the public. Of course, challenges remained. The public was still given too little information about food and drugs. No good system had been devised to track the effects of food and medicine once they were released to the public, including contaminated food and severe or fatal side effects caused by medicines.

Occasionally, the FDA could be seen overtly as heroes, as in the weeks of the Tylenol stalker, when in the face of national panic it quickly pinpointed the problem. Mostly, the work was becoming more intellectual and judgmental, which meant rarely pleasing everyone. But in 1981, Ronald Reagan had gained the White House, on a platform of deregulation. The mood in Washington changed suddenly. The FDA was among the first to feel it.

•

CHAPTER FOURTEEN

Deregulation

A FTER THE political confusion of the 1960s and 1970s, during which time Americans doubted their values, there was a great desire for simplicity and certainty.

The nation had rung up a large deficit in its budget. Inflation had begun a slow, rolling panic as it crept past 6, then 8, then 10 percent. By the time of the 1980 election, inflation was 12 percent. Americans, who had not worried about gas prices for decades, now had to wait in long lines for a few gallons as prices shot upward. America's international swagger also came to a humiliating end in a series of incidents including the capture of the ship *Mayagüez* and the ill-considered rescue that cost the lives of thirty-eight Americans. It got worse when mobs in Iran seized the American embassy and more than fifty hostages. The rescue mission never reached its target, as defective American helicopters were downed by a sandstorm. Americans were held captive abroad, and apparently we could do nothing about it.

The disillusionment with the government was made stronger by each succeeding failure, coupled with the economic woes. It seemed as if America was sinking to second-class status: we couldn't make reliable helicopters or automobiles; a recent president had departed in disgrace after he authorized bribes, as we had seen leaders of third world nations do. It was a moment set for electoral upheaval.

Voters had already opted for an outsider when they elected Carter in 1976. Now, in 1980, there was Ronald Reagan, whose image was that of a man of perfect confidence and certainty. He knew his role, to portray pride and purpose, and he had no doubts about either himself or his kind of Americanism. Those who were concerned that Reagan was recommending simple, facile solutions to complex problems, and that he was disconnected from those who wanted constructive reform, were swept aside in an electoral landslide. Moreover, the Republicans gained control of the Senate, and while Democrats didn't lose the House, they did lose thirty-three seats there. All barometers would have to be recalibrated. The nation, dissatisfied and worried, had turned sharply to the right.

Reagan wanted to rein in government, which he said was an obstacle to economic opportunity and human liberty. He repeated endlessly the quip that the federal government had "overspent, overestimated, and overregulated." The majority of Americans appeared to believe it. They thought "their government was choking them, wasting their money, forcing up prices, poking its nose in local affairs," as Theodore White writes. Estimates of the damage to America from regulators began to flow not only from conservative economists but from the White House itself. Murray Weidenbaum, Reagan's first chairman of the Council of Economic Advisers, said that government regulations were costing American businesses $100 billion annually (though benefits of regulation were not calculated). That number, though largely specious, was accepted as evidence that regulation was slowing growth and pushing up the cost of services.

Despite the rightward shift at the top, polls showed that American voters themselves were still making a distinction between good and bad regulation—they appreciated environmental, health, and safety protection, but rules governing competition between companies were seen as fundamentally different. The Reagan administration never acknowledged the distinction. It attacked any and all kinds of "regulation" and "social programs."

The reason for avoiding careful case-by-case judgments lay in the recent history of conservative politics. The New Right that elected Reagan, and later the Congress led by Newt Gingrich, was formed during the presidential campaign of Barry Goldwater in 1964. While the Goldwater campaign was an electoral failure, it was a social success in that it brought together figures from around the country who were not only opposed to the Democratic majority of the time, but dissatisfied with the moderate tone of the national Republican party as well. This wing of the party included those in the John Birch Society, but they wanted to steer clear of that extremist image. They wanted to mobilize conservatives, to rally different groups around the anger engendered by the rights movement—civil rights, women's rights, and consumers' rights. The disaffected groups were mostly white and male, and if well organized could be framed into majorities in many electoral districts. Their anger against minorities, government, and established elites—who were perceived to have produced the loss of faith and economic stability in America—could be marshaled to win elections. The appeal was to return to the America of tradition. Such a movement could not be forged without significant sums of money. And the brilliant stroke of the New Right was to blend together the angry religious fundamentalists and the lower classes with the angry among the new rich classes.

Theorists of the movement identified the origin of the modern conservative impulse deep in Western civilization, and said that moderate Republicans had abandoned those principles. The writers who helped join the old moral values of conservatism with the new principles of the free market were Richard Weaver (*Ideas Have Consequences*) and Russell Kirk (*The Conservative Mind*). Weaver said the troubles of the modern world began with the loss of a fourteenth-century philosophical debate between the idealists and the nominalists. The idealists were strong on moral values and Platonic discussions of the nature of human virtues. The nominalists said Plato's ideas were abstractions; they preferred more immediate facts. After the Middle Ages the idealists and their "values" were displaced from the monasteries, and those who favored the discovery of "facts" prevailed. After all the ages during which people were guided by clues from God, now humanity was turning to look for clues from nature.

Kirk identified the "mind of the conservative" not only with values but also with an elite in society—with the royalists against the French Revolution, for example—and said it is the natural order to have an elite. Thus, the New Right began with value-centered thought and added to it an allegiance to the new elite, the captains of society's greatest institutions, and the corporations. This elite was set against the pragmatic elite of scientists, lawyers, social workers, and others whose base was a belief in rationality.

"The leading conservative intellectuals seemed to share one strong conviction," writes James Smith. "Intellectual error—much of it to be found in the social science disciplines—was the root of modern problems. Conservative writers rejected the liberals' optimistic theories of historical progress . . . the conservatives attacked rationalism, 'moral relativism,' and the liberal obsession with scientific and technical solutions." The problems of the world cannot be resolved by a better understanding of how people or society work but must be resolved by "traditional" values. Thus, as moderate Republican leaders participated in running the nation, made compromises, and moved to the center, they lost their appeal to the New Right.

Among the most insightful inventions of the New Right in its push to power was a new kind of scholarship. It was based on "tradition" and "faith" rather than rational inquiry and investigation. The new conservatives realized that nonpartisan scholars had a disproportionate influence on both reporters and legislators. They were in universities and at private foundations such as the Brookings Institution and the Rockefeller Foundation. And in government, a carefully bipartisan and respected study office had been created as well—the Office of Technology Assessment. Information turned up by scholars could be extremely dangerous to conservative policy. If, for example, simple data collection could show that abortion was quite safe, and women wanted but did not have convenient contraceptives, then the message about abstinence would be undermined. If it is found as a matter of fact that fundamentalists get divorced as often as anyone else, and are unfaithful as often as anyone else, the conservative message is undermined.

So the solution was to begin a counter-scholarship. Data collection was stopped wherever possible. Studies on the safety of abortion were ended, for example. The Office of Technology Assessment was closed. Programs that funded the collection of social statistics at the National Science Foundation were cut back drastically. The outcome of research was now preordained. What might be called faith-based scholarship was created. The thinkers of the New Right created a new battery of think tanks, most notably the Heritage Foundation and the re-created American Enterprise Institute. In the 1980s and 1990s came the Competitive Enterprise Institute, the Citizens for a Sound Economy, the Cato Institute, and Gingrich's Progress & Freedom Foundation, among others.

These groups had a new understanding—that it was not necessary to start with disinterested work. The new scholarship extended the known truths from Christianity and free enterprise and brought them *to* society, rather than taking them from a reading *of* society. The challenge was marketing the known truths. From a distance, say the distance between a television and a viewer, it was difficult to distinguish these new kinds of groups from traditional scholarship. That required knowing how the research was conducted. For the most part, reporters through the 1980s and 1990s were aware that these new groups employed dubious methods, but it is not easy for a reporter to challenge the conclusions of such a group—it would require a good deal of work and would risk appearing needlessly hostile. It was easier simply to quote them and try to find other views as well. The advantage goes to the party making the assertions; it takes time to challenge them.

It seemed inevitable that the New Right in its heyday would go after the FDA. The agency not only represented the notion of science-based policymaking, which was contrary to the values-based policymaking of the right, but the agency was effective in taking on businesses. The FDA represented everything that conservatives disliked—regulation, the harnessing of business, and dedication to the public interest rather than received wisdom.

When Reagan took office, the Heritage Foundation produced a nearly 3,000-page blueprint for right-wing governance, an instruction manual for running a different—conservative—kind of government. A 1,000-page version was sold as a book, a bestseller in Washington called *Mandate for Leadership*. Its producers later bragged that two-thirds of its nearly 2,000 recommendations were adopted as policy or accepted as goals by the Reagan administration. The book is full of enthusiasm and certainty, but it is so short on support for its assertions that it was also described as the single greatest collection of unfounded statements on government and society ever compiled.

Mandate for Leadership contains the outline for the first wave of attacks on the FDA. The nation, the book says, was in a "crisis of overregulation," in which regulation has brought "mounting costs to society." Not that the authors had compared the costs of regulating to the costs of *not* regulating, or regulating *differently*. At least six dubious claims are rolled up into two sentences on the FDA: "The costs of regulatory compliance frequently work to depress competition and innovation by driving out small business and making private industry less willing to invest in new ideas and new products. The consumer bears the ultimate burden for excessive regulation, in higher prices for the goods he buys and decreased opportunity for choice in the marketplace."

The "costs" of regulatory compliance are not known. Only conservative economists have approached the subject, and they begin with the assumption that regulations entail only costs. The quantification of the trouble *avoided* by following the FDA's good manufacturing practice rules, for example, is not factored in, although many a manufacturer is saved from blunders and lawsuits by the rules. Economists have not attempted to account for gains in innovation by companies pressed to a higher standard by regulations.

The Reagan administration's plans to solve the crisis of overregulation included several bold steps, including stopping the creation of new regulations, cutting the budgets of regulatory agencies, and infiltrating the agencies with conservatives. The actions, like Nixon's but more extensive, were remarkable because the nation had been working to take politics out of the operations of government agencies since the days of Teddy Roosevelt and the progressives, and even before. The Civil Service Act of 1883 and other reforms over the next century were meant to give the president the power to set policy and to lead the agencies, but not to bring personal or ideological politics wholesale into the operation of their day-to-day activities.

It is unclear what Reagan himself understood about the history of public service, but many in his administration were committed to radical change in the government. Nixon had not gone far enough. Carter had made further, more successful efforts, asserting simultaneously that regulations should be reviewed to see if they cost too much, and that the president's budget office, the White House Office of Management and Budget (OMB), had the power to halt regulations if they were judged out of line. This was a new assertion of executive power, since it was Congress that had created the regulatory agencies and had given them detailed marching orders. Carter asserted for the first time that the president should be the final authority on regulation. He also began budget cuts at the federal agencies.

Carter's anti-regulatory action hardly rivaled Reagan's. Nine days after Reagan's inauguration, he ordered a sixty-day freeze on all new regulations. Within three more weeks, the president had signed Executive Order 12291, which went one better than Carter, declaring in law rather than just in rhetoric that the president had the power to control all regulations attempted by the federal agencies. He designated the OMB as the office to which every agency would have to apply if it wanted to implement regulation, and it was from OMB that orders emanated to dismantle regulations already in place. Agencies were required to review, analyze, and justify their regulations. (This was intended to tie up the *bureaucrats* with paperwork, instead of the businesses.)

FDA budgets for enforcement of the most essential rules—to prevent contamination of food, for example—were slashed. It was utterly demoralizing. Lawyers who had been busy day and night, working cases they believed in, suddenly were being told not to pursue investigations. In one case, for example, a company that produced canned mushrooms for large pizza chains decided to cut one safety step out of manufacturing. Previously, if the mushrooms had been in the cans long enough to develop the dangerous growth of botulin, the cans had to be reheated at high enough temperatures to kill the bacteria. The company decided just to drop the old cans back into circulation without reheating. An FDA inspector spotted the dodge, and investigators watched the plant for a time until they figured out a way to prove it: reheating caused the glue under the labels to reliquefy and run. The company was confronted, and denied everything. As the case was being put together, the lawyers were told to leave it alone, said one FDA attorney.

The lack of support from above and the lack of a proper budget were so severe that the situation turned grim. One lawyer recalled that investigators' cars were taken away; they were left with the choice of using their own cars to do their jobs or inspecting only plants within walking distance of the FDA regional headquarters. Lawyers were forced to buy their own supplies to make copies of court motions, and to buy their own covers and tabs to make presentations of court papers. Some of the more frustrated lawyers began to make lists of the cases canceled and the number of deaths that could be said to have resulted. "It broke their hearts," a lawyer said.

The OMB drew up a list that the United States Chamber of Commerce later called the "terrible twenty" regulations to be eliminated, those most offensive to American businesses. "This hit list included some of the regulations most critical to the health and safety of Americans: regulations for classifying hazardous waste, lowering air pollutants, licensing nuclear plants and classifying and restricting possible carcinogens," as Lou Cannon writes in his presidential biography of Reagan. (One of the terrible twenty was Goyan's plan to put information about drugs on package inserts for patients.) Needless to say, consumer and citizens' groups denounced the new policies and the arithmetic. They said that the calculations did not include the measure of lives, injuries, and illnesses that might be caused by reducing standards in factories, mills, and mines. Notorious opponents of regulation were appointed to run regulatory agencies. For instance, Thorne Auchter, vice president of a Florida construction firm and a noted opponent of regulation, was named to head the Occupational Safety and Health Administration.

The Reagan administration chose Dr. Arthur Hull Hayes, Jr., to run the FDA. He was a clinical pharmacologist by training, an M.D. who, unlike some appointees, was no ideologue. But he was camped out on the industry side of medicine. He had been a regular consultant for many drug companies, at high rates of pay, before joining the FDA (and he continued to accept industry money in the form of honoraria after he was in office, which was not illegal at the time). He shared the belief of earlier commissioners that industry should be regulated with its voluntary consent and cooperation. The conservative *Forbes* magazine counted him as a "moderate deregulator." Hayes made it a point to say he would get clearance from the political higher-ups if there were to be any new regulation.

He was a thin, heavy-browed man who sported slicked-down hair, standard-issue striped ties, and button-down shirts, with pens lined up in his breast pocket. He had studied at Oxford as a Rhodes scholar. He was cautious and soft-spoken, a conservative from Pennsylvania, the home state of the new secretary of health and human services (HHS), Richard Schweiker. He had been director of Penn State's Hershey Medical Center's hypertension clinic and was only forty-seven at the time of his appointment at the FDA. When a staffer for Secretary Schweiker was asked to produce names of possible FDA leaders, the staffer called a contact from the Pharmaceutical Manufacturers Association who turned out to be Joseph Stetler (of the Hussey-Stetler test of time). Stetler suggested a few people to call, including Hayes. Hayes got on well enough with Schweiker during his one interview that he was offered the job the next day.

Among his first priorities was canceling the new program to give patients information about the drugs they were taking, which had been put into effect only the year before. Industry opposition to it was fierce. It was a bit difficult to kill, as it was already in place as a federal regulation. But Hayes wrote a counter-regulation to kill the previous one. He himself had a conflict of interest because of money he had taken before joining the FDA from one of the companies involved, Hoffmann-LaRoche, maker of Valium and Librium.

Hayes also curtailed the FDA's efforts to require the new labels on processed foods. Hayes and the Reagan administration believed in voluntary programs and thought requiring new food labels was going too far. Hayes's background included years of work on high blood pressure, and he was aware that high salt content in the diet was an important risk for some patients. It was vital that patients at least be able to find out how much salt was in the food they were eating; not knowing could be dangerous. He suggested to industry that companies put on their food labels the amount of salt the foods contained. He made noises about putting in new regulations if the companies did not voluntarily comply. Industry responded over a period of two years by acceding less than half the time.

Like his predecessor and his successors, Hayes came under strong pressure to move drugs out faster. He voiced his willingness to consider a number of changes to get drugs to market more quickly, and "to . . . stimulate the marketing of important new drugs," as he said. But as he began to review the regulations, he found that the strongest measures being suggested by others in the administration were fundamentally irrational. On a number of issues, chiefly those involving fundamental principles of safety and effectiveness, whatever his own political allegiance, after some study he took a stand to preserve scientific standards. As Dr. Joe Levitt, a physician who has worked at the agency for more than a quarter century, described it, Hayes walked through each of the key proposals then designed to solve the "drug lag." Some of the solutions would be worse than the problem they were trying to solve, he found.

One was to eliminate the requirement that companies gain FDA approval before giving humans any experimental drug. It seems obvious given the history of human experimentation that new-drug experiments for toxicity should first be conducted in the lab and on animals. But the proposal at the time was to let private medical committees called IRBs (institutional review boards) be the sole determiners of whether a company could begin experiments on humans. As Levitt put it, "Hayes said, 'I've served on an IRB. They can review matters of ethics. But they can't do toxicology. They don't have the expertise, and they're not staffed to do that.'" Another proposal was to eliminate the requirement that a drug be tested to ensure it will do what its maker claims it will. Hayes would not waive it, saying, "I'm a doctor. When I treat a patient with a drug, I want to know whether it works." A third proposal was to eliminate prior tests of effectiveness, instead putting the drug on the market and gathering such data from doctors using it on their patients. Again, Hayes declined, ruling that clinical investigation was essential, if for no other purpose than instructing doctors on a drug's usage. A fourth proposal was to hand over the FDA's responsibility for reviewing drugs to outside committees. Hayes said he knew committees well enough to know they were not a good option.

On some specific issues, Hayes was not free to develop policies on the basis of medicine and science. He was faced with fairly bold political intrusion from above. Those at OMB were the hatchet men. One of the first issues they raised had to do with Reye's syndrome.

Reye's syndrome is a disease that comes on after a viral infection—flu or chicken pox. It appears mostly in children, and it is frequently fatal. About a week after the infection, nausea and vomiting begin. The mental changes in children vary from amnesia and lethargy to seizures and finally coma. Death results ultimately from liver failure. The illness has a high death rate—20 percent. And among those who survive, about a third suffer mental retardation or seizure disorders. Estimates had put the number of deaths of children from the disease between 120 and 360 per year.

There is apparently more than one trigger for the syndrome. The disease itself was recognized only in 1963, but by 1980 researchers had discovered that there appeared to be a strong connection between its onset and the taking of aspirin during the viral infection. The Centers for Disease Control announced publicly in 1980 that there might be a connection and that parents should "use caution" when giving aspirin during flu or chicken pox. The warning was not properly publicized, but even if it had been, what does caution mean to a parent in those circumstances?

But four studies in different parts of the United States between 1978 and 1980 had confirmed the link. The results were in by October 1981, and analyzed by an expert panel brought into the CDC for the purpose. The panel was alarmed. In uncharacteristically direct language, the scientists said that the data was strong enough for them to say that aspirin should *not* be used for children during flu and chicken pox outbreaks. Furthermore, the group said, aspirin bottles should carry a warning on their labels.

The panel's findings were quickly squelched inside CDC. The original data in the four studies—the original figures, interviews, and medical records—was no longer available to public health officials. Aspirin manufacturers had urged the CDC and, more important, those above them at the Department of Health and Human Services to say nothing until all the data could be reviewed again. By December, the CDC director passed on a pile of documents to the FDA, hoping Hayes could help. The FDA was aware of the new data, and had jurisdiction.

At the same time, the medical group most concerned, the American Academy of Pediatrics, appointed a committee to look into the matter. A month later, the committee had drafted a recommendation that was even stronger than the CDC panel's, urging doctors to instruct their patients not to use aspirin during the winter flu season, and to use acetaminophen instead. Immediately, the aspirin companies privately asked the academy to keep its report secret.

By January, lawyers at the CDC were warning top officials that they could not sit on the data—a warning of some kind had to be issued, regardless of its impact on aspirin makers. Of course, important secrets inside the government don't stay secret very long. Sidney Wolfe was outraged that children would continue to die while the aspirin industry kept damning reports bottled up, and he went public with the information in

February. He threatened legal action against the FDA if it did not act. The American Public Health Association weighed in by March, asking for FDA action. The CDC finally went public with its warning. Even the secretary felt compelled to say something. On June 4, Schweiker said the evidence was sufficient to warrant a warning to both doctors and parents. He ordered the FDA to change the labels on aspirin and said a major education campaign from HHS would begin. By September, the FDA had finalized an official labeling proposal.

But the Aspirin Foundation could still prevail. It knew that under Reagan's executive order, the White House Office of Management and Budget could stop the regulation in its tracks. The calendar of appointments at the OMB in those years was nothing short of a roster of the great companies in America. Consumer or health organizations were allowed very few visits. Five aspirin industry specialists were in the group that got an evening appointment with James J. Tozzi, deputy administrator of OMB's obscure but powerful Office of Information and Regulatory Affairs. The office was the repository of business information, and the place where regulatory measures were canceled.

Meanwhile, OMB officials, including statisticians, studied the data on Reye's syndrome. Denis Prager, a science specialist at OMB, advised the top OMB officials that the proposed labeling was a prudent public health measure. The data was more than solid, and he would even suggest making the warning clearer. Tozzi acknowledged that the risk was statistically significant in reporting to his boss, Christopher DeMuth. But he also larded his communication with anecdotal information and "ideas" from conservatives, such as if parents are warned about the problem with aspirin, maybe they will think Reye's is a disease curable just by avoiding aspirin. Therefore, a warning would be counterproductive.

DeMuth, working from Tozzi's memo, called Schweiker and told him to cancel the labeling rule. Simultaneously, the American Academy of Pediatrics board suddenly reversed its call for aspirin labeling. Schweiker soon announced that he was canceling his order to FDA. There would be no label. He cited the reversal by the American Academy of Pediatrics board as a key reason, and pushed for another study.

Schweiker left office shortly after that, in early 1983, and Margaret Heckler succeeded him. Aspirin manufacturers soon met with her to try to stop a campaign to educate parents about Reye's. On the day of their meeting, Heckler halted the distribution of pamphlets and radio spots on Reye's. The material itself was already so vague as to be useless, saying aspirin did not cause Reye's, but not saying to avoid aspirin during flu or chicken pox. Instead, the advertisements advised, "use caution when giving aspirin or other salicylate products for such illnesses." In fact, read literally, the ads suggested aspirin could be used if it was done carefully. Scientists and public health officials profoundly disagreed. By the fall of 1983, two years after studies had confirmed the problem and two panels had called for immediate action, it was possible to start counting deaths *after* action should have been taken. Reported figures are usually far below the number of actual cases; between November 1981 and November 1983, at least 361 new cases of the disease had been reported. One hundred thirteen children had died.

In the meantime, the aspirin makers, most notably Bayer, had begun a counter-advertising campaign aimed at parents. To do this, Bayer and others funded a front organization, the American Reye's Syndrome Association, which offered a novel solution to putting labels on bottles of aspirin. It actually suggested to parents that they diagnose Reye's syndrome themselves, and then tell their doctors how to diagnose it. This was a curious position from an association calling itself a "group of parents." In the tiny print at the bottom of their brochure, the "parents" said they were funded by Glenbrook Laboratories, the maker of Bayer aspirin for children.

The instructions in the brochure were an elaborate ruse. They said that no one knew the cause of Reye's and listed an array of possible causes, including "genetic factors . . . pesticides, chemical wastes, aflatoxins, etc., and medications used to control vomiting and fever such as antiemetics, aspirin and acetaminophen." That last bit was particularly nasty, because it diverted parents away from the proper treatment for fevers. The brochure went on to give a long explanation of what to look for in order to diagnose your child; it also said the disease was impossible to rule out or confirm without a blood test. It said, "Since many doctors are not familiar with RS, and the symptoms can be mistaken for meningitis, encephalitis, diabetes, poisoning, or especially in older children and adults, drug overdose, it is important to remind them about Reye's." The aspirin makers began to broadcast ads that started: "Stay tuned for a medical bulletin on Reye's Syndrome." The subsequent message declared that the cause of Reye's was unknown, and aspirin was *never mentioned*.

Over the following years, repeated warnings in news reports and independent educational efforts by public health groups gradually suppressed the rate of Reye's syndrome in the United States. But it came slowly—550 cases had been reported (out of an unknown number of actual cases) in 1980. By 1985 the number of reported cases had dropped to fewer than 200. Commissioners came and went before a resolution of the issue, and in 1985, Dr. Frank Young began a campaign to get the aspirin companies to voluntarily label their products. He failed.

Eventually it was found that aspirin increases a child's risk of contracting Reye's by thirty-five-fold—an extremely high correlation. A suit by the Health Research Group of Public Citizen against the FDA ended with a federal judge scolding the agency for failing to act early, but the judge declined to insert himself in the regulatory decision-making and stopped short of ordering labels on aspirin bottles. In March 1986 the FDA finally determined that mandatory labels were necessary, and they were introduced in June of that year.

By the 1980s, pasteurization (heating) was standard practice around the world to prevent salmonella contamination that often occurs in raw milk. The evidence for doing so was solid and long-standing, and pasteurization does very little to lessen milk's nutritive value. But now the "health food" and "natural food" crazes began in the United States, and raw milk was offered for sale once again. As it happened, only thirty states had actually gotten around to writing laws requiring milk to be sterilized to protect consumers. California was one of the twenty states that did not. One dairy there, Alta Dena, began to proclaim boldly that its milk was "pure," "the healthiest," and "certified." The health messages of fifty years before had apparently been forgotten. Their sales increased. Of course, the number of cases of sickness and death from salmonella around California also increased, from 46 in 1981, to 70 in 1982, to 123 in 1983.

In 1981 the FDA decided to ban the sale of raw milk as a potentially adulterated food. Doctors, scientists, and public health officials, including those inside HHS and the FDA, made it clear there was no case for raw milk. Alta Dena, however, was located in the district of Republican Representative Bill Dannemeyer, who had been general counsel for the company, and he took his pleading to the White House and HHS Secretary Margaret Heckler, as well as to the FDA. He recruited thirty-four other members of Congress from California to oppose the regulation of raw milk.

The FDA was ordered off the case. The assistant secretary of HHS who delivered the message, Dr. Robert Rubin, wrote that the HHS "nonconcurred" with the FDA ban. After all, he said, "persons who prefer raw milk are well aware that it is not pasteurized and are also aware of the risks they may be taking." It was an arguable proposition, especially regarding children.

In this case, Hayes made known his recommendation that raw milk be banned. But the Office of Management and Budget ordered the agency not to act, and it didn't. Again, the Health Research Group sued the agency, and by 1985 Judge Gerhard Gesell said in a written order that the HHS and FDA must act on raw milk: "The department's justification for its continued delay is lame at best and irresponsible at worst." While political officers of the HHS were saying more study was needed, Gesell retorted that "since its own top health officials are on the record to the contrary, this assertion can be given no credence." He noted that hundreds of illnesses and some deaths had occurred between the time the FDA first proposed a ban on selling raw milk in 1973 (it reproposed the measure in 1983 after new data on illnesses and death came in) and 1985. The battle continued until January 1987, when the court finally ordered the FDA to ban the sale of raw milk as a product that had been proved "conclusively" to be unsafe. Heckler, whose actions in 1984 had been found "arbitrary and capricious" by the court, protested that a ban was unnecessary. She said states could solve the problem if they wanted to. As for the raw milk sold interstate, she said it was a relatively small amount. This was an episode of deregulation at its ugliest.

•

CHAPTER FIFTEEN

The Medical Officer

DR. ROBERT Temple stepped out of a meeting with FDA staffers who were still peppering him with questions. He pointed to his next visitor "Just give me thirty or forty seconds." He walked out of the room, was immediately snared by another official, then made his way down the hall, to return a few minutes later. He was ready for his next appointment. It was early 2002; he had agreed to discuss some matters of the past thirty years of history.

His visitor entered Temple's office, a rabbit warren of paper stacks. Temple, the longtime guru of drug review at the FDA and a legend among those who carry out and study medical experiments around the world, is among the agency's most senior officers, so his office is one of the largest. It has a desk, a small round table, and three chairs; at least that is what the objects beneath the hillocks of paper appear to be. There are bookshelves, too, stuffed not only in rows but with volumes wedged horizontally between book tops and the next shelf. Further paper stacks grow from the bookcase top, heading toward the ceiling. The tops of the tall windows here serve as vents admitting air and light; tall, obscuring stacks block viewing.

"Something is different since I was last here," the visitor said.

"I cleaned up." Temple grinned. "Have a seat." He cleared stacks from a chair for his guest, then for himself.

The current era in medicine might be described as the pharmaceutical era, because that is the chief way we treat disease now. Getting a prescription is the most likely outcome of a visit to the doctor, and about 3 billion prescriptions are written annually in the United States alone. There are some 20,000 medical experiments conducted every year in the country, and probably more than 10 million people are subjects in them. The pivot upon which all of this turns is the medical experiment itself and the scientists who guide it, one of whom is Robert Temple.

Temple, sixty-one when we spoke, has had a career that spans the greater part of the entire era of scientific drug testing. He began his college studies in the late 1950s, at Harvard, where he graduated magna cum laude. He trained at New York University, and at the top training ground in the country at the time, the Columbia-Presbyterian Medical Center in New York. He then moved to the National Institutes of Health for three years. His career in medical research was progressing nicely, but he felt something was missing. Research was somehow a little too confining. "It just didn't light my fire. I didn't lie awake nights thinking about it," he said. He considered other work, from running a hospital clinic to working in the government. "I looked at FDA because I thought of myself as a consumer advocate; my wife had worked for Ralph Nader, and that had been positive. FDA provides direct protection to people," he said. He went to talk with Dr. Richard Crout, head of the bureau of drugs, liked him, and signed on. "I've been here ever since, and never regretted it for a moment."

He joined the FDA in 1972, at a crucial moment in the evolution of the agency. At one time, inspectors were the soul of the FDA—from the time they cracked the "dead horse" conspiracy in New York to their chasing down the bottles of deadly sulfanilamide from Texas to North Carolina. But over time, it is the medical reviewers who have emerged as the signature employees of the agency.

When he joined the FDA, Temple found himself walking into a new intellectual field. The occupation of "reviewer" or "theorist" of medical experiments was just being created. Since then, he has helped plan experiments and then pick them apart when they have run their course. He has theorized, taught, and helped write federal rules about them. He had made his mark, not just in American medicine but worldwide.

He is a man of medium size, perhaps five feet eight, with peppered black hair and mustache. He wears thick glasses. He smiles easily as the conversation begins, but clearly pressed by business, Temple jumps into the pool of data as soon as he can manage it. His daily work is the study of formations, patterns, and trends—"the puzzles," he calls them. Amid the data streaming out of the human experiments day by day, he must try to see clearly to the structure beneath. And because these puzzles involve matters of life and health, they often *can* keep him awake at night.

He recalled one case from early in his career. Calcitonin, a salmon hormone, had been shown to be effective in treating a rare disorder called Paget's disease, in which bone leaches away and is replaced with softer, more massive tissue. One company suggested that calcitonin could be used to reduce calcium in the blood when the levels were so high as to threaten severe damage to the organs.

In looking over the studies, Temple noticed wide discrepancies between the studies done in different clinics. Some seemed to show that calcitonin was quite effective at reducing calcium, while others showed little or no effect. How could such simple tests—blood drawn and tested for calcium—produce such disparate results? Temple began to sift through the records, patient by patient. Eventually, he spotted the pattern—the drug was typically given to patients early in the morning in all the different testing centers. But in some of the clinics, blood samples were taken soon after the patients got the drug. In others, patients did not get blood tests until hours later. Temple assembled the list of times when the drug was given versus when blood was drawn. When blood was tested immediately, the drug seemed to be effective and calcium levels dropped. But when patients were tested later, the results were insignificant. Temple realized that the drug worked for only a very brief time, far too short to be of any use to patients.

Another of Temple's detective successes concerned a terrifying pattern among those who have heart attacks—often they die suddenly and unexpectedly in the months after a first, warning attack. Doctors have long felt something could prevent these deaths. In 1980 an answer to patients' prayers appeared to come in the form of an experiment and its results announced in the *New England Journal of Medicine*. It appeared that a drug called sulfinpyrazone (or Anturane, the trade name given to it by its maker, Ciba-Geigy) could dramatically reduce the chances of sudden death after a heart attack. In one accounting, it appeared to cut the chance of death by 74 percent; in another, deaths were cut by 32 percent. The results were even more impressive because the study included 1,600 patients, a huge experiment at the time and a laudable undertaking for a drug company. Large trials then were conducted almost exclusively by government agencies; companies didn't want to risk the necessary investment.

After the report, doctors expected the FDA to approve the drug quickly, and an FDA advisory committee of experts soon voted to go ahead. Then, on April 25, 1980, as the *New England Journal of Medicine* put it, "The FDA surprised everyone by announcing that Anturane could not be [approved] for the prevention of death in the critical months after heart attack." Doctors were shocked and angry.

Temple, the key medical officer on the case, had stumbled over something that looked suspect. Some patients in the experiment had died, but their deaths had not been counted in the final report. Temple noticed that instead of simply comparing deaths among those who took the drug and those who did not, the researchers did something odd. Instead of just listing all cardiac-related deaths, they listed them in three categories: "sudden death," sudden death due to "acute myocardial infarction," or sudden death due to "other cardiac" problems. Temple also discovered that one patient who had died was listed in one category early in the study, then ended up in another. In fact, he found that misassignment was common. The mistakes just happened to strongly favor a positive result for the drug.

Temple and biostatistician Gordon Pledger ran the numbers again, with proper data entry. Now it was clear the drug did nothing to prevent sudden death after heart attack. Hence, the final FDA decision. (It was never determined whether the errors in the study resulted from mistakes or fraud.)

"That trial really changed our behavior," Temple said. For one thing, he and his colleagues were alerted to the creation of misleading statistical groups. "We realized that breaking it down into those groups was totally bogus. That was not their plan in the beginning; they came up with it after the fact. What they were doing was noodling around with the data" until the numbers came out the best way, he continued. He also learned that he had to account for every patient. "There were some patients in those original papers who died, but if you search the paper you cannot find them. They died but were not counted. So now, we say, if you randomize patients you have to tell us what happened to every one—we learned that from the Anturane trial: account for every patient," he said.

This kind of learning has proceeded, case by case, for decades. In 1940 the issues surrounding controlled experiments were largely theoretical; few such experiments had ever been tried. Over the next twenty years, practical experience showed what might go wrong, by accident or design. By 1970, the FDA wrote the first guidelines and prohibitions regarding "adequate and well-controlled" experiments.

Obviously, careful medical experiments are meant to separate the relative handful of discoveries that are true advances in therapy from a legion of false leads and unverifiable impressions. This is not a simple matter, because diseases do not always run the same course, treatment varies, and patients themselves differ in how they react. And there is fraud. But with years of accumulated experience, the process of designing and carrying out medical experiments has become more routine, if not foolproof. The path from lab to market now begins early—when the presumptive new drug is still just a chemical gleam in a flask.

Catastrophes like the one caused by Elixir Sulfanilamide have made it routine to check first whether the drug is an outright poison. Those tests are conducted on cells, then on two or more animal species. A drug's chemistry is considered—can the drug be made reliably, its components rendered stable so it does not deteriorate on the shelf? Exposing animals to a drug can show whether it interferes with the normal chemistry of organs, whether it breaks down into other chemicals, and whether those "metabolites" are hazardous. Will it get into the blood effectively, or is it quickly flushed from the body? If not enough is absorbed, very large doses may be needed to cause the intended effect, and large doses in turn are often toxic. Then there are the questions about how a drug affects behavior. Do the animals become agitated when taking it, or unusually sleepy? Do they go off their feed or lose weight?

All these studies can be completed in a period of months, providing proper standards are maintained. The scientists have to be good, of course, and the animals healthy and well cared for; unhealthy animals will complicate experiments. For the largest pharmaceutical companies, these matters are routine if rigorous, but for a substantial number of companies these tests are difficult to master.

A company pressing forward with a new drug will probably already begin talking to reviewers at the FDA early on. This was not always true. Until the late 1970s the independence of the FDA reviewers was deemed essential—they were not permitted to give company scientists guidance about what evidence would be sufficient to prove a drug's safety and effectiveness. In devising their own plans and conducting their own tests, companies risked the possibility that, after years of work, FDA reviewers might well simply tell them, "Sorry, but your designs from the beginning were faulty; you must start over."

This distance was abandoned by the 1980s, and reviewers were routinely offering detailed advice on what studies were needed and how they should be designed. Reviewers themselves believe that the cooperation helps make the approval process more efficient, more likely to produce the necessary kind of data. They often chart a new drug's development for two years or more by the time a final application is made to market a new drug, continually talking with company scientists from testing to final approval. They don't feel compromised by guiding company scientists through the needed tests. Rather, when there are problems, they tend to come from higher-ups within the FDA who want to press a drug forward. Reviewers have sometimes felt that their superiors too often side with companies rather than with their own review staff.

A review starts when a sponsoring company sends in an IND (investigational new drug) application to test its drug for the first time in humans. The company submits data from lab work and animal testing demonstrating this would be safe to do. It also outlines plans for how it will administer the new drug to people. If approved, the work on humans begins with a handful of volunteers. If there are no sudden and unexpected reactions (to the chagrin of hopeful researchers, toxic reactions occur as often as 40 percent of the time), the company quickly moves to conduct trials involving hundred of patients (phase II experiments). In the final round of experiments (phase III) before approval, thousands of patients are given a drug.

When the full set of data arrives at the FDA, reviews are typically conducted by teams of four: a chemist, a pharmacologist, a biostatistician, and an M.D. The data is most often sent in to the FDA as computer files; those companies unable to do that must submit their findings in binders that may run to three hundred volumes or more, mostly in data and tables of figures.

Safety comes first, and in a completed drug application there is an integrated safety summary, which can run up to ten thousand pages detailing all the results that might bear on a drug's safety. Looking at this document, and with other data as backup, reviewers first ask, how many patients who took this drug died during the experiment? Was the cause related to the drug itself? If patients dropped out of studies, reviewers want to know why. Was it because the side effects of the drug were intolerable? Could those effects lead to death or serious injury, and if so, in how many patients? Reviewers study the cases of participants who had serious "adverse events" along the way—severe reactions that are life-threatening, lead to hospitalization, or might result in cancer or some severe deformity.

Day after day at the computer screen, reviewers sift through seven or eight key categories of hazards, taking notes and making calculations, sometimes asking the company for more information. Similar sifting and calculating go on to determine whether a drug works as promised, and if there is a real benefit for the patients. This is difficult terrain. If the safety holds up, does the drug still do the patients any good? Most sick people are not stable but get better for periods of time, then worse again. Some people have more severe symptoms than others. How is it possible to sort out how much effect a drug is having in each individual case? How is success to be measured? In AIDS, for example, the first measure of the success of any drug was simply how many more patients survived while taking a drug compared with those who didn't. But later it was found that just measuring and tracking the number of HIV particles in the blood was a good measure of how well a patient was doing, and how likely the patient was to succumb to a severe episode of AIDS-related disease. So now, a drug that can measurably reduce the amount of virus in the blood is counted as one giving patients a benefit. The connection between virus particles and illness and death could not be assumed; it had to be shown by experiment.

The question of measuring patient benefit can easily become obscured, reviewers say. It is the most common source of disagreement between reviewers and companies pressing a drug forward. Doctors and medical researchers frequently begin to think in units of laboratory values—enzymes up, platelets down, blood pressure rising, heart rhythms settling down. These soon begin to stand in for the real objects—whether a patient survives longer, or may have fewer debilitating symptoms. Some guiding rules emerged over the years.

It is essential to develop in writing, at the outset, a careful plan for the experiment, making clear what you are setting out to prove and how you intend to prove it. Patients included must be selected carefully, so that it is clear that each has the same disease, diagnosed by the same methods, and usually equally advanced in the progression of disease. It is also essential to identify the tests used to diagnose the disease, how and when they will be conducted, and exactly what results will be counted. The idea is to limit the number of complicating factors and focus directly on the intended disease; if patients have widely varying problems and different diagnoses, the results of the experiment may depend on some extraneous factor and not on the all-important connection between the drug and its target.

Once patients are diagnosed and selected as similar enough to study, they must be assigned to one of two groups: one receiving the new drug, one not (possibly getting a placebo instead). It is essential to choose by an unbiased, random method. There must be an attempt to uncover previously hidden problems, like allergies, for example, or dietary differences. These people must be randomly distributed in both groups.

The underlying point is that ordinary human experience and observation are too unreliable to be the basis for medicine. The best proof of this inadequacy of experience and judgment alone is a crisis that occurred in

April 1989, arguably the worst drug disaster in American history, though it received little press coverage.

It began with a number of drugs that were able to correct irregular heart rhythms, such as Tambocor and Enkaid in their trade names, flecainide and encainide in their generic names. The FDA approved them for use in people who had severe heart problems and life-threatening electrical rhythms. But from 1981 on, doctors began to use the drugs in a way that was unintended, for patients who had mildly irregular rhythms. Some of this arrhythmia was so mild that patients did not notice it; only a heart monitoring machine, the Holter monitor, picked up the irregularities, called premature ventricular complexes. Doctors were putting mildly ill patients on the drugs as a precaution.

By 1988, doctors were putting several hundred thousand patients with mild rhythm disturbances on the drugs each year, even though it was not known whether it would do any good or any harm. But when the National Heart, Lung, and Blood Institute proposed to find out and scheduled a large study, doctors protested. Doctors who had taken a risk by putting patients on the drugs in 1981 were now firmly convinced by their "experience" that the drugs were benefiting their patients. It was even said that the experiment to test the drugs—in which some patients would be given the drugs and an equal number would be given a placebo—were unethical. At one meeting, a leader of the experiment, Dr. Raymond Woosley, endured shouts from the audience, "You are immoral! You are immoral!" for conducting the tests and "withholding" the drugs from some patients by giving them placebos.

In September 1988 calculations from the study showed that death rates were very different in groups getting the drug and those not getting the drug. Three patients died in one group, and nineteen in the other. It was assumed that the anti-arrhythmic drugs were working well, but by April 1989, the disparity in survival between the two groups continued despite the larger and larger number of patients enrolled in the study. Now the blind was broken, and patients taking the drug and the placebo were identified. The researchers were stunned. The drugs were not only failing to save patients, they were killing them. In the first 730 patients studied for less than a year, 33 patients taking the drugs died, while only 9 who were taking a placebo died. The death rate for those on the drug was three-and-a-half times greater.

Some 400,000 patients were now being given anti-arrhythmics annually to treat mild disturbances. The NHLBI study alone suggested that 5,000 people were being killed annually. Since several other drugs that were quite similar had not yet been studied and were used widely as well, it was likely that several times that number might be dying needlessly. Experts estimate that in the 1980s, tens of thousands to hundreds of thousands of people were killed in this misadventure by cardiologists.

When the experiment was halted and the news reported, doctors were overwhelmed by calls from patients. In a study of how doctors reacted to the news, Columbia University researchers found that more than 81 percent of cardiologists, despite news of the deaths, did not take their patients off the drugs. That, as one author noted, would have required calling patients and admitting to them that they had committed a life-threatening error. Rather, the heart doctors quietly changed their prescriptions for *new* patients.

The testing of drugs, and puzzling out the meaning of those tests, is plainly a matter of life and death. There are gray areas aplenty, and opportunities for mistakes.

The FDA's mistakes usually arise from bad judgments made in a state of uncertainty. If, for example, in a trial of a drug including three thousand patients, half a dozen have blood tests showing elevated liver enzymes, is that important? Is it a signal that the drug is damaging the patients' livers, or is it just a reflection of other medical problems the patients have?

There was little warning from pre-market tests for the drug cerivastatin, or Baycol. It is in a family of drugs called statins used to lower cholesterol and treat high blood pressure. The family defect is that all the drugs cause damage to the muscle cells, a condition called rhabdomyolysis. Some of the statins are worse than others. By the time Baycol came along, there were already five others on the market, so Baycol was not particularly needed. In fact, it appeared somewhat less effective than the others. But it was sold cheaply to undercut the market.

Within a year after the drug went to market, the hazards of the drug began to be apparent. First, there was a report of a death in Germany caused by rhabdomyolysis and the cascade of trouble it triggers in the body. As muscle cells disintegrate, the masses of cellular waste flow into the blood and then to the kidneys, which are then overwhelmed and may shut down altogether.

After the first reports, FDA changed the drug's label to warn of the problem. Letters were sent out to warn physicians. Many ignored them. As the number of deaths rose past twenty, it began to appear that Baycol was among the worst of the statins in causing muscle cell damage. A second warning was sent out, asking doctors not to start patients on the higher dose and also warning against using the drug in combination with another drug called Lopid. But some continued to ignore the warnings.

It wasn't until thirty-one deaths were confirmed that the FDA and the company felt there was no choice. The drug probably should have been pulled from the market sooner but was finally removed in August 2001.

Baycol's troubles were hard to spot ahead of time. Not so for Posicor, or mibefradil, a drug used to treat blood pressure and chest pain from angina. Six months before the drug was approved, the leader of the review team, Dr. Shaw W. Chen, wrote in his review that the clinical trials of the drug "cast a shadow of potential risk for serious arrhythmias." Six people had already died in the tests of the drug; it was not clear if the drug triggered any of the deaths, but it was possible. The company had already started a much larger experiment of congestive heart failure to better resolve the question of what was causing the sudden deaths. At the time the drug came up for approval, the large study was not finished. The company, Hoffmann-LaRoche, did not want to interrupt and therefore compromise the usefulness of the data from the experiment. It would take a year to finish. What was known was that of the 2,400 patients in the study, 268 were dead and 142 had died of sudden heart failure. Were the sudden deaths due to illness or the drug? The FDA could approve Posicor based on smaller studies in which it appeared safe, or wait until the agency could find out what happened to the 142 patients. Outside experts advising the FDA were split. After debate within the agency, the drug was approved in June 1997. After six months of use by tens of thousands of patients, it became clear that approval had been a mistake. The drug was dangerously lowering heart rates in some patients. It appeared that Posicor was interacting with other drugs to cause the problem. The label already had three drugs named that should not be taken with Posicor. The reports made clear that Posicor was triggering bad reactions to other drugs. When the number of drugs that could react fatally with Posicor reached twenty-six, including allergy medications, cholesterol-lowering drugs, and tranquilizers, the drug was withdrawn.

The company said that it would be impossible to write a sensible label involving warnings of so many dangerous interactions. In the larger experiment, ultimately it was also shown that Posicor wasn't as effective as other drugs while carrying a significant hazard of sudden death.

FDA officials were surprised by the turn of events but said in retrospect that they should have been able to anticipate them, and wait for better data, as the drug would not represent an advance over other treatments in any case.

Another problem drug was bromfenac, the pain reliever known by its brand name, Duract. With this one also, the FDA reviewers saw the trouble coming. In testing before approval, a few patients who took the drug had abnormal blood tests, showing that something was going wrong with their livers. Rudolph Widmark, one of the FDA reviewers, told his colleagues and superiors at the agency that the drug had problems, and if it was approved it should carry a strong warning that doctors not prescribe it for more than ten days at a time. A black box warning—the highest level of alert that can be put on a label—should be attached to it, Widmark recommended. After all, the market was already jammed with similar pain relievers, including over-the-counter varieties such as Aleve. But Widmark's boss, Dr. Murray Lumpkin, thought Widmark was being alarmist. The manufacturer, Wyeth-Ayerst, had been to visit Lumpkin, and he was convinced that the hazard was rare and could be handled by putting on the label a warning that the pain reliever should be used only for short periods. So the drug was approved. The label did mention the problem, but labels are not written by the FDA; they too are negotiated with the company. So the final warning on the label came in the fine print in which the drug was recommended "for generally less than 10 days." If doctors wanted to prescribe it for long-term use, they should check patients' liver functions with monthly tests. The drug was marketed, and doctors failed to heed the fine-print warnings; reports of severe liver damage came in, and some patients had total liver failure and required emergency transplants. Seven months after it went to market, the FDA finally decided that a black box warning was necessary. Still, the reports came in—17 deaths from liver failure, and an additional 50 deaths that looked suspicious. And these, of course, were only the voluntary reports, so the actual problems were likely to be ten to a hundred times greater for the simple painkiller. Ultimately, a year after approval, Duract was removed from the market as needlessly dangerous.

What is made clear by these examples is that, by the mid-1990s, the FDA, under pressure, was pinning its hopes on warning labels and doctors' care in prescribing. The burden of dangerous drugs thus shifted away from the agency. Good but worrisome drugs are sent to market, and worries are expressed on the label, rather than waiting for more data and proof of safety.

That system may work if doctors read and heed the labels. Reviewers say the crafting of the label and related information is one of the chief satisfactions of the job—it amounts to giving the official word on what science knows about a drug. But as one reviewer said, "Doctors aren't often paying attention. We may put crucial information in a label and have it end up as a dead letter." Studies confirm it: the labels are largely unheeded and often completely unread. At the same time, pharmaceutical manufacturers effectively use the full arsenal of advertising and promotion to tout a drug's good qualities and downplay its problems. They had hoped that warning doctors would help, but as one prominent pharmacologist, Dr. Alistair J. J. Wood of Vanderbilt University, said of Baycol, "If there is a dangerous cliff, and people keep falling off it, you have to stop relying on the sign that says 'Dangerous Cliff Ahead.' "

The problem drugs and FDA's errors remain relatively few. The agency now approves about sixty to seventy drugs per year. More than 97 percent of them are safe and effective. They are approved quickly and don't often come back to haunt reviewers, doctors, or companies. The number that do need to be pulled has remained essentially stable over the past twenty-five years at between 2 and 3 percent in the United States— a number noticeably better than in other nations reviewing drugs. The only exception to that stable record is one catastrophic year, a year of unprecedented political pressure, about which more later.

By the end of my hour's conversation with Robert Temple, he admitted that it is sometimes discouraging to try to guide the use of drugs only to have the guidance fail. But a regulatory agency's reach goes only so far; drug approvals are in the hands of the FDA, but medicine is in the hands of doctors. For his part, Temple is pleased to have been around for decades to watch medical experimentation progress. "Things have changed, changed for the better," he said. "At least I think so."

•

CHAPTER SIXTEEN

The Modern Plague

THE FDA was always accommodating itself to the warring demands of science and business, and to the minefield of political Washington. This was tough enough under usual conditions. But in the middle 1980s three events occurred that would severely test its mettle: the continuing onslaught of the incumbent anti-regulatory conservatives, a run of criminal activity within the FDA itself, and AIDS.

In the summer of 1981, the FDA's problems under the Reagan administration had hardly let up. The budget cuts and inflation were such that the agency's resources diminished year by year. In 1978 the FDA employed about 7,850 people. Carter cut the number to 7,500. Reagan's first budget reduced it to 6,800. The routine actions by which the agency kept contaminated foods and problem drugs off the market—seizures, injunctions, and prosecutions—dropped dramatically, year after year. Then, in the summer of 1981, the first sketchy reports of a new contagious disease began to be phoned in to investigators at the Centers for Disease Control.

A few doctors in Los Angeles and New York had seen patients infected by a germ called pneumocystis carinii, which caused a fatal pneumonia. It was an extremely rare disease usually; only one hundred cases had been reported in all the world's medical literature before the 1960s. The CDC saw an occasional isolated case, but now requests for help came for dozens, then hundreds of cases of pneumocystis in the United States alone. And while those with this form of pneumonia had usually been old and weakened, these new cases appeared strangely to be entirely in young men who were healthy and homosexual.

The CDC published its first notice of the outbreak on June 5, 1981. Almost a month later, it also reported an outbreak of forty-one cases in homosexual men of a rare and unusual cancer called Kaposi's sarcoma, also an opportunist that flourished only in humans whose defenses against disease were destroyed. The *New York Times* reported that story on July 3. A month later, the *Washington Post* reported that the outbreak was much worse, affecting 111 men with Kaposi's or the pneumonia. It was apparent that both the rare cancer and the rare parasite were piggybacking on some kind of immune system breakdown in the men, the *Post* said. In one of the first notes of alarm in a major newspaper, the *Post* said that the pair of diseases was rapidly surpassing toxic shock syndrome as a public health crisis; that disease had killed eighty-four women over a two-year period. By the end of the year, the number of "immune collapse" cases in homosexual men rose to 180. By the middle of 1982, the disease had jumped outside the category of homosexual men to Haitian immigrants and people who had received blood transfusions. By the end of the summer, 505 cases had been reported, with 202 dead. The disease was now officially called an epidemic.

The disease was eventually named acquired immune deficiency syndrome because its outstanding feature was that those who got it had disastrously weakened immune systems. That is usually an inherited trait, like that of the famous "bubble boy." But the immune system collapse in these cases appeared to be acquired, not inherited—the first time such a deadly loss of immune function had spread like an infectious disease. In other health crises such as toxic shock syndrome and legionnaires' disease, the outbreaks, once discovered, had been limited, and causes were found relatively quickly. But with this disease, it was soon clear that doctors were looking at something quite new. As would be learned gradually, a virus released from its rural reservoirs by encroaching civilization, the human immunodeficiency virus, triggered the disease. The virus not only infected people but also infected the one part of human biology that was nearly impossible to deal with—the body's defensive system itself. Worse, the virus actually entered the body's defensive cells themselves and lay dormant for years, until some signal set it to multiplying. Once this was triggered, every part of the body became susceptible to infections—the mouth, skin, eyes, nose, joints, muscles, and a variety of glands. A huge variety of disease organisms that were normally not much of a threat could now become fatal—bacteria, fungi, parasites, and other viruses. And the new disease apparently killed everyone infected.

The panic began rolling most quickly through the gay communities in New York and San Francisco. As the cause was unknown, and there were no treatments for the core disorder, the response at first was both to accept death (it was called by some the "beautiful death") and to build community groups that would care for the sick (the first and most effective of which was Gay Men's Health Crisis in New York). Soon, medical systems groaned under the demand for repeat services as patients appeared again and again with one potentially fatal disorder after another.

Art Hayes departed as FDA commissioner in the fall of 1983. The interim commissioner, Dr. Mark Novitch, was a first-rate candidate for the job. Both the Pharmaceutical Manufacturers Association and Public Citizen, a rare combination, endorsed him. It seemed urgent to name a new commissioner, and one generally respected, as AIDS was spreading and the burdens on the FDA would grow. But Novitch was a registered Democrat, so he was soon gone. The new commissioner would face slashed budgets, an epidemic in the making, an overburdened work force, and a whole lot of partisan politics. And for a public health official, needless to say, the pay is poor, and the person who holds the job can assume there will be regular public attacks on his or her reputation, intelligence, and integrity. At that moment, the agency was unable to fulfill the missions given to it by Congress. At least six people turned down the job.

Then Frank Young was unearthed at the University of Rochester. He was a former dean of the medical school, and then its vice president, who did not follow the politics of medicine or the FDA. He was a born-again Christian whose career moves had always been preceded by prayers for guidance and a search for signs. His name had been suggested by New York conservatives, but when first asked, he turned the job down. After a second call, he declined again. But by the time the third call came, he felt the job was a personal call from God for him to do public service. Young is a sincere man, with a round, welcoming face and an open smile. Born in Merrick, Long Island, he describes his strongest formative experiences—a childhood accident and his father's death—in terms that are both medical and spiritual.

He seems to be guileless. The difficulty of the job he was being offered didn't faze him. He was, however, pleased when he found he could wear the dress whites of the Public Health Service Corps, a snazzy uniform like that of a navy captain, at least one day a week. He was a man who appreciated such symbols, and who worked to speak in metaphors and parables that made issues simple. As one writer put it, he was "an accomplished politician and publicist . . . a fellow able to get on MacNeil-Lehrer all by himself. . . . He can spin one baseball metaphor after another." One FDA staff member said that Young's role as a publicist would be fine. After all, "the commissioner is not appointed for his expertise in drug review. That's the staff's job."

"I came in with essentially no baggage because I was totally unknown,"

238

Young says now. "I was the seventh commissioner or acting commissioner in seven and a half years. Commissioners were coming and going in the night like Greyhound buses." Early on he said his job would be partly to change the role of the agency from "umpire" or adversary to "catcher," just flashing signs and taking the pitches of the industry. He wanted to revive the agency with thoughts of the future, including biotechnology, and the creation of an "action plan," as he called it, to establish the agency's goals. He became a missionary, driving from one meeting to another in his white Chevy hatchback whose back seat was filled with papers and charts. They showed that the agency was being encumbered with more and more duties, that there were more new drug applications (and fewer FDA employees to deal with them). As news reports said, his favorite statistics were that twenty-one new federal laws had been enacted since 1979 giving the agency additional responsibilities, without any budget increases to finance the work. He said, with some sense of politics, that the decline was not Reagan's fault but started with Carter.

"I kept saying if we had two hundred more reviewers we would be able to deal with this," he said in regard to drug lag. He proposed that the pharmaceutical industry be made to pay some fees when they sent in a new drug application. With that money, the FDA could hire new reviewers and act more quickly on drug applications. Secretary Heckler liked the idea, and the pharmaceutical manufacturers were willing to entertain the notion if it would help get drugs approved faster. But the Office of Management and Budget was opposed. Such a step might actually strengthen the FDA, and the conservative ideologues at OMB wanted to dismantle the agency, not strengthen it.

Whatever plans Young had, AIDS soon dominated the agency's work. There was, first, the pressing issue of blood banks. Once it was suspected that AIDS is caused by a virus, it was essential to ensure that blood banks would not become pools of diseased and contagious blood. Proposed drugs for the treatment of AIDS and its associated illnesses needed to be tested. During the first six years of the epidemic, there were essentially no treatments for AIDS—none that attacked the virus itself, and few that could even treat the rapid onset of other diseases. Among the lessons of FDA history is that a fatal illness with no good therapy routinely draws out hundreds of fraudulent cures. AIDS was no exception. In a rush of comfort-seeking irrationality, many men began to ingest an array of substances touted by rumor. Some seemed rational, chemically and medically, but many did not. There were massage and meditation therapies, and herbal treatments of all descriptions. Human immune-system cells were sold by mail (presumably to replace the depleted ones). Some entrepreneurs sold tissue from pregnant cows; others sold injections of human urine (which is also a currently popular cancer remedy in Texas). Some advocated bathing in bleach, others suggested exposure of the testicles to the afternoon sun. Among the pseudo-pharmaceuticals were a long list of chemicals, including the one Rock Hudson flew to France to obtain, HPA-23, as well as ribavirin, suramin, dextran sulfate, and a disgusting milkshake of egg yolk containing something called AL-721.

AIDS activists in New York and San Francisco sought remedies from everywhere and anywhere. They soon began large-scale smuggling operations to bring to America remedies that had not been effectively tested, but that were nonetheless available in a number of countries with loose standards for drug marketing. There were regular runs to Mexico, Japan, and France. This was a direct challenge to the Food and Drug Administration, its law and regulations. But cautious by nature, overly so in the Reagan years, the FDA decided not to prevent the activists from obtaining the useless drugs. After all, the laws against importation of unapproved drugs were designed to attack commercial fraud, not to deter desperate individuals from seeking therapy. So the smuggling by plane and by mail continued. The FDA decided in the mid-1980s to step in only if enterprises began to profit grossly from the unregulated sales.

"If the medical establishment was unable or unwilling to put drugs into their hands," write Peter Arno and Karyn Feiden, "smugglers and bootleggers, kitchen chemists, and bathtub *braumeisters* were going to do it instead." And they did.

For many, this would be the dark time in America, between the coming of the disease and the time when medicines would be created to challenge it. There has been much argument about what hindered the nation's ability to address this modern plague. One barrier was the biology of HIV itself, and our ignorance of how to approach it. We had no effective drugs for any virus when the plague arrived, and many of our senior scientists believed that no drug treatment would be possible for decades. We simply knew too little, and the virus was able to change too quickly to make solutions like a vaccine possible immediately.

A second barrier was the failure of leadership from political leaders, chiefly those in the White House. It was probably rooted in prejudice against those who were first infected with the disease. In the first several years of the epidemic, long after it was clear that it was the worst epidemic in at least three-quarters of a century, the White House and many agencies of the government looked on AIDS with a collective cold stare. In the early days, the tone of those facing the disease had often been more pleading than angry, as at a candlelight parade in New York at which a young man named Bob Cecchi spoke to Reagan: "Like our first president, you are the father of this country. Do you hear me when I say your children are dying? This problem transcends politics. I ask for more than a simple release of funds; I am asking for an act of love. If you are my father, Mr. President, I am your son. Please help me save my life."

But Reagan refused to deal with it. He did not mention the disease or use the word "AIDS" in public until five years after the epidemic had started. It was seven years before he devoted a speech to it. No high-ranking federal official discussed the disease in public before the end of May 1983, when the assistant secretary in the Department of Health and Human Services, Dr. Edward N. Brandt, finally said that the disease was the first priority of the Public Health Service. He hastened to say that the disease was not one that should frighten the "general population."

At the time, 1,450 cases had been reported, including 558 deaths. Brandt pointed out that the disease was confined chiefly to homosexuals, drug users, Haitian immigrants, and those with the blood disorder hemophilia. "Our findings indicate that AIDS is spread almost entirely through sexual contact, through sharing of needles by drug abusers, and, less commonly, through blood and/or blood products." He said the government had spent $14.5 million on the disease, equal to the amount spent on eight years of work on toxic shock syndrome. What he did not say was that those dollars were spent by CDC doctors simply doing their routine chores in tracking an infectious disease—no additional money had been provided specifically for AIDS work. The Reagan administration had requested no additional funds. Further, the administration had not only failed to request additional funds but had also opposed requests from Congress to add money to the budget to cope with the rapidly spreading epidemic.

Elsewhere, however, public health officers were urgently requesting money to deal with the epidemic, and arguing with their superiors that something had to be done. Brandt passed along those requests to Secretary Heckler, who ignored them. As the AIDS epidemic was taking off, the NIH asked for 127 new positions to fight it. It was given eleven. FDA budgets, as we've seen, were slashed, rather than increased. It was the Democratic Congress, and two committee chairmen in the House, Representatives Henry Waxman of California and Ted Weiss of Manhattan, and in the Senate, Edward Kennedy, who held hearings and built momentum for the first significant funding to cope with the epidemic. With a kind of misplaced moral sternness, the administration refused to soften. "They tend to see health," said Stanley Matek, who had been president of the American Public Health Association, "in the same way that John Calvin saw wealth: it's your own responsibility and you should damn well take care of yourself." Suitable actions to supply money and moral support did not come from the administration until after it was clear to Reagan personally that those outside the gay community would be struck down as well.

The pharmaceutical industry's sluggishness also stood in the way. The free market, if it were true to the mythology, would have understood the risk and the opportunity and plunged into the development of AIDS drugs. Some scientists were predicting that tens of thousands of people would be infected by 1985, and the numbers would only go up from there. But in the summer of 1983, for example, with about 1,600 cases reported, some believed the epidemic would simmer but not boil, and businessmen listened to them. Dr. Norbert Rapoza, a senior officer at the American Medical Association, said he expected the epidemic to slow. "There are signs that the epidemic may slow because of the self-control of homosexual males," he said. By the end of 1984, the number of cases had passed 10,000, but still the pharmaceutical companies felt the target market would be too small. It was said that to develop a drug to treat an illness affecting fewer than 200,000 people would yield too small a profit.

Activists pressed businesses for action. The drug companies owned many thousands of the most biologically active chemicals; the many government and university scientists wanted these drugs to work with. One of them was Dr. Samuel Broder at the National Cancer Institute, a small, roundish, and mustachioed man with a soft and colorful if oddly paced way of speaking. "There was at the time a strong sense of therapeutic nihilism from the leadership in science," Broder said. "I think that kind of nihilism is dangerous. Fortunately the scientific environment allows a minority viewpoint to not only exist but flourish. We were fervently driven to see if we could find a positive result of some kind that would be an empirical antidote for that therapeutic nihilism we were hearing" from more skeptical scientists. Broder and other scientists went to one company after another, arguing that there were many approaches worth trying.

Finally, Broder found a company that believed viruses were not impenetrable, because it produced the only partially successful treatment to attack a virus then available—acyclovir, to treat herpes infection. The company was Burroughs Wellcome, the American subsidiary of Wellcome PLC, a British corporation. After a few unsuccessful attempts, Wellcome agreed to meet with Broder and Dr. Dani Bolognesi of Duke University in the fall of 1984. Government and university scientists offered the aid of their labs—talent of the highest rank—to test some of the thousands of chemicals sitting on the company's shelves to see if any worked against HIV. The company agreed to offer some of its compounds for testing. The AIDS virus was dangerous, however, so it would have to be handled in a laboratory specially designed to keep virus particles from floating in the air as scientists squirted and poured mixtures of them. Burroughs had no such labs, nor did the government or university scientists working on AIDS.

After some back-and-forth, the scientists at NIH and at Duke said they would shoulder the risk—they would take the virus into their own labs to work with it. Each researcher in the government and university labs made his or her own choice, and none declined to work with AIDS. These were simple acts of courage by people committed to science.

Burroughs began to ship parcels of coded but unnamed drugs from its labs in North Carolina to Broder's government lab outside Washington. There, one young and talented immigrant from Japan, Hiroaki Mitsuya, working for the usual dirt wages of $18,000 a year, devised a clever and rapid method to test the large number of drugs against the virulent virus. He sat at his bench hour after hour, day after day, hands in motion as he squirted drugs and the virus into tiny wells or onto dishes. In February, Mitsuya discovered that a chemical shipped from Burroughs labeled simply "compound S" seemed to attack the AIDS virus fiercely when it attempted to infect cells in laboratory flasks. Compound S was azidothymidine, or AZT for short. By June 1985, Burroughs Wellcome applied to the FDA to try a few doses in humans (phase I testing). After dutifully checking the facts, within a week the FDA approved the application to start the experiments. Small doses were to be used at first on eleven patients recruited in Broder's lab in Bethesda, Maryland. Then eight patients agreed to be tested in Bolognesi's lab at Duke.

The blood samples were to be sent from the government and university labs to Burroughs Wellcome for analysis, but the company reneged on that arrangement. Now, too committed to let the work stop, Broder reassigned scientists committed to other projects in his own lab, and had the analysis done at the NIH. The first patient, a furniture salesman, got the first dose of AZT on July 3, 1985.

After the initial trial showed that the drug was one the human body could absorb without a catastrophe, the real work started. Researchers had to find several hundred AIDS-infected patients for "phase II" testing who were relatively similar in age, background, and state of disease. This was to ensure that any result could be clearly attributed to the drug. The trial was started in February 1986 and scheduled to continue into 1987.

Usually, it is not until the end of "phase III" experiments in which more than a thousand patients may be monitored while taking a drug that the results begin to become clear. With AZT, the difference was fairly dramatic immediately. In experiments during which neither patients nor doctors know who is taking a drug and who is taking a placebo, it is customary in order to avert disasters to have a data safety and monitoring board periodically peek at the results as they are coming in. Only three months into the full AZT experiment, the data seen by the board was already clear. Nineteen of 137 patients taking the placebo had died. But only one of 145 taking AZT had died. The trial was stopped, and the FDA's long-standing policy of delivering any potentially important drugs to patients with life-threatening illnesses was triggered. Beginning on September 19, 1986, and over the next five months, the FDA and Burroughs Wellcome gave out AZT on a "compassionate use" basis, as it is called, to about 4,500 patients. That was at least one-third of all those in the United States who had AIDS at the time.

All of this occurred before the usual central review by the FDA to determine whether a drug is fully safe and effective. In the normal course of events, the next and most important step would be phase III experiments. This comes after the lab work, animal work, and brief tests of toxicity in humans; it usually includes two definitive experiments. If those go well, the company could then apply and get approval to sell the drug commercially. For most drugs—90 percent of which are merely slightly different copies of drugs already available—this phase of testing is essential to determine if there is any difference between a new drug and those already marketed, and whether it poses any needless risk given what is already available.

Things had moved quickly because it was a matter of life and death, but there was considerable worry about the consequences of the haste. Truth cannot be pulled out of nature when and how humans would like, with one truncated experiment. For example, dosage could not be properly evaluated in such a short experiment—too high, and many patients will be forced by severe reactions to stop taking it; too low, and the disease will resurge in some patients. And what happens to a patient when the drug is taken for more than a few months? Does the drug stop working at some point? Does the patient succumb to long-acting side effects from the drug? Was there another illness for which the drug could be effectively administered? Could the drug be fatal for some?

Taking a risk, the FDA decided to skip phase III experiments for the time being. The open questions were important, but the desperate need of an effective treatment for AIDS seemed more important. The company submitted its data and its final application for market approval in December 1986. The FDA reviewed it and approved the drug in March 1987, even as most patients who apparently could benefit from it were already receiving it.

Still businesses did not respond to the epidemic with large-scale research and cash. After Burroughs Wellcome demonstrated with AZT that AIDS drugs could be profitable, some have suggested the delay was because of anti-homosexual attitudes. They probably played a role, but most likely the companies were simply averse to taking risks. One money manager told *Barron's* magazine he would not bet on making money with AIDS drugs: "AIDS is beginning to peak. Not many more homosexuals are going to get infected—homosexuals are practicing safe sex. And because AIDS is always fatal, those who already have it are dying. Intravenous drug users aren't as cautious, but so many already have it that they're dying out. And women can't give it to men."

(Each sentence the moneyman spoke was incorrect. He did not have even the rudimentary facts in hand. At the time he spoke in 1989, there were 107,000 U.S. cases of AIDS recorded and 62,000 deaths. Five years after his remarks, there were five times as many cases recorded—535,000, with 332,000 dead. And life expectancy for AIDS patients had been not declining but increasing, from ten months to three years.)

Commentators on Wall Street had also been saying that the FDA was slow and the regulatory process "politically contaminated" against AIDS, so venturing into AIDS drugs would be especially risky. That was proved wrong with AZT, and then again with each AIDS drug following in the next several years. Approvals were quick and the drugs were profitable. But the drugs did not begin to flow from primary company work until a decade after the beginning of the epidemic. In fact, each of the first three drugs to market came out of work in government laboratories, where all the risks of working with the virus were borne by poorly paid federal scientists.

At first, there was a rush of excitement and hope regarding AZT. But when Burroughs Wellcome began selling the drug, it set its price so unexpectedly high—$10,000 per patient per year—that a wave of protests began over that issue. Many who needed the drug could not afford it. The company, for its part, feared that the epidemic might not take off as predicted, or that another company might soon come up with a competing drug, as at least two were already being tested. So the company had decided to try to recover all its expenditures immediately. It spent $86 million to develop and market AZT and reaped $100 million in sales in the first year. The epidemic, of course, cooperated, growing rapidly as expected, and returning to Burroughs many times its investment within a few years of going to market.

A backlash began. If anyone had been asked before the epidemic if such a feat was possible—a brand-new treatment for the most recalcitrant of disease organisms—no one would have thought it possible so soon. But now, with thousands dying every year and AZT so overpriced, the development period for new drugs seemed excruciatingly long. Anyone who expressed doubt or caution was quickly attacked as an obstacle to the hopes of the dying.

It also became clear now that the science *not done* because of the rush to get AZT to market was important. Some now said AZT was too toxic. As it turned out, the original dosage given in the experiment was too high: it worked, but it caused needlessly severe side effects and forced many off the drug entirely. A movement to refuse AZT treatment began, because of the drug's toxicity and short-lived usefulness.

So, ironically, by the end of 1987, just as the first effective treatment for AIDS had been formally approved, the anger and fear in the gay community were reaching their greatest intensity. In the beginning the epidemic had been concentrated among gay men, and hugely disproportionate suffering was visited there, not only on those who died but on survivors who found themselves attending funerals every week. As activist and playwright Larry Kramer had said, "I am angry and frustrated almost beyond the bounds my skin and bones and body and brain can encompass. My sleep is tormented by nightmares and visions of lost friends and my days are flooded by the tears of funerals and memorial services and seeing my sick friends. How many of us must die before all of we living fight back?" The government was hardly behaving as if the nation was facing the worst epidemic in its history. More than 71,000 had been infected by the end of 1987, and 41,000 were already dead.

On a March night in 1987, at a meeting in a basement in Greenwich Village, 250 people, mostly gay men and women, expected to hear a guest speaker, Nora Ephron. When she couldn't appear, the angry and articulate Kramer volunteered to speak. He pointed out that two-thirds of the people in the room were likely to be dead in five years. And he said, "If my speech doesn't scare the shit out of you, we are in real trouble." That talk led, two days later, to the founding of a group calling itself ACT UP, which was initially said to stand for AIDS Coalition to Unleash Power. The group adopted the motto "Silence = Death," and took as its symbol the pink triangle that the Nazis had forced gays to wear during the Holocaust, except that ACT UP's triangle pointed upward instead of downward. The group's first action came two weeks later, as demonstrators protested the price of AZT by blocking traffic on Wall Street; seventeen were arrested. Demonstrators hanged FDA Commissioner Frank Young in effigy from a gallows in Trinity Church. One of the activists, Peter Staley, a former stockbroker and Reagan Republican, was now part of the action. He said, "We think every minute counts. All we want is the same type of response that South Carolina got after the hurricane, what San Francisco got after the earthquake."

Meanwhile, the FDA after much debate among top staff and negotiation with protesters and scientists, determined in 1987 that some drugs, in extreme cases, should be made available before testing to prove their worth was complete. Of course, until then patients themselves could seek drugs from companies, one by one, on a "compassionate use" basis. But that meant patients had to know about drugs not on the market. And then, too, quite often the companies simply refused to give them the drug. So it was now necessary when a truly promising drug was coming along—not just some random herbal, but one that had proved itself in safety tests and had shown signs of effectiveness in life-and-death cases—to let that drug be marketed before it was approved. The new approach was originally called the "treatment IND" program, because it combined the terms "treatment" and "investigational new drug," suggesting it was both therapy and experiment.

At first, the new policy split not only FDA officers but doctors, scientists, and even AIDS activists as well. The more libertarian activists, such as Martin Delaney at Project Inform in San Francisco, generated a letter-writing campaign to thank Young for taking a bold step forward. Delaney found himself aligned with the extremist editorial page of the *Wall Street Journal,* which declared that the new policy was "a giant step for the sick and dying." Some were amused that the *Journal* ranked the decision as among the greatest Reagan administration decisions, along with massive tax cuts and the missile defense system ("Star Wars").

On the other side of the activist roster was, among others, Jeffrey Levi, director of the National Gay and Lesbian Task Force. He pointed to the danger of approving drugs that seemed safe in theory, and even in early tests, but proved later to be catastrophic. One of the many awful treatments that the AIDS underground had found and used in earlier days was suramin, traditionally used to treat African sleeping sickness. In the laboratory, it seemed to attack HIV effectively. It passed the first, very inconclusive safety tests. But Broder and his colleagues, in one of the first evaluations of the drug in a medical journal, said its action against HIV was limited and disappointing. Also, it had significant side effects, including urinary and liver abnormalities. Still, it seemed worth testing further. When the drug reached the next phase of testing, phase II, in which forty-one men were given the drug, its true character emerged. Two of the men died of liver failure, and several others had severe kidney and adrenal failures. It did nothing against HIV. Broder and his colleagues were eventually forced to write, "Suramin is a toxic agent that shows no virologic, immunologic or clinical benefit in patients with HIV-related disease." Levi suggested that another such dangerous and useless drug could easily be distributed widely in a "Treatment IND" program, only to find some months later that it was killing hundreds.

In 1988, ACT UP had decided to mount a major demonstration in Washington. It was not decided immediately who would be the target—Ronald Reagan, the Department of Health and Human Services, NIH, or the FDA. But eventually they chose the FDA because it seemed most immediate. The power of approval or disapproval seemed crucial, whether there was much to approve or not. The FDA also seemed more flexible, and so likely to change under pressure.

Young met with activists well before the demonstration, hoping to redirect it. But it nonetheless came on October 11, 1988, a sunny fall day in Rockville, Maryland. Demonstrators from around the country began appearing at 7 a.m. before the huge suburban office building that is the site of FDA headquarters. Each participating group seemed to have devised its own attention-getting slogan or visual presentation, and the theatrical event carried on through the day, with a thousand demonstrators ringing the building and staging visual events for cameras and reporters until 5 p.m. Demonstrators wore placards saying, "AZT is not enough." Reagan was hanged from a lightpost in effigy, and burned. Demonstrators wore white coats and rubber gloves; the gloves were covered with what looked like blood. People lay down in the street, and chalk outlines of their bodies were made to indicate deaths. A black flag was raised on the building's flagpole. Everywhere observers turned, there was something eye-catching. This was not a demonstration like those of the 1960s, in which violence routinely broke out. This was crafted to meet the needs of the media. Activists told reporters that the FDA was "actively blocking the delivery of promising therapies to people with AIDS." That was the theme of the day. The assertion was not strictly true; there were no promising therapies at that point with the exception of AZT. The dramatic pictures, slogans, and arguments were carried by network television and the major newspapers.

The demonstration marked the beginning of several years of turmoil in AIDS drug approval. Each new case seemed an object lesson of either too little testing or too much testing before approval. In hindsight, it is remarkable that one of the numerous highly toxic experimental AIDS treatments did not cause a thalidomide-scale catastrophe, because of quick approval. The pressure was intense.

There were several false starts. Ribavirin, for example, was announced with fanfare at a press conference. It seemed effective against the virus at first glance, but even some reporters at the press conference noted a major flaw in the statistics—too many of the people taking the drug were relatively healthy, so the drug's effects appeared better than they actually were. It was never determined whether the data presented in public was intentionally misrepresented, or if it was simply the result of sloppy research. But the drug proved ineffective against HIV, and if it had slipped into wide promotion and use without further tests, the result could have been catastrophic. As it was, some patients received it from underground supplies, thus delaying for months treatment with other, more effective drugs.

At the end of the 1980s, activists and regulators were looking for a new approach to drug approval that could be made into a clearer policy than the treatment IND, both to make it more certain that important drugs would get early distribution and that their makers would be certain to produce, at some time, the needed scientific data. AIDS activists Jim Eigo of ACT UP in the East and Martin Delaney of Project Inform in the West had talked with NIH's Anthony Fauci about such a plan. It was brought to Frank Young and accepted. A drug—not any drug, but one for a serious or life-threatening disorder—once proved safe in experiments with animals and humans, and with some reason to believe it was effective as well, could be given to thousands of patients as long as experiments to test it scientifically could go forward. This would be called parallel track, and it would eventually become the regulatory rule by which the FDA still operates.

Fauci had spoken to drug companies about the idea. They were cautiously receptive. It would be possible with some drugs, not others, they said. Activists were elated, though the plan was hardly without risk.

As Fauci said at the time, "Previously, there was a great concern that if we did this, then no one would be in the clinical trial." But he said he had changed his mind; he had become convinced by activist arguments that if both tracks began early enough, there would be volunteers for testing as well as for just receiving the drug. Patients would sign up for tests—they would still be given the new drug—out of a sense of public duty (they also hoped that being part of an experiment meant they would be handled by the best, most knowledgeable doctors).

Even as the details were being worked out, government scientists were making the path ahead clear. "The thing about a war," said Dr. Daniel Hoth, director of the AIDS division of the National Institute of Allergy and Infectious Diseases, "is that those who are fighting it are changed, maybe permanently." The fierce AIDS activist Martin Delaney said wryly, "I don't mean to suggest that we are now in sync totally, but the [FDA] has been humanized. When we were standing at the barricades we thought they were cruel Nazis, with no concern for people dying. On their side, they thought of us as wild-eyed radicals who wanted to flood the market with quack drugs."

The next major AIDS drug, another developed by Broder and Mitsuya at the National Cancer Institute, was called DDI, short for dideoxyinosine. It was the first to be reviewed under the new parallel track approach. It was a drug very like AZT, which provided some assurance. Mitsuya found that the body retained DDI longer than AZT, and even better, it appeared to have less dramatic side effects. DDI might not induce the fatal weakness and anemia that sometimes came with AZT, but it did have problems of its own. Careful studies would be required to determine their extent.

The FDA agreed to parallel marketing and testing. It also agreed that survival need not be the only measure of success in experiments. The FDA instead chose a "surrogate marker" to test DDI—whether the drug could maintain or restore to more normal levels the body's defensive blood cells called CD4 cells. These cells become depleted as the severity of AIDS increases. Most healthy people have between 800 and 1,500 or more of these cells per deciliter of blood; those with AIDS see these defender cells drop below 500, then below 100, then to 50. Below about 200, people are extremely vulnerable to repeated infection and are often counted as approaching death. Thus, if an antiviral drug could bring a patient's CD4 cells upward, or stop a downward trend, it was counted as successful therapy.

By 1991, a couple thousand patients had been in tests with DDI, and more than thirty thousand more had received the drug, free, from the manufacturer, Bristol-Myers, while the experiments continued. The studies revealed an increase in the body's immune defense, the CD4 cells—but only eleven cells on average. That did not establish that DDI allowed people with AIDS to live longer, nor would that be established for years. That was the essence of the parallel track trade-off; some questions would have to go unanswered for years. But the drug was approved, with some wringing of hands, on that slim basis.

Eventually, activists had to admit that during the years of crisis they had been overeager, and it was time to take a half step back. For example, they later endorsed the drug called DDC. But they soon found that the final data showed its effectiveness was poor, and some activists called for its recall. They were beginning to feel like FDA medical officers. "We have arrived in hell," said Gregg Gonsalves of the AIDS Treatment Action Group. "AIDS activists and government regulators have worked together, with the best intentions, over the years to speed access to drugs. What we have done, however, is to unleash drugs with well-documented toxicities onto the market, without obtaining rigorous data on their clinical efficacy."

The sad, desperate experiments in AIDS treatment and policy that were carried out, of necessity, in the 1980s revealed a great deal about drugs. No one with substantial experience of that time believes that no suffering was caused, no damage done by the rapid-fire use of one untested treatment or another. Drugs like suramin, dextran sulfate, and compound Q produced more harm than they were worth. But we were lucky—true disasters were averted. If dextran sulfate had been distributed much faster and more widely through an FDA approval process, the injuries and deaths that would have resulted could have run into large numbers. If the hepatitis B drug called FIAU had been an AIDS drug distributed under some early-release plan, a very sad spectacle might have ensued (among the fifteen patients given the drug on an experimental basis at the National Institutes of Health, five died). If Saquinavir, a drug dispensed at the wrong dose and with a mistaken formula that reduced its effectiveness, had quickly become the drug of choice to fight the virus, a public health nightmare might have resulted. As it was, AZT, the first drug to treat AIDS, was hurried to market at the wrong dose, and used at the wrong stage of disease by many. It was not a lifesaver but a drug that extended life by some months, and at the time it was essential to get it in the hands of patients. With life-threatening illness, haste is unavoidable. Some caution and testing is required nevertheless. No one knows that better than the activists who lived through the full nightmare of the sudden coming of the plague, and the fight to do something about it.

By the early 1990s, the FDA had accepted that something less than certainty was permissible in extreme cases. At the same time, activists learned to respect the importance of sound data produced by scientists and regulators, even if it seemed slow to emerge. This would be a permanent step forward in drug regulation. But a scandal within the FDA that had been brewing for a number of years finally broke the surface in 1990 and overshadowed, at least for a time, the progress on AIDS.

Generic drugs, chemical copies of brand-name drugs, were at the heart of the scandal. When a patent expires on a brand-name drug, competitors scramble to make inexpensive versions of it. Because the actual cost of making a drug from raw materials is usually extremely low—often one-hundredth to one-thousandth of the selling price—there is plenty of room for generic-copy manufacturers to reduce prices and still make a hefty profit. For the brand-name companies, of course, it is worth a significant amount of legal maneuvering to try to prevent a drug from losing its patent exclusivity. Prescription manufacturers fought for years to prevent the very existence of generics, and used a variety of tactics to prevent each generic drug from coming to market.

Most of those outside the pharmaceutical industry have sided with the beleaguered generic companies as they fought the giants of the industry. The fight for generics has seemed to be the good fight, given their lower cost. The huge price inflation that has always accompanied brand-name drugs in America strikes home when prices are compared. Generics are often enough one-tenth to one-half the price of the brand-name product, and in recent years they have proved to be completely equivalent therapeutically.

Unfortunately, during the 1980s the generic companies themselves also turned out to be something less than heroic. Companies began to cheat by putting out generics that were not equivalent to the brand-name drugs. It was not until 1983 that the agency was able to build up a record of court decisions, and finally a U.S. Supreme Court ruling, that made it clear that generics had to be biologically equivalent to brand-name drugs, and it was the FDA that would set the standard of equivalence. The year after, Congress passed a law to that effect, stipulating that generics could be marketed without any additional animal or human testing if they could demonstrate bio-equivalence.

To enforce bio-equivalence represented another huge challenge. One FDA lawyer, Donald Beers, wrote that the situation was unnerving. "The willingness of manufacturers to market these products without adequate evidence of bio-equivalence was chilling. Moreover, during the years in which FDA would seize unapproved generics whenever it could find them, some of those in the business began to engage in active evasion of law enforcement" that ultimately led to their prosecution and conviction.

During the late 1980s the more upright generic companies began to notice that generic drugs did not seem to be approved on a first-come, first-served basis. Some shot through while others languished. Some seemed to be assigned to lenient reviewers, while others were judged more stringently. The products of Mylan Laboratories of Pittsburgh, which apparently had played the game honestly, had sailed through FDA approvals until 1986, when suddenly they began to be tied up. Mylan had heard rumors of payoffs and special deals for those who offered money and gifts to FDA reviewers and decided to investigate. They got hints from FDA officers that something was expected in return for speedy approvals. Talking to one FDA staffer who had recently left the generic drug division, the company received confirmation of gifts arriving for a few FDA officers in generics, most notably, Charles Y. Chang and David Brancato, group leaders within the division. Gifts included tens of thousands of dollars, travel, a fur coat, and a VCR.

"We knew there were payoffs. We knew we were being pushed back behind other companies' applications and discriminated against," Mylan's chairman, Roy McKnight, later told the *New York Times*. McKnight was certain enough that Mylan hired a private investigator to track Chang. The investigator began to sift through Chang's garbage carefully, day after day, for weeks. Twice a week over a month and a half, he found shreds of a picture—an incriminating photo of Chang with generic drug company officials in Hong Kong—that Chang was dropping in the trash bits at a time. The trip was one of a number of bribes Chang received in return for his quick approvals.

The scandal was first made public when, in May 1989, hearings held by the Subcommittee on Oversight and Investigations of the House Energy and Commerce Committee, led by Representative John Dingell of Michigan, brought in Mylan and two other generic manufacturers, Barr Laboratories and Barre-National, to make their charges public. The whistle-blowers said that some companies got quick approvals if they paid bribes to a few FDA officials. They also said the arrangements put customers at substantial risk because some test data was faked. Required by law to show their drugs were equivalent to the brand-name drug they were imitating, a number of companies bought bottles of the brand-name product, dumped it into their generic capsules, and then tested them.

Eventually, the hearings led to further investigations and arrests as well. More than two hundred generic drugs were pulled from the market, at least temporarily. Fifty-five employees of fifteen generic drug companies were convicted of felonies, along with five FDA officials.

Frank Young was stunned. He had heard rumors but had not acted on them. When he learned the extent of the corruption during the hearings, he had harsh words for those insiders who brought corruption to an agency that had been relatively free of it for many decades. As was his way, he put the matter in religious terms, reading to the subcommittee a quote from Romans: "All have sinned and fallen short of the glory of God."

During his five years in office, Young appeared to have made an honest attempt to understand the law and the FDA, and many in the industry and Congress felt he had been blindsided, but nevertheless, he would have to go. Officially, he left office at the end of 1989, but his replacement was not sworn in until the latter days of 1990.

•

CHAPTER SEVENTEEN

A Progressive

B Y 1990, the FDA was in desperate shape, an organizational disaster waiting to happen. The industries the FDA regulated were booming. The number of applications for approval of drugs, devices, and other products shot up from 4,200 in 1970 to 12,800 in 1989. Over the same period, the reports of serious reactions to drugs increased from about 12,000 to 70,000 per year, not including the 16,000 reports of problems with medical devices, for which the FDA was now responsible. In 1970 the Freedom of Information Act did not exist; by 1989, as a result of its passage, the FDA was fielding 70,000 consumer inquiries, 40,000 FOIA requests, 3,000 queries from members of Congress, and 180 citizen petitions for action. In the decade between 1980 and 1990 alone, Congress passed twenty-four laws giving the FDA new responsibilities and requiring diversion of at least 675 staffers from other tasks. And the AIDS crisis forced the agency to divert 400 people to deal with it, from blood transfusion issues to the testing of viral drugs.

But it was a conservative era, with George Bush now president. Budget deficits had piled up. The Bush administration continued to hold down FDA budgets. The total number of employees had been cut from about 7,960 in 1978 to 6,960 in 1987. Enforcement was decimated. The total number of seizures, injunctions, and prosecutions in 1980 was 500, but by 1989, it had dropped to 173. Though it had been suggested that the pharmaceutical industry should be left to police itself voluntarily, during this grand opportunity the voluntary actions by industry dropped from about 5,100 to 4,300 a year. No surprise, the complaints against the FDA for its inability to act, or act quickly, increased. In fact, it is remarkable that, given its added burden, the agency's drug review times had actually dropped. The agency had improved its efficiency to the point that it could handle more drugs with fewer staff.

But with the explosion of the bribery scandal in the generic drug division, the wheels came off. A *New York Times* headline described it as "A guardian of health buckling under stress." Dr. Samuel Thier, then head of the Institute of Medicine at the National Academy of Sciences, said, "The Food and Drug Administration is a demoralized group, being asked to do too much with too few resources." Peter Hutt, the conservative general counsel under Commissioner Edwards, refused to blame the agency's problems on deregulation but said simply, "The FDA's problem is resources. There has been a very serious erosion of resources across the board. It is a non-partisan issue. This is the single most important regulatory agency in the world. If we harm it, we are taking chances with the public health. Of all the agencies, this is the one we cannot afford to tinker with. It affects our health most directly. This is a wounded agency that we have already bled too much."

In Congress, Representative John Dingell, a Democrat and then chairman of the key House Energy and Commerce subcommittee that helped expose the generic drug scandal, said, "This has been a slow, persistent strangulation of an agency, and it has led to the damnedest, most unfair, and inconsistent regulations. This is a terrible mess, the denigration and emasculation of a fine and once-proud agency." The cry came not just from Democrats. Senator Orrin Hatch, Republican of Utah, said the FDA was "an overburdened and underfunded agency" and that something had to be done soon. And, as Hutt added, this was also just the time when the industry and the FDA were looking forward to a whole array of entirely new products made from biotechnology, tissues, and biological substances engineered in the laboratory, or products based on new understandings of human genes. If the agency couldn't keep up with the current workload, what would happen in the future?

The situation was so bad that even leaders in the pharmaceutical industry created a support fund for the beleaguered agency. The companies acknowledged privately that they depend for their credibility on the FDA's reputed toughness. If the FDA falters, the reputation of their own products falters with it. Conflicts were set aside for the time being, and the companies actually began using their wiles on behalf of the FDA— they set up a new lobbying group in Washington, D.C., called the FDA Council, backed by professional societies and a number of major companies including Merck & Company, Johnson & Johnson, Pfizer Inc., the Upjohn Company, and Procter & Gamble. Its brochures called for strengthening the agency's "infrastructure . . . so that it can efficiently carry out its mission."

Further emergency action came from the Department of Health and

Human Services. A committee to review the crisis and make recommendations was formed. Recruited for it were former commissioner Charles Edwards, to be chairman, along with an array of knowledgeable conservatives including Louis Lasagna, head of the pharmaceutical industry's think tank at Tufts University; Alan Nelson, former AMA president, and Sherwin Gardner, then head of the Grocery Manufacturers of America. Another member of the committee was David Aaron Kessler, a young man who was both a doctor and a lawyer. The committee reported to the nation that the FDA was being starved of resources and support, and now was the time to make changes, before the problems at the FDA led to damage to American industries that worked with and depended on the FDA.

With that as background, the Bush administration chose a new commissioner for the FDA—David Kessler. A graduate of Amherst College, he had obtained his M.D. from Harvard. His specialty was pediatrics. But he had also attended law school at the University of Chicago to prepare for work in making medical policy. By the time he was thirty-two years old, he had become the very young director of medicine at the Albert Einstein College of Medicine in New York, while teaching a course in food and drug law at Columbia University. He had further bolstered his credentials for policy work by serving for several years in Washington as a part-time assistant on the staff of Senator Orrin Hatch. Kessler was capable of a prodigious amount of work.

Because he was so task-oriented, no one knew whether he was a Democrat or a Republican. In other times that might have been thought a plus. But in the White House of George H.W. Bush, his indeterminate political gender raised eyebrows. (In fact, Kessler is a moderate, progressive Republican who had been on different sides of FDA issues. He believed in regulation and enforcement, but also that some reform was in order.)

Before landing on Senator Hatch's staff, he did not care which side he worked for in Washington. He wanted to work on issues, not sides. He had applied for work elsewhere to get his Washington experience—in the office of liberal Republican Senator Jacob Javits, and then of Senator Ted Kennedy—but there were no openings. When the Senate passed into Republican hands, he was waiting in line for a job.

Eight years later, in 1990, when he was working with the Edwards committee, he began to think there was no job he'd like better than that of commissioner of food and drugs. The job was still vacant into that fall, and he began to speak to friends about offering his name for nomination. He got a warm endorsement from Hatch, which was crucial. Hatch knew essentially nothing about Kessler's political tendencies but knew he was smart, and a problem-solver. Kessler also got enthusiastic references from Edwards, who was counted as reliably conservative, and from Peter Hutt, the most prominent food and drug lawyer in Washington. They had been impressed not by his allegiances but by his dogged analysis of issues and his understanding of the FDA's history and laws. Hutt, whose rhetoric never flags, said of him, "If you had to write a fictional résumé for the perfect person to hold this job, it would turn out to be David Kessler's résumé. If he can't do it, no one can." Kessler got the nod.

He has an unassuming appearance, with a reddish-sandy beard and eyeglasses with lenses like magnifying glasses. The ensemble yields an overall impression of a genial owl. Kessler speaks in bursts of directness and enthusiasm, though he never seems to finish a sentence, stopping just before the end to see if he has made his point without punctuation. When asked a question, he often contemplated it for an unusually long time before coming out with a measured reply. He was rather exacting professionally, but distinctly eccentric personally. He was, in fact, unlike any commissioner in recent memory, and perhaps the closest of all commissioners in temperament to Harvey Washington Wiley himself.

He says he grew up with an excitement about science, and largely speaking, he is the scientific type—socially awkward, swimming in internal enthusiasms, and most important, able to bear huge amounts of boring, detailed, obsessive work to ferret out a new fact. His parents joke that he did not smile until he was three, and that he was so shy the barber had to come to their house and crawl under the table where little David hid. He read history and science—he spent one summer building a giant model of a molecule—and not much fiction except *To Kill a Mockingbird*, which he read repeatedly, trying to absorb the dignity and simple decency of the lawyer Atticus Finch. As a young man, he was not greatly political, but he enthusiastically supported Barry Goldwater in his season.

During college at Amherst he broke away from the regular course of study to pursue a great fascination of his, the relationship between certain viruses and kidney cancer in frogs. When Kessler tells of that time, he describes his need for an unending supply of frogs with tumors. "I traveled to large frog farms where I put on thigh-high wading boots and squeezed the bellies of thousands of animals" in hopes of finding a few animals with tumorous growths. He recalls the first time he met his future wife, Paulette Steinberg, on the porch of a Victorian manse where she was living while a student at Smith College. They talked for a time that evening, and then he invited her down to his Oldsmobile. He wanted to show her the trunk, which was filled with croaking frogs, "hundreds of specimens," he says. She was uncharacteristically silent.

Two mentors—Oscar Schotté, the developmental biologist under whom he worked at Amherst, and Henry Steele Commager, the noted historian ensconced at the school—shaped his young view of the world. From Schotté he learned that great patience and a meticulous attention to detail are as important as grand visions. From Commager, who fought against the influence of Joseph McCarthy and was an early opponent of the Vietnam War, he learned to think of a life's work by the long view, combining scholarship with a sense of public responsibility.

Kessler was named to head the FDA in November 1990, but he asked the acting commissioner to keep making the key decisions for a while. The new commissioner spent time meeting the department heads, listening to their problems, and planning strategy. But it quickly became clear that there wouldn't be much time for strategy. Crises are the order of the day at the FDA, and planning happens in the cracks between. The first major public crisis during Kessler's service came about midnight on March 2, 1991, a week after he was sworn in. He was watching *Saturday Night Live* when FDA public affairs chief Jeff Nesbit called saying that cyanide had been found in Sudafed capsules in the Pacific Northwest; one woman was dead already, and another woman had narrowly escaped. Kessler soon learned that at the time about three hundred product tamperings a year were reported. Not many resulted in deaths, but all had to be investigated. He immediately organized a conference call of top advisers, and the agency's expert on product tampering, Dick Swanson (nickname: Dr. Doom), who had dealt with contamination dozens of times, including botulism in Bon Vivant soup and the dumping of salmonella bacteria into salad bars in Oregon.

Ruth Johnson, a scientist at one of the FDA's nineteen district offices around the country, came up with the first break in the case. She had examined the suspect Sudafed package and capsules that had killed the Washington State woman, under a microscope and chemically as well. Everything appeared in order. But it was the serial numbers on the box and the blister pack inside that caught her attention. They should have been the same but were different. That meant capsules from one box had been inserted into another. Soon, by comparing the numbers on the Sudafed taken by the second victim, it became clear that the two victims who had purchased their medicine in different stores and different towns nevertheless had capsules from the same box, which had been tampered with.

Before 1 a.m., Kessler and the FDA chiefs had decided on the first, relatively easy step: a warning would be issued in the Seattle region, announcing the code number on the tampered box—8U2846. The harder decisions—should there be a product recall? should it be national?—had not yet been made by 3 a.m. Then, another death by Sudafed had been reported. So, by 4 a.m., Kessler was on the phone with the CEO of Burroughs Wellcome, manufacturer of Sudafed, suggesting a full recall might be necessary. Because a national recall had been highly effective during the Tylenol crisis—it quickly assured the public that the problem was isolated to a single product and also showed the company to be a responsible citizen—a recall was implemented a few hours later. Eventually, three more cyanide-contaminated capsules would be found—one on a store shelf and two in home medicine cabinets. The case was Kessler's welcome to the agency. "The morning after the national recall," he said, "a reporter asked me why we had not moved sooner. I began to understand what I was facing."

The first issues focused on by Kessler were enforcement of the law, and fairness and honesty in labeling. These were the issues of Harvey Wiley's food and drug campaigns. Kessler's first important speech was given before a meeting of the Food and Drug Law Institute, an association of specialists in food and drug issues, mostly lawyers. Many are former FDA employees, and almost all work for industry. The group embodies the connection between the regulators and the regulated, and it often provides a stage for the announcement of FDA attitudes and policies.

The speech was unusual, and not particularly friendly. It had been many years since anyone from the FDA spoke about getting tough in carrying out the law. Since the late 1970s the rhetoric had been that of conciliation and withdrawal. The words "cooperation" and "partnership" had probably been used a thousand times for every time the term "enforcement" was. Kessler now said that things were going to change. "Deregulation" might be a popular word, but no longer at the FDA. "The FDA is the regulator, and you should know that I have no problem stating that fact. The FDA *must* stand for, it *must* embody, strong and judicious enforcement. . . . Let me remind all of you neither to underestimate the vigor of this agency nor the strength of its resolve." He said he intended to hire a hundred new criminal investigators to reestablish serious enforcement of food and drug laws. The speech was reported in some newspapers, but the public splash came only a few weeks later on the subject of food labeling.

Under FDA law, it had been a violation to make a false claim on a food label; for example, to claim that a product was raspberry juice when it was mostly apple juice. But over the years the FDA had also begun to make positive use of food labels, to offer vital health information about the foods that carry the label. In the 1970s the agency began to require companies to give some basic information to consumers—for example, to list the number of calories per serving in a package.

Consumer groups, led by the Center for Science in the Public Interest (CSPI), had pushed for this new approach to labels and nutritional information. They had done studies and filed petitions regularly on one issue or another—to get salt and fat content put on labels, to define often misleading terms like "light" or "lite." The group scored significantly when its testing turned up the fact that Sara Lee's "light" cheesecake actually contained substantially more fat and cholesterol than its regular brand.

The CSPI in 1988 set a strategy that was to be crucial over the next few years. It said food labels were not just about honesty and fairness, but that good, detailed labeling could reduce disease. It would be necessary to give consumers information package by package about fat, calories, salt, and vitamins, and some guidance about how to use the new information, say, to determine how much fat should be their daily limit. The label would no longer be just another forum for hawking products. To help accomplish this, the leaders at CSPI, Michael Jacobson and Bruce Silverglade, were able to bring together a coalition of more than twenty notable groups, including the American Heart Association, the American Cancer Society, the American Public Health Association, the American Dietetic Association, and the Society for Nutrition Education.

At the time, the executive branch had not much interest in consumers' views. The prevailing feeling was that food companies should not be required to carry nutritional information on their labels if they didn't think it was to their advantage, and, at the same time, should be free to make claims about how healthful and disease-defeating their products were, without having to justify the claims scientifically to the FDA. In 1984, Kellogg had broken the ice with its cold cereal All-Bran, which it claimed could help prevent cancer.

The FDA had for eighty years said that if a food company claims one of its products can prevent cancer or heart disease, it was to be treated in the same manner as a drug claim. Thus, the company would have to submit an application for the product, and it would have to go through the same painstaking review process as any drug would. But within a few years after Kellogg broke through that barrier, it was estimated that 40 percent of all newly introduced food products had asserted some kind of claim to aid health and reduce disease. All sorts of products were included in the rush to make health claims: breakfast cereal, juice, margarine, fish oil, pizza. By 1989, it was estimated that one-third of the entire $3.6 billion spent on food advertising contained some health message.

But the free-for-all ended up, as many deregulatory orgies do, pleasing only unscrupulous entrepreneurs. Luther McKinney, a vice president of Quaker Oats, explained the problem that had been created for industry: Quaker Oats had scientists on its staff, carried out serious research, and adhered to rigorous scientific standards. The company made use of its own work and that of science in general to make claims for its products. But most companies, he said, had little interest in science. "They just sprinkle a little oat bran on their product and ride this train without any backing for their claims."

Consumer advocates, for their part, were unhappy about the baseless claims and the food label's descent into meaninglessness. But they weren't ready to buy Quaker Oats' claims either. One of those protesting the company's claims was Deputy Attorney General Stephen Gardner of Texas. "They are promoting oats as the magic bullet. But the studies only show oats reducing cholesterol with minimal statistical significance, after you monkey around with the numbers, by three percent." And this, he said, only if you are eating a healthy diet at the same time.

The FDA tried to stem the tide of the worst claims and finally went to court to prohibit one small manufacturer, Phoenix Laboratories on Long Island, from asserting on the label of its lecithin-based food supplement that the product was useful in treating heart disease. The FDA said that the claim was unfounded. The company lawyers did not disagree; instead, they argued that the FDA was acting prejudicially. The government had made clear that it was not going to enforce rules against health claims when big companies made them, whether it was Kellogg, with its claims about All-Bran, or Fleischmann, with its claims on margarine, so why shouldn't smaller companies get the same treatment? The judge agreed. The FDA quickly alerted the White House that its position in favor of total deregulation had become untenable. The court had declared, in effect, that claims, no matter how baseless, were permitted; the failure to establish rules by which one claim was sound and another was not had left the market open to all claims.

But while federal regulators were inactive, state regulators were willing to take up the slack. More than a dozen states filed suits against Kellogg, Kraft, Coca-Cola, and others, claiming false and misleading labels and packaging. Food companies imagined the chaos stretching off into the future, with the prospect of fifty separate court systems in which they would have to fight their cases. Deregulation had gone too far, and food companies now wanted uniform rules—federal rules that would pre-empt state enforcement, exactly as they had at the end of the nineteenth century.

Now, the consumer coalition led by the CSPI came into its own. It succeeded in persuading Representative Henry Waxman, chairman of the House Commerce subcommittee on health and the environment, to make food labeling one of the committee's top issues. Waxman held hearings, and by July 1989, he, with twenty-five members of the House as co-sponsors, introduced a broad reform bill, the Nutrition Labeling and Education Act. Simultaneously, Senator Howard Metzenbaum of Ohio introduced a companion bill. The bills would require not just a comprehensive list of ingredients but also a detailed list of how much (or little) nutrition each food provided. Health claims would be allowed but limited to what was supported by strong evidence. It was the most comprehensive law on these issues with a chance of passage in more than fifty years.

By March 1990, the Bush administration also began to act, finally setting aside the objections of OMB officials and listening to the pleas of businesses for a level playing field. The administration permitted the FDA, which had been working on the issue for years, to put out a broad reform proposal to compete with the bill proposed in Congress. Health and Human Services Secretary Louis Sullivan announced the administration's newfound faith in regulation in a speech at a food policy conference, saying, "The grocery store has become a Tower of Babel, and consumers need to be linguists, scientists, and mind readers to understand the many labels they see. Vital information is missing, and frankly some unfounded health claims are being made."

Congress, faster than the administration, passed a food labeling law before the end of 1990. The law called for detailed nutritional information—from salt to saturated fat—to be listed on all labels. The law designated the FDA to write up the details and work out just how such a mass of information should be best crammed into a small area on a label.

263

But Congress went a step further. Because there had been a decade of anti-regulatory maneuvering from the Bush and Reagan administrations, lawmakers decided to insert into the law what is known as a "hammer." Fearing that conservative OMB officials might water down all the FDA regulations implementing the law, or delay them for many years, or both, Congress ordered the administration (that is, the FDA) to finish writing regulations by 1991 and to put them into effect by 1992. If the administration failed to enact regulations, the strongly worded proposals of 1990 would simply be declared the official regulations that spelled out the letter of the Nutrition Labeling and Education Act. It is rare for Congress to add such forceful language to a new law, but the labeling law was widely popular and the administration's hostile attitude toward regulation was well known.

At this point, David Kessler had been commissioner for just a few months. He was making it clear that deregulation was over and enforcement was back in style.

Kessler had chosen to emphasize the point in his first "public stage" event, an address to food company lawyers at a meeting in Florida. Beforehand, he had asked staffers to produce an example or two of deceitful food labels. He was soon buried in them. A particularly aggravating one was the claim a food was "fresh" when it was both processed and months from the field. In the increasingly artificial environs of the supermarket, consumers were desperate for foods that were fresh and natural but were confronting clever and copious misdirection in labeling. It was not really a safety issue, but it spoke to the base level of fairness that consumers might rely on. It harkened back to Harvey Wiley's speaking of glucose passed off as honey, of colored raw alcohol being labeled whiskey.

The mega-corporation Procter & Gamble had among its products an orange juice called Citrus Hill. The label was a marvel of misdirection. The official name of the product was Citrus Hill's Fresh Choice orange juice, but the words "Fresh Choice" were triple the size of "Citrus Hill." And the words "from concentrate" were tiny. Fresh Choice was trying to pass itself off as orange juice freshly squeezed from oranges, a more expensive product. Below "Fresh Choice," it said, "Pure squeezed 100% orange juice." Cartons also contained the claim, "We pick our oranges at the peak of ripeness. Then we hurry to squeeze them before they lose their freshness." What was not mentioned was that they then stopped hurrying, evaporating the liquid from the juice and leaving behind a heavy mush. Then the residue was shipped; later, sometimes months after squeezing, it was finally prepared for containers by adding water, pulp, oils, and flavoring. There was nothing fresh about Fresh Choice.

The FDA warned the company that the product was "misbranded," the legal language for mislabeled. Procter & Gamble protested that the words "from concentrate" were on the package, that the label did not actually say the juice was fresh, or freshly squeezed. Besides, the company maintained, the kind of fudging it was engaged in had become standard in the industry. More important, Procter & Gamble was aware that the FDA had not enforced the law against deceptive labeling in years. After FDA lawyer Denise Zavagno sent the firm a warning to which it did not respond, she sent FDA inspectors to a P&G plant in Minneapolis to take samples of concentrate being made into Fresh Choice. That got the attention of the company's lawyers, and negotiations began. FDA set a deadline of April 24 to change the label.

Kessler was already scheduled to address the group of food industry lawyers in Palm Beach Gardens, Florida, on the twenty-fourth. He planned to announce a settlement with the company, and hoped to emphasize the point that the FDA was once again going to be serious about enforcement. But at nine o'clock on the night of the twenty-third, P&G lawyers walked away from the negotiations, making it plain that the company did not believe the FDA would take the action it had threatened. When Kessler was told he was initially taken aback. He didn't have any experience staring down multi-billion-dollar corporations. The agency's chief counsel, Margaret Porter, asked him what he wanted to do. "What did we tell them we would do?" he asked. "We said we would seize the product," she said. Kessler said, "Well, go seize it."

In FDA terms, a seizure is a symbolic action rather than a national recall. The agency takes possession of a sample of a product in order to bring the company and its product into court. In this case, the FDA brought U.S. marshals to Super Valu warehouse in Minneapolis, where they put yellow police-line tape around 24,000 cartons of Citrus Hill Fresh Choice orange juice. It had been years since the FDA had made any serious attempt to enforce honesty in food labeling. But Kessler's strategy was to regain the high ground for the agency. That meant a series of charges up the hill, and victories in court and in the public eye. There was no shortage of opportunities, as the FDA had pulled back from many frontiers of enforcement, and this had led to egregious abuses.

Late in the evening, in Florida, Kessler began revising his speech for the next day. When he stood before the group, they were not expecting anything unusual. "The food industry lawyers were dressed for golf," he said later. In his speech, he said, "I am here today to tell you that I place a high priority on enforcing the law. This is not the idle talk of a new commissioner. . . . Today, the U.S. Attorney's office in Minneapolis is filing on the FDA's behalf a seizure action against Procter & Gamble's Citrus Hill Fresh Choice. . . . The use of the term 'fresh' on their product is false and misleading, and confusing for consumers." Reporters later said that those in the room froze at first; then there was an intense sound of whispering. The challenge was made, and within two days Procter & Gamble admitted its mistake and changed the label.

A series of similar actions followed as Kessler tried to draw a new line where an old one had been obscured or erased. Unilever Corporation sold a spaghetti sauce called Ragu Fresh Italian. But, of course, it was not fresh—the tomatoes had been heated until they were reduced to solids, which were then shipped to regional plants, where water and other ingredients were added to reconstitute the sauce. After its first warning Unilever tried to dodge the issue by adding to its label that the word "fresh" in the name referred to "fresh taste," rather than fresh sauce. Unilever soon agreed to change its label to "Fino Italian."

When Kessler returned to the headquarters building in Maryland after the Citrus Hill flare-up, someone had put up a banner for him to see: "The watchdog is back and it has teeth." Morale was improving quickly. But Kessler saw it not as a triumph but as a successful first skirmish. Conservatives spoke up quickly, ridiculing as meaningless the FDA's attempts to make labels honest, a needless harassment of business. Within the next few weeks, the FDA was busy. It sent warning letters to three food manufacturers, telling them to stop putting "no cholesterol" on their labels of vegetable oil as a hint that it might help prevent heart disease. Of course, vegetable oil does not contain cholesterol, but it does contain 100 percent fat, the number one suspect in causing heart disease. Also put on notice was a company producing doughnuts with a sprinkling of oat bran, accompanied by a misleading claim that its product reduced cholesterol and thus helped prevent heart attack. Syntex was forced to carry out a multi-million-dollar advertising campaign to correct misleading claims for one of its anti-arthritis drugs. Bristol-Myers Squibb agreed to stop promoting an anti-cancer drug for a separate, unapproved use.

"We're just putting some of these outrageous claims back in the box," Kessler told *Time* magazine. "And there's some grumbling. I recognize that. But we mean business, and I believe that in the end it is the credibility of the industry that will be enhanced by a stronger agency." Dr.

Louis Lasagna, who worked for drug companies for forty years and has been a harsh critic of the FDA on many issues, said that what Kessler was doing was truly different. "I have never sensed in previous FDA commissioners—and I have known them all since the 1960s—the sense of purpose that Kessler exudes."

The sense of purpose was soon put to use in the behind-the-scenes fight to write the regulations for the newly passed food labeling law. As is usually true, the language of the law itself was broad. Congress had been right to assume that the conservatives in the White House and the Agriculture Department would try to undercut the importance of the law by writing loose rules. So it would be the detailed regulations written later that would determine whether this law would be a tough or a weak one. It was the job of the FDA, as Kessler saw it, to act on behalf of consumers and resist the gutting of the law.

The fight over the shape of the new food regulations would become complicated. Twenty thousand food items were under the FDA's jurisdiction, but meat and poultry were still under the rules of the Agriculture Department. The FDA regulated pizza, the main ingredients of which are cheese and tomato. But if pepperoni slices—meat—were added, then the Agriculture Department technically had jurisdiction with regard to labeling. In order to end this kind of tangle, it was agreed early on that the FDA would write the rule, but Agriculture would consult on it and thereafter would abide by it, so that there would be only one set of food labels put out by the federal government.

In theory this was fine, but it soon pointed up one of the grotesqueries of what history had wrought in government. The FDA was not an independent agency nor a cabinet-level department. It was two ranks below cabinet level. In Congress, its budget was subject not to health committee approval but rather approval of an agriculture committee. The Agriculture Department was huge, well funded, and powerful. It had 110,000 employees to the FDA's 7,500. Agriculture had more beef inspectors alone than the FDA had employees. This doesn't make rational sense, but it developed historically in a country that was once an agricultural nation. So when it turned out that any battle over the food label would be fought between the FDA and Agriculture, it was clearly going to be an unequal battle in terms of political weight.

The challenge was to make the new labels sensible and readable. To begin with, the key words on a label were to be defined under law to mean pretty much what they mean in common English usage. Under the law "fresh" would mean raw food, not frozen, preserved, or processed food.

"Low fat" would mean less than three grams of fat per serving. "Reduced fat" would mean a reduction of no less than 50 percent from the industry's similar products. Kessler said, "We want to do three things. We want to end the confusion. Second, we want to make it easier for people to choose healthy food. And third, we want to give companies an incentive to encourage innovative products."

Some matters that had become tangled under earlier rules would be untangled. For example, there was the question of serving size. In the 1970s the FDA had asked manufacturers to list a number of facts on labels, including serving size and calories. But manufacturers soon realized that manipulating the serving size could offset giving nutritional bad news. So a potato chip company would declare arbitrarily that a small bag of potato chips usually eaten with a sandwich at lunch actually contained, say, three servings. That way, the company could report the number of calories as 75 per serving rather than 225.

If a label on a package said a serving of twenty chips contained five grams of fat, you needed some gauge as to whether that was a lot or a little fat. The FDA approach was to include that frame of reference on the label, what it called the "daily value." That is the amount of calories, fat, salt, and other nutrients in an average American diet each day. This new kind of label would not only say that microwavable hamburger contains fifteen grams of fat, but that fifteen grams of fat is about one-third of all the fat a person should consume for the day. Salad dressing, the number one source of fat in the diet of American women, would now be labeled as two tablespoons per serving, with one serving equal to one-quarter of the proper fat intake for a day.

Since the average diet varies greatly depending on the size and metabolism of each person, this approach came under attack as being too vague. Moreover, the average man's intake is 2,350 calories per day, and the average woman's, 2,000. After much debate, the FDA settled on 2,000 calories as the number to use for the reference. This, obviously, could only be a general guideline, but helpful as such.

Kessler and his assistant commissioner, Mike Taylor, went to Louis Sullivan with flip charts to explain their approach. The top staff at Agriculture had proposed a fundamentally different approach to the label, one that gave no daily values and no frame of reference. Taylor explained to Sullivan that the Agriculture Department's approach was like the old, muddled labels: A consumer concerned about fat and ready to ingest a bag of chips would have to know his or her own calorie requirements, then carry out five separate mathematical steps on a calculator to determine the import of the grams of fat. The five-step calculation would have to be repeated for every nutrient—once for fat, once for saturated fat, once for carbohydrates, once for protein, and so on.

As Kessler put it, "I was looking for an easy-to-grasp consumer guide, not an exercise that required a calculator. . . . For USDA [United States Department of Agriculture], the concern about labeling revolved around one word—fat. It was not uncommon for meat products to have nearly half the desirable level of daily fat calories in a single serving. Once the meat industry realized that our proposed label would make it far simpler for a shopper to gauge fat intake, it vigorously lobbied the USDA to follow a different course. One hint of the thinking within the USDA was reflected in a staffer's comment about the term 'low fat.' 'The problem is that our products won't be able to make that claim,' he said. Our products. A confusion between the interests of the industries it regulated and the interests of the consumers it was supposed to protect seemed ingrained within USDA. It was not going to be easy for the two agencies to agree on a rule."

The conflicts over fat and the design of the label were only two of several sticking points, but they became central. One meeting after another was held, and the OMB was assigned to facilitate agreement between the two agencies. By the fall of 1992, Kessler and the FDA were completely committed to their approach, and with each succeeding argument, their position became hardened. Kessler decided he could not win the struggle behind the scenes but instead needed to make clear publicly the nature of the struggle taking place and who was on which side. He could not get his message out to consumers unless the conflict was covered as news, so he gave background briefings and an array of off-the-record details to reporters, such as food writer Marian Burros of the *New York Times*.

At the same time the OMB was obtaining comments from food companies and ordering changes, often adopting verbatim industry wording. A compromise was nowhere in sight, and the "hammer" set in the law, the deadline of November 1992, was fast approaching.

News stories about the battle began to paint Agriculture Secretary Edward Madigan as a representative of the meat industry rather than of consumers—in one *Times* story, a source said Madigan was just "fronting for fat"—and he could not escape the label. That November, Bush lost the election, but the White House, the HHS, and the FDA all wanted to bring the issue to finality before the president left office, so it was agreed that Bush himself would decide matters. The president's staff was briefed, and materials were prepared for arguments. Clippings were collected to show how the fight was playing out in the media. A meeting to lay the issue before the president was set.

Key officials at the meeting were Madigan and Louis Sullivan, the two cabinet secretaries who would face off. Madigan had brought along Vice President Dan Quayle, who headed the president's Council on Competitiveness, to make it clear that hard conservatives opposed label reform. Supporting Sullivan was FDA Deputy Commissioner Taylor. The president listened, and Chief of Staff James Baker was the referee.

The meeting was tense, and dragged on for an hour. Sullivan presented the case for the new labels as drafted by the FDA. Madigan made his case for looser labels. Near the end, Madigan was disputing the 2,000-calorie "average diet" when Sullivan suddenly pulled out a sheet of colorful paper, a tray liner from a McDonald's restaurant Kessler had picked up when vacationing at the New Jersey shore. The HHS secretary was struck by what good evidence this paper alone provided for the FDA position. It laid out nutritional advice and fat content, and put it in the context of an average diet—of 2,000 calories per day, with a footnote on the liner that cited the National Academy of Sciences' National Research Council. Madigan was caught by surprise. There could hardly be a better advertisement for the FDA position than a meat merchant like McDonald's not only giving out tray liners that might have been printed by the FDA, but flatly accepting the "daily values" for consumers and the 2,000-calorie average as well. The meeting ended with no decision.

Kessler was prepared to resign if the decision went against the FDA. His wife, Paulette, a former litigator and one of Kessler's most trusted advisers, said there was really no option. Taylor had already said he would resign if the decision went against the FDA, and Sullivan was considering a similar protest. As Kessler said, he didn't believe he was considering resigning over the details of a policy, 2,350 calories versus 2,000, or any similar calculus. "I was going to resign because a decision against us would have meant the meat industry had asserted undue influence over the White House. I felt that the FDA's credibility and influence were at stake. From the outset, I insisted that we were not going to allow political interests to outweigh public health."

A few days later, President Bush decided in favor of the FDA. The food labels would be reformed. In some ways it was the most important food regulation ever. It was the kind of regulation the FDA had worked toward over the century—a balance of rules that protected consumers, ensured that ample information was available to them, and encouraged businesses to compete on the basis of health and nutrition. It not only stopped dishonest promotional practices but also used high standards to help create new markets. A floor had been set; food companies would have to work upward from it.

Winning the fight over food label reform was a major boost for the FDA. It was a popular measure that earned the agency credit for working to make reforms that industry could live with, and earned Kessler respect as a fierce advocate for consumers. It was clear the FDA was serious about its advocacy of consumer and public health positions.

As these battles were playing out, a much nastier struggle was starting—the argument over silicone-filled breast implants. For the FDA the issue was fairly direct, even though the maneuvering around it became both wild and complex. The FDA did not have responsibility for monitoring the safety and effectiveness of medical devices until 1976. Then, along with other medical devices, breast implants became subject to safety regulation. The law allowed the current breast implants to be sold but said testing data would be required later. In 1982 the FDA alerted companies that data would be needed and they should start gathering it. In 1988 the agency officially put implants on the list of devices that would require solid scientific studies establishing their safety. The companies could not produce these studies; tests showed their commercially successful products would fail scrutiny. They hoped the issue would die.

By the time the FDA insisted on seeing the data in 1991, the companies could produce only data demonstrating a number of serious safety problems with the implants. The companies, after thirty years of putting the implants in women, had no more than a handful of "studies," and those were more like surveys of plastic surgeons. Dow Corning, for example, simply asked plastic surgeons who had implanted the devices to review the medical charts of women who had implants, and counted the number of problems the doctors had recorded. The weakness of the data gathering was obvious.

When the data review was complete, Kessler said:

We still do not know how often the implants leak, and when they do, we do not know exactly what materials get into the body. We still do not know how often the implants break, or how long the implants last. We still do not know how often women with the implants suffer adverse effects. For example, there are reports that painful hardening of the implant can occur in anywhere from 10 to 70 percent of patients. We still do not know to what extent the implants interfere with mammography examinations. We still do not know whether the implants can increase a woman's risk of developing cancer. And we still do not know enough about the relationship between these devices and autoimmune and connective tissue diseases.

Kessler held several public hearings in the fall of 1991, not only to hear testimony on the implants from women and doctors but also to let the public hear the data, or about the lack of it, at the same time. During the debate at the hearings, a bin full of damaging documents from inside Dow Corning was leaked to newspapers, confirming that the company had known of serious problems with the implants for many years, from their own studies and from reports from doctors observing severe problems. But the company had decided not to investigate.

The situation turned awkward for the FDA because it was difficult to convey to the public what the basic issue was. The companies and doctors were putting medical devices into humans; the law said that the companies had to conduct serious, controlled studies of the devices and the women. The studies had to show the devices were safe. The full burden was on the companies. But to some, with scanty knowledge, it appeared that the FDA had simply decided to try to take the breast implants off the market even though the agency didn't have data that supported the decision.

To confuse matters, the plastic surgeons' society was pressing a campaign to drive home this erroneous picture. The group offered spokesmen who said that, based on their experience, they didn't see any reason to take the implants off the market. They were ignorant of both what the law required and of what had happened to their patients. It was a lobbying campaign to save their businesses, and they gave no quarter. The companies had evaded the issue, and now they were staring at a potential major loss of business. From a public relations perspective, the FDA was ineffective in this instance.

Leading the charge against the FDA was the American Society for Reconstructive and Plastic Surgery, under the direction of Dr. Norman Cole. He levied a membership tax of more than $1,000 per doctor to finance a public relations and lobbying campaign to keep all implants on the market without restriction. Cole's group spent at least $4 million on the effort. The plan had two parts essentially: first, to lobby Congress and the Bush administration, and second, to discredit David Kessler personally. The plastic surgeons hired several lobbying firms with direct connections to President Bush (Deborah Steelman, Roger Stone, and Charles Black of Black, Manafort, Stone and Kelly). Cole, who had trouble getting his phone calls returned by Kentucky congressmen, was stunned at the access he could get by hiring Washington lobbyists. Meetings were arranged and briefing papers delivered up and down the line in the administration, from Chief of Staff John Sununu, domestic policy advisor Roger Porter, and Vice President Quayle, to Louis Sullivan and his staff. Members of Congress received substantial cash donations. Four hundred women with implants who had been flown to Washington visited their congressmen. The women spoke of their need to have augmented breasts and in press sessions offered reporters a chance to feel them.

The campaign was blunted by the first jury verdict on the implants which initially went against Dow. A California jury awarded $7.3 million to a California woman who had sued Dow Corning over its misbehavior—marketing but not testing the implants. Documents showing that the company had not done the required scientific testing and had lied about safety problems reported to them were central to the case.

After these documents were made public, Kessler suggested a moratorium on the use of implants while an investigation and decision were pending. A moratorium, Cole said, was "unconscionable—an outrage," and with it, the FDA had created "hysteria, anxiety, and panic" among women (not to mention in Cole's office). Cole unleashed the personal part of the attack. He called for Kessler to be dismissed, and sent fifty thousand letters to surgeons, urging them to besiege HHS with requests to do so. Charles Black, who was now with the Bush reelection campaign, wrote a personal note to Sullivan asking him to intervene against Kessler. The surgeons also began a rumor campaign that suggested Kessler was opposed to implants because his wife had them and had had trouble with them. One of the surgeons' lobbyists, Nancy Taylor, even called Paulette Kessler at home to question her about whether she had problems with implants.

Plastic surgeons were working to convey the impression that the burden of demonstrating safety was on the FDA, not the device makers, and that surgeons had established from experience that implants were safe. As Dr. David Hidalgo wrote in a *New York Times* op-ed page article, "Critics charge that silicone implants harden . . . and that they rupture and leak with unknown effect to the body. Though these complications do happen, it is only in a very small percentage of cases." The surgeons had no hard data but presented their impressions as evidence. At the AMA, the loudest voice was that of Dr. Mitchell Karlan, who told Kessler at a press conference that if implants were not kept on the market, "There will be absolute hysteria among women," and said doctors did not need any more evidence of implant safety. "We already have the data—the experience of physicians," he said. Dow Corning asserted, and the plastic surgeons agreed, that the rate of rupture was half of one percent, though the company had in its own files reports from doctors giving rates of rupture from 10 to 32 percent. At the time Hidalgo wrote his article for the *Times* and Karlan was speaking up for the AMA, we now know that the rate of problems from implants was hardly "a very small percentage of cases." The rate at which the implants ruptured and dumped silicone into women's chests, abdomens, and arms was between 60 and 96 percent, based on studies of women over years. In 1999 the Institute of Medicine of the National Academy of Sciences wrote the most comprehensive report to date on the safety issues, and it noted that contrary to the reports of the companies and the surgeons, the rate of rupture was "very high, in fact unacceptable." Essentially, all the implants would rupture or cause inflammation and hardened breasts over time. The surgeons and the companies had said the implants were good "for a lifetime." But even in the best cases research showed that women who want implants must have new ones implanted and reimplanted two or three times at least because of defects and hazards; some have had as many as sixteen surgeries to keep implants in place.

And the effect of implants on breast-feeding is apparently large. Though definitive studies have not yet been done, in the key study to date, 64 percent of women with implants were unable to breast-feed. Women without implants were unable to breast-feed only 7 percent of the time. Though it is known that breast-feeding infants ingest silicone from the implants when mothers are able to breast-feed, it is not clear whether the silicone has any effect on the nursing infant. On the question of mammograms, Dr. Melvin Silverstein, in studies done between 1986 and 1991, showed that viewing of malignancies was completely obscured in 39 percent of cases, a false negative four times higher among women with implants than without them.

Representative Ted Weiss of Manhattan said at a hearing he held on the implants, "For thirty years, more than one million women have been subjects in a massive, uncontrolled study, without their knowledge or consent. It's almost a perfect case of how patients ought not to be treated."

In the end, as the law requires, the agency declared there was not enough data to show that the implants were safe—the benefits did not outweigh the risks. But rather than ban them outright, the agency picked a middle road: It permitted saline-filled implants to be sold freely. Silicone-filled implants could also be used by women who wanted the devices for breast reconstruction after cancer surgery. And silicone implants for cosmetic augmentation of breast size would be allowed as long as women and their doctors were willing to be part of a large study on the safety of implants.

•

CHAPTER EIGHTEEN

Drug Lag Revisited

D URING DAVID Kessler's term as commissioner, whatever the headlines about the FDA and its actions (the polls of citizens were positive; the comments from politicians were often negative), there was a
continuing controversy about the weather-worn issue of drug lag. It per-
sists to this day. It had all begun with the faulty reports of drug lag in
1972, and reports funded by the drug companies and work from conservative economists multiplied through the decade afterward. The reports
were amplified as conservatives running for office seized the figures to
demonstrate that the government had gone too far, that regulation
needed to be curtailed.

There was a lesser voice in the background, from scholars not financed
by the drug companies, which asserted that drug lag was an odd notion to
begin with, since every nation has a drug lag, and the one in the United
States was not disproportionate. After all, no country approves every
drug, and some drugs get approved ahead of others for good and understandable reasons. Very few drugs indeed are approved in multiple countries simultaneously. Then, too, some of the drugs hastened to market
elsewhere turned out to be unsafe, and most of the others were unimportant copies of existing drugs.

The General Accounting Office of Congress, a nonpartisan and generally reliable investigative agency, conducted the first investigation by a
neutral group into what exactly led to delay on any given drug. Its early
report, published in 1980, was headlined "FDA Drug Approval—A
Lengthy Process That Delays the Availability of Important New Drugs."
The headline appeared to be a confirmation that regulation was halting
innovation and creating problems for America's health. It reinforced the
already long-held belief among some critics that the FDA was slow and
needed to change. But, in fact, the report provided a significant amount

of ammunition for supporters of regulation and the FDA. The report made clear that the slowness was *not* due to excessive caution and over-regulation, as conservatives had asserted. The GAO spelled out in some detail that the drug industry itself was quite often responsible for the long delays for which the FDA was blamed. The report identified three general problems that were the source of the delays: a disastrous lack of staff at the FDA, incompetent and uninterested industry research departments, and a lack of communication between the two sides.

The GAO found that in 1979, during the time of the longest "drug lags," the FDA reviewers were stretched so thin—meeting with company researchers, setting out guidelines for data presentation, resolving disputes, handling unexpected safety problems—that they were able to spend less than 40 percent of their time actually working on a company's new drug application. The impression that companies were pressing ahead with their work and impatient with the FDA delays was also false, the GAO noted. Investigators checked on twenty-seven drug applications that had taken more than three years to work their way through the system and were not yet approved. In these cases, the FDA reviewers said the applications were unfinished, with vital information missing. The companies involved confirmed this for the GAO. The manufacturers had not given the data to the FDA sooner in a number of cases because they felt the drugs would not pass muster. Instead, they put the blame on the FDA. In other cases, manufacturers gave higher priority to other drugs and let some applications slide. In still other cases, company staffers had simply botched the work; they handed in applications with big chunks of data missing. In the cases of delays longer than forty months, the GAO found, between two and three years of that time had been due to company delay. Moreover, as FDA staffers told the GAO investigators:

> It would appear that almost half of the original New Drug Applications submitted to the FDA and initially rejected are considered by their sponsors to be so lacking in profitability, therapeutic gain, proof of efficacy, or otherwise unapprovable, that the sponsors do not intend to pursue them further. . . . It would appear that some drug companies use FDA reviewers as sounding boards to see if they have produced an acceptable drug rather than submitting applications for only those drugs that they are really committed to marketing. This industry practice dilutes the effectiveness of the FDA review process and causes delays in approving other, more promising, drugs.

Between the time of the GAO report in 1980 and the time David Kessler was named FDA commissioner, the situation appeared to have improved gradually. The FDA had put significant effort into speeding up approvals, chiefly by working with companies to get questions asked and answered quickly on both sides, and to be sure that applications coming in were fit to be read and dealt with in the first place. The median approval time for a new drug (a new chemical, not just a copy of one already on the market) had dropped from about thirty-three months in 1987 to twenty-two months in 1991. Just as important, other nations were getting more serious about scientific standards, so their approval times were growing longer. A consensus among nations was gradually developing about how to review and approve drugs so as to avoid facile approvals that let dangerous and useless drugs on the market or lethargic approvals that held back some useful medicines.

Negotiations began quietly among the FDA, industry, and members of the key congressional committees. The FDA's aim was to avoid the corrosive rhetoric about "overcaution," "deadly regulation," and "bureaucrats," and instead target what appeared on sober analysis to be the real issues—getting enough qualified doctors onto the FDA staff to carry out drug reviews, and getting the company staffs to cooperate in meeting higher standards. The solution that emerged was one intended to bypass the anachronistic and unreliable congressional system that always underfinanced the FDA. The plan worked out by the agency and industry was not ideal but had the virtue of getting directly to the issue—money to hire drug reviewers. It proposed a "user fee" like that paid by visitors to national parks to help maintain them. In this case, the industry would pay a fee for each drug submitted for approval, and the money collected would go to hire medical officers to review drugs. The fees were set to cover the cost of more than two hundred additional reviewers—an indication of just how understaffed the FDA was. But by law money given to the FDA under normal circumstances could not be handed over to one small unit—the drug review group. It would have to go into the general funds, from which money would then be parceled out. The companies, understandably, feared that all the money they were prepared to pay out would never find its way to the right program. Congressional staff members eventually addressed these concerns satisfactorily. The FDA was now ready to meet a strict series of deadlines when the additional manpower was on board.

Then the Council on Competitiveness in Vice President Quayle's office, along with a few other conservative stalwarts in the White House, put a halt to things. John Cohrssen and Boyden Gray on President Bush's staff attacked user fees, saying, "The gridlock that exists at FDA is not the result of a lack of funds." Even Peter Hutt, former FDA chief lawyer, now an increasingly conservative food and drug industry lawyer, said user fees would do no good. He blamed the "bureaucrats' " attitudes for the delays and said giving them more money would lead to longer, not shorter, review times.

For David Kessler, this sort of thinking was a revelation. "I was amazed," he said. "Here we had a workable, cooperative deal. It seemed to work in everyone's interests—a really creative solution to a problem. But there were people who did not want to solve it. They wanted the agency to fail for other, ideological reasons." But Kessler, industry representatives, and some Democratic and Republican members of Congress pressed their case with the White House and finally won agreement.

The law that resulted, the Prescription Drug User Fee Act, passed in 1992. It was written with an array of "hammers," to ensure that the agency acted with alacrity. It was expected to take five years to hire and train more than two hundred reviewers. Actually, review times began dropping as soon as the new reviewers joined the FDA, even before they finished their training. Only two years into the program, standard drug approval time dropped from nineteen months to sixteen; drugs identified as particularly important had their approval times drop from fifteen to six months. Two years after the passage of the law, head-to-head comparisons with Britain—the kind of study that started the drug lag debate—showed that the United States was now ahead in the race, and had a better safety record besides. Between 1990 and 1994, of the drugs approved by both the United States and the United Kingdom, 30 were approved in the United States first, 28 in the United Kingdom first. A similar comparison showed the United States ahead of Germany 31 to 13, and the United States was ahead of Japan 10 to 4. Most important, however, was the comparison of drugs that actually had therapeutic importance. Between 1990 and 1995 no drugs of therapeutic importance approved in Britain were not also on the market in America. In contrast, nine important drugs had been approved in America that had not been approved in Britain. Britain now appeared to have a drug lag.

Over the next few years of the program, the drop in review times continued steadily, until by 1999 the median for all drugs was less than twelve months, and priority drugs were approved in under six months. Ironically, within a decade of the introduction of user fees, news reports were suggesting that the speedup of drug approvals caused a number of unsafe drugs to reach market that later had to be recalled. Notwithstanding such tangential objections, in the light of day it seems clear that user fees will eventually lead to serious problems. One effect of having drug companies support the FDA is that every time the user fee act is reapproved, the industry, since it is now bearing a substantial financial burden, can ask for additional favors and will likely get them. There is also the problem that Congress, already having shirked its responsibility, will continue to shift its burden. Because drug review is taken care of by industry dollars, the tendency in Congress will be to reduce its overall funding for the FDA.

As the issue of new drugs was being resolved, the oldest drugs of all began to create a problem. Herbals and remedies given as supplements to the diet had created some confusion since the 1906 law. The substances were not food and not exactly medical drugs either. But their advocates insisted that they could be used successfully to treat human ailments, even if no data proved it.

The popular food labeling law passed at the beginning of Kessler's term became the instrument that roused this sleeping beast. The labeling law stipulated that health claims could be displayed on food packages— such as "helps prevent heart disease"—provided there was scientific agreement on the facts underlying the claim. It seemed natural when the law was passed that producers of herbal medicines, supplements, and other assorted substances sold as remedies—feverfew, comfrey, ephedra, ginkgo biloba, extracts of animal organs, amino acids, and enzymes— should also be asked to provide evidence before they could claim health benefits. And so the law was written.

But these items were produced by a different breed of manufacturer from the large food and drug companies of America. These products carry with them a swirl of associations suggesting they are "natural" medicines, remedies discovered by wise folk over the past few thousand years. Their marketing often invokes the secret knowledge of the ancients, the wisdom of folk healers, the honesty and safety of traditional remedies, and neighbors helping neighbors heal. The aim is to evoke plain values in a world that appears to be otherwise dominated by masses of technical information, cold and haughty doctors, sterile corridors in modern hospitals, and aggressive drug corporations. These substances are meant to be a refuge and a comfort. What consumers had not noticed over the years was that these items were now produced by large corporations that had adopted homey appearances but were pharmaceutical houses just the same, though freed of certain scientific or ethical standards when producing herbal remedies.

Scott Bass, a supplements industry lawyer, traces the origin of the self-medication craze in America to Samuel Thomson, though he may not be entirely familiar with Thomson's sociopathic character and his attempts to bleed his cult followers of large sums of cash.

Many of today's remedies are not just like the nineteenth-century remedies; they are the *same* medicines—lobelia, echinacea, pennyroyal, ephedra. Other, newer ones have been created in imitation of genuine scientific advances. (When it became known that amino acids were biological chemicals essential to the body's operations, amino acids became available as remedies; never mind that the body can't use them in the form in which they are swallowed.) It was no less true in the nineteenth century. Each advance of science produced new "cures" on the market. The discovery that the body uses electricity produced totally useless "electrical stimulation" cures. The discovery of germs as the source of disease was soon followed by thousands of "germ killing" medicines; these medicines could kill germs in lab dishes but were ineffective within the body.

The psychology of the remedy business was analyzed bluntly and with great insight by one of the great American entrepreneurs, Phineas T. Barnum, who had worked the folk remedy circuit himself when he started out in business. Writing about the advertising of these medicines, he said, "Fortunes equaling that of Croesus, and as plenty as blackberries, were dangling from many an advertisement. Applicants were invited to cellars and dark attics, where temporarily impoverished capitalists asked them for money and ingenuity in distributing patent medicines, new microscopes, or directories providing vital information sure to be purchased by every citizen." He was aware that the greatest appeal of medical scams came from the appeal of science, the wonders of new knowledge itself, and the optimism that came with it.

Barnum became famous for his circus, but most of his entrepreneurial adventures were less innocent. He found a wry and spry woman who looked far older than her years, advertised her as George Washington's 161-year-old nurse, and charged admission. He found a child who looked older than his five years, and called him Tom Thumb, the world's smallest man at twenty-five inches high. He indentured Tom and his entire family for $7 a week, while making $90 a week himself from their appearances. He displayed the body of a fish, with a monkey head and arms sewn on, as the corpse of the Feejee Mermaid.

What was remarkable about his deceptions was not so much who or what he put on display, but the *manner* in which he did it. He created the public relations scheme that is still used today by some manufacturers of herbals. Instead of declaring the mermaid genuine, he offered her up as a puzzle to modern science. He said simply, the evidence is not in. Science was always discovering amazing new facts, creatures, and cures. All the great discoveries, he said, had been disbelieved or mocked. The pitch sounded at once reasonable and irrefutable. Commandeering a line from Alexander Pope, Barnum put it to service in shady commerce: "Who is to decide when doctors disagree?" It was intended to suggest that if the final authorities cannot agree, there is room for each of us to make a judgment.

Barnum counted himself the new model of the American business-man. He acknowledged that this type of business was not a good school for morals but accepted it as a given in America. He wrote that the age that produced this kind of trade was not to be admired; readers should avoid emulating it if possible in the future. It was the most vulgar, unscrupulous, and foolish era in America, he said.

He was pointing out, with his mixture of idealism and cynicism, something unpleasant about the nature of the new commerce in nineteenth-century America. Despite the wish of the founders, there was to be no noble and virtuous society of farmers. Banishing royalty and hereditary nobility did not dispose of kings and barons; it merely sent them into business. The common man would now have to make some judgments on his own. And between the businesses and the common man, it would not exactly be a fair fight. "When credentials, coats of arms, and university degrees no longer guaranteed what passed for truth, it was difficult for him to know whom and what to believe. Everything was up for grabs," writes Neil Harris in his biography of Barnum. P.T. did, however, make a distinction between his kind of small-time cheating and the corporate organization of lying and cheating. One businessman may cheat another, and a small merchant may be sly with his customers when he faced them, he said, but corporations were something else. They were like royalty and were not to be tolerated.

The FDA, beginning early in the twentieth century, had cracked down on patent medicines, chiefly by attacking the most dangerous ones— those with high alcohol and opium content, and those with the most fla-grantly fraudulent claims to cure disease. But the bulk of the remedy trade was untouchable, largely because of the huge number of products available. There were never enough FDA employees to contemplate a broad effort to stop false claims and fraudulent medicines. The FDA had to take on the patent medicines one by one, bringing each one to court in laborious, drawn-out actions.

Over time, the folk remedies were counted as a variety of food, or "supplements to the diet." They were like vitamins, as the reasoning had it, supporting the body with useful chemicals and botanicals so that it could remain healthy, and disease and disorder could be avoided. The practical effect of grouping the supplements with foods was to avoid undergoing the tough safety and effectiveness tests that true medicines did. Occasional actions were taken against some of them, and dangerous ones were banned from the market, such as L-tryptophan, an amino acid that was billed as a natural tranquilizer and a sleep medication. The supplement, or at least one company's version of it, killed some thirty-eight people and injured 1,500 more that we know of.

In the early 1990s, when foods became subject to new rules about what may and may not be on their labels, it was a broad change for products that had been regulated by the 1906 and 1938 laws, as well as numerous smaller laws passed over the years on such matters as food colorings. The broad new approach in the food labeling law included (at first, before the trouble started) food supplements, folk remedies, and herbal products. They were now to be part of a general standard that required testing for any claims made on labels, as well as explicit statements of ingredients, amounts, and so on. Before the 1990s the food supplements and herbals had made a tradition of flying under the regulatory radar, changing labels, ingredients, and companies, even moving from jurisdiction to jurisdiction when health department investigators came after them. The manufacturers had for years been niche marketers whose ads ran in alternative publications or classified advertising sections. The supplements and remedies were very cheap to make and could be sold dear, so in the 1960s and 1970s, even though the markets were not large, a few small companies managed. Then, in the 1980s, the business began to grow rapidly. By 1992, the remedy business was big and corporate—and still growing very rapidly.

On Capitol Hill, as in society more broadly, supplements were thought of as somehow *different* from foods and drugs when it came to labeling. Between 1992 and 1994 the companies making them began requesting that they be officially exempted from all tests of safety and effectiveness. They wanted, in their words, "a more lenient standard." Senator Orrin Hatch of Utah, a senior Republican, said that there was $700 million worth of supplement companies in his district, and he himself owned part of one of them. (He also spoke at one fund-raiser for groups lobbying Congress on the bill that he would profit from.)

Hatch was the leader in Washington of the "lower standards for supplements" movement. The campaign was exactly in keeping with the history and character of the remedies. The companies offered no evidence that supplements were more useful or safer than foods or drugs that were already regulated. Rather, they simply asserted it. "I use supplements daily and I believe in them," said Senator Hatch. "And there is ample reason to do so. You can't pick up a newspaper without seeing studies indicating the benefits of supplements," he testified before a House subcommittee in 1993. And they "have been safely used for centuries."

There were, of course, no studies to support these assertions. But when the debate over supplements heated up from 1992 to 1994, some scientific testing was begun. Though the initial studies were not in hand until after a new supplement labeling law was enacted, the results were what skeptics expected. For example, it had been repeated often that St.-John's-wort was effective in relieving depression and was not harmful. When rigorous scientific tests were conducted, the data not only showed that it does not work but that it has some extremely dangerous side effects in that it blocks the effects of other medicines. (It counteracts the lifesaving effects of AIDS treatments, for instance.) It was a good example that to claim "centuries of use" meant nothing. Antioxidants, such as vitamin E and beta-carotene, were said to help block "free radicals" in cells, and free radicals were thought to cause cell damage that resulted in cancer. A variety of small, poorly done studies seemed to support the claim. But the best evidence now available shows that vitamins C and E and beta-carotene do not protect against cancer.

As each of the venerable remedies is subjected to testing, more hazards are found, and there is less evidence that the substances work. Royal jelly, the seemingly harmless substance secreted by worker bees, has been found to trigger dangerous reactions in asthmatics. Comfrey, used by the ancients to heal external wounds and in recent years to counteract indigestion, can cause severe liver damage. It is unclear how many of the supplements would remain on the market if all were tested rigorously for safety or effectiveness.

In the early nineties, the lobbying to set a looser standard for the remedies, in keeping with the history of patent medicines, was aggressive and nasty. At the time, FDA officials did not think they were making a very threatening gesture in their new labeling requirements. After all, the giants of the American food business had agreed to them. It seemed perfectly reasonable that herbals and supplements should be held to the same standard. But in this assumption, the FDA misjudged. These remedies are part of a social attitude, and their adherents could be roused to anger and action.

In February 1992 leaders of the newly rich corporations in the supplement industry decided to mount a forceful campaign to evade studies of their products. They formed the Nutritional Health Alliance (NHA) with Gerald Kessler (no relation to the FDA commissioner) as its head. This Kessler is head of the company that makes Nature's Plus products, a wide variety of supplements, including L-tryptophan and Cardio-Maxim. Gerald Kessler and the NHA were aware of the rebellious streak in their clientele and decided to make use of it in going after the FDA.

"THE FDA WANTS TO PUT YOU OUT OF BUSINESS," said the headline on one NHA flyer sent to health food stores. The text of the item went on, "Every health food store is under immediate threat of siege. Congress wants to give FDA police powers so they can seize products without notification and use heavy fines and court penalties to close you down. FDA wants to destroy your supplement business by making many items prescription only. FDA wants to make it illegal for you to sell the majority of your best selling products." "DON'T LET THE FDA TAKE YOUR VITAMINS AWAY," said one action alert from NHA.

In other materials the NHA said the FDA was planning to turn vitamins into prescription drugs. Another piece, entitled "Fight for Your Family's Rights," said that the FDA "in preparation for increased enforcement activities has hired 100 criminal investigators." The flyer went on to say, "These new G-men will be unleashed on the supplement industry." "Write to Congress today or kiss your supplements goodbye," said another mailing piece.

The claims were false, of course, but the FDA was caught flat-footed. Belated denials seemed only to make things worse. Gerald Kessler steadfastly asserted that the FDA wanted to shut down supplement companies and take away the nation's vitamins even when reporters noted that the FDA was not proposing anything of the kind. Scott Bass was more sophisticated in asserting the "disastrous effects" claim. He acknowledged that it was not the FDA that would take supplements off the market, but rather the *manufacturers* who had declared they would take them off if their claims had to be tested like other foods. "If the regulations go into effect, the products will be taken off the market because the manufacturers won't take health-claim labeling off. They are the lifeblood of the industry," he said. The line had been drawn.

The industry fed money and materials to their supporters, including ubiquitous supplement stores. The campaign that was cranked up included radio and TV spots, fax blitzes, "hot lines" for call-in persuasion, celebrity videos, petitions, and "grass roots" lobbying kits. Stores offered 20 percent discounts on purchases if the customers would send a letter of protest to Congress. The stores would supply the pencil, the paper, and the language. The industry staged a nationwide "blackout" day in supplement stores, on which black draping was hung from doors and aisles to draw media coverage.

Thousands of letters flooded Capitol Hill, and the *Washington Post*'s wry monitor of Washington activities, Al Kamen, noted, "The supplements battle has been wacky even by Hill standards. The enormous lobbying effort against the labeling law, which swept health food stores and generated tidal waves of calls, was directed at an outcome—loss of access to such remedies without a prescription—that the law never contained."

On May 6, 1992, a blunder by the FDA hurt its cause. Dr. Jonathan Wright, a Harvard-educated medical renegade, was the leader of the Tahoma Clinic in Kent, Washington, where he illicitly manufactured "natural" medicines according to FDA and court records. One of his devices was something he called the Interro machine. It was billed as a machine of medical diagnosis, but it was really a galvanometer that measured electrical conductance of skin—in other words, whether there was moisture such as sweat on the skin. The device is used in lie detectors on the theory that people sweat when they lie. This device, created in Germany, was used by Wright to "read" the medicinal "needs" of his customers.

An FDA investigator had gone to the clinic undercover to be tested with the machine. A young female employee there "probed" points on one of the investigator's fingers. She said that her probes with the Interro machine would determine which substances he was allergic to. Supplement salesmen claimed allergies caused many diseases, and they sold remedies accordingly. The computer attached to the Interro machine produced a printout that indicated which medicines the investigator should buy.

Wright was also an advocate of L-tryptophan. The FDA had banned sales of the supplement, but he declared he believed tryptophan was deadly because of a contamination of the substance in one manufacturer's plant. He sued the FDA, stating he had the right to sell tryptophan despite the ban. In February 1992, Wright took a further step and posted on his clinic door a militia-style notice that said he was exempt from U.S. law. The notice added, "No employee, agent, or inspector of the FDA shall be permitted on these premises."

The FDA had evidence that Wright was manufacturing remedies in his offices. Since the Elixir Sulfanilamide catastrophe, the manufacture of remedies has been taken quite seriously, and renegade drug factories that operated without health or safety inspections have been closed down when possible. Wright's operation was on the FDA's list of serious violators, and the agency asked a U.S. magistrate for a search warrant, given that Wright was refusing inspection. On May 6 the local sheriff's office carried out the warrant against Wright's clinic. The sheriff's deputies knew that they were there to investigate "illegal drugs," but the deputies made the unfortunate assumption that the drugs being manufactured were heroin or cocaine, requiring a different type of approach to the shop. When employees at the clinic refused to let the sheriff's deputies and FDA inspectors in, despite the warrant, the deputies broke open the door. The defiance suggested to the deputies that the situation was dangerous, and one drew his gun. The gun, the sheriff's office said, was never pointed at anyone, and was quickly reholstered when it was clear that the defiance was merely verbal.

The investigators searched the clinic and took away the Interro devices, 103 bottles of L-tryptophan, and assorted other materials related to the illegal manufacture of drugs. In the days that followed, the state of Washington suspended Wright's pharmacy license for illegal and unsafe manufacture and sales to both "patients" and other practitioners. Wright pleaded no contest to federal charges, and the tryptophan bottles were destroyed. He paid the costs of the court action.

News of the raid was put out over the PR Newswire, saying: "Fifteen Food and Drug Administration agents in black flak jackets, with guns drawn, backed by a contingent of armed King County police, broke down the door and stormed into the Tahoma Clinic of Dr. Jonathan Wright. In a scene that resembled a television drug bust, agents shouted at bewildered clinic employees and patients, 'Drop everything and put up your hands.' "

The FDA has no agents and no guns. There was a legal warrant for a search, and the clinic employees refused to honor it. But that was lost in the public relations blitz. Activists had videotaped the raid, which they distributed to the media, along with selected photographs of the clinic employees immediately after the raid. It became a national TV event overnight, complete with erroneous information that the FDA was after vitamins in the raid. Eventually, even the *New York Times* ran a confused, error-filled story on the front page that completely missed the point of both the raid and the debate over the labeling of supplements. The story, which was reprinted in newspapers around the country, reported that a videotape of the raid "shows FDA agents, dressed in bulletproof vests, bursting into the clinic and commanding clinic employees to freeze." A correction ran soon afterward.

Industry advocates were soon asserting that several such raids had taken place. Actually, the other raids referred to were actions by state health departments, not federal agencies, against other medical scams. The coup de grâce was a sixty-second commercial featuring actor Mel Gibson, and showing a SWAT team with guns drawn raiding his house to get his vitamin C in the bathroom cabinet. The voiceover said, "The federal government is actually considering classifying most vitamins as drugs."

The lobbying campaign was a complete success—the new rules for supplements were stalled. Many members of Congress were persuaded that any effort expended on behalf of supplement labeling would produce a small army of enemies and a series of unneeded political headaches. So Congress voted, first, to delay the label rules, then to enact a law written by supplement industry lawyers that carved out a completely new category of law for supplements, vitamins, and herbal remedies. In Congress, it was referred to as the Dietary Supplement and Health Education Act. The *New York Times* called it "The Snake Oil Protection Act." It was opposed by all the public health, medical, and professional nutrition groups, including the American Cancer Society, the American Dietetic Association, and the Consumer Federation of America, as well as the health watchdog groups at the Center for Science in the Public Interest and Public Citizen's Health Research Group.

The law that emerged in 1994 stipulates that companies are permitted to put "health" remedies on the market with no safety testing or any review by the FDA, just as in the days of Elixir Sulfanilamide. Claims that the products improve health and strengthen the body against disease are permitted. Thus, a claim for saw palmetto can say it helps the prostate, but cannot say it treats prostate disease. If the FDA finds a product has an "unreasonable risk of injury or illness," the agency must notify its manufacturer and allow it a hearing. Then, if the agency still wants to go forward, it must present its evidence to a U.S. attorney, who will decide whether to take the matter to court. In court, the burden of proof is entirely on the FDA to investigate and prove that a remedy is dangerous.

If an emergency develops, and it is clear that there is an imminent danger to the public health, such as the wave of sudden deaths that occurred in the case of sulfanilamide, the FDA is not permitted to take the remedy off the market but must ask the secretary of HHS to do so. After the secretary acts, an extensive evidentiary hearing is required.

One of the most salient facts about the whole supplement episode is the fiction that underlies it. The law says that supplements can advertise their power to "enhance" the body and its health. It says the supplements can be seen to "support" health. But it also says the remedies are *not* to be sold as medicines designed to prevent, treat, or cure disease. But, of course, that is exactly how they are sold. In one article in the publication *HerbalGram* of the American Botanical Council, Mark Blumenthal writes, "As many in the botanical community are aware, people use herbs and other supplements in a variety of ways, sometimes for the prevention or treatment of disease." In the tall stack of books about what remedies people should use, the tables of contents and the indexes are often organized by the *diseases the remedies are intended to treat.*

In point of fact, the labels on remedies remain vague enough to avoid prosecution under the law. The salespeople deliver the treatment pitch. For example, the supplement Cardio-Maxim, sold a few years ago by Nature's Plus, contained nothing useful for the heart except a tiny amount of niacin, which can easily be absorbed from a normal diet. The promotional material for the supplement read, "Cardio-vascular disease is the number one killer in America. Therefore, strengthening the body's vital organs is an essential part of preventative health." The material went on to say that Cardio-Maxim is a "sophisticated foundation of nutrients for those who are interested in this very special supplementation." No direct claims were being made, but the pitch was plain enough.

Alex Schauss, one of the founders of Citizens for Health, which lobbied against the FDA and for supplement deregulation, freely tells stories about how patients have been cured of AIDS by supplements. Senator Hatch, for his part, has routinely claimed supplements prevent disease; he offered the example of vitamin A preventing breast cancer in women. The pattern holds in some consumer surveys of practices at supplement stores. For example, in 1989 a group called the Consumer Health Education Council in Houston conducted a casual survey of supplement stores by telephoning forty-one of them. The caller said she had a brother with AIDS who was looking for an effective alternative to taking standard drugs. The caller explained that the brother's wife was still having sex with her infected husband, and was seeking products that would reduce her risk of being infected. All of the stores offered remedies that would help the brother's immune system, improve his wife's immunity to AIDS, and protect her from infection. The products recommended were vitamins and an array of substances such as coenzyme Q10, germanium, lecithin, and blue-green algae. Thirty of the stores said they had products that would cure AIDS. None recommended sexual abstinence or use of a condom. "Immune boosters" remain one of the most popular items in supplement stores.

The FDA did its own survey, a broader, more scientific study that covered all regions of the country and asked standardized questions of supplement store operators. They asked straightforward questions about what items the stores sold to prevent or treat disease. Among the questions asked were, "What do you sell to help high blood pressure?" "Do you have anything to help fight infection or help my immune system?" and "Do you have anything that works on cancer?" One hundred twenty-nine requests for treatment yielded 120 offers of dietary supplements to treat disease.

Testing by Consumers Union after the dietary supplements act was in effect focused on ten brands of ginseng. It found that the active ingredients, the chemicals called ginsenosides, varied from .4 milligram per capsule to 23.2 milligrams per capsule. Extracts from three entirely different plants were being sold as ginseng, and different parts were used in different remedies. There was also no agreement about what to use ginseng for. It is promoted for treatment of stress, high blood pressure, ulcers, diabetes, depression, impaired memory, and menopause, among other maladies. There are thousands of "studies" of the value and safety of ginseng, but as with most other supplements, there are none of the essential long-term, controlled trials.

Surveys, including one carried out by the Congressional Research Service, show that Americans believe that anything sold in pill form or as medicine in this country has been tested for safety and approved by the FDA. The supplement industry benefits from the impression of safety. But because the substances are untested, a catastrophe could emerge at any time. Ironically, the law opposed by the FDA has now begun to make supplement makers very nervous. They have begun to complain that some among them are selling potentially hazardous supplements, and the FDA is not doing all it could to police them.

•

CHAPTER NINETEEN

An Anti-regulatory Campaign

THE FDA had now rebounded from the attacks of the Reagan years and the self-inflicted wounds of the generic drug scandals. It fought publicly on the side of consumers and had won more than once.

One victory involved the Red Cross. In 1992 the system of blood banking that had been built up from a loose network of volunteer-staffed clinics was clearly in danger. The system had broken down repeatedly through the 1980s, and blood contaminated with AIDS had been distributed with fatal effects. Then in the early 1990s the Red Cross let the system decline to the point that inspections found numerous potentially fatal errors and a system unable to correct itself. The organization neared collapse. The FDA, over Elizabeth Dole's objections, pulled the system back from the brink, using a court order to force the Red Cross to reorganize and upgrade its safety systems.

Then came another key victory. When X-ray mammography became standard to help detect breast cancer in women, the mammography business grew rapidly and chaotically. The testing could be lucrative, and the mammography machines proliferated in hospitals, clinics, and doctors' offices. As the tests spread, quality control lapsed. Medical societies tried to rein in the trade, but failed, and high error rates were found in many clinics—10 percent or more of cancers that could be spotted were being missed. Republicans, led by Senator Nancy Kassebaum of Kansas, opposed setting higher standards because that might hurt business. The FDA, working with the medical societies, established new standards, put them into effect, greatly increased the quality of mammography, and put the worst offenders out of business over a short time. It was a regulatory blitz. The howls of Republicans ceased when the General Accounting Office of Congress investigated and found that the cooperative programs between the FDA and doctors' groups had quickly produced better mammograms with business disruption for only the most recalcitrant abusers.

Kessler and his staff had previously discussed investigating the subject of tobacco, addiction, and public health. Some staffers, including the smart and conservative aide Jeff Nesbit, had been urging the agency forward. The nation's top two preventable public health problems, and the nation's two top killers, were bad diet and smoking. A significant step forward on diet had been taken with the new food labels. Now, it seemed time to further consider tobacco. The FDA had not actively pursued the subject before, not because Congress had prevented it, or because of anything in the law, but simply because it was a hornet's nest. There was no nastier political tangle.

By late 1993, the staff's investigation had dug up enough information about the hidden practices in tobacco manufacture to conclude that cigarettes were designed and manufactured specifically as devices for delivering addicting levels of nicotine. If the FDA was to assert jurisdiction, it had to show that the companies made and sold the cigarettes with the *intention* of delivering a drug, nicotine, to smokers to addict them or keep them addicted to their products. That would officially make the nicotine in cigarettes a drug under the law's definition, and cigarettes a drug-delivery device. Over the years tobacco companies had devised elaborate strategies to reduce costs. As a result, modern cigarettes contain a relatively low percentage of tobacco and a high percentage of extracts sprayed on paper shredded to look like tobacco. The product is highly engineered, through the many manipulations of "tobacco," paper (with and without holes), and filters (chemically treated). But one feature was consistent—the precise amount of nicotine that reached smokers' mouths and lungs. When the FDA investigators had enough data to make that clear and to show how it was done, it was obvious what the central object of cigarette making was.

In February 1993 the agency announced that it had made substantial progress in gathering proof that the companies intended to deliver nicotine to smokers, and carefully controlled it to keep smokers satisfied. The agency put that conclusion in a letter written to the Coalition on Smoking or Health (an amalgam of the American Heart Association, the American Lung Association, and the American Cancer Society). It said, in a carefully crafted message, "Although it has been well-known for many years that some people smoke for the drug effects of nicotine . . . cigarette vendors have in the past been given the benefit of the doubt as to whether they intend cigarettes to be used for this purpose." The intention of the companies was the issue. With that letter, the agency crossed the Rubicon.

At first, Kessler intended to draw this conclusion, then punt—a draft of the letter said the proper forum for deciding what to do next was Congress. But on second thought, he decided to press the issue harder. The final draft said, "It is vital in this context that Congress provide clear direction to the agency." So the agency asked for guidance from Congress and suggested that the FDA was ready to act.

At the same moment, Representative Henry Waxman was also looking into tobacco. As chairman of the House Commerce Committee's subcommittee on health, he had organized an investigation of secondhand cigarette smoke as a public health hazard. There were further hearings after a tobacco company whistle-blower, Merrell Williams, had procured thousands of pages of damning internal documents from the companies, and managed to get them to the *New York Times,* where they appeared on the front page in an extended series. Among the documents were unusually candid admissions by tobacco executives that they did indeed make cigarettes for both the drug pleasure and the addiction. "We are, then, in the business of selling nicotine, an addictive drug effective in the release of stress," wrote one Brown & Williamson company executive in the summer of 1963.

The executives even declared that they could think of themselves as drug companies. An executive at R.J. Reynolds wrote in 1972, "In a sense, the tobacco industry may be thought of as being a specialized, highly ritualized and stylized segment of the pharmaceutical industry. Tobacco products, uniquely, contain and deliver nicotine, a potent drug with a variety of physiological effects." He and other executives had been made nervous by the increasing number of tranquilizers and other mood-altering drugs on the market. But he said, "Happily for the tobacco industry, nicotine is habituating and unique in its variety of physiological actions, hence no other active material or combination of materials provides equivalent 'satisfaction.'" In the tobacco business, the word "satisfaction" was used as code for addiction. He said that eventually other drug companies would catch up. He also said that the regulatory climate made it impossible to go directly to their chief customers—the "youth market," as he put it—with a message about the drug pleasures of nicotine. Rather, the companies would have to continue to find clever ways to disguise their direct intent, and advertise to teenagers by indirection.

"Brands tailored for the beginning smoker should emphasize the desirable psychological effects of smoking [looking older, looking cool], also suggesting the desirable physical effects to be expected later. Happily, then, it should be possible to aim a cigarette promotion at the beginning smoker."

The tobacco companies' own extensive research showed that tobacco smoking was specifically a habit acquired by children, not adults. The tobacco industry's research showed that people who had never smoked but tried to start when they were adults—that is, after age twenty-one—almost always dropped the habit quickly because of its unpleasant side effects. Those who became lifelong customers almost exclusively started when they were young—89 percent of steady smokers were already recruited by age nineteen. Three-quarters were habituated by age seventeen. So it was clear to the FDA staff members that, in public health terms, the problem was not just that a drug was intentionally being delivered to smokers, but that the companies intentionally hooked smokers when they were children. At bottom, smoking was a *pediatric disease,* even if the illness and death finally struck during adulthood.

Thus, ultimately, the object of planned FDA regulation was not to ban smoking or to go after adult smokers, but simply to try to reduce the number of children who started. Banning cigarettes entirely was never entertained as an option. If tens of millions of people are addicted, the best medical strategy is not to cut off their source of drugs suddenly and without recourse. It would be bad medically, and it would be catastrophic socially. A solution geared to the public health, therefore, would not contemplate sudden national withdrawal. And by law, just because cigarettes are hazardous does not mean they have to be banned, any more than alcohol does, or dangerous cancer drugs. The FDA, under law, has a wide range of options. Alcohol, under IRS jurisdiction, had been placed under regulations. Similarly, the FDA wanted to require that tobacco be sold under regulations that discouraged promotion to children, and made it easier for smokers to quit when they wanted to (perhaps by requiring tobacco companies to subsidize medical quitting programs). The plan also included large financial penalties for companies if the number of children smoking did not decline gradually, by set amounts, over the years.

Though the law clearly allows latitude for FDA action, the conservative Supreme Court halted FDA regulation of tobacco in March 2000. The Court said Congress should decide the matter, and there the issue has sat since. But the FDA can take some credit for the extraordinary national debate, one that continues to this day, and has given a boost to smoking restrictions passed at all levels of government.

By the fall of 1994, the revitalized FDA had effectively restated the progressive philosophy of government. Bill Clinton was president, but after the election that year Congress was controlled by Republicans, who had substantial majorities in both houses, so the new, resurrected FDA, headed in one direction, soon met the rolling conservative resurgence coming back in the other.

It is hard to say which of the FDA's positions or actions riled the conservatives most, and whether, as some have said, tobacco was the trigger for the next fierce charge from the right. Whatever the pretext, the attack was, for the FDA, the most blatant and nasty public assault since the turn of the century. In fact, in many ways, the whole episode recalled the fight to establish food and drug regulation in the first place. The arguments of the right were similar and were delivered with similar vitriol. It was as if a century of regulation, compromise, and advances had simply been erased.

Polls have been conducted about the FDA and about some of its specific actions since 1937, when the first showed that 88 percent of Americans were in favor of government regulation of food and drug advertising. Since then, few agencies have remained so rock-steady in opinion polls. Since the 1970s, when people have been asked about their general feelings, positive or negative, about the agency, the responses have remained, with little variation, at 75 percent positive. The Roper Organization has tracked the FDA and government issues consistently, and found that among all government agencies, the FDA has been among the most popular, and routinely number one among regulatory agencies. In addition, during the years of heavy criticism from conservatives under Ronald Reagan, the FDA's approval rating every year was both higher and more stable than that of Reagan himself. President Bush's approval figures rose above those of the FDA once, when he took the country to war against Iraq, but otherwise, the FDA's numbers were better than his uniformly.

Some have suggested that the warm feeling for the FDA did not extend to specific issues. But that has not been the case even during the years of the most severe anti-regulatory rhetoric from conservatives, according to Roper and others. Most were satisfied, but among those who were dissatisfied, most believed the agency needed to be stricter; the anti-regulatory sentiment has remained isolated on the right and never gotten above a quarter of those polled. The action against the FDA had nothing to do with public attitudes. But for the New Right in Congress, polls could be rationalized. For them, it was not a matter of representing their constituents, or a matter of history, or of public health data, it was a matter of personal moral certainty.

The public assault began just after the election of 1994, and started essentially with salvos from Newt Gingrich just before and immediately after the election. Gingrich said the FDA was the "No. 1 job-killer" in America (a hard statement to support). He charged that the FDA discouraged innovation and prevented profitable products from coming to market. Gingrich also went after the commissioner personally. He called David Kessler "a thug and a bully." The low level of the rhetoric was startling. Though American politics can be rough, this kind of rhetoric was unusually nasty, and was born of no apparent provocation to Gingrich.

The goal was to dismantle the FDA, to roll back the scientific standards of the 1962 law and turn over the "review" of drugs to private companies hired by the drug manufacturers themselves. Information about drugs was largely controlled by those who made and sold them; now, the review of the safety and effectiveness of drugs was also to be handed back to the manufacturers. The battery of organizations built up after the Reagan election and still going strong were now concerted in their efforts to discredit regulation in general and the FDA in particular. The groups shared two general sources of funds. There were half a dozen foundations of the extreme right that provided several million dollars annually to the cause. In addition, the new Republican leadership made it clear that industry's traditional ploy of giving to both sides to hedge bets would no longer be acceptable. Gingrich stated plainly that businesses should choose their side and stick to it, because he and the new leaders of Congress intended to hold them accountable for donations to the opposition. Having made this assertion in public, the Republicans then went out to collect funds from the traditional adversaries of the FDA. They had no trouble raising millions from the tobacco companies, and though the drug companies were wary of the New Right programs because injury to the FDA could mean injury to the credibility of their own products, they felt obliged to contribute some additional millions to those who would be leading the Congress for, it seemed, at least a few years.

And from this fount of cash issued a coordinated attack. From the Washington Legal Foundation (WLF) came a series of ads (in the *New*

York Times and the *Wall Street Journal,* among other venues) that showed tombstones in a graveyard. The text said: "If a murderer kills you, it's homicide. If a drunk driver kills you, it's manslaughter. If the FDA kills you, it's just being cautious." The text continued, "Our own federal government's bureaucratic and apparently unaccountable Food and Drug Administration" blocked drug approvals while Americans "died in agony from a disease other nations have controlled for years." As evidence, the group cited six cases, which were referred to repeatedly by other groups and by members of Congress and conservative activists. All of the claims misrepresented the facts.

Interleukin-2: This cancer treatment achieved great attention in the mid-1980s based on early test results. Eventually, researchers writing in medical journals condemned the enthusiasm as premature. Because it was intended to treat a life-threatening condition, the FDA made the drug available to patients in 1987, before its proponents were willing to recommend it and a year before its manufacturer even *applied* for drug approval. Nevertheless, the WLF declared in a 1995 ad that "2,500 kidney cancer patients died during the 3½ years it took the FDA to approve the drug Interleukin-2. It had already been approved in nine European countries."

The FDA approach—early availability for those who felt they needed to take the risk, but careful assessment before final approval and labeling—turned out to be the right one, however. The drug was found to be extremely toxic, and useful to only a small number of patients. At best, about 15 percent of cancer patients were helped by the drug, in the sense that their disease progression slowed, usually temporarily. In the long view, it is possible to say that the chief value of the drug (and of the testing of it) is that a new field of research in kidney cancer was opened in which the new drug, combined with other treatments, might eventually yield better results. But that argument was not made by WLF. (In any event, to use Interleukin-2 more effectively would require years of investigating the drug, not a sudden rush to market.)

The CardioPump: This suction device, like a toilet plunger, was created by a company called Ambu to make emergency cardiopulmonary resuscitation easier. CPR done by hand does not give heart attack victims a great chance of survival. The device was intended to replace that, for it does mechanically what emergency medical teams do before heart attack cases reach the emergency room. Before the basic studies were done, the WLF in its ads had made up its mind. The ads said, "14,000 heart attack victims so far have died who could have been saved by the CardioPump during the two years the FDA has delayed approval."

Sam Kazman, the chief of the Free Market Legal Program at the Competitive Enterprise Institute, gave a lecture on the squat, squarish plunger on Newt Gingrich's television show. Gingrich said: "This increases by 54 percent the number of people with CPR who get to the hospital and have a chance to recover. . . . so the FDA makes illegal a product used in eleven countries that minimizes brain damage, increases the speed of recovery, saves money." It is unclear where Gingrich got his data, but most likely it came from an incomplete study of a few patients conducted by one of the inventors of the device.

When patients' records were checked after their hospitalization, the company conceded at hearings that no additional patients survived. Those who used the device and those who did not had the same survival rate. Some of Ambu's studies showed a very small number of patients who had been treated with the CardioPump surviving for an extra hour, but it was unclear whether that was the result of the device's work. Moreover, for about 18 percent of users, when the device was attached to their chest, it quickly slipped off; precious time was lost. In addition, the early studies showed the CardioPump caused damage to the chests.

When the device was produced, American law did not permit experimentation on patients who could not give their consent or have their relatives give consent. Conservatives called such informed consent rules "silly" in this case. Ambu ignored the rules. When the issue of waiver was raised with the FDA in 1995, over protests from advocates of strict ethical rules in human experiments, the agency set a new policy in which informed consent could be waived in order to do studies in emergency medical situations.

The waiver, however, didn't help Ambu. In 1998, three years after conservatives began defending the device, the company was still unable to put together a study that showed the device was useful when used alone. (In Paris, emergency teams did help a few patients with the CardioPump, but those teams used other measures at the same time.) Seven other studies showed there was no difference between traditional and mechanical CPR. New studies are under way.

Tacrine: As with cancer and AIDS, a substantial body of patients suffering from Alzheimer's disease and their families have taken risks in search of alternative treatments. By 1993, the FDA was routinely permitting early access to treatments that would, under tougher scrutiny, not be found useful. Such a case was tacrine (or Cognex), a drug that causes liver damage in a large number of patients; it does nothing at all to treat the underlying disease and very little to treat the symptoms. Warner-Lambert, the maker, conducted studies showing that some patients taking the drug were able to score a few points higher on tests such as word memory. But the effect disappeared in a few months, and the progression of the disease was unhindered. The medical experts asked to review the drug in 1991 wrestled mightily with their decision whether to recommend that the FDA approve the drug, but ultimately they voted against it. Advocates said any help would be welcome, even if it caused liver damage. Opponents said the drug was merely an attempt to extort billions of dollars from already suffering families. The FDA approved emergency access to the drug. By 1993, the agency gave full approval to the drug after acquiring more data on its dangers and benefits (some of those tested showed a very small and temporary improvement in cognition). It appeared that Tacrine could be used safely if patients were closely monitored.

Again, conservatives seemed unaware of what was transpiring. The WLF ads said, "During the seven years it took to approve Tacrine, thousands of Alzheimer's patients gradually lost their memories. Nobody knows how many died." Tacrine would not have prevented *any* deaths. Nor would it have halted the progress of Alzheimer's disease. The United States was first to approve the drug, but many countries have not followed its example.

The heart defibrillator: A WLF ad read: "The American Heart Association estimates that at least 1,000 lives were lost during the time an approved heart defibrillator was delayed. Why was it delayed? The FDA prohibited shipments because of paperwork problems."

The American Heart Association immediately denounced the ad, saying it had said no such thing, and that the number quoted did not seem credible. The heart association wrote: "The American Heart Association is dismayed by the use of its name in a January 12 advertisement by the Washington Legal Foundation. The advertisement essentially accuses the Food and Drug Administration of killing thousands of Americans by delays in the approval process for drugs and medical devices. Comparing the FDA to murderers and drunken drivers is irresponsible and incorrect."

The figure of a thousand deaths, first cited on a television show, came not from the heart association but from a doctor who was paid by the device's manufacturer to testify in a lawsuit. The "paperwork" problem referred to was a lawsuit over safety issues; the company lost in court.

The Sensor Pad: This product is intended for use by women while conducting self-exams for lumps in the breast. It is a plastic pad with silicone inside that is to be draped over the breast as the woman kneads the breast tissue, feeling for unexpected, BB-sized nodules. Self-examination can be effective in detecting breast cancer early, and the usual recommendation is that women perform self-exams routinely, using soapy water for lubrication, as they take a shower, for example. The maker of this device was a pair of fellows, Grant and Earl Wright, who felt they did not need approval to sell the device, nor did they need to do tests to determine whether the device made it easier or harder for women to detect the lumps. Their company, Inventive Products of Illinois, claimed that the fluid feel of the silicone "enhanced" a woman's ability to detect lumps. The FDA first ordered the product off the market, then asked for hard data in support of the claim. It raised the possibility that if women felt as if they were doing self-examination by using the pad, and they missed lumps because of the interference of the device, then the device was plainly harmful. The company responded with tests in which women were asked to detect lumps in plastic breasts, which meant nothing.

The conservatives loved the device anyway. A WLF ad said, "In spite of criticism in *The Wall Street Journal* and on ABC's '20/20,' and in the face of 96,000 deaths per year from breast cancer, the FDA has obstructed approval—for nine years—of the Sensor Pad, a device that magnifies the sensation of lumps in women's breasts. In Canada, the product was approved in less than sixty days."

Canadian authorities don't normally give approvals for medical devices; they can be marketed without it. But in this case Canada specifically banned the product until the manufacturer produced proof that it worked. Data that had been submitted to the FDA showed that the device appeared to *decrease* sensitivity to lumps. The FDA stood its ground, and the company finally agreed to do proper tests and submit the results to the agency. The tests demonstrated that the device did not enhance a woman's ability to detect lumps—it did about as well as a good manual exam—but it did aid some women psychologically. The device was therefore approved.

TPA (tissue plasminogen activator): TPA, made by the genetic engineering company Genentech, is a drug that dissolves blood clots. It was introduced as a very expensive new biotechnology product, and heavily promoted as a lifesaver for heart attack victims. Because blood clots often figure in heart attacks as they cut off blood flow to the heart muscle itself, it was assumed that dissolving them with TPA would be an effective treatment. There was already a good clot-dissolving drug on the market—streptokinase—but at the time it had been proved effective only when it was injected directly into the affected artery of the heart. This took some skill, and meant a brief delay in getting the drug into the patient. In a head-to-head comparison over a brief time, the tests showed that streptokinase dissolved clots only 40 percent of the time if delivered intravenously and quickly. By contrast, TPA was quicker and effective 65 percent of the time in the same period.

But that was misleading. The real issue was not clot-dissolving power but whether more patients survived heart attacks. The financial section of the *New York Times* reported that TPA, to be sold under the name Activase, "has proved extremely effective at breaking up clots and could save the lives of thousands of heart attack victims each year. Some analysts have estimated that sales of TPA for Genentech . . . could be as high as $1 billion a year, making it the first blockbuster product created by the new technology of gene splicing. Virtually everyone expects TPA to win approval later this year." The reporting was accurate, including a mention of TPA's dangerous side effects. The problems were not trivial, and though TPA's power to save lives after heart attacks was assumed, it was not proved.

Stories on the "miracle drug" appeared in April and May, just before an advisory committee including the usual array of expert physicians and medical researchers from around the country met on May 29, 1987, to review the data on TPA and streptokinase and make a recommendation to the FDA. The manufacturer of streptokinase now had data backing up its effectiveness in saving lives after heart attacks if the drug was given intravenously, rather than just injected into the blocked heart artery. Streptokinase was making a bid to stay alive in a market dominated by the popular biotech company Genentech. The committee meeting was the longest on record, and one of the most difficult, not because the experts were in doubt, but because they were under great pressure, given the public relations effort on behalf of TPA. The committee determined that the recommended dose of TPA appeared to be wrong—it caused not only the dissolving of clots, but also extraneous bleeding, and bleeding into the brain, which could be fatal. The rate of severe bleeding into the brain was one to two patients per hundred treated—unacceptable. The committee also noted that Genentech had data confirming that the drug could dissolve clots but not that it could save lives. The streptokinase data was about saving lives. So, after 10 p.m., the advisory committee voted unanimously to approve streptokinase for intravenous injection immediately after heart attacks; and the committee voted ten to one *against* recommending TPA for the same use.

The commissioner at that time, Frank Young, had to explain the decision to the White House. The Associated Press story said the advisory committee voted to ask FDA not to approve "a drug that proponents say can save the lives of heart attack victims." The story did not mention the problems with TPA, nor did it give the views of the vast majority opposing approval. It did not even mention the approval of streptokinase, which had been shown to be effective for the same use. The most extreme view of the situation came from the *Wall Street Journal* editorial page, which said the decision "should be properly viewed as throwing U.S. medical research into a major crisis."

The editorial conceded it had not been demonstrated that TPA "helps people with heart attacks." It also said that such data from a controlled experiment with 11,712 patients proved streptokinase did reduce deaths. That, said the editorial, was the outrage. Streptokinase, the editorial writer was sure, was inferior, and Genentech would certainly have excellent data in hand on TPA within months.

"So the advisory panel decided to approve intravenous use of streptokinase, but not approve the superior thrombolytic [clot-busting] TPA. This is absurd," the editorial said. "Patients will die who would live longer." The editorial made the attack personal, excoriating Dr. Robert Temple, the chief of the bureau of drugs, who was not involved in the decision. But he had become known as an advocate of having scientific evidence in hand before making decisions. Here, the matter of faith was arising; the *Journal* was ready to accept early, incomplete data that had not quite proved the new drug's value, the facts be damned. Business was being impeded! As the *Journal* editorial said, "Are American doctors going to let people die to satisfy the bureau of drugs' chi-square tests? The gods of pedantry are demanding more human sacrifice."

The outrage among doctors and journalists to the *Journal's* attack was sufficiently great that an array of former FDA leaders, including the previous eight commissioners and acting commissioners, wrote to the *Journal* that the editorial was "misguided." They explained that the vote was among top experts from outside the FDA, not from the FDA. They pointed out that soliciting expert opinion from outside the agency had proved a very useful exercise. "Controversial recommendations from advisory committees are an inevitable outcome of open government and of the scientific peer-review process at work," they wrote.

When the data from Genentech came in later, it was clear that the committee was correct. The dose used by the company was too high, and it did cause unnecessary deaths. News stories less than two years later suggested that the expectations for TPA expressed by the *Wall Street Journal* were out of line. New studies that measured whether TPA and streptokinase saved lives after a heart attack found that both had about the same level of effectiveness, despite TPA's far greater cost. Hospitals were paying about $2,250 per dose of TPA, $80 for streptokinase. As a *New York Times* story noted, "A highly publicized and expensive drug to treat heart attack is no better than one that costs only a fraction as much." Still later studies showed that TPA could surpass streptokinase in effectiveness if another drug was added to it when delivered.

This case was a perfect example of what happens when conclusions are drawn before the data is in, and before approval. But the industry can rouse enormous public clamor for shortcuts. The irony is that if the FDA had given in to pressure, a wrong dosage of TPA could have been authorized, and worse, the discovery of just what would make TPA *really* useful—the second drug that made its effect significantly better—might never have taken place.

Nevertheless, the WLF failed to let the facts get in the way of a good ideology. In 1995 it said, "The lives of more than 100,000 heart attack victims may have been saved had the FDA not delayed approval of the emergency blood-clotting drug TPA by a year and a half."

The legal foundation's ads were completely consistent with the style of argument and the level of accuracy of the New Right advocates. An example from the same period was a radio advertisement run by the Competitive Enterprise Institute:

(VOICES): Help! Man overboard!

FIRST MAN: Hang on, I've got a rope!

SECOND MAN: Hold it! What do you think you're doing?

FIRST MAN: What do you mean? That guy's gonna drown if I don't get him this rope!

SECOND MAN: Rope? Let me see the paperwork on it.

FIRST MAN: Paperwork? But he's drowning!

SECOND MAN: I don't care what his condition is, he can't have that rope till I say it's safe. So get me the files.

FIRST MAN: Yes, sir, but . . .

SECOND MAN: Okay, put a tensile-strength meter on it and see what it'll hold. Better safe than sorry.

PAUSE

SECOND MAN: . . . and there's minimal fraying as well. Okay, we're ready. Ahoy out there! The rope I'm about to throw you meets all federal standards. Hello? Hello?

VOICEOVER: When it comes to approving new medical drugs and devices the federal government's overcaution can be deadly. Think about this: If the government approves a drug that will start saving lives tomorrow, then how many died yesterday waiting for the government to act?

In this ad, the strong underlying assumption—that rigorous scientific testing does not matter—becomes explicit with the last line. Fourteenth-century philosophers who staked out the conservative position would no doubt have been comfortable with that point of view. And we know what happens when we leave the decisions about safety and effectiveness in the hands of industry. The simple fact is that the FDA is, at least for now, the best hope we have. Given the complexity of the challenges it faces, it will inevitably make mistakes along the way, or on occasion take more time than commercial interests would like. But the proper tests and experimentation should not be jettisoned. We just don't know what we know until we test.

Sam Kazman of the CEI, three years after his organization produced the drowning man ad and the anti-FDA campaign, expressed surprise that the conservative campaign could not enlist the AIDS community for the onslaught. AIDS activists had criticized the slowness of the FDA and succeeded in making some changes. Why would they not join the movement to make all kinds of drug more available without tests? His speculation was that AIDS activists in their brief combat with FDA officials had grown close to the agency and didn't want to jeopardize the relationship by continuing the attack. In fact, the activists are quite clear about what happened, and it wasn't love for the FDA that intervened.

"We were wrong," said Mark Harrington, founder of the AIDS Treatment Action Group in New York. "We learned. But even by the time [1988] of our big demonstration at FDA, despite the rhetoric, we didn't see ourselves as against the FDA or against regulation. I think we saw ourselves as wanting them to be flexible and intelligent about development and approval of drugs."

Jim Eigo of Act Up New York, in response to one conservative proposal to allow the FDA to conduct only minimal safety testing, said, "We are not against all drug regulation of any sort. We don't want ourselves or our friends to die from taking unsafe drugs, and we disagree with the radical deregulators of the right who would abolish all efficacy requirements, and risk flooding the market with safe but ineffective AIDS drugs."

The AIDS activists, many of them outspoken adversaries at the outset, emerged from their engagement with the FDA's believing in good scientific data. After the appearance of the first useful treatment, it became clear that the solution to the problems lay in the details of the science, not in pumping more unknown drugs onto the market. What was the right dose? Could one drug be combined with another effectively? Could the side effects be lessened? Should the drug be given immediately or only when symptoms became very bad? By the time the anti-FDA campaign of the New Right was launched, the AIDS activists were as sophisticated as any medical researcher. They understood the details and the necessity of testing.

The difference between the attacks on the FDA by the AIDS activists and by the New Right is telling. The AIDS activists were serious about truly useful treatments and saving lives. They had no interest in ideology for its own sake. So they learned quickly; they held the FDA to account where it made sense to them to do so, and eventually embraced the agency in holding to high standards. Ultimately, they were the strongest advocates for careful science and public regulation in a century. They were smart, they had a vital stake, and they had no ulterior motives—who could be a better critic or advocate?

On the other side, the conservatives were arguing against the FDA because they disliked government, and were against its efforts to provide public services and hamper private profit. But food and drug testing is a popular public service; the assumption that business is paramount, self-correcting, and good for society, all outdated simplicities, led them astray.

If a company said a drug was a cure and was ready to sell it, why shouldn't it be made available immediately? Conservatives saw scientific testing as an impediment, not an essential service. Once in a while they even said so explicitly. In an article in the *New York Times Magazine,* Jeffrey Goldberg wrote:

Among FDA critics like [Utah Senator Orrin] Hatch, it is an idea as inviolate as Scripture itself that people die because David Kessler refuses to release the drugs that could save their lives. But the commissioner's most prominent critics are often stumped when asked to cite a particular drug. C. Boyden Gray, the former Bush White House counsel, who is now the chairman of Citizens for a Sound Economy, could not name any such drug, even though his organization regularly bashes the FDA for laggard approval times.

Perhaps Gray was just being cautious. Some months before, soon after the Republicans gained control of the House and the leadership was calling for the "privatization" of the FDA, Gray testified before a House Appropriations subcommittee. He said privatization would be the answer to the terrible effects of the FDA on business profits, and suggested possibly eliminating altogether the requirement that, to be approved, drugs must work as claimed. He cited the usual canard—data from previous decades that suggested the FDA was slow—and said that "this kind of delayed approval kills American citizens." He gave some examples, including the time taken to review Interleukin-2, which he said cost 3,500 lives. As it happened, a Democratic congressman listening to the recitation knew better. Richard Durbin of Illinois recited for Gray the recent data showing that FDA approval time was quite fast. He also pointed out that the latest data on Interleukin-2 showed that 4 percent of patients using it had a complete remission of their cancer (at least for a time), but that the treatment itself also killed 4 percent of patients immediately. Durbin asked Gray, "Does it raise any question in your mind as to why the FDA took the time to study a drug like Interleukin-2 when the success rate and the death rate are the same?" Gray seemed confused; he said, "I suppose you could make the same claim about almost any approval. Yes, it's got to be studied. But couldn't these same conclusions have been reached quicker? Weren't the data there quicker?" It was about as plain an admission that he had no idea how the FDA or drug companies worked as you will ever find in public debate. Durbin took up another of Gray's examples of delayed approvals, nitrazepam, one of many copies in the benzodiazepine tranquilizer family, of which several were already in wide use in the United States. Gray said its approval was "delayed" in the United States; in fact, its manufacturer didn't bother applying for approval in the United States until fourteen years after putting the drug on the market in Britain. Nevertheless, Gray claimed that if the FDA had approved it "earlier," then "more than 3,700 Americans would have been saved." Saved? The drug was a tranquilizer.

In the *Times* article, Goldberg also named Sam Kazman as someone who stumbled when asked to identify an important drug whose approval was delayed by the FDA. Kazman named Elmiron, a drug for chronic bladder disease. But the FDA had cleared the drug for approval, and even the manufacturer had pointed out that the FDA and the company had been cooperating to make the drug available during the years it was being tested. In a letter to the editor of the *Times* a bit later, while protesting ("This is nonsense") that he was not stumped by the question, Kazman blundered again. He listed streptokinase, TPA, misoprostol, and Interleukin-2 as drugs whose slow approval by the FDA caused a minimum of fifty thousand deaths. The letter as published did not spell it out, but in interviews he explained that what he was saying was not that the FDA took a bit too long, but that *all* review time kills patients. He was back to the Peltzman Proposal, under which it is not necessary to know what works or doesn't, and thalidomide-like events are acceptable to preserve company "innovation." Thalidomide-scale damage is acceptable as the collateral damage of entrepreneurial business.

If there are dangers, the New Right was arguing, people will find out about them soon enough. (Soon enough *for the businesses.*) Bad products would be weeded out by competition. But in matters of health, life, and death, the values of commerce are not the starting point. It is not permissible to knowingly cause a certain number of deaths and injuries in order to keep companies profitable. Sam Peltzman and the several New Right groups in Washington kept reiterating what Peltzman, older but no wiser two decades later, asserted in a conference run by the American Enterprise Institute in 1995: "It does not take sophisticated cost-benefit analysis to understand that a risk management system that filters out almost all harm has gone too far."

In the creation of medicines, this kind of thinking is grotesque. The throwaway mistakes are human lives. With the present FDA system that Peltzman describes as overcautious, drugs that are *reviewed and approved* kill about 100,000 people annually and seriously injure more than a million in the United States. The system has not filtered out all risk, apparently. No other cause of accidents approaches the level of injury attributed to pharmaceuticals. (A table of risk put together by Thomas Moore of George Washington University estimates the lifetime chance of being put in the hospital by accidents: severe injury by prescription drugs, 26 in 100; auto accident, 2 in 100; murder, one in 100; commercial air crash, one in 35,000.) And the vast majority of deaths occur not among people knowingly taking a risk, but among the innocent. We accept this high level of risk because we are seeking the greater benefit—

saving lives and preventing or minimizing illness. The FDA is not an overcautious agency by nature.

It is vital to build a system of making and selling drugs much more carefully than the making and selling of brooms. "Let the customers decide" or "let the free market function unfettered" may be acceptable for brooms, but it is unacceptable in the realm of prescription drugs. Sometimes health must be counted first, and business second. Newt Gingrich didn't see it that way.

•

CHAPTER TWENTY

The Argument Is Joined

B Y THE end of 1995, after a stream of advertising, forums, press con-ferences, and reports, the New Right rhetoric led to a proposal that would soon be cast into bills to be offered in Congress, in particular, to the House of Representatives. There, the Republican leadership was expected to drive the FDA "reform" through in short order. It was, as the conservative Republicans saw it, a battle of monetary and political force in the service of moral certainty.

Several pharmaceutical companies, the tobacco companies, and an array of extreme-right foundations supplied several million dollars to argue in Congress that the FDA was working too slowly. Conservatives were quoting lines from Gray, Gingrich, Peltzman, and Kazman, and saying it seemed obvious that major FDA reform was necessary. One conservative group found a polling firm that, using a battery of biased questions, was able to announce that some doctors, a substantial minor-ity, believed that the FDA was working too slowly. Peltzman said the FDA record "is nothing short of a continuing national disaster." The con-servative Republican leaders said they wanted a law to end it.

In the spring of 1996, as the New Right foundations ran a second blitz of anti-FDA advertising, the drug industry made its contribution. The Pharmaceutical Research and Manufacturers of America (PHARMA), which represents all the major drugmakers in America, had arranged a fly-in to bring about 140 "real people" to Washington to talk about why they were living proof that FDA reform was essential. Disease victims and family members were to make the point that the FDA was holding up vital treatments. The fly-in of patients hit a snag, however. *Washington Post* reporter John Schwartz, following the FDA reform campaign, decided to interview a sampling of the scores of patients flown in to lobby Congress. "PHARMA provided the *Washington Post* with the names of some of the people it had brought to Washington to meet with lawmakers," the *Post* reported. "All of those contacted by a reporter told of problems obtaining treatment for themselves or family members, but it appeared that none of those problems would be addressed by FDA reform proposals."

Among those lobbying Congress were:

• Julie Full-Lopez from Illinois, with multiple sclerosis. MS is a degenerative disease in which patients gradually lose control of their muscles. Full-Lopez said that a drug called Betaseron saved her life. The drug was new, and was first approved in the United States. Not exactly an argument against the FDA.

• Stephanie Hudson of St. Louis, whose child suffered from sickle cell disease. Her child was taking hydroxyurea, which has been available in the United States since the 1960s. Hudson's complaint was that the drug had been approved for another use, and her insurance company wouldn't pay for it to treat sickle cell disease. The insurance company said it pays only for primary, approved uses of a drug. The manufacturer, Bristol-Myers Squibb, had never sought approval from the FDA for the additional usage. The agency cannot, under law, review or approve drugs not submitted to it for consideration.

• Janet McDermott of Marshfield, Massachusetts, whose daughter had epilepsy severe enough that she sometimes had a hundred seizures a day. The girl took four medications a day, twenty-one pills, but her mother wanted her to get Sabril, a new treatment. Hoechst Marion Roussel, maker of the drug, had not yet applied for approval in the United States. Nevertheless, she should have been able to get the drug, as so many AIDS and cancer patients do, under the compassionate use program; a letter from the girl's doctor to the FDA should have seen to that. But the company refused to permit compassionate use, saying, according to the *Post*, that giving the drug to patients in need "would divert resources from the ongoing large clinical trials and 'that would delay the ability to get the drug approved for the population at large that could benefit from it.' "

Other cases included a complaint that the FDA was not releasing therapies for Parkinson's disease; none existed. Another fly-in was worried about budget cuts that would reduce the quality of home nursing care for his wife, suffering with Alzheimer's; the FDA has nothing to do with nursing care, and what marginally useful drugs had been produced were available.

The patients had visited Congress and told of their suffering as if the FDA were the issue, and it is not clear to what degree the *Post* story corrected the misrepresentation. At the time, there were serious patient groups working on the issue and attempting to get their message across to Congress. They did not have the funds to fly members to Washington, but more than seventy-five groups, including the Alzheimer's Association, the Arthritis Foundation, the United Parkinson Foundation, and the Wilson's Disease Association, joined together in a group called the Patient Coalition to fight the anti-FDA action. Particularly incensed about the attempt to dismantle the FDA were the AIDS groups and the many disease constituencies organized under the National Organization for Rare Disorders. The leaders of these organizations had direct experience working with the FDA and Congress. They said that the FDA was, by and large, doing its job; they knew the myths of miracles being delayed by the FDA were false and destructive, and said so.

Reports surfaced in newspapers and trade publications that the leaders in the pharmaceutical industry itself did not believe the conservative mythology and did not like the kind of reform being promoted. As the drug industry's chief lobbying group in Washington, PHARMA was in a bit of an odd position. The major drug companies were doing quite well—business was good and getting better, profits were high, the FDA was moving faster than ever—but the companies had no desire to alienate the new Republican leadership. At the beginning of the anti-FDA campaign, some company leaders felt that a public discussion of FDA reform from zealots wouldn't hurt; they stood to gain, relatively, if the FDA's public image was tarnished and the drug companies were seen to be miracle workers. But as the campaign went on, company insiders began to worry that the conservatives might do significant damage to the FDA.

A few knowledgeable insiders talked to the press, most of them anonymously, and clarified the industry's position. The chief regulatory official at one of the largest American drug companies said the drug companies were quietly going along for the time being with Gingrich's initiative. But "I know the people who have made these proposals, and they are not knowledgeable about FDA affairs. They are summer soldiers. What I worry about is the vitriolic rhetoric." He feared that there was an inverse correlation between the degree of rhetoric and the positive change that would come of it. At Merck, Dr. Eve Slater, chief of regulatory affairs, was willing to say a few things on the record. Dismantling the FDA and cutting back on its critical drug reviews would be a mistake, she said. "The tenets the FDA enforces, and we live by, ought to remain in place."

W. Virgil Brown, a Georgia Republican and a supporter of Gingrich, was also a former president of the American Heart Association. He wrote to Gingrich to say that he and the heart association had great concern about efforts "underway by some special interest groups to move to quickly dismantle the Food and Drug Administration." He said the conservative groups' agenda "could set public health back into the dark ages."

If the conservative members of Congress had checked with the reputable polling firms they would have been told some disappointing news: Harris, Gallup, and other polling firms asked Americans about the plans to "reform" the FDA. The plans were rejected two to one.

At first the conservatives conceived the simple abolition of the agency. But the official proposal, published in February 1996, said the FDA need not be eliminated. Instead, companies could just bypass it; they would be allowed to market drugs when they saw fit, without FDA review, provided they hired a commercial service to "review" their drugs. These rent-a-review services would not be independent but could be bargained with, and hired and fired by the companies marketing the drugs.

The document outlining the proposal was "Advancing Medical Innovation: Health, Safety and the Role of Government in the 21st Century," published by Gingrich's Progress & Freedom Foundation in Washington, D.C. The text began: "The United States leads the world in the discovery of the new drugs, biologics, and medical devices that offer the promise of longer and healthier lives for our citizens. But the process of actually developing these products and getting them approved for marketing has become increasingly lengthy, expensive and complex. . . . America's regulatory procedures are among the slowest and most expensive in the developed world." The statement was false, relying as it did on figures one to three decades old; at the time the proposal was written, the FDA was in truth both the fastest and safest drug approval agency in the world even by the industry's own measures.

In a nod to the statistics of the 1990s, the report did acknowledge that the FDA had already streamlined the drug review system. "But, they have failed to yield significant improvement in the only meaningful bottom line: total development times and product availability. . . . (Recent evidence may suggest that marketing approvals recently may have become slightly more expeditious, but no impact has been seen on the overall time and cost of development.)" Development times and product availability are the only meaningful bottom lines? Safety isn't meaningful? Effectiveness of a drug is unimportant? Cost doesn't matter? I doubt that the writers intended to put the matter so baldly, but the sentence suggests the underlying ferocity of the conservatives' faith in the power of business, and their near-total lack of interest in public health or the concerns of people who are actually sick. These matters are often lumped together with the marvelously dismissive term from economics—they are "externalities."

In the House of Representatives, three bills were created: one to cover food, one for drugs, and one for medical devices. The first stage of activity, the heart of all lawmaking in Congress, is in the committees. It is there that the expertise in Congress resides, usually in the committee staff members who have studied, followed, and even written previous law on the questions that come up. It is also here that Democrats and Republicans search for the key elements of an issue, and the common ground on which they might be able to agree. Generalities and platitudes are set aside in favor of working legal language. It is also here that lobbyists press their case in detail and suggest language for a proposed law. Consumer and public interest groups are often consulted as well, but sometimes they are intentionally excluded.

The hearings in the House of Representatives about dismantling the FDA began on May 1, 1996. The venue was the House Commerce Committee, led by Representative Thomas Bliley of Virginia. The committee, under Gingrich's eye, was at the center of the Republican revolution, and this was seen as the most important front in the battle. Hard-right commentator James Brovard wrote: "Kessler has overseen an unprecedented expansion of regulatory interference and meddling by the agency . . . zealotry seems a weak term for the intrusive and deadly bureaucracy of Kessler's FDA." He said, "One of the clearest tests of whether a Republican Congress can begin to rein in big government will be the forthcoming battle over the future of the FDA."

On that first day, David Kessler walked the three blocks from a downtown Washington outpost of the FDA up to Capitol Hill to appear before the committee. A headline that morning in the *Washington Post* read, "FDA Reforms Have Momentum As Hearings Open." The attack had been going on for months, longer if you counted the adversary relationship with Reagan and Bush. This was the moment Kessler was going to lay out in public his defense of the FDA. "This is as serious as it gets," Kessler said to a reporter, who thought the commissioner looked unusually grim. "This is about weakening a century's worth of food and drug laws. This is about undermining the safety of the drugs Americans take." He walked along heavily trafficked boulevards, up a hill, and into the edifice of bright white marble that is the Rayburn House Office Building.

Jeffrey Goldberg, writing for the *New York Times,* noted that as Kessler took his seat at the witness table, with the members of Congress looking down from the dais, he was "quite literally surrounded by foes. Before him were Congressional critics, some of whom are committed to a near-libertarian vision of a self-regulating public sector. Behind Kessler, in the audience, sat the private sector itself, a blue-suited battalion of lobbyists representing the drug and medical device industries, food-additive and dietary supplement makers, grocery and tobacco conglomerates." Kessler, Goldberg noted, had developed some kind of immunity, an ability to remain unemotional when attacked even in the nastiest terms.

The attacks came with the opening statements. Representative James Greenwood of Pennsylvania had been asked by Bliley to lead the FDA reform project for the committee, gathering information and drafting the proposed law. Greenwood started by picking up the themes from the hard right. Ignoring the large and legitimate patient groups that opposed his "reform" proposals, he talked instead about the patients and families who had been flown in by the drug companies, and "patient groups" funded by industry and recruited to support the attack. (By the middle of the 1990s, this sort of "cultivated grass roots" had become routine in Washington. The public interest and consumer advocacy groups held the moral high ground, but these phony grassroots groups were often slick enough to pass for the real thing.) The "patients" had delivered a message to Congress, he said. "Their message was powerful. Americans are dying of red tape."

He replayed the deception that the pharmaceutical industry was ready to bring miracles, but that the demon FDA was standing in the way. He said it was vital to make sure safe and effective products "are made available to people who need them. . . . That's not happening now, not when it takes twelve years and more than $350 million to get each new drug from the research lab to the American patient who needs it. It's not happening when two-thirds of the drugs approved by the FDA in the past five years were first available overseas and when 21 percent of those were available abroad for at least six years."

It is not clear whether Greenwood understood the numbers he was parroting, but his suggestion was false, even by the lights of the industry analysts who produced the numbers. It sounded as if he was saying that the FDA took twelve years to approve a drug, which, of course, was not true. As we've seen, only two years can be counted as largely under the control of the FDA. Even the human testing is not under the control of the FDA, though the agency must make clear what will be needed to show safety and effectiveness. But as even industry analysts report, companies do many more studies than are necessary for the FDA's purposes. They are done for many other reasons, including economic and planning within the company, or meeting other countries' requirements.

Only the final phase of drug development is actual FDA review. The numbers Greenwood was using were out of date by at least five years. Moreover, the Republicans never raised the question of the industry's role in the delays. But some of the answer comes from industry analysts themselves. A poll of FDA reviewers, published in *Pharmaceutical Executive,* reported that, in their opinion, the quality of new drug applications turned in by companies was rated as excellent 7 percent of the time; good, 30 percent; fair, 42 percent; and poor, 21 percent. And for the time Greenwood was referring to, about a quarter to a third of drug applications were so bad they were essentially unreadable and could not even be considered. The General Accounting Office also noted that companies' work significantly affects the total review time at the FDA. The difference in total review time between "inexperienced" and "experienced" companies in submitting applications was 20 percent or more.

Industry managers had sometimes complained that FDA reviewers were often unclear about what they expected, that backlogs of drugs waiting to be reviewed built up (at least in years past), and that reviewers were sometimes needlessly critical of applications. Each of these can lead to delay. But it was eminently clear that the blame for slow drug approvals could hardly be laid at the feet of the FDA alone.

Greenwood understood little about the issues involved, and relied on studies that had an industry bias. For example, a central fount of data on the FDA and drug review is the Tufts Center for the Study of Drug Development. It is paid for by industry. It has produced scores of papers on drug lag issues, but not one detailing how much of the delay is industry's fault. Tufts studies routinely refer to the time between when a drug is first tested in humans and the time the drug is approved at the "regulatory" phase. This is plainly misleading, especially to novices, such as poorly prepared members of Congress.

Untangling the numbers, the proper "delay" Greenwood should have attributed to the FDA is a few months. Moreover, the delay was worse in other countries. The United States had a better record of first approvals than any other nation in the world at the time Greenwood was speaking. In 1994 there were twenty-eight new therapeutic chemicals approved in the United States; of these, ten were approved here first. Second best was the United Kingdom, which approved just three first. Greenwood said none of this.

But as the Republicans began their hearings, they needed a victory. They had just been pummeled for trying to dismantle substantial parts of America's environmental regulation. They had to pull out all the stops. Richard Burr, a freshman congressman from North Carolina, a marketing manager, warned Kessler, "If you are here today to say that no, the FDA will not or cannot make America's access to life-saving drugs the best in the world, don't waste my time."

As Kessler began, he was not apologetic. He did not rely on the usual formula in testifying before Congress, which would be to say that while he disagreed with some parts of the proposals, he was ready to work with the committee. Instead, he addressed the issue of public health. He went straight to the point:

> Mr. Chairman, Americans rightfully expect public health decisions to be made in their interest, and to be based on the best science and medicine. Reform ought to be about improving and strengthening the public health. It should not be a gamble with the public's health and safety. The House bills you are considering today do not meet those tests.

He had listened to and read endless times the claims of slowness on the part of the FDA, and heard data years old dragged up to support it. He introduced the newer data into the record at this hearing. It seemed unlikely that it would move his opponents, but it was necessary to try to put matters straight:

> Today the FDA is a world leader in both the quality of its drug reviews and the timeliness of its approvals. That undeniable fact has been demonstrated once again by the latest analysis of international data by the Centre for Medicines Research, an industry-funded, not-for-profit research group in the United Kingdom. FDA's median approval time for new drugs approved in 1994 and 1995 was as fast as the United Kingdom and faster than those in France, Spain, Germany, Australia, Japan, Italy, and Canada. . . . That performance is the result of hard work and the commitment of Congress, the industry and the Agency in passing the Prescription Drug User Fee Act in 1992. That was reform.

In his written remarks, Kessler added:

> Unfortunately, too many of our critics justify the call for "reform" based on how the FDA did its job in the 1980s or earlier. They have missed the substantial progress that the dedicated doctors, nurses, engineers, chemists, microbiologists, biostatisticians, nutritionists, and others at the FDA have achieved over the past several years. They would have us ignore the important lessons we have learned about the kind of change that will result in getting safe and effective drugs and devices to the market more quickly. Those who fail to recognize the Agency's performance and achievements threaten to undermine the real progress the Agency has made.

"Let me explain what we have done," Kessler said. He noted the results of the three most recent studies that demonstrated that the drug lag was gone, though it still seemed to be haunting the House chamber. He described a new study by the General Accounting Office which found that by 1994, "FDA review and approval times were faster than those in the United Kingdom—a country whose regulatory system many critics like to cite as a way of doing things faster and better." The FDA had also done a study, one that might have been suspect, but that was rigorous enough to be accepted and published in a peer-reviewed journal. The agency review looked at the truly new chemicals among drugs, not the drugs produced to copy others. Among these, called the New Molecular Entities, between 1990 and 1994, were 58 approved in both the United States and the United Kingdom. The United States approved 30 of them first, the United Kingdom approved 28 of them first. Making the same comparison with Germany, there were 44 new chemicals approved in both countries—31 were approved first in the United States and 13 were approved first in Germany. There were similar numbers for Japan. The study also concluded that several drugs with important therapeutic value were on the market in the United States but not in these other nations; conversely, there were no important therapies available elsewhere that were not available here directly or in copies.

"What these three studies demonstrate," Kessler added, "is that if you are an American patient, you have access to therapeutically important new drugs that have been proven safe and effective sooner than any other country's citizens." On the subject of the most important drugs, Kessler noted that the United States was routinely ahead. "Of the eight new anti-AIDS-virus drugs, the FDA was the first agency in the world to approve seven of them. Beyond AIDS, America was first to approve Taxol for ovarian cancer, Fludarabine for leukemia, Pulmozyme for cystic fibrosis, Betaseron for multiple sclerosis, Riluzole for Lou Gehrig's disease, and somewhat dubiously, Cognex (tacrine) for Alzheimer's disease."

Kessler had a tougher sell on medical devices. The user's fee plan that worked effectively for drug producers had been offered as a solution to the medical device industry as well, thus guaranteeing speedy review. At first the industry agreed to cooperate with the FDA and press through a similar plan to hire additional medical officers to review devices. But with the rise of the New Right, the industry's leaders reneged. They figured the Republican Congress might well dismantle the FDA or do enough damage that approvals would be easier to obtain. Because of a lack of resources, an FDA backlog had developed about which the industry complained bitterly. But even without additional resources, by the time of the congressional hearing, the backlog had been erased. Review times for devices had been reduced substantially (for one category of device, for example, review time had been reduced to 138 days on average, from 182 days the year before; Kessler said another 48 days should still be cut from the review time). New and potentially dangerous devices, which were subject to a full safety and effectiveness review, were reviewed in 20 months on average. "Still too long," Kessler said, "but we are making progress there as well." He finished his review of agency performance with a plea that the user's fee program be applied to devices.

In his testimony, after asserting that the FDA was moving forward rapidly on its own, Kessler then turned to the details of the bills being offered in Congress. They began with a brand-new "mission statement" for the FDA that added for the first time a business agenda to the agency's historic mission to "protect the public health and safety." The added language said the FDA shall "promptly and efficiently review and approve clinical research and marketing of products in a manner that does not unduly impede innovation or product availability."

But the most publicized provision of the bills was the one that took away the FDA's power to fully review and approve products. Even the remaining canard—the FDA was permitted a "veto"—was absurd. If the FDA wanted to object to any approval, it had only sixty days to do so, and it wouldn't have access to the detailed information needed to check a drug application. Rather, it would get only sanitized summaries. Yet the FDA, limited to summaries, would have to show that there was a lack of safety, not just raise questions about the safety or usefulness of a drug. Where would the information come from? The drugs in question would be under the control of the companies, like all the data. In addition, the industry would control the questioning in any review. As FDA officers had learned the hard way over a century's work, the only successful approach to safety was asking the proper questions and getting answers. Data about harm does not exist unless reviewers seek it. Would the companies do so?

Any role for the FDA in drug approval in the bills had been retained only as a political cover for the conservatives. It would make the bills appear less radical. The FDA's safety and effectiveness checks were still in place, they said. In reality, the new bills eliminated the "adequate and well-controlled investigations" required to approve a drug, the standard set in 1962. As for drugs meant to treat serious and life-threatening diseases, the bill said that such drugs could be approved if it could "fairly and reasonably be concluded by experts that 'there is a reasonable likelihood that the drug will be effective in a significant number of patients.' " Furthermore, once a drug had been approved for one condition, it could be approved for any other use under an even lower standard, merely the "demonstration that the new use is common among clinicians experienced in the field and represents reasonable clinical practice based upon reliable clinical experience and confirmatory information." That provision alone would ensure that disasters would occur.

The bills forbade drug reviewers to compare the effectiveness of two commercial drugs with one another in determining whether to approve a new one. In some situations, such comparisons are essential to the public health. Treatments for gonorrhea, for example, currently kill 95 percent or more gonococcal bugs. If a new drug doesn't, it presents a risk, because patients using it will be more likely to remain infectious, and a rolling infection in a community is more likely to continue. This provision, while understandable among companies unwilling to compete for effectiveness, would guarantee a decline in the public health over time.

Companies would no longer have to notify the FDA or reviewers when they made a manufacturing change in a drug. The number of catastrophes caused by just such small manufacturing changes would fill a book, beginning perhaps with Elixir Sulfanilamide and continuing through Cutter Laboratories' polio vaccine. The authors of these bills were not aware of the history, but they were aware of what was irritating to current business.

The FDA would no longer have the power to investigate or stop dangerous human experiments. The question whether injuries to patients were caused by a drug under study or by something else would be resolved solely by the companies and their hired reviewers.

The bills required no conflict-of-interest review or financial disclosure among those hired by a company to do drug reviews. The FDA had such safeguards in place for its employees and advisors.

In his testimony, Kessler suggested that the human experience gained within the FDA of working with drugs and data over long periods was in itself valuable. Institutional memory matters, he said. FDA reviewers learn a good deal by studying products from different companies. The reviewers look at all heart valves, at all arthritis drugs, and gain essential knowledge beyond their training as doctors in each specialty. That would be lost if commercial reviewers took over the task, with no likelihood that they would review two drugs in the same field. Another vital piece of medical knowledge lost permanently would be the long experience FDA reviewers have with each individual drug, Kessler continued. They follow it from its development, through its approval, and into the years after it is used by thousands of patients. Commercial reviewers would see a drug for only a brief time in its life and would not be responsible for it afterward.

Kessler pointed out that the bill's mission statement on foods spoke of prompt review of business matters, but the authors completely disregarded the agency's historical responsibility to ensure that food is wholesome and properly labeled, and that consumers be protected from fraud. The food labeling laws recently put into effect would be deflated by these bills, once again allowing a vast array of unchecked claims and inadequate language to substitute for what was now defined by law. The FDA would be prohibited from acting regardless of a food company's claims.

With regard to medical devices, the proposed bills completely eliminated checks for safety and effectiveness, the commissioner said, and instead would have required reviewers merely to check the quality of engineering. The FDA would be prohibited from investigating whether a medical device was effective in practice.

The list of potential hazards and the lowering of standards created by these bills went on for more than thirty pages. But the most far-reaching section of one bill provided that companies could ask for and receive a judicial review for "any written decision respecting any aspect of an investigational new drug, or any written decision respecting any aspect of an application, petition, or notification for marketing review or approval of a drug." Needless to say, using this power, a company could publicly challenge anything and everything FDA employees did, from a minor criticism in an internal memo to an attempt to take a drug off the market.

And finally, Kessler testified, the bill would simply "move us away from an evidence-based approach that is the greatness of our system."

The conservatives were proposing that the hard-won gains of the previous century to establish testing and the standards of science be erased in a few paragraphs. America would enthrone the judgment of doctors and companies again, and opinion rather than science would rule. The system they proposed to replace the FDA was a fragmented, information-light system that might well be slower than what it replaced, and could certainly lead to medical catastrophes. It reflected a rejection of science and statistics, a discomfort with the plainly sectarian nature of science. Or maybe, as some critics said, the bills were about nothing but greed.

As Kessler stepped away from the witness table, the basic elements of the historical conflict had been outlined. Then, for two days of hearings, the Republicans quizzed witness after witness, probing for evidence that the FDA was withholding vital medicines. They kept looking for the smoking gun. One leading doctor, Robert Young of the Fox Chase Cancer Center, said the FDA needed reform, and it was a tragedy that so many drugs used in cancer treatment were approved not for that disease but for some other purpose. That meant insurance companies wouldn't pay for them. He wanted the FDA to fix the problem of insurance. But when the Republicans asked whether there were drugs that patients couldn't obtain because of the FDA, he said no, not in his experience. Frederick Goodwin, the former head of the National Institute of Mental Health, told the story of imipramine, a drug developed to treat depression. It had turned out to be a very good drug to treat a different problem, panic disorder. But it hadn't been approved for that use, so doctors, again, had to prescribe it off-label and insurers wouldn't pay. Again, a Republican asked, So you mean because the FDA hadn't given its approval for the other use, patients weren't getting this important medication? Goodwin didn't want to disappoint the congressmen. "Basically, yes," he said. Basically no—the FDA cannot under law offer an approval if its maker hasn't asked for one. Meanwhile, patients were getting the drug, though they had to pay for it. One of the witnesses representing the Pharmaceutical Manufacturers, Gordon Binder, chairman of Amgen Corporation, worked hard to sound positive and supportive of the Republican efforts. But eventually, he too was asked the question, What exactly do you want that you are not getting under current law?

"Well, at Amgen," Binder said, "we do have a close working relationship with the FDA. Our first two working products were both approved in about fifteen months, which was particularly rapid at that time. . . . We'd just like it to be done faster. It's being done well, I think."

The committee brought before the dais a pitiable young woman with

AIDS who had decided to stop taking the newest and best drugs available for the disease, but instead was taking something that she admitted had never been tested. She got it from France, she said. Eagerly, the Republicans asked about its availability in the United States and whether the FDA was blocking it. No. She bought it in America through a local buyer's club, against the advice of her doctor. But, of course, that sort of access to drugs was worked out more than a decade earlier between AIDS activists and the FDA.

The Republicans had chosen the witnesses, questioned them, and completely struck out. They had brought forward many witnesses saying reform was an excellent idea, but none who could seriously attest to the slowness, the foot-dragging, and the bad regulatory behavior upon which the conservatives' "reform" movement had been premised.

One of the witnesses, Dr. Sidney Wolfe of Public Citizen, opened his statement by acknowledging that he had been the most outspoken critic of the FDA for twenty-five years. But he wanted to talk about the danger of quick approvals and a weaker agency. He had done a study of all the drugs put on the market, then removed, because of the deaths and injuries to patients, in the United States, Britain, France, and Germany between 1970 and 1992. Fifty-six drugs fell into that category. The quicker-approval countries had the worst records: 31 drugs were withdrawn in France, 30 in Germany, 23 in Britain. The United States had to pull back only 9, and 3 of those would not be on the list if the companies had not lied and withheld damaging evidence to get them to market, and for which executives were later prosecuted and convicted.

Wolfe also pointed out that before the 1962 standards went into effect in the United States, the rate of hazardous drugs withdrawn was the same in both the United States and Europe. It was the standards put into effect that made the difference. There was little reason to abandon the higher standards, especially now that approvals were quicker even with high standards, he noted.

Those who have attended many long congressional hearings know that most of what is said tends to become a blur after a while, but later what sticks in the memory is the testimony of one person who seemed to grasp the issues better and express them more effectively than anyone else present.

In the May 1996 hearings, that person was a George Washington University teacher, Thomas J. Moore. He had long studied the issues of drug hazards and public health, and had written several books on the topic. He began by noting that near his home there is a supermarket that sells a deadly rat poison, and a drugstore next door that sells the same substance as a drug to prevent fatal strokes. That rat poison was helping people because of a series of "expensive, lengthy, well-designed clinical tests that had demonstrated that for a specific medical use, this rat poison had benefits that greatly outweighed its risks." Determining the correct dosage was critical, because the drug can cause hideous birth defects, hemorrhaging, and gangrene. He named other drugs that seem benign and familiar but also have potentially crippling or fatal effects. "There is no such thing as a safe drug," he said. "They do not exist. We do have drugs with benefits that greatly outweigh their risks for specified medical uses. This basic idea lies at the heart of current law. . . . The legislation before this committee would do great damage to it . . . it would eliminate much of the required testing that has been essential to protecting consumers for thirty-four years."

The first principle of drug safety declares that the facts about drugs can be determined only through scientific evidence from well-controlled trials. Other kinds of information are not reliable enough. Patient testimonials, the clinical experience of doctors, and expert opinion have been proved wrong with such tragic consequences that this nation long ago abandoned them as a guide to the safety or benefits of drugs.

"On the basis of reliable clinical experience, the drug DES was prescribed to prevent miscarriage in pregnant women, and it caused over 1,000 cases of cancer in their babies," Moore testified.

A consensus of experts recommended the drug phenformin as beneficial for mild elevations of blood sugar, he said. As a result, thousands of patients died of lactic acidosis before the drug was finally withdrawn. A panel of experts told patients with hemophilia to keep taking their blood-clotting factor drugs, even after they knew these drugs might be contaminated with the HIV virus. That only increased the number of hemophiliacs who will die of AIDS, a total now estimated at 7,000. Expert opinion also said it was beneficial to treat mild irregular heartbeats with anti-arrhythmic drugs. As a result, Moore estimated 50,000 heart patients died of drug-induced cardiac arrest, though others say the number is somewhat lower.

Since 1962 the Food, Drug and Cosmetic Act, Moore said,

has wisely required that experts support their opinions with scientific evidence from well-controlled trials. This bill abandons those essential standards. It would permit the approval of drugs without any well-controlled trials if a waiver were obtained. New drugs for serious illnesses [might] be approved on the basis of expert opinion. Drugs [might] be approved for new medical uses on the basis of reliable clinical experience but without formal testing. . . . If Congress abolishes all these important requirements for drug testing, the whole process becomes fatally flawed. The facts needed to judge risks and benefits would simply not exist. In approving the Prescription Drug User Fee Act of 1992, the House of Representatives demonstrated how to speed the approval of drugs without compromising standards for safety and efficacy. But if Congress abandons the vital principle of drug safety that guided the User Fee Act, there is no limit to the damage that can result.

A few minutes after Moore finished, and the last panel of witnesses left the long table before the dais, Representative Greenwood wrapped up the hearing with a remark that suggested he had not even been present for the testimony. The words had probably been written before the hearings started: "This concludes our second day of hearings on FDA reform. We have had in excess of thirty witnesses. I believe the testimony has been overwhelming that we need some reform of FDA." He promised to press ahead with the FDA reform, taking into account the "concerns of the minority."

CHAPTER TWENTY-ONE

•

Old-fashioned Politics

A FTER THE public hearing ended, the chairman of the Commerce Committee could have taken a vote (holding the majority, he would win the vote, of course) and then press the House leadership to put the matter before the whole House. The stars seemed properly aligned for such a movement, given the ascendancy of conservatives. But something went awry with the leadership's plan.

After the hearings the committee staff, Democrats and Republicans, met to talk about the final shape of the package. One of the leaders on the Republican staff at the time was Howard Cohen, a longtime committee professional and a conservative. He has a cloud of dark, wiry hair and he speaks in clipped, half-finished sentences. He had been opposed to many of the Democratic initiatives over the years, but he was uncomfortable with the new, mean attitudes that began to seize Congress after Gingrich took power. He saw the work of bringing together personalities and philosophies into the legal language of a law as high drama, an adventure. Of course, the work can be tedious, and the details of issues and language of the law are the kind of material that can kill a conversation at dinner. But Cohen loved the work of government. Even if there are weeks, months, years of work for a few memorable and useful laws, if you care enough, the good ones can supply sufficient satisfaction to allow you to believe you have made a difference in the world.

As Cohen and others tell it, the Commerce Committee in the House—both in the days of its Democratic majority and beginning in 1995 with its Republican majority—had kept an eye on the FDA. And most often, proposals to change things at the agency originated in that committee. During the fifteen-year run of the Democratic majority, John Dingell, chair of the full committee, and Henry Waxman, chair of the health and environment subcommittee, had devoted disproportionate amounts of time to the FDA and its issues. Even when the Democrats could press bills through committee and get them through votes of the entire House on the strength of their majority, most often they did not; the desire was for bipartisan decisions.

When the investigations of the tobacco companies heated up, for example, Waxman, as chairman of Commerce's subcommittee on health and environment, held one hearing after another demonstrating through documents and testimony the disregard of public health and outright deceit by tobacco company executives. But at the end of the revelations, when it came time to vote on a bill to crack down on tobacco, Waxman did not act unilaterally. Rather, Republicans and Democrats on the subcommittee met, talked, negotiated, stalled, and negotiated again. They were looking for common ground. By the time there was an agreement on how tobacco companies should be regulated—an agreement that may yet serve as a useful template—it was too late, as the House leadership passed into the hands of fierce partisans, and the committee that had done so much to bring the tobacco companies into the dock was prevented by Newt Gingrich, over the objection of Bliley, from carrying any action forward.

But before the rancor reached the House, agreements on several contentious issues were hammered out within the Commerce Committee and became law. There was the Orphan Drug Act. Democrats wanted the pharmaceutical companies to turn their attention in part to making drugs for the many diseases that affect 10,000 or 20,000 or 100,000 patients. The companies initially thought those markets were too small. They didn't want to invest several hundred million dollars in developing a drug only to break even, not when there were other ways to spend the money that brought very large profits. So the Democrats and Republicans in the Commerce Committee worked on a bill to change the economic incentives. They offered the companies tax breaks and longer patent monopolies if they would go ahead with the development of these vital medicines. The result was largely a success. In ten years, forty new drugs for "orphan" diseases were developed and marketed. The Prescription Drug User Fee Act was another remarkable cooperative success, as was the highly successful law that again used profit and patent incentives to get scores of new generic drugs to market.

According to both Republican and Democratic staff members, when the Republicans gained the majority in the 1994 election, and the power shifted within the Commerce Committee and its subcommittees in 1995, the fundamental operative rules did not change. Bliley became chairman of Commerce, Michael Bilirakis of Florida became chairman of the health and environment subcommittee, and within the committees, the rules of political civility and practicality were maintained. "In the Commerce Committee, even though it looked like Bliley and Waxman hated each other," Cohen said, "it was not that way really. The committee was actually built on the idea that we could produce bills, and at the proper time, come together on both sides and understand the issues."

That sense of cooperation and respectful dealing in private, despite public disagreement, of course, was something that the hard conservatives led by Gingrich attempted to destroy in Congress and elsewhere. But when the longtime Republican staff and key committee chairmen such as Bliley said an issue or a bill was not ready, it was difficult to override them. Then, too, there was the likelihood that even if the bills passed, they would face a veto by President Bill Clinton.

The basic understanding in the Commerce Committee had always been, Cohen said, that the FDA "was a public health agency and a public health statute. You must have bipartisan action on a public health statute. You cannot have a Republican-only or Democrat-only bill, and just force it through. You have to go to the center. Find something that the Republicans can live with, that Dingell and Waxman can sign off on for the other side. And you know, bring Kennedy along in the Senate later."

As to the FDA's role as guardian of the public health, its drug approval process, Cohen said, "It gets very technical . . . but there would always come a point where you just think of who it affects . . . you think about your spouse, or your kid, or your mother. At some point you sort of make this mental test of what you are doing. If this is going to be used on my mother . . . I want to be careful. I don't want it tied up forever, either. But you have to get away from ideology, and apply this sort of commonsense test. That guided us."

The staff members met regularly for weeks to go over the details of the proposals to weaken the FDA. They met with agency officials, with industry groups, and others. On the Democratic side, a key committee staff member was Kay Holcombe, a quick-talking woman who in twenty-four years of government experience had worked at the NIH, the Public Health Service, on Senator Hatch's staff, and at the FDA. She is a person in constant motion, and her conversation about even serious issues is often touched with humor.

Holcombe and Cohen had both felt the wind shift in congressional rhetoric on the topic of regulation. "Starting in 1994, people began saying that the function of the regulatory agency should be to stay out of the way of the profit-making industries, versus the view that existed prior to that, which was that the function of a regulatory agency was to protect citizens from harm," Holcombe said. Discussions before 1994 about drug lag were very academic in nature. There were tensions because the two sides were adversaries, but nothing like what came after the hard-right conservatives arrived in Congress. Before, Holcombe said, "Nobody was really thinking of blowing up the FDA to solve the problem. But that changed. We got much more hyperbolic and lost the sense of what good policy was."

She recalled one staff member at the Tufts Center saying that something had to be done about restrictions in American regulation because in other countries so much more could be done. "He used to say you could just basically drop out of the sky in planes and start injecting people with stuff. And we as a country were going to be left behind, shipping out all our brainpower to these other countries. I didn't buy it. But then, I'm a skeptical person," she said.

So in the Commerce Committee staff meetings in 1996, as one proposal after another was rolled out for discussion, Cohen and Holcombe sat listening. They had long been adversaries, respectfully, across this table and could just about guess what the other was thinking.

"Howard—all he had to do was look at my face to know I already had the talking points done in my brain," Holcombe said. "Some of the proposals put on the table were going to get creamed. When the chips were laid out, they would have to explain to the people beyond the Beltway why it was that we were going to put drugs on the market that no one has tested, and their children were going to be exposed to them. There was no defense."

For Cohen, looking for some firm ground in these proposals to stand on, it was painful. There were so many extreme postures. "It was just a long wish list," he recalled. "And there was no way to take the bills apart to find the sections with common ground either—they were just too far out." Images danced in his head of front-page stories in the *New York Times* and the *Washington Post* about the catastrophes that could be caused by the loopholes.

"In the first couple weeks of meetings I was just trying to see if there was a deal to be had in all this," Cohen said. But by summer, Cohen went to Bliley with the bad news. "I said, 'Mr. Bliley, there is no deal here. You know, if we try this, they're just going to take our heads off. And there's no reason to end the year that way, after all we have accomplished. It's not ready.' So, we never went to markup"—the session in a committee where a final bill is amended and voted on.

In public, Representative Greenwood was still saying that the proposals would go forward, and a bill would be ready soon. The New Right rhetoric kept on for a time in the absence of public reports about committee action. Gradually that too deflated. Fundamentally, Gingrich and his supporters made the error all true believers in politics make: they became certain and aggressive to the point that compromise became impossible, as the New Republicans were finding out on one issue after another.

In the Senate, the staff did not have the same kind of intra-committee relationships that would have stopped the proposals in committee. So there, the Senate Labor and Human Resources Committee approved a radical bill. The chairman, Senator Nancy Kassebaum, tried to press the bill into law. Then, as Cohen said, "she got pummeled pretty good." Senator Edward Kennedy, the ranking minority member on Kassebaum's committee, gave a speech in opposition on the Senate floor, one that went largely unreported by the media:

Mr. President, today when Americans get up in the morning and brush their teeth, they do not think about whether the toothpaste they are using is safe. When they eat their breakfast they do not think about the safety of the food they are eating. When they take a pill to treat an illness they do not worry about whether the drugs are safe. They do not worry about whether those drugs work. Americans have confidence in all of these products because the Food and Drug Administration is an independent agency with enormous credibility.

Yesterday, the Senate Labor and Human Resources Committee approved an FDA reform bill, S. 1477, that will destroy that confidence. S. 1477 will cripple the FDA, and turn many of its functions over to private industry.

The history of food and drug legislation is that we have learned from the tragedies of the past. The United States was fortunate to avoid the Thalidomide tragedy in the 1950s. But in the 1950s and 1960s we did not avoid the tragedy of DES, Diethylstilbestrol, which causes cancer in the daughters of the women who took it.

In the 1970s we did not avoid the tragedy of the Dalkon Shield, which caused thousands of cases of infertility in women who used it. In recent years, we did not avoid the tragedy of the Shiley Heart Valve, which broke and caused many deaths.

As a result of the Thalidomide tragedy, we strengthened our drug laws in 1962. As a result of the Dalkon Shield tragedy, we strengthened our medical device laws in 1976 and we strengthened them again in 1990 after the Shiley valve tragedy.

Most recently, we reduced the delays in approving prescription drugs with user fees. As a result, we are now approving drugs faster than the United Kingdom. We have fixed the drug lag. In fact, the United States approves more important new drugs faster than any other country in the world.

But equally important, we have the best record in the world of blocking the approval of unsafe or ineffective drugs that have to be withdrawn after patients have been killed or injured.

The bill reported from the committee goes in the wrong direction. The lessons of the past have been turned on their heads, and those who have failed to learn from the history of Thalidomide, Dalkon Shield, and DES will condemn the American public to new device and drug tragedies. The basic theme of the legislation the committee approved is privatization. It says, "Let us return to the days when drug manufacturers decided what was safe and effective." It says, "Let device manufacturers pay private bodies to determine if their heart valves and pacemakers will help or harm patients, instead of relying on the scientists at the FDA, who have no interest except the public interest." If this bill is enacted into law, the Food and Drug Administration will no longer have the principal responsibility for making crucial decisions about the safety of the food supply and the safety and effectiveness of drugs and medical devices. Instead, those decisions will be made by private companies.

In the cases of medical devices those companies will be selected and paid by the medical device industry to decide the safety and effectiveness of the products. No company that is paid to do product reviews can be objective, if future business depends on whether it grants a favorable decision. And to make the conflict of interest even more blatant, it will be up to the regulated industry to determine how much compensation the regulator will receive for the review.

Do you get this? That the medical device company will make the judgment as to which individual will come and inspect their particular medical device, and they, the inspector and the company, will work out the terms of payments.

If you were one of those inspectors, how long do you think you will make adverse judgments against those companies if you ever expect to get paid or hired again? You have a basic, fundamental conflict of interest. Compare this with the current situation where an inspector has no financial interest in making the judgment and bases decisions only upon pure science. That is how we do it at the present time. . . .

How ironic that just a few days after the mad-cow disease disaster [in the United Kingdom] came to light, legislation was approved by our committee to dismantle the regulatory agency that is universally recognized abroad as the gold standard for the world. The FDA is our strongest defense against this kind of crisis in the United States. We have the safest food supply and the safest medical products in the world. We should not take any steps that jeopardize the confidence of American consumers in the safety of food and medical products. Yet this bill would seriously weaken current protections.

By the fall of 1996, the attack on the FDA had been derailed. The challenge ended on the merits, in the hands of experienced government leaders, and it was moderate Republicans who helped lead the way. It was taken up again the next year, but enthusiasm was lower, the wild character of the claims cut back. Even commentators sympathetic to changing the FDA made it clear that, ironically, it was the high passion of the right, and their parade of false claims, that was the single most damaging factor to their cause. The conservative groups were deflated and soon felt themselves less welcome in serious discussions of public health policy. They were bitter, and made a few protestations. Under the headline "Failed FDA Reform," the hard-right magazine *Regulation* ran an article by Henry Miller, one of the authors of the Gingrich plan that had been killed in Congress. "The failure of the 104th Congress to accomplish any FDA reform . . . means that the time and costs of drug development will continue to rise, fewer drugs will be developed, market competition will erode, and prices to patients will increase. Ultimately, patients will be the victims."

With the end of this episode, a cycle in FDA history had concluded. In 1997, even with conservative free-market rhetoric at high pitch, and conservative lawmakers holding power in the legislature, the foundations of regulation stood.

David Kessler left the FDA in 1997, after more than six years as commissioner, the longest reign since Larrick dominated the 1950s. He left because his wife, Paulette, couldn't take it anymore, he said, only half joking.

The assessments of his work were split. *Time* magazine said: "In six tumultuous years at the FDA, David Kessler did the unexpected: He improved the public health." The *Washington Post* recalled the state of the

FDA when Kessler arrived, and said he had "transformed the beleaguered agency, and U.S. public health policy." The National Academy of Sciences gave him its top award, the Public Welfare Medal, for pursuing a public health mission in the face of fire from formidable special interests. On the other side, conservative papers said he was a tool of big government and a traitor ("back-stabbing" was the term used in the *Washington Times*) because he was a Republican appointee. (That was not unlike both Harvey Wiley and Theodore Roosevelt, who started their careers as Republicans and left the party over the issues of special interests and their power.) Orrin Hatch was upset, at least partly because conservatives blamed him for Kessler's rise in Washington. Hatch seemed puzzled by the betrayal, and concluded that Kessler's mission had been not about health but only about Kessler's own personal aggrandizement. Peter Hutt of Covington & Burling, one of those pressing for FDA reform in Congress, declared Kessler the worst commissioner he could think of in the agency's history.

It took more than a year to find a successor to Kessler who was acceptable to both Democrats and Republicans. Ultimately, Dr. Jane Henney, an oncologist who had spent a fair part of her career at the National Cancer Institute, was chosen. She was a Kessler deputy, and worked to make the user's fee program and speedier drug reviews possible.

It was only after Kessler was gone that the trouble sowed in the long anti-FDA campaign began to be reaped. Health reporters around the country began to note a disturbing trend. Two drugs were pulled off the market in 1997 after a significant number of deaths and injuries were traced to them. Then in 1998 three more drugs had to be pulled for safety, and in 1999, two more. In 2000 the apparent trend got worse: four more drugs had to be pulled. The drumbeat of safety breakdowns appeared alarming. The FDA had never had to pull back eleven drugs in less than four years before. News reports began to speak of the FDA rushing drugs through to market carelessly.

The news stories with the greatest impact appeared in the *Los Angeles Times* beginning in 1998 and running through a long Pulitzer Prize–winning package of stories in December 2000. They described how pressure from industry, and acquiescence from some top agency officials, allowed some drugs to make it to market that the *Times* suggested never should have.

One example was that of the diabetes drug Rezulin. It was created as a one-pill-a-day treatment to lower blood sugar for diabetics. In adult-onset diabetes (unlike juvenile diabetes, in which the patient must get injections of insulin or die), the body has insulin but it does not work efficiently. One method of keeping blood sugar from skyrocketing when insulin doesn't work effectively is to control the intake and use of sugar with diet and exercise. Another is to use drugs to stimulate the body to make more insulin. There were eight drugs on the market to do that when Rezulin came along. Rezulin seemed promising because it was convenient to take and worked by a different mechanism, making the body use insulin more efficiently. It was hoped that it might offer some advantages in the long run.

The trouble was that diabetes drugs sometimes cause liver damage. (The early diabetes treatment phenformin was pulled from the market in 1977 for that reason.) So, from the beginning, FDA reviewers looked for signs that Rezulin might cause it. The medical officer assigned to the case was Dr. John L Gueriguian, who in late 1996 said that his review of the data from the drug showed that it did not offer major advantages over other drugs, and also showed the signs of serious liver toxicity: some patients' liver enzymes shot upward after taking the drug. Gueriguian recommended denying market approval to Rezulin because of the toxicity. The company complained about him to higher-ups at the FDA. They did not like his analysis, and the company reported that, in a meeting with company officials Gueriguian called Rezulin "shit." He was removed from the review.

An advisory committee of outside experts was not given a copy of Gueriguian's negative review that flagged the liver toxicity. Warner-Lambert told the committee that the liver damage seen in diabetic patients on the drug was essentially the same as the liver damage seen in diabetics taking only a placebo. (That was not true, as FDA officials learned; the rate of liver damage was double or more on the drug.) The committee voted for approval, and within a month the drug was on the market.

Up to that point, the FDA had only a scattering of high liver enzyme tests to indicate that the drug might be a hazard. But within eight months of the drug's marketing, reports began to come in of patients who had total liver failure caused by damage from the drug. Four deaths were known by October 1997. By December, six deaths had been confirmed, and the British Medicines Control Agency banned the drug.

The FDA said the liver hazard with the drug was still very rare and possibly avoidable. It hoped to stem the problem by warning doctors and suggesting that they give their Rezulin patients liver tests periodically in their first year of use in hopes of catching any damage before it was too late. So instead of pulling the drug, the FDA went with the advice of the company and simply put new warnings on the label. The warnings suggested that doctors who prescribe it should give their patients liver tests to ensure that they are not getting into danger. But soon a scattering of reports, including one from a study at the National Institutes of Health, made it clear that liver tests would not protect patients either. Researchers there found that even though patients in a trial of Rezulin were being closely monitored, the fatal liver damage came on very quickly, largely without warning, in less than two weeks.

Gradually the FDA's faith in the drug waned and the company's assurances became untenable. The FDA dragged the matter out with four separate instances of more and more stringent warnings and calls for more intensive monitoring of patients. Inside the agency, gradually more reviewers and top officials lined up against the drug as the death reports continued to come in at a steady pace. By June 1999, as the number of deaths approached twenty, the FDA attempted another approach beyond warnings and tests—it downgraded Rezulin's status. It said it no longer should be the first or only therapy used to lower a patient's blood sugar—it should instead be used as a backup only.

That change failed as well. By March 2000, with confirmed reports of 58 deaths, Jane Henney called a series of emergency meetings and finally, belatedly, halted the sale of Rezulin. The FDA's final count was 94 confirmed total liver failures from the drug, and 66 deaths.

In the end, Dr. Janet Woodcock, chief of the FDA's center for drug evaluation, acknowledged the FDA failure with Rezulin. She had hoped that the issuing of warnings and information would get doctors to be cautious, and that tests would help avoid trouble for patients. But neither proved reliable. Doctors neither heeded the warnings nor, in the vast majority of cases, did they ever test their Rezulin patients for signs of trouble. (Of course, the warnings came even as the company was continuing a massive advertising campaign including direct payments to doctors for switching their patients to Rezulin, so perhaps the failure of cautions might have been expected.)

"We learned something from that experience," Woodcock said. Safety cannot be managed through labels and warnings. The agency must sometimes make the hard choice and not leave it to doctors and companies when safety is at stake.

Rezulin was one drug from what is widely referred to as "the nightmare year" of 1997 in terms of the worst drug disasters on record at the FDA. Five drugs were approved that had to be withdrawn because of deaths and injuries. In addition, two more required black box warnings (Trovan, an antibiotic, and Orgaran, an anticoagulant). Still another doubtful drug approved that year was Meridia, a dangerous drug that both the FDA review officer and an advisory committee of experts warned against approving, but which has not yet been removed from the market.

That year, of course, was the year that the most intense anti-FDA campaign peaked, and the year that the FDA "reform" law was passed. One pharmaceutical company official made the political nature of the pressure on the FDA explicit. When the FDA staff resisted approval of a flu treatment called Relenza in 1998, Dr. James Palmer, the director of medical, regulatory, and product technology for Glaxo Wellcome, wrote to FDA officials, declaring that the FDA reviewers' position against Relenza "is completely at odds with the will of Congress that drug development and approval proceed swiftly and surely." (Not surprisingly, the company that declared it was the "will of Congress" to approve its drug was also the company with the worst record of drug disasters of recent years. Besides Relenza, Glaxo was responsible for three drugs withdrawn because of death and injury in the past four years: Raxar, Lotronex, Hismanal, and with Bayer as distributor, Baycol.)

Relenza, in fact, reduces the symptoms of the flu, at best, by a day. Reviewers were skeptical of its value, but felt it was commendable for a company to be exploring treatments that might one day actually seriously challenge influenza viruses. The drug was approved.

Soon after approval, though, some who took it experienced severe breathing problems. A number of deaths from the drug were reported in patients who had other respiratory problems, such as asthma, prompting the FDA to warn doctors about the minimal usefulness of the drug. By 2000, it was suspected as a cause of death in twenty-two patients.

With headlines like "Perilous Rush at the FDA" and "Hidden Risks; Lethal Truths" in the *Los Angeles Times,* and "Questions Raised on Ability of FDA to Protect Public" in the *New York Times,* the rhetoric of the "slow bureaucracy" began to disappear in news reports, to be replaced by talk of FDA haste. Commentators were soon drawing the conclusion that the relentless pressure from conservatives and the pharmaceutical industry had finally pushed the agency over the edge.

The user's fee program, little noticed when it was put in place in 1992, suddenly became a focus of scores of news stories. Reports noted that the user's fee law set strict deadlines for reviewers to meet regardless of the complexity of the safety problems reviewers were looking at. News reports said the atmosphere within the FDA had become tense, and that even Janet Woodcock admitted that the deadlines made the FDA feel like "a sweatshop."

When the FDA asked its medical reviewers about their experiences, a third felt the pressure to approve drugs had become too great, and said cautions were not being taken seriously enough. As the FDA survey put it: "About one third did not feel comfortable expressing their different scientific opinions." A number of reviewers told those doing the survey that "decisions should be based more on science and less on corporate wishes."

In some of the cases, approval or rejection was not an easy call. And 1996 and 1997 were not normal years in another respect: a huge glut of drug applications was filed. So, as a percentage, it was natural for there to be both more approvals and more withdrawals. But even accounting for that, there is the extraordinary number of bad drugs from the class of 1997. The *Los Angeles Times* list of likely FDA mistakes from the period includes seven drugs.

But however the cases are counted, there is no doubt that by 2000 and 2001 the old alarms had rung again, as they had in earlier episodes through the FDA's history. Newspapers, magazines, talk shows, and the Internet buzzed with it.

The message was clear enough. The FDA was reminded that citizens, who don't often speak up, were back in it, raising the question whether the FDA was doing its job. Soon, the number of "me too" drug applications was down again. Some of the FDA officers most solicitous of industry views had left the agency. By 2002, tentatively, critics suggested that, after the conservative storm, the FDA was back to steering a more usual regulatory course.

By 2003, another turn of the wheel had begun at FDA. President Bush named a member of the White House Council of Economic Advisers, Dr. Mark B. McClellan, as FDA commissioner. His appointment followed nearly two years of struggle over one nominee, then another, and another. McClellan is chiefly an economist, the first to be named to head the FDA, but he is also an M.D. He has been counted as a free-market enthusiast, and an independent thinker at the same time. If history is any guide, the agency will shape him as much, or more, than he shapes the agency. Previous leanings count for little at the FDA, and so he took up the job in 2003 accompanied by hopeful remarks from both liberals and conservatives.

For a period in the last two decades of the century, regulation had become one of the most contentious and even inflammatory issues in politics and society. It was asserted that regulation, regardless of its type or apparent usefulness, cost society money and freedom. But now after the fever has passed, in looking back over the whole history of the agency, it is clear that regulation has become a vital part of society for both citizens and business. It has elevated the debate and the standards. It has added to freedom as it has made medicines more reliable and safe to take. It has helped establish a base upon which more advanced medicines can be found and developed, guided by principles of medicine and science rather than hype. The lesson we can see through the past century of conflict is not that businesses may sometimes exploit citizens for profit, or that government agencies will sometimes make mistakes, but that regulation and commerce are part of the same equation of progress. The scientific facts and social understandings needed for progress are not created in industry, or in universities, or in government, but in all of them together.

The FDA began as an agency to protect consumers from cheats; it has evolved into the body that sets the scientific marks against which progress is measured. It is fair to say that the FDA is not brilliant in all respects. The agency has suffered from some bad leadership at times, and a lack of support in Congress. It cannot now effectively monitor herbal medicines and supplements. The agency has failed to press for a single independent and reliable source of data on drugs and their dangerous side effects. The FDA has nevertheless effectively handled many parts of its increasingly complicated role. It has created a base of medical testing, and has stood for public health standards against storms of self-interest. It is accountable in that it records its actions in detail and in public, as they are being made. The FDA makes decisions with routine consultation with teams of outside experts, and is as broad and open an agency as seems possible in this conservative time in American history.

Whether the agency has always remained independent enough from the industry it regulates, the general thrust and purpose of the FDA has never been lost. The employees of today go to work with a sense that they are doing something useful for the public, much as the employees of 1906 did. And more often than not, they succeed.

Epilogue: Greed and Goodness

IN LOOKING over the history of food and drug regulation, and the little agency that was created in the progressive years, there is one story that, for me, still stands out. It is the tale of the drug called Panalba.

The drug, made by the Upjohn Company from 1957 to 1970, was an antibiotic combination measurably less effective than other antibiotics on the market at the same time for the same uses. Some patients who took Panalba instead of one of its competitors simply didn't get better as they should. In the worst cases, that led to permanent injury or death. The FDA and, independently, the National Academy of Sciences said the drug had no use in modern medicine.

But Panalba was a big seller for Upjohn, yielding 12 percent of the company's entire gross income. Doctors who should have known better had been persuaded by company salesmen that by giving two drugs in one, they were giving better therapy. So, despite the clear judgment of medical science, and despite clear evidence that some were suffering needlessly, and while the FDA sought a ban, the company kept Panalba on the market. In fact, Upjohn knew of the problems before they became public, and had concealed them. Now, every additional month of sales before Panalba was forcibly pulled from the market meant an additional million dollars. The company's decision was supported by the American Medical Association. Its leaders acknowledged that the drug was not a good one, but the AMA said it was important to assert the authority of doctors rather than government regulators over the health of patients. They must be able to prescribe any medicine, even a bad one, if they choose.

There was an essential conflict: on one side, solid scientific data supporting a policy judgment; on the other side, two powerful special interests. The company intervened politically and twisted arms in government to derail any FDA action. There was a deadlock. Faced with the evidence

338

and the public requests from some scientists to stop selling the drug, a special board meeting was called at Upjohn. The board chose not only to keep the dangerous drug on the market, but to vigorously fight in court to keep it available as long as possible.

When Professor J. Scott Armstrong, a teacher of management at the Wharton School at the University of Pennsylvania, read a story by Morton Mintz in *Science* magazine about this fiasco, he was struck by the behavior of the Upjohn managers during their crisis. Armstrong's students were all bright prospective managers of American business or prospective teachers of the theory of business. They were in his classes to learn how to think about managing businesses effectively. When he finished Mintz's article, Armstrong said, "I thought, well, I don't believe my students, faced with that situation, would have acted the way Upjohn did. I just don't think so." He asked his students if they had ever heard of the case; they said no. So he designed a little experiment to test his faith.

First, he described the case to a sample of seventy-one students and businessmen and told them of Upjohn's choice to keep Panalba on the market, and further, to fight in court to keep it on the market, and to lobby behind the scenes in Washington to defeat the FDA. He asked them whether Upjohn acted in a socially responsible manner. Not one of those asked counted Upjohn's behavior as socially responsible. Ninety-seven percent said it was irresponsible, and 3 percent offered no opinion.

It seemed clear enough; this was business behavior that was out of bounds. Then Armstrong asked a different group of students to act out the situation in a brief role-playing episode. Each was to take a role as one of the seven members of the Upjohn board of directors. Each player was told that the FDA wanted to remove the drug from the market as a hazard, and that that decision was based on a twenty-year study and a conclusion by an unbiased group of medical scientists whose recommendation was unanimous. The "board" was given other information about the company's profits and revenues from the drug, then met for forty-five minutes to make one of the following decisions: (1) recall Panalba immediately and destroy it; (2) stop production of Panalba immediately, but allow what had been made to be sold; (3) stop all advertising and promotion of Panalba, but provide it for those doctors who request it; (4) continue efforts to market Panalba most effectively until sale is actually banned; and (5) continue efforts to market Panalba most effectively and take legal, political, and other necessary actions to prevent the authorities from banning Panalba.

Playing the role of Upjohn board members instead of simply judging them, 79 percent of the students came to the same decision as Upjohn—number five. Armstrong tried again. With another group, he made it crystal clear to those playing Upjohn managers that the product was killing a number of people every year, and cured infections no better than several similar products that were safer. Adding this information changed little; three-quarters of the students chose to keep up sales as long as possible to earn $19 million a year from the drug.

"I was stunned," said Armstrong. "My students were making the same decisions Upjohn had, even when it was laid out clearly that patients were dying. No matter how I put the case, hardly anyone decided to take the drug off the market. In one case, I even [arranged for] someone to rush into the meeting, and say, 'I'm the research director. Our own studies were suppressed until now, and they show that they are right, this drug is killing people.' Even that didn't do it."

Armstrong was not the only one surprised; those who participated in the experiment were dismayed with their own behavior after they realized that the experiment had not been simply a teaching exercise about decision-making in a crisis, as it had been presented, but a measure of social responsibility.

The results were so unexpected to Armstrong that he decided to continue the experiment. Thus began years of repetitions and variations of what he had seen but had difficulty believing. Was this really the way people behave when it is their role to be a manager, in apparent disregard of their social responsibility? He asked other researchers to carry out versions of the experiment. The experiment was also conducted in other nations, and among role players of different ages and experience. The results held firm.

Armstrong focused on what he felt was the key issue—what the "board members" thought their role was. In America and, in recent times, around the world, the standard belief among business managers is that they should work to maximize profits, and let the market take care of the social outcome of their choices. The idea has been most famously expressed by the barons of commerce themselves. William K. Vanderbilt, asked about the harm to the public of his closing a railroad line, replied, "The public be damned! I am working for my stockholders!" This view, in less harsh words, is strongly supported by the teaching of business schools and the strong "free-market" culture that has developed in business. It is the standard view, explicitly stated by many companies and found in polls to be the majority opinion of businessmen. In fact, it has often been said that the business manager's duty is only to the stock-holder. This, of course, relieves the manager of the responsibility to think about society in general. Furthermore, the attitude has been repeatedly backed up in the view of courts since the 1920s. In other words, as Arm-strong notes, air pollution is acceptable if it represents no threat to profit maximization. Only a boycott triggered by reports of pollution from a company should get the manager's attention.

In later versions of the experiment, Armstrong asked role players to consider not only stockholders' interests but also the interests of a few other specified groups directly affected by the directors' decisions. They were asked not to think of the interests of society in general, but to weigh the effect of their decisions on stockholders and on company employees, customers, retailers, and the community where the company is located—the "stakeholders." This had no significant effect. Seventy-six percent chose the most irresponsible course, and none chose to take the haz-ardous drug off the market.

Trying yet another approach, Armstrong imagined a situation that exists in a few Swedish corporations. Armstrong altered the composition of the "Upjohn" board to include a public representative, an employer representative, and a supplier representative. This, finally, had an effect on the outcome. Adding stakeholders to the board and providing a spe-cific accounting of the possible harm their decision could have, board members voted quite differently. Only 22 percent chose the most irre-sponsible course. Fifty percent chose a middle course, such as marketing and promoting the drug until an FDA ban took effect. Still, only 29 per-cent chose to make the moral choice—to take the drug off the market.

The experiment was repeated 91 times, in 10 countries, with 2,000 subjects and 23 different experimenters. If the membership of the com-pany's board was not artificially altered to include outsiders and specific details about harm were not given, in North America and Europe, 76 per-cent of the board members took the most irresponsible course. None chose the most responsible course.

Some years before Armstrong's odyssey, Stanley Milgram of Stanford University carried out a series of experiments testing how much harm people would do to their fellow citizens if asked to by a figure of author-ity. Milgram devised a simple test. One subject, the "learner," would be asked questions. A second, the "teacher," would put the questions. Each time the learner gave a wrong answer, the teacher would administer an electric shock. The shock was mild at first. But as the number of wrong answers from the learner increased, the shocks became more powerful. What the teacher did not know was that he or she was the only subject in the experiment. The learner was in league with the psychologist running the experiment, instructed to give wrong answers on a schedule.

Milgram expected that none of his recruited teachers would actually deliver the most dangerous shocks. He guessed they would tell the attendant psychologist that they would not participate after a certain level. But it did not happen. The teachers jolted the learners up to the limit with hardly a hesitation.

Milgram watched the episodes with surprise, as Armstrong did later when observing his own experiments. Milgram was viewing something about human behavior that was simply not entertained in current psychology. Good people will behave badly as they perform their expected roles.

But we do not need to confront the worst implications of the work of Milgram and Armstrong to understand their meaning for regulation. In reflecting on human history, it is not hard to see the fundamental lesson. As people become more distant from those affected by their decisions they can lose the personal and moral sense of what they are doing. In Milgram's words, "Ordinary people, simply doing their jobs, and without any particular hostility on their part, can become agents in a terrible, destructive process. Moreover, even when the destructive effects of their work become patently clear . . . relatively few people have the resources needed to resist authority."

This is the reason for regulation. We must recognize the roles business managers are required to play, and simply set in counterposition to them a group with a fundamentally different role. Against businesses, whose first job is profit, we must set groups whose first job is safety. It is, after all, common sense. Warren Kiefer, a public relations executive for Pfizer International, several decades ago spoke before Congress, and then wrote, in a letter to *Saturday Review,* "It was my experience in the drug industry that most executives were honest most of the time. But they were businessmen, who, in the old American tradition, placed company interest first. Public interest was the FDA's lookout," he said. It is the "regulatory officials who are responsible to the people."

In contrast to the FDA's poor resources but dedication and openness, American corporations overall have failed to evolve much as organizations. They have remained rigid hierarchies, with little input from the public or stakeholders when key decisions are made. Some management experts have begun to press for more open corporations, ones that include as members of the board some workers, or members of the communities where the companies reside, or suppliers. Essentially, though, the logic of "profit alone" that dominated the companies in the nineteenth century dominates them today. This is one reason the FDA's job is difficult, and necessary.

•

Notes

Sources for this book included substantial interviews with more than two hundred people, including all the living former FDA commissioners, and a variety of FDA officials, pharmaceutical company officers, congressional aides, and university scholars. Especially helpful were the oral histories of former FDA officials held at the National Library of Medicine on the NIH campus in Bethesda, Maryland, and the back issues of the *Food Drug and Cosmetic Law Journal* held at the offices of the Food and Drug Law Institute in Washington, D.C.

INTRODUCTION: THE BEGINNING OF REGULATION

ix In 1882, Theodore Roosevelt: Nathan Miller, *Theodore Roosevelt.*

x His tour of tenements was his first adult confrontation: Theodore Roosevelt, *An Autobiography.*

xiii As one writer found, the FDA's work may be vital: Some examples of the FDA's work as well as an overall view of the agency come from Joshua Wolf Shenk, "Warning: Cutting the FDA Could Be Hazardous to Your Health," *Washington Monthly,* January 1996.

PROLOGUE: THE CHALLENGE

3 One day in the fall of 1992, novelist Diane Ayres: This section is based on an interview with Stephen Fried and Diane Ayres; the fuller story is written up in Stephen Fried, *Bitter Pills.*

5 It was four years ago that Michael Hill was raised from the dead: based on interviews with Michael Hill and Dr. Jerome Groopman.

8 On a fall day in 1994, Jennifer Bilger: based on interviews with Jennifer and Burkhard Bilger; a review of numerous pamphlets and books that mention pennyroyal, most of which fail to mention its potentially disastrous effects; and Burkhard's review, "The Secret Garden," in *The Sciences,* January/February 1998, pp. 38–43. The book reviewed was John M. Riddle, *Eve's Herbs: A History of Contraception and Abortion in the West* (Cambridge: Harvard University Press, 1997).

CHAPTER ONE: DR. WILEY'S TIME

11 a tall, stringy young fellow named Harvey Washington Wiley: The biographical material relies largely on Harvey W. Wiley, *Harvey W. Wiley: An Autobiography;* Oscar E. Anderson, Jr., *The Health of a Nation;* James Harvey Young, *Pure Food;* Maurice Natenberg, *The Legacy of Doctor Wiley and the Administration of His Food and Drug Act;* William MacHarg, "Speaking of Dr. Wiley . . . ," in Donald Elder, ed., *The Good Housekeeping Treasury,* pp. 118–41. Also useful were reminiscences and reports in the files of the Food and Drug Administration records and the *Food Drug and Cosmetic Law Journal.*

The most recent historical treatment of Harvey Wiley and the beginnings of the FDA is Clayton A. Coppin and Jack High, *The Politics of Purity: Harvey Washington Wiley and the Origins of Federal Food Policy* (Ann Arbor: University of Michigan Press, 1999), a work of propaganda funded by the extreme-right-wing Koch Foundation, during the period when Koch and other extremist groups mounted an extraordinary and vicious attack on the FDA. Its general thesis is that Wiley was working not because he cared about pure food or the public interest, but because he was selfish and out to build a bureaucratic empire and his own reputation. Like the other material published in the extremist wave from which it came, it is filled with transparent propaganda, non sequiturs, and enough evidence to destroy the authors' premises. The book does offer the possibility of many laughs and gasps, as the authors stumble forward trying to make one point while actually demonstrating the opposite and their own strong biases.

11 new, large operations, called combinations: Background in Alfred D. Chandler, Jr., *The Visible Hand,* introduction and chap. 9; Charles Sellers, *The Market Revolution;* and David F. Noble, *America by Design.*

11 The commercial market, and new attitudes toward money in particular: Richard Hofstadter, *The Age of Reform,* and Eric F. Goldman, *Rendezvous with Destiny.*

12 Locally produced foods were now shipped into the great maw of city factories: MacHarg, "Speaking of Dr. Wiley"; Wiley, *Autobiography;* Mark Sullivan, *Our Times: The United States, 1900–1925,* vol. 2, *America Finding Herself;* and Young, *Pure Food.*

12 The modern estrangement between the people who create goods and the people who consume them: Sellers, *The Market Revolution,* chap. 1, "Land and Market"; Hofstadter, *The Age of Reform,* pp. 23–36.

12 The corporations were developing a reputation not only for lack of accountability, but also for ruthlessness in competition and hardness toward their workers: Sean Dennis Cashman, *America in the Gilded Age.* Cashman also notes the famous comment of Clemenceau that the United States, in its rush from a colony to industrial power, "had gone from a stage of barbarism to one of decadence without achieving any civilization between the two" (p. 3).

12 The voice of the farmers, originally a voice of stability, was becoming a national voice of protest: Hofstadter, *The Age of Reform,* chap. 1.

15 "The Senate, instead of representing geographical areas": Cashman, *America in the Gilded Age,* p. 259. Also Arthur M. Schlesinger, Jr., *The Age of Jackson,* p. 46: President Jackson told Congress, "Office is considered as a species of property and government rather as a means of promoting individual interests."

15 "and rode over the hills of Trimble County": Anderson, *The Health of a Nation,* pp. 1–9.

18 There were already protests, marches, and lobbying: Mitchell Okun, *Fair Play in the Marketplace,* and Lorine Swainston Goodwin, *The Pure Food, Drink, and Drug Crusaders, 1879–1914.*

CHAPTER TWO: COMMERCE, COMMERCE, COMMERCE

19 "Under our system of government, no shackles or fetters are placed upon your investigations": Harvey W. Wiley, *Harvey W. Wiley: An Autobiography,* p. 102.

19 in commerce deceit seemed to be an accepted tactic to achieve profits. There was some disjoint here: On the land, families labored cooperatively, and from farmer to farmer, there was little difference in status. But in the market, wealth accumulated quickly, sharp differences of status developed, and the values of cooperation were displaced by those of competition. Deceit can have a positive value in competitive commerce. "The market fostered individualism and competitive pursuit of wealth by open-ended production of commodity values. But rural production of use values stopped once bodies were sheltered and clothed and bellies provided for. . . . Therefore subsistence culture fostered family obligation, communal cooperation, and reproduction over generations of a modest comfort." Charles Sellers, *The Market Revolution,* chap. 1, "Land and Market"; and Richard Hofstadter, *The Age of Reform,* pp. 23–36.

20 "The voice of the people and their government is loud and unanimous for commerce": Gordon S. Wood, *The Radicalism of the American Revolution;* discussion continues over pp. 325–40.

20 It "was frightening and bewildering to many": Wood, *The Radicalism of the American Revolution,* p. 326. Wood also suggests that thoughtful leaders in business and government began to fear that the entire nation would fall apart in an orgy of selfishness, or worse, turn to socialism (pp. 325–40).

20 "Corporations have been enthroned": Lincoln quoted in David C. Korten, *When Corporations Rule the World,* p. 58. At first, the architects of the new era, from Thomas Jefferson to Adam Smith, believed that society would now be under the stewardship of the great landowners, the educated elite, essentially as an agrarian nation.

At the mere suggestion that the government of the new era would also grant corporate charters to some favored citizens, howls of protest were heard from every quarter just before and just after 1800. The "republican revolution" was supposed to have created "a separate public authority free from private interests" (Wood, *The Radicalism of the American Revolution,* pp. 319–20).

But there was nothing to restrain the deluge. There had been no more than half a dozen business corporations chartered during the entire colonial period; now they became popular entitlements. Between 1800 and 1817 in Massachusetts alone, 1,800 corporate charters were granted for every kind of business, from establishing banks, to building bridges, to manufacturing a wide variety of goods. The argument against privilege changed accordingly: Grant not one or two, but many *competing* corporate charters. Thus, if anyone can begin a corporation, it will no longer be a privilege.

William Frederick of the University of Pittsburgh, in a column in the *Wall Street Journal* (January 11, 1999), wrote incisively that societies throughout history have always imposed social controls on business and economic activity through civil or religious authority. "But during the 19th century when unfettered capitalism dominated the scene, the long historical relationship was reversed, and society was ruled by economics, with all the attendant problems."

21 would be sufficient to tame the excesses: Charles Sellers writes that producing a livelihood from the land and producing one from manufactured goods for sale were fundamentally different, and tended to force people apart in the new nation. Cooperation was downplayed and competition was emphasized.

By the second half of the nineteenth century, pioneering capitalism had begun the complete breakdown of barriers of distance and difficult travel that had separated farmers and allowed each small group to remain sovereign in their area. The shift drew more resources from the farmers and townspeople to the marketers and the cities. The government began to supply both legal and financial support to businessmen, including the opening of roads and waterways, as well as lay down new rules for money that benefited the new businesses. Charles Sellers, *The Market Revolution.*

21 New forms of cheating were now possible on a large scale: James Harvey Young, *Pure Food;* Wiley, *Autobiography;* Mitchell Okun, *Fair Play in the Marketplace;* and Lorine Swainston Goodwin, *The Pure Food, Drink, and Drug Crusaders, 1879–1914.*

21 These substances became available: The discussion of adulteration, the pure food crusades, and patent medicines in this chapter relies chiefly on James Harvey Young, *The Toadstool Millionaires* and *Pure Food;* Oscar E. Anderson, Jr., *The Health of a Nation;* Okun, *Fair Play in the Marketplace;* Goodwin, *The Pure Food, Drink, and Drug Crusaders;* and Wiley, *Autobiography.*

23 A new category of drugs: The best description of the creation of quack products as a business phenomenon rather than a medical one is in Young's *Toadstool Millionaires,* pp. 38–43, chap. 8, and elsewhere.

25 The drugs "flourished in direct ratio to the availability of cheap newspapers": John Duffy, *From Humors to Medical Science,* pp. 92–93.

26 The remedy faced stiff competition and did not turn a profit: Young, *The Toadstool Millionaires,* p. 102.

26 "medicines were worthless merchandise until a demand was created": Ibid., p. 101.

26 "the walls of our inns": Ibid., pp. 112–13.

27 a year-long investigation by Dr. M. J. Bailey: Okun details some of Bailey's results in *Fair Play in the Marketplace,* as does Young in *Pure Food.*

27 America "has become the grand mart and receptacle of all the refuse merchandise": Young, *Pure Food,* p. 12.

28 "No one can believe that adulteration here would be carried to the extent practiced by foreigners": Okun, *Fair Play in the Marketplace,* p. 14.

28 Dr. Edward R. Squibb: Okun describes the struggle between physicians and patent medicine sellers, e.g., *Fair Play in the Marketplace,* pp. 26–31, as does the biography of Squibb by Lawrence Blochman, *Doctor Squibb.*

29 For drugs made and sold in America: The tale of the pharmacists' struggles with greed and nostrums is described in several volumes. Okun gives a brief sketch in *Fair Play in the Marketplace,* and Jonathan Liebenau et al., eds., *Pill Peddlers: Essays on the History of the Pharmaceutical Industry* (Madison, Wis.: American Institute of the History of Pharmacy, 1990), contains two illuminating articles on the subject: John Parascandola, pp. 29–48, and John P. Swann, pp. 73–90. Also Parascandola, *The Development of American Pharmacology,* chap. 5, and Swann, *Academic Scientists and the Pharmaceutical Industry,* pp. 25–35, discuss the conflict.

31 "Practically all the industries have now been taken from the home": Goodwin, *The Pure Food, Drink, and Drug Crusaders,* p. 48.

33 Few doubted that the slough of American politics needed dredging: Samuel Eliot Morison, *The Oxford History of the American People,* vol. 3, *1869 Through the Death of John F. Kennedy, 1963,* p. 132.

CHAPTER THREE: THE PROGRESSIVE ERA

35 what is an "agricultural scientist" anyway?: Oscar E. Anderson, Jr., *The Health of a Nation,* p. 106.

37 These famous "midnight rambles": drawn from Edmund Morris, *The Rise of Theodore Roosevelt.* Cf. H. Paul Jeffers, *Commissioner Roosevelt,* pp. 109–10.

38 "There was sent to Porto Rico [*sic*] 337 tons of what was known as, or called, 'refrigerated beef,' which you might call embalmed beef": James Harvey Young, *Pure Food,* p. 136.

39 Wiley selected young men as the guinea pigs: The work of the poison squad ran over about seven years, and the data collected from the experiment is contained in the volumes of the U.S. Department of Agriculture, Bureau of Chemistry, bulletin no. 84 (1902–1908).

At the time of the poison squad, doggerel was commonly attempted, and numerous ballads about the squad were written. Part of one of Wiley's favorites, written by S. W. Gillian, read:

> . . . *We are the Pizen Squad.*
> *On prussic acid we break our fast; we lunch on morphine stew;*
> *We dine with a matchhead consommé, drink carbolic acid brew;*

Corrosive sublimate tones us up, like laudanum ketchup rare,
While tyro-toxin condiments are wholesome as mountain air.
Thus all the "deadlies" we double-dare to put us beneath the sod;
We're death-immunes and we're proud as proud—
Hooray for the Pizen Squad!
. . .

If you ever should visit the Smithsonian Institute,
Look out that Professor Wiley doesn't make you a recruit.
He's got a lot of fellows there that tell him how they feel,
They take a batch of poison every time they eat a meal . . .

CHORUS
. . . They may get over it, but they'll never look the same.
That kind of bill of fare would drive most men insane.
Next week he'll give them moth balls, à la Newburgh, or else plain.
They may get over it, but they'll never look the same.

41 By the 1820s, Paris physician Pierre Louis challenged doctors: described in Lester S. King, *Transformations in American Medicine,* and in Guenter Risse, "The Road to Twentieth-Century Therapeutics: Shifting Perspectives and Approaches," in Gregory J. Higby and Elaine C. Stroud, eds., *The Inside Story of Medicines.*

42 "the generalissimo of a coalition": James Harvey Young, "The Science and Morals of Metabolism: Catsup and Benzoate of Soda," *Journal of the History of Medicine* 23: 1 (1968).

43 shouldn't the industry begin to be more careful?: Some companies did come out in favor of legislation. They were chiefly the larger companies with more capability to carry out research and maintain standards of cleanliness, such as the H. K. Mulford Company and Smith, Kline, as described in Jonathan Liebenau, *Medical Science and Medical Industry,* beginning with a comment on p. 3.

44 One such industry witness was Walter H. Williams: quoted from his testimony before the Committee on Interstate Commerce of the House of Representatives, Feb. 13, 1906.

45 "While deodorized eggs": James Harvey Young, "The Social History of American Drug Legislation," in Paul Talalay, ed., *Drugs in Our Society.*

46 Sullivan discovered: In addition to the *Ladies' Home Journal* articles, Mark Sullivan compiled his musings about the time in his multi-volume memoir, *Our Times.*

48 The articles had an instant impact: They also began a history of publications by the American Medical Association on quacks and quack remedies: *Nostrums and Quackery,* vols. 1 and 2 (Chicago: American Medical Association Press, 1912 and 1921).

49 Upton Sinclair's novel *The Jungle:* Discussions of the muckraking of the time and of Sinclair's work in particular come from Sinclair, *American Outpost* and *My Lifetime in Letters,* as well as David Mark Chalmers, *The Muckrake Years* and *The Social and Political Ideas of the Muckrakers,* and the fine old

anthology of the best muckraking articles edited by Arthur and Lila Weinberg, *The Muckrakers*. James Harvey Young also chronicled the events in his article "The Pig That Fell into the Privy: Upton Sinclair's *The Jungle* and the Meat Inspection Amendments of 1906," *Bulletin of the History of Medicine* 59 (1985) 467–80.

50 Finley Peter Dunne wrote: I have taken the quotes from Barbara Schaaf's anthology *Mr. Dooley*, but I have taken the liberty of tidying up the quotes slightly to make them more readable. This will undoubtedly outrage my father, Edward L. Hilts, who is a nephew of Finley Peter Dunne and one of the keepers of the Dooley flame. Nevertheless, I couldn't resist trying to make them as clear and funny on a quick read as they are when labored over for a time to decipher them.

51 Wiley had despaired of ever getting a law: Young, *Pure Food*, p. 172.

51 "Has there ever been in the history of this country a more universal demand for action upon the part of Congress": Wiley, *Autobiography*, p. 224.

53 Biologics Control Act: See chap. 4 as well. It was a groundbreaking law that required manufacturers of diphtheria antitoxin to be regulated and submit their antitoxin to government testing before releasing it to the public. This pre-market testing for safety was not a model followed in the 1906 law.

55 "gradually awakening to the fact of its own improvability": Young, *Pure Food*, p. 147.

CHAPTER FOUR: THE LAW SUCCEEDS, AND FAILS

56 According to the overenthusiastic editorial writers: The news quotes are from James Harvey Young, *Pure Food*, pp. 269–72.

57 "dead-horse" racket: told in the fifty-page booklet "Paul B. Dunbar Shares Memories of Early Days of Federal Food and Drug Law Enforcement," in the *Food Drug and Cosmetic Law Journal*, February 1959. Also told in the little book are the tales of ketchup and oysters, pp. 108–9.

58 Cuforhedake Brane-Fude: follows the version in James Harvey Young's *The Medical Messiahs*.

60 The case at hand was *Johnson v. the United States:* James Harvey Young describes the case in *American Health Quackery*, pp. 94–96, and *The Medical Messiahs*.

62 "You must make the manufacturers call a spade a spade": Oscar E. Anderson, Jr., *The Health of a Nation*, p. 206.

63 The officials "must make adequate explanation or else be considered liable": Anderson, Ibid., pp. 213–14.

63 "Mr. Secretary, my what?": Harvey W. Wiley, *The History of a Crime Against the Food Law*, p. 157.

64 Some manufacturers had sided with Wiley: The fullest tale comes in Andrew F. Smith's *Pure Ketchup: A History of America's National Condiment* (with recipes) (Washington, D.C.: Smithsonian Institution Press, May 2001). His book contains telling statistics from small surveys of the time. In 1898, when benzoate preservatives were at the peak of their popularity, a sampling of

fifty-five preserves and ketchups in California found forty-eight to be adulterated with hazardous substances. From other figures, it appears that a
majority of makers used benzoate to conveniently mask rotting tomatoes,
but a substantial minority dedicated to quality foods always managed without it. By 1915, the tables had turned at least in some places; in a sampling in
Pennsylvania, fewer than 2 percent of 138 samples were found adulterated or
illegal in any respect.

68 The problems were inevitable: After Wiley, Carl L. Alsberg became commissioner, from 1912 to 1921. His approach was conciliatory, not enforcement-
oriented. As Aaron Ihde writes in *Food Controls Under the 1906 Act, Food Drug
and Cosmetic Law Quarterly,* September 1946: "He sought to still the controversy and work by persuasion and cooperation." During his nine years in
office, problems developed as more and more pesticides, including arsenic,
were used. Occasional seizures of fruit coated thickly with arsenic were kept
quiet by the FDA. When Walter G. Campbell took over as commissioner, he
reversed the trend and tried again to openly enforce pesticide limits.

68 The model for a law: The 1902 law was simple and effective in making diph-
theria antitoxins safe for use. The story is told by Ramunus A. Kondratas in
"The Biologics Control Act of 1902," in the collection of essays edited by
Glenn Sonnedecker, *The Early Years of Federal Food and Drug Control.*

69 "commence to prepare the serum as a business enterprise": Kinyoun letter
cited in Kondratas, "The Biologics Control Act of 1902."

71 Wiley was bitter: By contrast, industry leaders went from opposition to the
1906 law to praise of it. For example, Clarence Francis, chairman of the
board, General Foods Corporation, wrote of the 1906 act, "Its Basic Value to
the Food Industry," pp. 379–400, *Food Drug and Cosmetic Law Quarterly,*
September 1946: "In examining the testimony [before passage of the act],
one comes again and again upon the statement that most manufacturers
wanted sincerely to operate honestly, and urgently sought some means of
curbing the unscrupulous competitors whose practices were discrediting the
entire industry." The FDA supplied the fulcrum that helped dislodge the
worst business practices, he said. "It would be an exaggeration, of course, to
attribute all of the food industry's splendid gains of the last 40 years
[1906–1946] to a single regulatory law. . . . Nevertheless, I believe sincerely
that we must give the greatest recognition to the effect which the Food and
Drug Act had in *setting the stage* for the progress of industry. [emphasis in the
original] . . . I can only echo the expression of one of the businessmen who,
40 years ago, went to Washington and, perceiving the potential benefits of the
act, testified in its behalf by exclaiming that such a law would be a 'grand,
good thing.' "

CHAPTER FIVE: CAPITALISM IN CRISIS

74 "The great knife of the depression": Robert S. Lynd and Helen Merrell
Lynd, *Middletown, A Study in Contemporary American Culture* (New York:
Harcourt, Brace and Company, 1929).

74 There was no great sense that science would join with business: One notable incident in the story of progress in food safety came with the olive scare of 1920. After the law was passed in 1906, the canning industry in America, long behind its counterparts in other nations, began to expend some money and thought on research. Industry leaders, though as divided after the law as they were before, began to feel more and more that a detailed knowledge of what went into their cans and jars, and just what might grow there accidentally, could be vital to avoid future legal problems. An industrywide research board was set up in 1913 to begin work, and more people with technical expertise began to be hired, including Wiley's former chief of the food division, Willard Bigelow, to direct industry research. By 1916, the canning industry had begun a voluntary system of inspecting factories for cleanliness.

But more than cleanliness was necessary to safety. After scattered outbreaks of what appeared to be olive-related illness, three outbreaks hit quickly in 1919. In Canton, Ohio, olives were served at a country club dinner to honor a war hero; the feast ended with many of the guests sick and six of them, including the honored military man himself, dead. A few weeks later, olives served at a private formal dinner in Detroit caused the death of five guests. In each case, the cause appeared to be botulism poisoning. The illness was relatively new in the nomenclature of medicine, but it was becoming clear that the toxin produced by the botulism bacterium was among the most deadly poisons ever encountered by humans.

The FDA began an investigation immediately after the Ohio tribute dinner and had taken biological samples. When the second set of deaths occurred, the FDA found that the olives causing them came from the same California plant and were from the same batch. A little later, a Memphis outbreak was traced to the same factory and the same batch.

The agency had the power to remove that lot from the shelves, but no general recall was allowed, and the most the agency could do was issue a warning about canned or bottled ripe olives.

In early January, after a large meal at an Italian household in New York City, the mother suddenly became ill. She vomited repeatedly and then began to experience severe choking. Her vision blurred. Her breathing suddenly became difficult. The next morning she was dead.

The doctor ascribed it to kidney problems, but three days later the family assembled again for dinner, this time in honor of the dead woman. The husband and his two brothers were there, along with his daughter and two of his three sons. They had macaroni with tomato sauce, and a salad of oil, vinegar, peppers, anchovies, and olives.

One of the sons, Dominica, became ill first and was dead an hour after he arrived at the hospital the next morning. That day, the father, one of his brothers, and another of his sons fell ill. The next day, the father's other brother became sick with the same symptoms. By the third day, all four were dead of botulism poisoning.

The canners did not know what to do. The California Health Department called them together and gave them new data from the FDA compiled by the western chief, R. W. Hilts (no relation as far as I know). It appeared that the temperature to which the olives were heated in canning and bottling was not high enough to eradicate the bacteria. Hilts said, particularly in bottling, the heating was cut short because the companies had found that glass could not withstand long boiling. At the emergency meeting in California, his suggestion that canners stop packing olives in glass for the time being was met with blankness. The canners, as Hilts wrote back to Washington, were "nonplussed." They refused to go along. The outbreaks continued, and soon 95 percent of the trade in canned and bottled olives had been wiped out. By 1922, when all the scientific and trade issues were finally understood, there had been eighty-three outbreaks and 185 deaths.

Eventually, canners agreed to higher temperatures for olive processing—240°F for forty minutes. At this temperature, most of the problem was eliminated, and the industry wanted to begin a broad national campaign declaring the outbreaks ended. The new process "removes all danger from ripe olive poisoning," it declared. But again, the FDA warned that even at that high temperature, experiments showed that a few containers of olives became contaminated. The point was proved when a new round of outbreaks occurred, and the reason for all the difficulty was finally sorted out. Unlike most bacteria familiar to canners, botulinum bacteria grow best in the dark interior of foods *where there is no oxygen.* So all attempts to seal containers better were useless. Both early processing and high heat would be necessary, chemistry proved.

It was clear that the problems of modern technology in foods and drugs were beyond the ability of any company, or even of all the industry's brainpower together, to manage. Outside scientists with the power to act were vital. But in those years, the federal agency charged with ensuring food safety simply didn't have the power to prevent deadly outbreaks that carried on for years and caused many deaths.

77 Before the inauguration Tugwell said, "One of the first problems I shall meet": Michael Namorato, ed., *The Diary of Rexford G. Tugwell,* p. 85.

77 Tugwell fired his first rocket in early March 1933: The fullest account of the 1933 to 1938 battle for a new FDA law comes from Charles O. Jackson, *Food and Drug Legislation in the New Deal.* In addition, a great number of reminiscences of the 1930s from FDA staff survive, including articles by Dunbar.

79 The attack on the bill was carried out largely under the generalship of the two trade groups of secret-formula drug makers: Jackson describes some of this on pp. 30–35 of *Food and Drug Legislation in the New Deal,* and Ruth deForest Lamb, in *American Chamber of Horrors,* devotes more space to the issue in her chap. 11 and appendixes. The propaganda quoted here comes from Lamb.

84 Among the cases in the exhibit was one dealing with a cosmetic called Lash Lure: described by Jackson, *Food and Drug Legislation in the New Deal,* and by Lamb, *American Chamber of Horrors.*

85 Crazy Water Crystals: following Jackson, *Food and Drug Legislation in the New Deal,* pp. 6–8.

89 For example, the use of dinitrophenol as a quick weight-loss agent: Though

the drug catastrophe caused by dinitrophenol has never been well documented, the medical literature does contain reports of at least nine deaths and several hundred injuries. Maurice Hardgrove and Nancy Stern, "Dinitrophenol: A Review of the Literature," *Industrial Medicine* 7, no. 1 (January 1938), focuses on the descriptions of symptoms and fails even to add up the number of deaths reported in the open literature. Many of the other reports are questionable, as they were written by doctors who advocated the treatment of obesity with dinitrophenol and apparently hoped to minimize their role in the suffering which followed. But collecting information from report to report produces a stark picture. Unfortunately, this extremely dangerous drug is now being hawked for weight loss and bodybuilding, chiefly on the Internet, without any apparent cognizance of the drug's historical record.

90 It was apparent to those present that he would have been in excruciating pain: In writing about the elixir tragedy FDA commissioner Jere Goyan quoted from a letter which he said was "one of the most poignant expressions of social failure in the annals of medicine." The letter was from a mother whose child had been poisoned by Elixir Sulfanilamide:

Dear Sir,

Two months ago I was happy and working taking care of my two little girls, Joan age 6 and Jean age 9. Our byword through the Depression was that we had good health and each other. Joan thought her mother was right in everything, and it would have made your heart feel good last November to have seen her jumping and shouting as we listened to your re-election over the radio.

Tonight, Mr. Roosevelt, that little voice is stilled. The first time I ever had occasion to call in a doctor for her and she was given the Elixir of Sulfanilamide. Tonight our little home is bleak and full of despair. All that is left to us is the caring for of that little grave. Even the memory of her is mixed with sorrow for we can see her little body tossing to and fro and hear that little voice screaming with pain and it seems as though it would drive me insane. . . . Tonight, Mr. President Roosevelt, as you enjoy your little grandchildren of whom we read about, it is my plea that you will take steps to prevent such sales of drugs that will take little lives and leave such suffering behind and such a bleak outlook on the future as I have tonight. . . . Surely we can have laws governing doctors also who will give such a medicine not knowing to what extent its danger. . . .

CHAPTER SIX: THE BIRTH OF THE MODERN PHARMACEUTICAL TRADE

95 The revolution in medicine took place between that summer afternoon in 1938 and an October day in 1951: The Food, Drug and Cosmetic Act was passed in the summer of 1938, and the Durham-Humphrey law establishing

the prescription drug system was passed in 1951. Between the two dates the modern pharmaceutical system with its reliance on research, patents, and promotion was invented.

97 Representative of this was a war between the pharmacologists in universities and those who worked for industry: The split between academic and commercial science is described in both Jonathan Liebenau, *Medical Science and Medical Industry*, and John P. Swann, *Academic Scientists and the Pharmaceutical Industry*.

98 Gerhardt Domagk at Farbenindustrie rediscovered the chemical in the early 1930s: This account follows Irmengarde Eberle, *Modern Medical Discoveries*, and M. Weatherall, *In Search of a Cure*.

100 It is often written that Sir Alexander Fleming discovered penicillin in 1928: The adventure of taking penicillin from the lab to the pharmacy is best described by Trevor I. Williams, *Howard Florey*, and by Gladys L. Hobby, *Penicillin*. The American part of the venture is in Williams's chap. 4 and Hobby's chaps. 4 and 5.

104 the myth that business is solely responsible for medical progress: Harry F. Dowling, *Medicines for Man*, pp. 42–43, also believed that credit should be shared:

Which one of these groups—universities, government, or the drug industry—deserves the greatest credit for these new drugs? . . . The threads of collective achievement cannot be disentangled. . . . Penicillin was discovered in one university laboratory with the assistance of a grant from a private foundation and perfected in another university; then, under the stress of war, it was produced as a collaborative effort by twenty-two industrial firms in the United States under the sponsorship of the federal government, which provided subsidies. The program was spurred by the discovery in a research laboratory of the Department of Agriculture that corn steep liquor would increase the yield of the antibiotic one hundred-fold and also that one of the strains of penicillium from the laboratory would do a better job than those used before. Who then is responsible for penicillin?

107 The companies also used the 1938 law to devise the concept of prescription drugs: Conservative commentators, notably Peter Temin in his poorly researched book, have often made the mistake of assuming that the FDA devised the prescription system because the 1938 law contains the provision on which it was based. In fact, the pharmaceutical companies and proprietary drug makers initiated the drive for a prescription system, with pharmacists soon joining them in support. Negotiations that shaped the system took place over several years and were finally codified in 1951. The story of these events is described in two papers: Harry M. Marks, "Revisiting 'The Origins of Compulsory Drug Prescriptions,' " *American Journal of Public Health* 85, no. 1 (January 1995); and John P. Swann, "FDA and the Practice of Pharmacy: Prescription Drug Regulation Before the Durham-Humphrey Amendment of 1951," *Pharmacy in History* 36, no. 2 (1994).

CHAPTER SEVEN: NEW DRUGS, NEW PROBLEMS

108 The story of one drug, chloramphenicol: This chapter follows the account of
the drug given by Thomas Maeder in his well-researched and well-written
book *Adverse Reactions*. It also draws on material from Morton Mintz's
reporting and from Harry F. Dowling, *Medicines for Man*, as well as personal
interviews.

112 Suggested Details / Chloramphenicol: quoted from Maeder, *Adverse Reactions*.

115 after a thousand deaths: As for the sales of chloramphenicol, they began in
1950 at about 25 million grams sold annually (about 1 million to 2 million
courses of treatment). In 1960, 55 million grams were sold. The company
said in 1960 that about 40 million people had been given chloramphenicol;
by conservative estimates, that means that about thirty-five times as many
people got it as should have. The sales fluctuated after that, but even in the
mid-1960s, 30 to 50 million grams were being sold annually.

CHAPTER EIGHT: THE INDUSTRY ASCENDANT

120 Most important, President Eisenhower's close friend and political operative
in Minnesota, James Bradshaw Mintener: Sometime after he was assured
that Larrick was appointed to the FDA, Mintener began private practice in
food and drug law. His clients included some of the drug manufacturers,
such as E. Fougera and Company, and Richardson-Merrell, which had run
into trouble from regulatory agencies.

120 "George Larrick's fundamental objective": Oral history interview with Winton Rankin, in the National Library of Medicine.

121 Patent law was made tame: The other key element in the formation of the
modern drug industry was patents. If companies could gain control of one of
these new miracle drugs under a patent, the profit would be spectacular. The
way had been laid for just such a development over the years.

To begin with, patents were not intended to produce monopolies by corporations. The American plan for patents was novel in its conception at the
time the Constitution was written. It provided that only inventors personally,
not companies, could gain patents on their inventions. The notion was to
give an incentive to inventors, a chance to gain exclusive profit for a time
from anything they invent. It was in keeping with the hope of fostering individualism and self-reliance in America, and as Abraham Lincoln commented, it "added the fuel of interest to the power of genius." Monopolies
were not permitted in America except in such cases.

The patent system flourished, but as corporations rose in America, they
soon began to buy out inventors and hold the patents themselves. In 1885
corporations held only 20 percent of patents; by 1950 more than 75 percent.
Although the original intent of the patent provision in the Constitution has
by now been shredded, the form is still observed—each patent must be in
the name of an individual. So it became common practice for corporations

to require scientists and engineers to surrender any patent rights they might create while employed. Even though there was no compensation for turning over their rights, inventors, always insecure, were willing to do so as long as they could have a steady job and get some credit, if not cash, for their work. Companies then began to accumulate patents in given areas of interest. They sought the patent not only for the invention but for the processes used to make it, and for any related products or processes they could think of. As monopolies per se were not legal, the companies had to create them by bundling patent rights together. The tactic was plainly laid out in 1906 by Edwin J. Prindle, a mechanical engineer and patent lawyer. "Patents are the best and most effective means of controlling competition," he wrote. They will even "occasionally give absolute command of a market, enabling their owner to set the price without regard to the cost of production. . . . Patents are the only legal form of absolute monopoly."

This history is described in detail by David F. Noble, *America by Design*.

122 "It is becoming exceedingly difficult for physicians to keep things clear": Morton Mintz, *By Prescription Only*, pp. 170–71.

123 He said that the single most striking thing about the new pharmaceutical business was its enormous expenditure on promotion: Pierre Garai in Paul Talalay, ed., *Drugs in Our Society*, p. 191.

123 "According to some experts, it would be expected that advertising for drugs would be relatively small compared to other industries": Seymour E. Harris, *The Economics of American Medicine*, p. 86.

125 "How in the world can any physician be expected to keep up with the new pharmacy?": Morton Mintz, *By Prescription Only*, p. 50.

126 the AMA suddenly changed its approach: A description of the events is given in Harry F. Dowling, *Medicines for Man*, chap. 8.

127 It was as if Prometheus had stolen the fire of the gods: Stuart B. Levy, *The Antibiotic Paradox*.

CHAPTER NINE: THE GRAND BARGAIN

129 It began with a sore throat on a winter day in 1951. It was irritating enough to send Walton Hamilton: This section relies in the main on Seymour E. Harris's account, *The Economics of American Medicine*. In addition, I interviewed several journalists, and FDA and congressional staffers involved in the events, and drew on the voluminous transcripts of the Kefauver hearings, beginning with *Part 1: AMA and Medical Authorities, Hearings Before the Subcommittee on Antitrust and Monopoly of the Committee on the Judiciary*, United States Senate, 87th Cong. (Washington, DC: U.S. Government Printing Office, 1961). The bill in question was the Drug Industry Anti-Trust Act, S. 1552.

132 In this case, the kind of steroids discussed: The substances were made naturally, in tiny amounts, in the adrenal bodies of the kidney. The excitement over the drugs began with a false but very stimulating report from a spy in Argentina in 1941. The report to the American military said that the German

military was purchasing large quantities of adrenal glands from slaughter-houses in Argentina. The drugs extracted from the glands were to be used to help Luftwaffe pilots withstand the stress of flight at high altitudes.

The Office of Scientific Research and Development, the group also responsible for leading the charge on penicillin, recruited top American chemists to start experimenting with likely adrenal steroids. The spy reports turned out to be wrong. Merck management saw the possibilities quickly, and they were confirmed when the fifth compound that researcher E. C. Kendall developed was given to a young woman desperately ill with arthritis. She was immobile, in pain, and not expected to live. After her third shot of the drug, she rose from her bed without suffering for the first time in five years. A further week of treatment allowed her to leave the hospital walking.

141 "Most people—in and out of the medical profession—were not unhappy": Louis Lasagna, in John B. Blake, ed., *Safeguarding the Public*, pp. 171–72.

142 it appeared to be permanently interred: Columnist Drew Pearson ferreted out a key aspect of the situation. He reported that Spencer Olin, of Olin Mathison, the chemical combine that was sole owner of Squibb, asked Republicans in Congress to strongly oppose Kefauver's bill. Olin was not only a heavy contributor to Senator Everett Dirksen's campaigns, but for some years had been financial chairman of the Republican National Committee. The Pearson column disturbed White House advisors when they realized they had fallen into step with the hard right of the Republican party. The day after the Kefauver bill was killed in committee, the president wrote to Eastland suggesting that the bill had merit and it should be enacted by Congress—too late, it appeared.

142 The object is to appear to have responded to the call for reform: Unnoticed at the time, one day after Kennedy's letter went to Eastland, the *New York Times* ran a small story about the rising incidence of deformed children in Europe. The story quoted Dr. Helen B. Taussig of Johns Hopkins University as saying a drug that had been touted as a harmless sleeping pill was the cause of 3,000 to 5,000 birth deformities so far recorded in a European epidemic. Taussig said the FDA had not yet approved the drug. While the story was not widely noted, Jo Anne Youngblood in Kefauver's office brought it to the attention of other members of Kefauver's staff. John Blair began to think about making strategic use of it. When Taussig came to Washington to testify at a hearing on the European misadventure, some reports have it that Blair asked the committee chairman not to notify the press of her appearance or its import. That way Blair could release the news on his own, when and to whom it seemed most useful.

CHAPTER TEN: THALIDOMIDE

144 The source of thalidomide and other drug disasters: The best accounts of the tale of thalidomide, on which this chapter relies, are in order of importance: *Sunday Times* of London Insight Team, *Suffer the Children*; Richard E. McFadyen, "Thalidomide in America: A Brush with Tragedy," *Clio Medica*

11, no. 2 (1976): 79–93; John D. Archer, "Suffer the Children: The Story of Thalidomide," *Forum on Medicine,* February 1979; Frances O. Kelsey, "Thalidomide Update: Regulatory Aspects," *Teratology* 38 (1988): 21–226; and Morton Mintz, *By Prescription Only.*

144 the Vick Chemical Company: The Vick Chemical Company acquired the drugmaker William S. Merrell Company in the 1930s, but Merrell kept its name until 1960, when it was merged with another part of the company and changed its name to Richardson-Merrell, Inc.

145 By June came reports that in studies done by university scientists the drug caused cataracts in animals: At Merck & Company, where there was also great interest in drugs that lower cholesterol, some tests were done on MER-29, comparing it to their own potential product. The scientists were surprised to find that a large proportion of dogs developed cataracts when using the drug, and rats were blinded by it. Merck quickly passed on the information to Richardson-Merrell. But the latter was not ready to give up. It continued to report publicly, the *Times* team wrote, that no evidence of toxicity had been seen in animals and that the drug was quite safe for people.

146 With the evidence of felonies in hand, Larrick was able to persuade Richardson-Merrell executives to voluntarily remove the drug from the market: In subsequent prosecutions, company executives and scientists pleaded no contest to the charges; the company was fined $80,000 and the executives were given six months' probation. The company later estimated that 420,000 people took the drug and 4,200 of them had been injured by it, chiefly a combination of cataracts, extreme rashes, and loss of hair.

146 Merrell did not invent thalidomide: The account of the development of thalidomide used here follows the London *Sunday Times* account in *Suffer the Children* and Mintz's description in *By Prescription Only.* Additionally, I conducted personal interviews with participants.

148 When the researchers checked the drug's toxicity, they could not find any, they said: It is common to start out such studies by giving animals large doses, and establishing the dose at which 50 percent of the animals are killed by the compound (it's called the LD-50). They gave doses up to fifty times the calming dose and observed no detrimental side effects. At least, that is what the published data showed.

149 In the company's promotions for the beginning of 1960, it told doctors and patients buying the over-the-counter package that the drug was "non-toxic" and "completely harmless even for infants": Eventually, the salesmen who had to face doctors day by day were alarmed. They told their superiors that they were getting more and more reports that could not be ignored, especially reports of peripheral nerve damage, according to the *Times* team. The head of the clinical research section wrote in a memo, "Sooner or later we will not be able to stop publication of the side effects of Contergan. We are therefore anxious to get as many positive pieces of work as possible." That meant getting doctors to write glowing reports on use of the drug. These were submitted to scientific journals. One executive wrote to the company's Portuguese licensee about the urgency of publication, "To be quite clear about it: a quick publication, perhaps in three months, with reports of fifteen

to twenty successful cases who have tolerated the drug well, is more important to us than a broadly-based large work."

151 Dr. Roy Nulsen: Nulsen and other doctors in the Richardson-Merrell "experiments" were informed that whether they submitted results to the company or not, the official launch date of Kevadon would be March 6, 1961.

158 Altogether, there were about 40 cases: Although Richardson-Merrell had failed to get the drug to market in America, the company had succeeded in Canada and had kept it on the market there for three months after both Germany and England pulled it from their markets. In Canada, 100 cases of thalidomide deformities were reported, and a similar number of fetal deaths is presumed.

161 But in an unusual admission, he added that the new rules would pose no serious problems: Behind the admission was the knowledge that, despite all the fuss, the pharmaceutical industry really put out two completely distinct products. There were drugs marketed to copy others already available, in the hope that clever promotion could be used to steal some of the market. And then there were the truly new drugs, the ones that were original molecules. In 1962 about 250 "new" drugs were approved, only ten of which were original molecules. In fact, of the ten, only one offered any real advance in medical treatment. The industry had been arguing to save the 249 unimportant products from tests that might unmask them. They had no worry that the really useful drugs would be threatened. But with stricter standards, profits from the copycat drugs might decrease. Then, in theory, less money would be available to spend in the discovery of important drugs, making it less likely they would be found. So, after a couple of little leaps of logic, the industry came to the conclusion that the mission of bringing life-giving drugs to market would be hurt by strict regulations. In fact, that did not happen. The number of drugs that represented important medical advances remained the same year to year.

CHAPTER ELEVEN: SCIENCE MEETS POLICY

166 "I know the pressures that you feel and the duties you must discharge": Morton Mintz, *By Prescription Only,* p. 95.

167 "*this thing*": James Goddard, personal interview.

167 "Look, . . . there are three elements here": Goddard, personal interview.

168 "I am very uneasy": Goddard, from text of speeches collected in the library of the Food and Drug Administration.

171 "Why is this, Joe?": Goddard, personal interview.

171 (The study was known as the Drug Efficacy Study of the National Academy of Sciences, National Research Council.): National Research Council, Division of Medical Sciences, "Drug Efficacy Study, Final Report to the Commissioner of Food and Drugs, Food and Drug Administration" (Washington, D.C.: National Academy of Sciences, 1969).

The final report, while it was a massive review, was only the beginning of another elephantine undertaking. After the National Academy and the FDA had rendered initial judgment on drugs, each company started the work of defending its drugs. Their job was largely to delay the day of reckoning on which a drug must be pulled from the market as worthless, hazardous, or both. So, whether there was any data to support their position or not, companies filed positive reports on their drugs and requested formal hearings before the FDA.

For the agency, the review of drugs had now turned into a review of whether each drug should get an administrative hearing as well. To defend itself against the possibility of an endless series of frivolous hearings, which could last decades, the agency set out minimum standards. The evidence in favor of a drug had to meet minimum standards in order to earn another review after the academy and the agency had already determined a drug worthless. As Dr. Robert Temple says, the task of setting minimum standards of evidence had a good side effect—the agency wrote out in detail, for the first time anywhere, a set of guides as to what constituted an "adequate and well controlled" medical experiment. The first version of these standards was published in 1970. If a drug was not supported with adequate studies, and the existing evidence suggested it had little or no value, then it did not get another hearing.

The whole process, including the hearings, ultimately dragged on for twenty-two years, not counting a few odd cases and not counting the review of over-the-counter medications. By 1984, about 3,500 drugs had been reviewed fully, and more than a thousand worthless drugs (in about 7,000 different formulations or packages) had been removed from the market. (See, for example, Irvin Molotsky, "U.S. Review of Prescription Drugs Ends," *NewYork Times,* Sept. 15, 1984, p. 52.)

CHAPTER TWELVE: PARTISAN POLITICS

180 And so it was in the FDA: A primary source for this chapter was "Report of the Review Panel on Drug Regulation, Investigation of Allegations Relating to the Bureau of Drugs, Food and Drug Administration" (Washington, D.C.: Department of Health, Education and Welfare, April 1977)—"The Dorsen Report." It was named after the chairman of the panel that wrote it, Norman Dorsen of New York University Law School. He led a two-year investigation into irregularities at the FDA.

I also interviewed several FDA officials in the agency at the time.

189 And the dissension inside the FDA broke into a public free-for-all when Senator Edward Kennedy held surprise hearings in August 1974, just a few days after Nixon had resigned the presidency: The hearings were *Joint Hearings before the Subcommittee on Health of the Committee of Labor and Public Welfare and the Subcommittee on Administrative Practice and Procedure of the Committee on the Judiciary, United States Senate, 93rd Cong., First and Second Sessions, on S. 3441 and S. 966, Legislation Amending the Public Health Service Act and the Federal Food, Drug, and Cosmetic Act,* August 15 and 16, 1974 (Washington, D.C.: Government Printing Office); and *Joint Hearings before*

the Subcommittee on Health of the Committee on Labor and Public Welfare and the Subcommittee on Administrative Practice and Procedure of the Committee on the Judiciary, United States Senate, 93rd Congress, Second Session, on Examination of New Drug Research and Development by the Food and Drug Administration, September 25 and 27, 1974 (Washington, D.C.: Government Printing Office).

190 Prior to the Kennedy hearings, in 1972, one enterprising physician, Dr. William Wardell: W. M. Wardell, "Introduction of New Therapeutic Drugs in the United States and Great Britain: An International Comparison," *Clinical Pharmacology and Therapeutics* 14 (1973): 773–90.

191 so-called drug lag: Sources for information on the drug lag issues and its history are in the endnote to p. 276.

192 Conservative economist Sam Peltzman of the University of Chicago now produced a couple of papers that electrified both the right and the free market advocates: See Sam Peltzman, "An Evaluation of Consumer Protection Legislation: The 1962 Drug Amendments," *Journal of Political Economy*, September/October 1973, pp. 1049–91. Also, a version with fewer equations, and from which most quotes in this book are taken: "The Benefits and Costs of New Drug Regulation," in *Proceedings of the Conference on Regulation of New Pharmaceuticals* (Chicago: University of Chicago Press, 1974).

194 About two or three truly useful new drugs were approved annually from 1960 on: Harry F. Dowling, *Medicines for Man*, pp. 97–101.

196 It has been estimated that before 1969, 90 percent of FDA files were secret: Carolyn Morgan helped change that: Troetel describes the opening up of the agency to Freedom of Information Act requests and more citizen access generally. Barbara R. Troetel, "Three-Part Disharmony,"

CHAPTER THIRTEEN: THE LIMITS OF POLICY

202 It was the last decision of an era: Barbara R. Troetel, "Three-Part Disharmony," chap. 1.

203 It took place at a policy forum sponsored by the American Enterprise Institute in 1977: American Enterprise Institute for Public Policy Research, Center for Health Policy Research, *The Saccharin Ban: Risks vs. Benefits* (Washington, D.C., 1977). The historical background can be found in James Harvey Young, *Saccharin: A Bitter Regulatory Controversy, Research in the Administration of Public Policy* (Washington, D.C.: Howard University Press, 1975).

CHAPTER FOURTEEN: DEREGULATION

212 "The leading conservative intellectuals seemed to share one strong conviction": James Allen Smith, *The Idea Brokers*, p. 170.

212 The problems of the world cannot be resolved by a better understanding of how people or society work but must be resolved by "traditional" values: This conflict with a science-based agency was not over details or practices,

as the quarrel between the FDA and industry was, but was deep. These conservatives were opposed to science itself and science as a basis for policy.

214 A 1,000-page version was sold as a book, a bestseller in Washington: *Man-
date for Leadership; Policy Management in a Conservative Administration,* ed.
Charles L. Heatherly, foreword by Edwin J. Feulner (Washington, D.C.:
Heritage Foundation, 1980).

215 Within three more weeks, the president had signed Executive Order 12291:
Susan J. Tolchin and Martin Tolchin, *Dismantling America.*

216 as Lou Cannon writes in his presidential biography of Reagan: Lou Cannon,
President Reagan, pp. 736–50.

217 the Hussey-Stetler test of time: Morton Mintz, *By Prescription Only,* pp.
72–77. The phrase was coined by Mintz to refer to the time-honored but
utterly irrational argument that if a drug has been used for years, by virtue of
that use it must have been found safe and effective by doctors and patients,
otherwise they would have dropped it. This conjecture has been disproved
many times over as harmful drugs and treatments have remained in use not
only for years but for centuries. Mintz names the "test of time" argument
after two of its most vociferous advocates of the 1950s and 1960s, Hugh
Hussey and Joseph Stetler, who were both, not by coincidence, officers of the
American Medical Association.

217 "to . . . stimulate the marketing of important new drugs": Arthur Hull
Hayes, Jr., personal interview.

218 Hayes walked through each of the key proposals: Joe Levitt, personal interview.

220 But the Aspirin Foundation could still prevail: The *Wall Street Journal* broke
the story of the political inference with a public health decision, and later
accounts of how the pressure was applied appeared in a United Press International account by Larry Doyle, "A Reye's History," on May 12, 1987, and
in the *Washington Monthly* by David Segal, "Lemon Laws," in January 1993.

CHAPTER FIFTEEN: THE MEDICAL OFFICER

224 Dr. Robert Temple stepped out of a meeting with FDA staffers: based on
FDA documents and interviews with FDA medical officers.

225 He recalled one case from early in his career: from a personal interview and
Thomas J. Moore, *Deadly Medicine,* pp. 103–4.

227 Temple and biostatistician Gordon Pledger ran the numbers again, with
proper data entry: Robert Temple and Gordon W. Pledger, "The FDA's Critique of the Anturane Reinfarction Trial," and Arnold S. Relman, "Sulfinpyrazone after Myocardial Infarction: No Decision Yet," *New England
Journal of Medicine* 303 (December 1980): 1488–92, 1476–77.

229 Reviewers have sometimes felt that their superiors too often side with companies: A 1998 survey of FDA medical officers by Wolfe's Health Research
Group found that of those willing to comment, many more felt drugs were
approved when they should not be, rather than the reverse, and a quarter of
them cited pressure from superiors to approve drugs as a problem. See Peter

Lurie and Sidney M. Wolfe, "FDA Medical Officers Report Lower Standards Permit Dangerous Drug Approvals" (Washington, D.C.: Public Citizen's Health Research Group, December 1998).

231 The drugs were not only failing to save patients, they were killing them: The results are reported in D. S. Echt et al. and the CAST Investigators, "Mortality and Morbidity in Patients Receiving Encainide, Flecainide, or Placebo: The Cardiac Arrhythmia Suppression Trial," *New England Journal of Medicine* 324 (1991): 781–88; and The Cardiac Arrhythmia Suppression Trial II Investigators, "Effect of the Anti-arrhythmic Agent Moricizine on Survival after Myocardial Infarction," *New England Journal of Medicine* 327 (1992): 227–33.

234 Rudolph Widmark, one of the FDA reviewers, told his colleagues and superiors at the agency that the drug had problems: This account relies chiefly on the reporting of David Willman and the *Los Angeles Times* story series headlined "The New FDA: How a New Policy Led to Seven Deadly Drugs," Dec. 20, 2000.

234 What is made clear by these examples is that, by the mid-1990s, the FDA, under pressure, was pinning its hopes on warning labels and doctors' care in prescribing: The Reagan administration prevented patients from getting reliable information directly from the FDA with their medicine. This maintained the pharmaceutical industry's control over key drug information. The basic reference book on drugs is the *Physicians' Desk Reference,* and it contains, for each drug, a copy of the official FDA labeling information. It is a fat volume that lists in detail the uses of a drug and its problems. Unfortunately, this is an industry publication. The listings in the book are the legal "labeling" for each drug, but it is not written by the FDA, as it should be. It is written by the companies, with the FDA acting as editor. Thus, the language and format is obfuscatory by nature, and each warning is the subject of litigation-style negotiations between the manufacturer and the FDA. Further, the volume lists the best data about a drug—the data used to gain approval—and very often fails to include later, more pertinent data until years after it is published. Thus, the book that is the basic reference to drugs is unreliable and heavily biased toward the favorable. Two more reliable sources exist but are far from complete. For doctors, *The Medical Letter* reviews drugs from the point of view of public health–minded physicians, but it can review only a handful per year. For consumers, *Worst Pills, Best Pills,* a publication of the advocacy organization Public Citizen Health Research Group, is plain and reliable but again not as complete as a full compendium.

CHAPTER SIXTEEN: THE MODERN PLAGUE

238 "I came in with essentially no baggage because I was totally unknown": Frank Young, personal interview.

239 He wanted to revive the agency with thoughts of the future: Young studied at Syracuse University, then at Case Western Reserve in Cleveland, before going to the Scripps Institute in California to work on genetics. He then went

to Rochester, again basing the choice on prayer and signs. When he had agreed to take the job, he did so on the condition that he be allowed to outline the administration's policy on biotechnology, which was then as unformed as the commercial ventures into it were. Secretary Heckler agreed.

240 "If the medical establishment was unable or unwilling to put drugs into their hands," write Peter Arno and Karyn Feiden: Peter S. Arno and Karyn L. Feiden, *Against the Odds.*

242 "There was at the time a strong sense of therapeutic nihilism": Samuel Broder, personal interview.

245 One money manager told *Barron's* magazine he would not bet on making money with AIDS drugs: The quote was from 1989. The skepticism remained even after two AIDS drugs had been profitably marketed. AIDS has resulted in more than a hundred drugs and many billions of dollars in profit. Each of the first companies to work on AIDS drugs began its work because it was being pressed hard to do so, not because it was willing to take risks on its own.

247 Of course, until then patients themselves could seek drugs from companies, one by one, on a "compassionate use" basis: At the time, the FDA required companies to give drugs free of charge if they were not yet approved. The company later reported the compassionate use program cost $10 million. A quick calculation suggests that when the company later charged patients $10,000 per year for AZT, that was at least four times its cost.

250 "Previously, there was a great concern that if we did this, then no one would be in the clinical trial": Anthony Fauci, personal interview.

250 Mitsuya found that the body retained DDI longer than AZT: The manufacturer of DDI was Bristol-Myers. This time, when Broder and the NIH had turned over their work to a company, they wrote a clause in to their agreement that any drug produced as a result had to be priced reasonably. (When it came on the market, DDI was priced at about one-fifth of the original price of AZT.)

252 Generic drugs, chemical copies: In the 1970s the FDA had few resources to check up on companies that made generic copies of the drugs, and it decided to give those companies a break. It allowed them to market their copies immediately after the brand-name patent expired, but before the generic copy had been tested—a regrettable leap of faith.

CHAPTER SEVENTEEN: A PROGRESSIVE

256 A *New York Times* headline described it as "A guardian of health buckling under stress": The article laid out the agency problems described here. Philip J. Hilts, "Ailing Agency: The FDA and Safety; A Guardian of Health Is Buckling Under Stress," *New York Times,* Dec. 4, 1989, p. 1.

258 "If you had to write a fictional résumé": Philip J. Hilts, "New Chief Vows New Vitality at FDA," *New York Times,* Feb. 27, 1991.

258 "I traveled to large frog farms": David Kessler, *A Question of Intent,* p. 4.

259 Kessler was named to head the FDA in November 1990: Parts of this chapter follow Kessler's *A Question of Intent*. At the time, I was also a Washington science correspondent for the *New York Times*, and my beat included regular coverage of the Food and Drug Administration, which gave me access to many other sources and materials on these issues.

260 "The FDA is the regulator, and you should know that I have no problem stating that fact": Kessler, *A Question of Intent*, pp. 18–19.

261 The CSPI in 1988 set a strategy that was to be crucial over the next few years: The Center for Science in the Public Interest was a significant player in food issues at the FDA, and I interviewed its leaders several times. See also Laura S. Sims, *The Politics of Fat*, pp. 145–50, 179–212.

262 "They just sprinkle a little oat bran on their product and ride this train without any backing for their claims": Luther McKinney, personal interview for *New York Times* coverage.

262 "They are promoting oats as the magic bullet": Stephen Gardner, personal interview for *New York Times* coverage.

265 "What did we tell them we would do?": Kessler, *A Question of Intent*, p. 22.

265 "The food industry lawyers were dressed for golf": Kessler, personal interview and text of speech. Cf. Kessler, *A Question of Intent*, p. 23.

CHAPTER EIGHTEEN: DRUG LAG REVISITED

276 the polls of citizens were positive: Poll data was provided largely by the archives at the Roper Center for Public Opinion Research, University of Connecticut.

276 Its early report, published in 1980: The issue of how quickly a drug can be tested and found safe and effective will remain permanent. It is a pressure point simply because it seems as if every extra day spent in review and testing is a day patients and doctors do not have the benefit of a drug, and companies cannot profit from it. In fact, the judgment must be made case by case. And it can go both ways—taking more time than the necessary minimum can lead to more patients' receiving a valuable drug, and it can sometimes lead to fewer patients' being harmed by a bad drug.

On the positive side, a somewhat later marketing of a drug that is supported by better data might well lead to more patients' getting and benefiting from it, as company marketing experts have discovered. Each drug does not have a defined market; that market must be won by proof of the value of a drug, plus convincing doctors and formulary managers of the value of the drug.

On the negative side, when substantial doubts about a drug's safety remain, it is sometimes best to pause, because mistakenly sending a bad drug to market not only causes harm to the patients who take it, but diverts patients from getting the drug treatment they should have. The time and energy lost to companies, doctors, and patients when a bad drug makes it to market can be substantial.

During the era when the FDA was struggling to set standards and build a professional staff—during the 1970s, essentially—a number of useful drugs were delayed. Various estimates have been made of how many drugs were delayed and what the impact was of that delay. Because the FDA was leading the way to higher standards, and had to invent the process of review, it is not clear that the FDA deserves blame for its failures while its innovations were being made. But a reasonable estimate of how many mistakes were made while the innovations were under way would put the number at between a half dozen and two dozen.

In reviewing the issue of drug lag, a handful of sources are useful or interesting:

Sam Peltzman, "An Evaluation of Consumer Protection Legislation: The 1962 Drug Amendments," *Journal of Political Economy,* September/ October 1973, pp. 1049–91. Also "The Benefits and Costs of New Drug Regulation," *Proceedings of the Conference on Regulation of New Pharmaceuticals* (Chicago: University of Chicago Press, 1974).

W. M. Wardell, "Introduction of New Therapeutic Drugs in the United States and Great Britain: An International Comparison," *Clinical Pharmacology and Therapeutics* 14 (1973): 773–90.

O. M. Bakke, W. M. Wardell, and Louis Lasagna, "Discontinuations in the United Kingdom and the United States, 1964 to 1983: Issues of Safety," *Clinical Pharmacology and Therapeutics* 35: 559–67.

Joseph A. DiMasi et al., "New Drug Development in the United States from 1963 to 1992," *Clinical Pharmacology and Therapeutics* 55 (1994): 609–22.

Kenneth I. Kaitin et al., "The Drug Lag: An Update of New Drug Introductions in the United States and in the United Kingdom, 1977 Through 1987," *Clinical Pharmacology and Therapeutics* 46 (1989): 121–38.

Kenneth I. Kaitin and Joseph Di Masi, "Measuring the Pace of New Drug Development in the User Fee Era," *Drug Information Journal* 34 (2000).

Donald Kennedy, "A Calm Look at 'Drug Lag,' " *Journal of the American Medical Association* 239, no. 5 (1978): 423–26.

U.S. Food and Drug Administration, "Timely Access to New Drugs in the 1990s: An International Comparison" (Washington, D.C., 1995).

Peter Lurie and Sidney M. Wolfe, "FDA Medical Officers Report Lower Standards Permit Dangerous Drug Approvals" (Washington, D.C.: Public Citizen Health Research Group, December 1998).

Sidney Wolfe, "Differences in the Number of Drug Safety Withdrawals, United States, United Kingdom, Germany, and France, 1970–1992" (Washington, D.C.: Public Citizen Health Research Group, February 1995).

John Parker, "Who Has a Drug Lag?" *Managerial and Design Economics* 10 (1989): 299–309.

U.S. General Accounting Office, "FDA Drug Approval—A Lengthy

Process That Delays the Availability of Important New Drugs" (Washington, D.C.: U.S. Government Printing Office, May 28, 1980).

———, "FDA Drug Approval—Review Time Has Decreased in Recent Years" (Washington, D.C.: Government Printing Office, Oct. 20, 1995).

Mary R. Hamilton, "FDA Review and Approval Times" (Washington, D.C.: U.S. General Accounting Office, Feb. 21, 1996). Testimony before the Committee on Labor and Human Resources of the U.S. Senate. Pharmaceutical Panel, Committee on Technology and International Economic and Trade Issues, Commission on Engineering and Technical Systems, National Research Council, "The Competitive Status of the U.S. Pharmaceutical Industry: The Influences of Technology in Determining International Industrial Competitive Advantage" (Washington, D.C.: National Academy Press, 1983).

281 Scott Bass, a supplements industry lawyer, traces the origin of the self-medication craze in America to Samuel Thomson: A good account of Thomson's cult is in James Harvey Young's *The Toadstool Millionaires,* pp. 44–57, and Paul Starr's *The Social Transformation of American Medicine,* pp. 51–54.

281 The psychology of the remedy business was analyzed bluntly and with great insight by one of the great American entrepreneurs, Phineas T. Barnum: The discussion of Barnum relies on Neil Harris, *Humbug.*

286 Dr. Jonathan Wright, a Harvard-educated medical renegade, was the leader of the Tahoma Clinic in Kent, Washington: This discussion relies on personal interviews and Stephen Barrett and Victor Herbert, *The Vitamin Pushers.*

CHAPTER NINETEEN: AN ANTI-REGULATORY CAMPAIGN

293 There were further hearings after a tobacco company whistle-blower, Merrell Williams, had procured thousands of pages of damning internal documents from the companies, and managed to get them to the *New York Times:* Philip J. Hilts, *Smokescreen: The Truth Behind the Tobacco Industry Cover-up* (Reading, Mass.: Addison-Wesley, 1996).

296 There were half a dozen foundations of the extreme right that provided several million dollars annually to the cause: The foundations that ran the attack ads against the FDA got their funding for the attacks from a few extreme-right foundations, some drug companies, and tobacco companies. It is probably not a coincidence that the three foundations most active in attacking the FDA were each funded in part by the family and company that produced thalidomide and MER-29: The money came from the Smith Richardson Foundation, which earned its money from the Vick Chemical Company, parent company of Richardson-Merrell. (The company's name changed from William S. Merrell to Richardson-Merrell in 1960, but Vick remained the parent company.)

A small sampling of the groups that led the attack on the FDA, and a few of their funding sources:

Washington Legal Foundation, with money from the Smith Richardson and Scaife family foundations, R.J. Reynolds, Eli Lilly, and the John M. Olin Foundation.

The Competitive Enterprise Institute, with funds from the Smith Richardson Foundation, Koch family foundations (started by Fred Koch, a founder of the John Birch Society), Scaife family foundations, and the Olin Foundation.

Progress & Freedom Foundation, with funds from the Smith Richardson Foundation, Scaife family foundations, Genzyme Company, Searle, Glaxo Wellcome, Philip Morris, and R.J. Reynolds.

Citizens for a Sound Economy, with funds from Scaife family foundations, the Olin Foundation, Philip Morris, and Koch family foundations.

299 "The American Heart Association is dismayed": quoted from a letter to the editor of the *New York Times*, Jan. 21, 1995.

304 "We were wrong": Harrington echoed, rather frankly, the views of a number of men who were prominent activists in the 1980s and early 1990s, and whom I interviewed for this book.

305 "Among FDA critics like [Utah Senator Orrin] Hatch, it is an idea as inviolate as Scripture itself": Jeffrey Goldberg, "Next Target: Nicotine," *New York Times Magazine*, Aug. 4, 1996.

CHAPTER TWENTY: THE ARGUMENT IS JOINED

309 *Washington Post* reporter John Schwartz, following the FDA reform campaign, decided to interview a sampling of the scores of patients flown in to lobby Congress: Schwartz, "FDA Often Blamed for Problems That Aren't Agency's Fault," *Washington Post*, July 15, 1996, p. A17.

312 The document outlining the proposal: *Advancing Medical Innovation: Health, Safety and the Role of Government in the 21st Century*, Progress & Freedom Foundation, Feb. 7, 1996. The authors are listed as Ralph A. Epstein, Thomas M. Lenard, Henry I. Miller, Robert D. Tollison, W. Kip Viscusi, and William M. Wardell.

314 The attacks came with the opening statements: U.S. House of Representatives, Committee on Commerce, Subcommittee on Health and the Environment, *FDA Reform*, beginning May 1, 1996 (Washington, D.C.: Government Printing Office).

CHAPTER TWENTY-ONE: OLD-FASHIONED POLITICS

325 After the hearings the committee staff, Democrats and Republicans, met to talk about the final shape of the package: This chapter is based largely on interviews with a number of participants in the negotiations and on records of the House committee.

332 She was a Kessler deputy, and worked to make the user's fee program and

speedier drug reviews possible: She had left the Kessler staff and become a vice president at the University of New Mexico, where she worked to unite disparate health, science, and education establishments at the university. Her strength was her ability to listen and to manage without stirring partisan fights.

332 They described how pressure from industry, and acquiescence from some top agency officials, allowed some drugs to make it to market that the *Times* suggested never should have: The *Los Angeles Times* list of likely FDA mistakes from the period includes seven drugs. FDA officials acknowledge mistakes in these cases but dispute the broad claim that reviewers should have held them all off the market. Each of the drugs is a case study on its own; however, the *Times* did identify the key problem drugs of recent years. The *Times* list comprises drugs for which safer alternatives were already on the market at the time of approval. All eight drugs were mentioned in the story series, which began December 20, 2000.

Troglitazone, trade name Rezulin. Warner-Lambert (now owned by Pfizer). A drug to lower blood sugar in diabetes. Problem: liver damage. On the market from January 1997 to March 2000.

Bromfenac, trade name Duract. Wyeth-Ayerst Laboratories. A painkiller. Problem: liver damage. July 1997 to June 1998.

Grepafloxain, trade name Raxar. Glaxo Wellcome (now Glaxo Smith-Kline). An antibiotic. Problem: heart rhythm disturbance. November 1997 to October 1999.

Mibefradil, trade name Posicor. Hoffmann-LaRoche. A drug to lower high blood pressure. Problem: heart rhythm disturbances that can cause sudden death. June 1997 to June 1998.

Losetron, trade name Lotronex. Glaxo Wellcome. A drug to ease irritable bowel syndrome. Problem: ischemic colitis, a potentially dangerous shutdown of blood flow to the colon. February to November 2000.

Cisapride, trade name Propulsid. Janssen Pharmaceutica. A drug for heartburn. Problem: heart rhythm disorders. The company sold it for use in children; eight deaths were recorded.

Dexfenfluramine, trade name Redux. American Home Products. A diet pill that was used in combination with Phentermine, an amphetamine-like drug. The combination was called Fen-Phen. Problem: Caused damage to heart valves and triggered off a dangerous variety of high blood pressure, primary pulmonary hypertension. April 1996 to September 1997.

Zanamivir, trade name Relenza. Glaxo Wellcome. A drug to shorten by one day the duration of the flu. Problem: breathing difficulties, some deaths reported. On the market since July 1999.

332 One example was that of the diabetes drug Rezulin: Since the text of the book was written, information revealed in trials suggests that Warner-Lambert officials may have lied to the FDA and withheld key data about liver damage, a federal crime. Preliminary criminal investigations have begun.

335 "is completely at odds with the will of Congress that drug development and approval proceed swiftly and surely": quoted from David Willman, "Relenza: Official Asks If One Day Less of Flu Is Worth It," *Los Angeles Times*, Dec. 20, 2000.

EPILOGUE: GREED AND GOODNESS

339 The board chose not only to keep the dangerous drug on the market, but to vigorously fight in court to keep it available as long as possible: According to Peter B. Hutt and Richard Merrill, *Food and Drug Law* (Westbury, N.Y.: Foundation Press, 1991), the sequence was roughly as follows. In December 1968 the FDA gave notice it was considering removing Panalba from the market because it was ineffective, and in May 1969 it officially withdrew its approval. Upjohn went to court to get a hearing on the evidence. A flurry of action followed in court as other manufacturers piled on with court actions to prevent their drugs from being ruled useless by the FDA. The FDA responded by saying Upjohn hadn't demonstrated any evidence that a formal hearing was needed for Panalba. The agency also published regulations defining in detail what was necessary in "adequate and well-controlled clinical investigations" to show that a drug was worthy of approval. The FDA's rules were upheld in *Upjohn v. Finch*, 422 F.2d 944 (6th Cir. 1970). The drugmakers then attacked as a group in *Pharmaceutical Manufacturers Association v. Finch*, 307 F. Supp. 858 (D. Del. 1970). After another round of fights, the Supreme Court finally upheld FDA rules in June 1973 in *Weinberger v. Hynson*, 412 U.S. 609 (1973).

339 So he designed a little experiment to test his faith: Armstrong published a long series of papers in this landmark work on management and responsibility. The latest, updated paper was published in his book *Principles of Forecasting*. The earliest complete paper was J. Scott Armstrong, "Social Irresponsibility in Management," *Journal of Business Research*, Sept. 5, 1977, pp. 185–213.

Selected Bibliography

Abraham, John. *Science, Politics, and the Pharmaceutical Industry: Controversy and Bias in Drug Regulation*. New York: St. Martin's Press, 1995.

Ackerknecht, Erwin H. *A Short History of Medicine*. Baltimore: Johns Hopkins University Press, 1982.

Anderson, Oscar E., Jr. *The Health of a Nation: Harvey Wiley and the Fight for Pure Food*. Chicago: University of Chicago Press, 1958.

Armstrong, J. Scott. *Principles of Forecasting: A Handbook for Researchers and Practitioners*. Norwell, Mass.: Kluwer, 2001.

Arno, Peter S., and Karyn L. Feiden. *Against the Odds: The Story of AIDS Drug Development, Politics and Profits*. New York: HarperCollins, 1992.

Barrett, Stephen, and Victor Herbert. *The Vitamin Pushers: How the "Health Food" Industry Is Selling America a Bill of Goods*. Amherst, N.Y.: Prometheus, 1994.

Blake, John B., ed. *Safeguarding the Public: Historical Aspects of Medicinal Drug Control*. Baltimore: Johns Hopkins University Press, 1970.

Blochman, Lawrence. *Doctor Squibb: The Life and Times of a Rugged Idealist*. New York: Simon & Schuster, 1958.

Burkholz, Herbert. *The FDA Follies: An Alarming Look at Our Food and Drugs in the 1980s*. New York: Basic Books, 1994.

Cannon, Lou. *President Reagan: The Role of a Lifetime*. New York: PublicAffairs, 2000.

Cashman, Sean Dennis. *America in the Gilded Age: From the Death of Lincoln to the Rise of Theodore Roosevelt*. New York: New York University Press, 1993.

Chalmers, David Mark. *The Muckrake Years*. Huntington, N.Y.: Krieger, 1980.

———. *The Social and Political Ideas of the Muckrakers*. Salem, N.H.: Ayer, 1984.

Chandler, Alfred D., Jr. *The Visible Hand: The Managerial Revolution in American Business*. Cambridge, Mass.: Belknap, 1977.

Chase, Stuart, and F. J. Schlink. *Your Money's Worth*. New York: Macmillan, 1936.

Chetley, Andrew. *Problem Drugs*. London: Zed Books, 1995.

Diner, Steven J. *A Very Different Age: Americans of the Progressive Era*. New York: Hill and Wang, 1998.

Dowling, Harry F. *Medicines for Man: The Development, Regulation, and Use of Prescription Drugs*. New York: Knopf, 1971.

Duffy, John. *From Humors to Medical Science: A History of American Medicine.* Urbana and Chicago: University of Illinois Press, 1993.

Eberle, Irmengarde. *Modern Medical Discoveries.* New York: Crowell, 1968.

Edelstein, Ludwig. *Ancient Medicine: Selected Papers of Ludwig Edelstein.* Baltimore: Johns Hopkins University Press, 1967.

Eden, Robert, ed. *The New Deal and Its Legacy: Critique and Reappraisal.* New York: Greenwood, 1989.

Edwards, Lee. *The Conservative Revolution: The Movement That Remade America.* New York: Free Press, 1999.

Fine, Ralph Adam. *The Great Drug Deception: The Shocking Story of MER/29 and the Folks Who Gave You Thalidomide.* New York: Stein and Day, 1972.

Fried, Stephen. *Bitter Pills.* New York: Bantam, 1998.

Galbraith, John Kenneth. *The Good Society: The Humane Agenda.* Boston: Houghton Mifflin, 1996.

Goldman, Eric F. *Rendezvous with Destiny: A History of Modern American Reform.* New York: Vintage, 1961.

Goldsmith, Margaret. *The Road to Penicillin: A History of Chemotherapy.* London: Drummond, 1946.

Goodwin, Lorine Swainston. *The Pure Food, Drink, and Drug Crusaders, 1879–1914.* Jefferson, N.C.: McFarland, 1999.

Groopman, Jerome. *The Measure of Our Days: New Beginnings at Life's End.* New York: Viking, 1997.

Harris, Neil. *Humbug: The Art of P. T. Barnum.* Boston: Little, Brown, 1973.

Harris, Richard. *The Real Voice: The First Fully Documented Account of Congress at Work: Senator Estes Kefauver's Investigation of the Drug Industry and the Battle over a New Law to Protect the Neglected American Consumer.* New York: Macmillan, 1964.

———. *A Sacred Trust: The Story of America's Most Powerful Lobby—Organized Medicine—and Its Forty-Five-Year Multi-Million-Dollar Fight Against Public Health Legislation.* New York: New American Library, 1966.

Harris, Seymour E. *The Economics of American Medicine.* New York: Macmillan, 1964.

Higby, Gregory J., and Elaine C. Stroud, eds. *The Inside Story of Medicines: A Symposium.* Madison, Wis.: American Institute of the History of Pharmacy, 1997.

Hobby, Gladys L. *Penicillin: Meeting the Challenge.* New Haven, Conn.: Yale University Press, 1985.

Hofstadter, Richard. *The Age of Reform.* New York: Vintage, 1955.

Jackson, Charles O. *Food and Drug Legislation in the New Deal.* Princeton, N.J.: Princeton University Press, 1970.

Jeffers, H. Paul. *Commissioner Roosevelt: The Story of Theodore Roosevelt and the New York City Police, 1895–1897.* New York: Wiley, 1994.

Kallet, Arthur, and F. J. Schlink. *100,000,000 Guinea Pigs: Dangers in Everyday Foods, Drugs and Cosmetics.* New York: Vanguard, 1933.

Kessler, David. *A Question of Intent: A Great American Battle with a Deadly Industry.* New York: PublicAffairs, 2001.

King, Lester S. *Transformations in American Medicine: From Benjamin Rush to William Osler.* Baltimore: Johns Hopkins University Press, 1991.

Korten, David C. *When Corporations Rule the World.* West Hartford, Conn.: Kumarian Press; San Francisco: Berrett-Koehler, 1995.

Kuttner, Robert. *Everything for Sale: The Virtues and Limits of Markets.* New York: Knopf, 1997.

Lamb, Ruth deForest. *American Chamber of Horrors: The Truth About Food and Drugs.* New York: Farrar & Rinehart, 1936.

Lasagna, Louis. *The Doctors' Dilemmas.* New York: Harper & Bros., 1962.

Levy, Stuart B. *The Antibiotic Paradox: How Miracle Drugs Are Destroying the Miracle.* New York: Plenum, 1992.

Liebenau, Jonathan. *Medical Science and Medical Industry: The Formation of the American Pharmaceutical Industry.* Baltimore: Johns Hopkins University Press, 1987.

MacHarg, William. "Speaking of Dr. Wiley," in Donald Elder, ed., *The Good Housekeeping Treasury.* New York: Simon & Schuster, 1960.

Maeder, Thomas. *Adverse Reactions.* New York: Morrow, 1994.

Mahoney, Tom. *The Merchants of Life: An Account of the American Pharmaceutical Industry.* New York: Harper & Bros., 1959.

Mann, Charles C., and Mark Plummer. *The Aspirin Wars: Money, Medicine and 100 Years of Rampant Competition.* New York: Knopf, 1991.

McElvaine, Robert S. *The Great Depression: America, 1929–1941.* New York: Times Books, 1984.

Milgram, Stanley. *Obedience to Authority: An Experimental View.* New York: Harper Colophon, 1975.

Miller, Henry I. *To America's Health: A Proposal to Reform the Food and Drug Administration.* Stanford, Calif.: Hoover Institution Press, 2000.

Miller, Nathan. *Theodore Roosevelt: A Life.* New York: Morrow, 1992.

Mintz, Morton. *By Prescription Only: A Report on the Roles of the United States Food and Drug Administration, the American Medical Association, Pharmaceutical Manufacturers and Others in Connection with the Irrational and Massive Use of Prescription Drugs That May Be Worthless, Injurious, or Even Lethal,* originally published as *The Therapeutic Nightmare.* Boston: Beacon, 1967.

Moore, Thomas J. *Deadly Medicine: Why Tens of Thousands of Heart Patients Died in America's Worst Drug Disaster.* New York: Simon & Schuster, 1995.

Morison, Samuel Eliot. *The Oxford History of the American People,* vol. 3, *1869 Through the Death of John F. Kennedy, 1963.* New York: Meridian, 1994.

Morris, Edmund. *The Rise of Theodore Roosevelt.* New York: Coward, McCann & Geoghegan, 1979.

Namorato, Michael V. *Rexford G. Tugwell: A Biography.* New York: Praeger, 1988.

———, ed. *The Diary of Rexford G. Tugwell: The New Deal, 1932–1935.* New York: Greenwood, 1992.

Natenberg, Maurice. *The Legacy of Doctor Wiley and the Administration of His Food and Drug Act.* Chicago: Regent House, 1957.

Noble, David F. *America by Design: Science, Technology and the Rise of Corporate Capitalism.* Oxford, Eng.: Oxford University Press, 1977.

Okun, Mitchell. *Fair Play in the Marketplace: The First Battle for Pure Food and Drugs*. DeKalb: Northern Illinois University Press, 1986.

Parascandola, John. *The Development of American Pharmacology: John J. Abel and the Shaping of a Discipline*. Baltimore: Johns Hopkins University Press, 1992.

Parrish, Michael E. *Anxious Decades: America in Prosperity and Depression, 1920–1941*. New York: Norton, 1992.

Pendergrast, Mark. *For God, Country & Coca-Cola: The Definitive History of the Great American Soft Drink and the Company That Makes It*. New York: Basic Books, 1993.

Porter, Roy. *The Greatest Benefit to Mankind: A Medical History of Humanity*. New York: Norton, 1998.

———, ed. *Cambridge Illustrated History of Medicine*. Cambridge, Eng.: Cambridge University Press, 1996.

Ricci, David M. *The Transformation of American Politics: The New Washington and the Rise of Think Tanks*. New Haven, Conn.: Yale University Press, 1993.

Roosevelt, Theodore. *An Autobiography*. 1913; reprint, New York: Da Capo Press, 1985.

Ross, Walter S. *The Life/Death Ratio: Benefits and Risks in Modern Medicines*. New York: Reader's Digest Press, 1977.

Sanders, Elizabeth. *Roots of Reform: Farmers, Workers and the American State, 1877–1917*. Chicago: University of Chicago Press, 1999.

Schaaf, Barbara, ed. *Mr. Dooley: Wise and Funny—We Need Him Now*. Springfield, Ill.: Lincoln Herndon Press, 1988.

Schlesinger, Arthur M., Jr. *The Age of Jackson*. Boston: Little, Brown, 1945.

———. *The Coming of the New Deal*. Boston: Houghton Mifflin, 1988.

Schlink, F. J. *Eat, Drink and Be Wary*. New York: Grosset and Dunlap, 1935.

Sellers, Charles. *The Market Revolution: Jacksonian America, 1815–1846*. New York: Oxford University Press, 1991.

Shapin, Steven. *A Social History of Truth: Civility and Science in Seventeenth-Century England*. Chicago: University of Chicago Press, 1994.

Shryock, Richard Harrison. *Medicine and Society in America, 1660–1860*. Ithaca, N.Y.: Cornell University Press, 1972.

Sims, Laura S. *The Politics of Fat: Food and Nutrition Policy in America*. Armonk, N.Y.: Sharpe, 1999.

Sinclair, Upton. *American Outpost: A Book of Reminiscences*. New York: Farrar & Rinehart, 1932.

———. *My Lifetime in Letters*. Columbia: University of Missouri Press, 1960.

Smith, James Allen. *The Idea Brokers: Think Tanks and the Rise of the New Policy Elite*. New York: Free Press, 1991.

Sonnedecker, Glenn, ed. *The Early Years of Federal Food and Drug Control*. Madison, Wis.: American Institute of the History of Pharmacy, 1982.

Starr, Paul. *The Social Transformation of American Medicine: The Rise of a Sovereign Profession and the Making of a Vast Industry*. New York: Basic Books, 1982.

Sternsher, Bernard. *Rexford Tugwell and the New Deal*. New Brunswick, N.J.: Rutgers University Press, 1964.

Sullivan, Mark. *Our Times: The United States, 1900–1925,* vol. 2, *America Finding Herself.* New York: Scribner's, 1927.

Sunday Times of London Insight Team. *Suffer the Children: The Story of Thalidomide.* London: Deutsch, 1979.

Swann, John P. *Academic Scientists and the Pharmaceutical Industry: Cooperative Research in Twentieth-Century America.* Baltimore: Johns Hopkins University Press, 1988.

Talalay, Paul, ed. *Drugs in Our Society.* Baltimore: Johns Hopkins University Press, 1964.

Temin, Peter. *Taking Your Medicine: Drug Regulation in the United States.* Cambridge: Harvard University Press, 1980.

Tolchin, Susan J., and Martin Tolchin. *Dismantling America: The Rush to Deregulate.* Boston: Houghton Mifflin, 1983.

Troetel, Barbara R. "Three-Part Disharmony: The Transformation of the Food and Drug Administration in the 1970s." Ph.D. diss., City University of New York, 1996.

Urquhart, John, and Klaus Heilmann. *Risk Watch: The Odds of Life.* New York: Facts on File, 1984.

Wardell, William M., ed. *Controlling the Use of Therapeutic Drugs: An International Comparison.* Washington, D.C.: American Enterprise Institute, 1978.

Wardell, William M., and Louis Lasagna. *Regulation and Drug Development.* Washington, D.C.: American Enterprise Institute, 1975.

Weatherall, M. *In Search of a Cure: A History of Pharmaceutical Discovery.* Oxford, Eng.: Oxford University Press, 1990.

Weinberg, Arthur, and Lila Weinberg, eds. *The Muckrakers: The Era in Journalism That Moved America to Reform—the Most Significant Magazine Articles of 1902–1912.* New York: Putnam's, 1964.

White, Suzanne Rebecca. "Chemistry and Controversy: Regulating the Use of Chemicals in Food, 1883–1959." Ph.D. diss., Emory University, 1994.

Wiley, Harvey W. *Harvey W. Wiley: An Autobiography.* Indianapolis: Bobbs-Merrill, 1930.

———. *The History of a Crime Against the Food Law: The Amazing Story of the National Food and Drug Law Intended to Protect the Health of the People—Perverted to Protect Adulteration of Food and Drugs.* Washington, D.C.: Harvey Wiley, 1929.

Williams, Trevor I. *Howard Florey: Penicillin and After.* Oxford, Eng.: Oxford University Press, 1984.

Wilson, James Q., ed. *The Politics of Regulation.* New York: Basic Books, 1980.

Wolfe, Sidney M., Larry D. Sasich, and Rose-Ellen Hope. *Worst Pills, Best Pills: A Consumer's Guide to Avoiding Drug-Induced Death or Illness.* New York: Pocket Books, 1999.

Wood, Gordon S. *The Radicalism of the American Revolution.* New York: Vintage, 1993.

Young, James Harvey. *American Health Quackery.* Princeton, N.J.: Princeton University Press, 1992.

———. *American Self-Dosage Medicines: An Historical Perspective.* Lawrence, Kans.: Coronado, 1974.

————. *The Medical Messiahs: A Social History of Health Quackery in Twentieth-Century America*. Princeton, N. J.: Princeton University Press, 1992.

————. *Pure Food: Securing the Federal Food and Drugs Act of 1906*. Princeton, N. J.: Princeton University Press, 1989.

————. *The Toadstool Millionaires: A Social History of Patent Medicines in America Before Federal Regulation*. Princeton, N. J.: Princeton University Press, 1961.

Acknowledgments

I want to thank the Alicia Patterson Foundation and the Kaiser Family Foundation for support during my work on this project.

I would also like to offer thanks to those who provided vital help along the way: Suzanne White Junod and John Swann, historians at the Food and Drug Administration; Doug Starr and Ellen Shell at Boston University, and James Harvey Young, historian emeritus at Emory University. Thanks also to Louise Gordon at Writeup Communications, Rosalie Prosser at Alice Darling Secretarial Services, and Troy Kitch and Mike Vatalaro.

Gloria Loomis, my agent, provided essential advice and support. Jonathan Segal, my editor, provided what is most unusual, both broad criticism and sharp line-by-line aid.